*RACE AND THE QUESTION*
*OF PALESTINE*

Stanford Studies in Middle Eastern and
Islamic Societies and Cultures

# RACE AND THE QUESTION OF PALESTINE

*Edited by* **Lana Tatour**
*and* **Ronit Lentin**

STANFORD UNIVERSITY PRESS

*Stanford, California*

Stanford University Press
Stanford, California

Library of Congress Cataloging-in-Publication Data

Names: Tatour, Lana, editor. | Lenṭin, Ronit, editor.
Title: Race and the question of Palestine / edited by Lana Tatour and Ronit
    Lentin.
Other titles: Stanford studies in Middle Eastern and Islamic societies and
    cultures.
Description: Stanford, California : Stanford University Press, [2025] |
    Series: Stanford studies in Middle Eastern and Islamic societies and
    cultures | Includes bibliographical references and index.
Identifiers: LCCN 2024042781 (print) | LCCN 2024042782 (ebook) |
    ISBN 9781503642133 (cloth) | ISBN 9781503642973 (paperback) |
    ISBN 9781503642980 (ebook)
Subjects: LCSH: Racism–Palestine–History. | Zionism–Palestine–History. |
    Settler colonialism–Palestine–History. | Jewish-Arab relations–History. |
    Palestine question (1948-) | Palestine–Race relations–History. |
    Palestine–Colonization–History.
Classification: LCC DS113.2 .R33 2025 (print) | LCC DS113.2 (ebook) | DDC
    305.80095694–dc23/eng/20241231
LC record available at https://lccn.loc.gov/2024042781
LC ebook record available at https://lccn.loc.gov/2024042782

Cover design: Michele Wetherbee
Cover painting: Tayseer Barakat, *Nagham*, 2003
Typeset by Newgen in 10.5/14.4 Brill Roman

The authorized representative in the EU for product safety and compliance is: Mare
Nostrum Group B.V. | Mauritskade 21D | 1091 GC Amsterdam | The Netherlands | Email
address: gpsr@mare-nostrum.co.uk | KVK chamber of commerce number: 96249943

# Contents

*Preface*

As we finish work on this book, we witness the annihilation of Gaza in what the International Court of Justice has referred to as plausible genocide.[1] Since October 2023, every day has seen a horrifying progression of genocide, the destruction of Palestinian life, the dehumanization of Palestinians, and the escalation of anti-Palestinian racism. Israeli officials, including at the highest levels of government, have called for a "second Nakba,"[2] describing the Palestinians in Gaza as "human animals," "the children of darkness," "monsters," and an "evil" to be "uproot[ed] so that there will be good for the entire region and the world."[3] Israel's prime minister, Benjamin Netanyahu, declared that the war on Gaza is "a battle of civilization against barbarism."[4] Articulating Israel's genocidal intent, on October 9, 2023, Israel's minister of defense, Yoav Gallant, said: "Gaza won't return to what it was before. We will eliminate everything."[5]

Ever since, day and night, Israel has been doing exactly that. This is the first genocide in history to be livestreamed. No one will be able to say that they did not know what was happening. Acting with impunity, in complete disregard of international law, and with the active support of the United States and other Western powers (indeed, as I write, Netanyahu is receiving a standing ovation in the US Congress, a reminder that, in the words of Palestinian doctor Ghassan Abu Sitta, this genocide belongs as much to the United States, itself a settler colony founded on genocide, as it does to

Netanyahu),[6] Israel has been mass killing Palestinians. Israeli soldiers have been broadcasting their war crimes on social media as a badge of honor, with Israeli civilians joining in and relishing the killing of Palestinians.[7] At the time of writing (July 25, 2024), Israel has killed 40,000 Palestinians in Gaza, including more than 15,000 children, and the bodies of at least 10,000 more lie under the rubble.[8] Experts estimate that the actual number of dead is at least 186,000, constituting 8 percent of Gaza's entire population.[9] The spread of disease is threatening the lives of tens of thousands more.[10] Entire families and bloodlines have been erased. Twenty-one thousand children are missing: buried in the debris or in mass and unmarked graves, held as hostages, or separated from their families.[11] Israel has even bombed Gaza's main IVF center, destroying most of its frozen embryos and a thousand more specimens of sperm and unfertilized eggs, thereby preventing Palestinian lives from ever coming into existence.[12] Miscarriages are at a record high due to severe stress, anxiety, and malnutrition.[13]

It has been ten months of nonstop bombardment. Most Palestinians are now displaced, many of them multiple times. They live in tents, in schools established by the UN Relief and Works Agency for Palestine Refugees in the Near East (UNRWA), and on the streets. Israel regularly issues evacuation orders, forcing hundreds of thousands of exhausted and starved civilians to leave their temporary shelter immediately and go to so-called safe zones, only to then bomb them—a practice that Francesca Albanese, the UN special rapporteur on the situation of human rights in the Palestinian territories occupied since 1967, called a "humanitarian camouflage."[14] Israel is making Gaza unlivable, targeting anything that can sustain life. So far, it has destroyed or damaged half of the homes in Gaza, most schools, and all universities, as well as hospitals, libraries, bakeries, shops and markets, pharmacies, hundreds of places of worship, municipal buildings, cultural heritage sites, archives, and essential civilian infrastructure—including electricity, telecommunications equipment, water wells, desalination plants, over half of all road networks, and even farmlands.[15] Israel is deliberately denying food and water to an entire population, using starvation as a weapon of war.[16] But it is not only the state that is restricting the entry of essential humanitarian aid: Israeli civilians are also actively blocking and destroying deliveries of food and medical supplies intended for the starved and besieged population.[17]

And Palestinians desperately seeking food for their children and families have been killed by Israel in what have come to be known as the "flour massacres."[18] As I write, Palestinian babies and children are being starved into skeletons, dying in pain from human-made starvation and lacking even the energy to cry.[19]

The Gaza-based Palestinian journalist Hossam Shabat has described daily life in Gaza as "slow death." Slow death, he writes, is

> waiting for days to get drinking water under the scorching sun . . . to search for wood sticks for fire so you can prepare food for the family, to watch your child die of starvation, to be displaced tens of times and look for a safe place, to have the occupation army burn your tent, bomb your house, and kill your child. Slow death is living this suffering.[20]

These unparalleled conditions led the UNRWA commissioner-general to refer to the war on Gaza as "a war of all the superlative, everything is unprecedented,"[21] with other humanitarian organizations and professionals calling it "a crisis of humanity,"[22] a "living hell,"[23] "apocalyptic,"[24] "a graveyard for thousands of children,"[25] and "the most dangerous place in the world to be a child."[26]

What we are witnessing in Gaza is race at work: the treatment of Palestinians not just as less-than-humans, but also as nonhumans. On a daily basis, we see how Israeli lives are valued over Palestinian lives. While the October 7, 2023, attack was considered by politicians, the media, and even human rights organizations in the West as unconscionable, barbaric, and monstrous, Israel's ongoing genocidal violence against Palestinians—both before and during the current genocide—is ignored and denied, or, when it is acknowledged, it is described in cold and sanitized terms. This, of course, is not new. Palestinians, as nonwhite, are treated as statistical and logical figures of suffering, displacement, dispossession, and death, while Israelis, due to their proximity to whiteness, are seen as natural embodiments of life. Palestinian death is unfortunate; Israeli death is unacceptable.[27]

Reflecting on this moment, Sherene Seikaly writes: "In the face of death, life, Palestinian life and Palestinian futures continue."[28] This continuance is the people—children, women, men, the elderly—doing the impossible to survive slow death. It is the doctors, nurses, and medical and rescue teams providing care under impossible conditions. It is the volunteers feeding people, organizing activities for kids, and more. It is the journalists covering the worst that humanity has to offer and showing us what true journalism looks like, and the human rights defenders documenting the atrocities. It is the teachers insisting on teaching children in tents and partly destroyed buildings and the children who are going through hell but are still eager to maintain a semblance of life and of childhood. It is the students defending their MA and PhD theses in tents and Gaza's academics insisting on their future and reaffirming their "collective determination to remain on our land and to resume teaching, study, and research in Gaza, at our own Palestinian universities, at the earliest opportunity."[29]

This is admirable, but no people should have to endure so much. As the Palestinian Gazan scholar Malaka Shwaikh writes, we need to be careful "expecting supernatural 'coping mechanisms.'" She reminds us to keep our focus on ending the violence: "The conditions in Gaza are inhumane. They are also human made. And they can and must be removed to enable justice and freedom to prevail."[30]

The war on Palestinians also continues in other parts of Palestine. In the West Bank, violence by the Israeli military and settler militias has reached new heights, and the Israeli police has escalated its violence against '48 Palestinians too. And in the diaspora, especially but not only in the West, Palestinians and their allies are facing new levels of suppression. As the violence against Palestinians continues to escalate, on July 19, 2024, the International Court of Justice ruled in a landmark Advisory Opinion that the occupation of the West Bank, East Jerusalem, and Gaza is unlawful, and that Israel is in violation of Article 3 of the Convention on the Elimination of All Forms of Racial Discrimination,[31] which prohibits both racial segregation and apartheid.[32]

As we sign off on this book, there is still no end in sight for the genocide in Gaza. Its impact on Palestinians and on Palestine will last for generations, even after a ceasefire. At this horrifying moment, we continue to hope for a free Palestine.

*Lana Tatour*
July 25, 2024

*Contributors*

**Yasmeen Abu-Laban** is a professor of political science and Canada Research Chair in the Politics of Citizenship and Human Rights at the University of Alberta. She is also a fellow at the Canadian Institute for Advanced Research. Abu-Laban is coauthor (with Abigail B. Bakan) of *Israel, Palestine and the Politics of Race: Exploring Identity and Power in a Global Context* (I. B. Tauris, 2020).

**Seraj Assi** teaches Arabic studies at American University in Washington, DC. He is the author of *The History and Politics of the Bedouin: Reimagining Nomadism in Modern Palestine* (Routledge, 2018) and the novel *My Life as an Alien* (Tartarus Press, 2023). Assi also writes for *Jacobin* magazine.

**Abigail B. Bakan** is a professor in the Department of Social Justice Education at the Ontario Institute for Studies in Education, cross-appointed to the Department of Political Science, and an affiliate with the Anne Tanenbaum Centre for Jewish Studies at the University of Toronto. She is coauthor (with Yasmeen Abu-Laban) of *Israel, Palestine and the Politics of Race: Exploring Identity and Power in a Global Context* (I. B. Tauris, 2020).

**Zvi Ben-Dor Benite** teaches Chinese and Middle Eastern history at New York University. He is the author of *The Dao of Muhammad: A Cultural History of Muslims in Late Imperial China* (Harvard University Press, 2005) and *The Ten*

*Lost Tribes: A World History* (Oxford University Press, 2009) and the coeditor of *Modern Middle Eastern Jewish Thought: Writings on Identity, Culture, and Politics* (Brandeis University Press, 2013), *The Scaffolding of Sovereignty: Global and Aesthetic Perspectives on the History of a Concept* (Columbia University Press, 2017), and *Time and Language: New Sinology and Chinese History* (University of Hawai'i Press, 2023).

**Yinon Cohen** is a professor of sociology and Yosef H. Yerushalmi Professor of Israel and Jewish Studies at Columbia University. His recent publications focus on income inequality in the US, socioeconomic ethnic gaps in Israel and Israeli emigration to the US, and are available on his webpage, yinoncohen.com.

**Noura Erakat** is a professor at Rutgers University in the Department of Africana Studies and the Program in Criminal Justice. She is the author of *Justice for Some: Law and the Question of Palestine* (Stanford University Press, 2019). In 2020, she completed a nonresident visiting fellowship in the Religion, Conflict, and Peace Initiative at the Religious Literacy Project at the Harvard Divinity School. Erakat was a 2022 Mahmoud Darwish Visiting Fellow in Palestinian Studies at Brown University. Also in 2022, she was selected as a Freedom Fellow by the Marguerite Casey Foundation.

**Michael R. Fischbach** is a professor of history at Randolph-Macon College. Among his many publications are *Black Power and Palestine: Transnational Countries of Color* (Stanford University Press, 2018) and "Black 1968 and Palestine: Transnationalism, Anti-Imperialism, and Revolutionary Culture," in *Black 1968*, edited by Timothy Parsons (Routledge, forthcoming).

**Neve Gordon** is a professor of human rights and international humanitarian law at Queen Mary University of London. He is the author of *Israel's Occupation* (University of California Press, 2008) and the coauthor of *The Human Right to Dominate* (Oxford University Press, 2015) and *Human Shields: A History of People in the Line of Fire* (University of California Press, 2020).

**Alana Lentin** is a professor of cultural and social analysis at Western Sydney University and a member of the Founding Collective of the Institute for the Critical Study of Zionism. She is the author of *Why Race Still Matters* (Polity Press, 2020); *The Crises of Multiculturalism: Racism in a Neoliberal Age* (Zed Books, 2011); and *Racism and Antiracism in Europe* (Pluto Press, 2004).

**Ronit Lentin** is a former associate professor of sociology at Trinity College Dublin. Her books include *Conversations with Palestinian Women* (Mifras, 1982); *Women and the Politics of Military Confrontation: Palestinian and Israeli Gendered Narratives of Dislocation,* coedited (Berghahn Books, 2002); *Thinking Palestine* (Zed Books, 2008); *Co-Memory and Melancholia: Israelis Memorialising the Palestinian Nakba* (Manchester University Press, 2010); *Traces of Racial Exception: Racializing Israeli Settler Colonialism* (Bloomsbury Academic, 2018); *Enforcing Silence: Academic Freedom, Palestine and the Criticism of Israel,* coedited (Zed Books, 2020); *Racial Capitalism and Palestine,* coedited (journal special issue, 2024).

**David Palumbo-Liu** is the Louise Hewlett Nixon Professor and a professor of comparative literature at Stanford University and also a longtime activist. His latest book is *Speaking Out of Place: Getting Our Political Voices Back* (Haymarket Books, 2021). With Azeezah Kanji, he produces the *Speaking Out of Place* podcast.

**John Reynolds** teaches at Maynooth University in Ireland and writes about international law and colonialism. His book *Empire, Emergency and International Law* (Cambridge University Press, 2017) was awarded the Kevin Boyle Book Prize for Outstanding Legal Scholarship. He is a member of the editorial collective of the *Third World Approaches to International Law Review* (*TWAIL Review*) journal and website.

**Lana Tatour** is a senior lecturer in the School of Social Sciences at the University of New South Wales and previously held the Ibrahim Abu-Lughod postdoctoral fellowship in the Center for Palestine Studies at Columbia University. She is currently completing her monograph, provisionally titled *Colonized Citizens: '48 Palestinians and the Paradoxes of Domination and Resistance.*

**Kieron Turner** is an independent researcher and public educator. He has edited a special issue on Palestine in the *Journal of Holy Land and Palestine Studies* (2024). Turner has published in the journal *Interfere* on the subject of direct action and Palestine (2022) and has a chapter on racial capitalism as a theory of history in the *SAGE Handbook of Decolonial Theory* (SAGE, 2025).

*RACE AND THE QUESTION OF PALESTINE*

# *Introduction*

LANA TATOUR

BETWEEN JANUARY 2021 AND MARCH 2022, FOUR REPORTS PUBLISHED by human rights organizations determined that Israel is practicing apartheid against Palestinians, a crime against humanity under international law. Written by B'Tselem, Human Rights Watch, Amnesty International, and the UN special rapporteur on the situation of human rights in the Palestinian territories occupied since 1967, the reports finally caught up with what Palestinian activists, intellectuals, human rights organizations, and their allies have been saying for decades: that Israel subjects Palestinians to a systematic racial regime of domination and segregation that treats Jews and Palestinians differently. The reports show that Israel's land and planning policies, its demographic engineering to ensure a Jewish majority, its practice of targeted extrajudicial killings, its movement restrictions, its segregated roads and towns, its policies of expulsion and forcible population transfer, its institutionalized discrimination, and its denial of citizenship to most Palestinians are all part of a planned system of racial domination tantamount to the crime of apartheid. Israel, according to the UN special rapporteur, conforms to the legal definition of apartheid as a political regime that "intentionally and clearly prioritizes fundamental political, legal and social rights to one group over another, within the same geographic unit on the basis of one's racial-national-ethnic identity."[1]

Inherent to this system is the exercise of differentiated racial citizenship regimes based on a system of racial distinction between Jews and Palestinians. In Israel, citizenship and civil and human rights are racial entitlements. All Jews—whether they reside in Israel or not—are entitled to citizenship, while the vast majority of Palestinians, inside historic Palestine and in the diaspora (what Palestinians refer to as the *shatat*), are denied citizenship and a right of return to their homeland. The minority of Palestinians who do hold Israeli citizenship are systemically discriminated against in all areas of life, including political rights, access to land and housing, public services, and resource distribution, with discrimination being institutionalized in law. Israel's citizenship regime and its control of Palestinians rely on the fragmentation of Palestinians into separate groups with differing legal statuses: Palestinians with Israeli citizenship, Palestinian Jerusalemites with Israeli residence status, Palestinians under military occupation in the West Bank, Palestinians under occupation and siege in the Gaza Strip, and Palestinians in the diaspora.

Importantly, the four reports and the growing use of the apartheid framework to conceptualize the Israeli state have brought to the fore race and its applicability in the Palestinian context. Accordingly, this book asks: What is the relevance of race analysis to the study of Palestine? How do modalities of racialization inform the durability of Zionist colonization in Palestine? How does race structure Zionist/Israeli settler colonialism in Palestine? And how has the intersection between colonialism and racism shaped the Palestinian struggle along anticolonial and antiracist registers?

The apartheid reports grapple with whether race is a relevant category and, if it is, how it should be understood and conceptualized. The report by B'Tselem, the leading Israeli human rights organization, differs from the others in its conclusion that race is an inappropriate category for conceptualizing Israeli apartheid.[2] B'Tselem draws on an understanding of race as a biological attribute that is signified by skin color, noting that "the division in South Africa was based on race and skin color, while in Israel it is based on nationality and ethnicity."[3] Even though the B'Tselem report speaks of Israel as a "regime of Jewish supremacy," it refrains entirely from using the term "race" and related terms—such as "racism," "racial domination," "racial discrimination," "racial rule," and "racial system"—to describe Israel's regime and policies.

The reports by Human Rights Watch, Amnesty International, and the UN special rapporteur are not as quick to dismiss race because the definition of "apartheid" under international law requires showing that Palestinians qualify as a "racial group" and that they are subject to a system of domination and institutionalized discrimination. They therefore mainly address race through the question of what constitutes a "racial group" in international law. As pointed out by Amnesty International, "if a group is perceived and treated as a distinct racial group, it would qualify as a racial group in the meaning of the crime of apartheid."[4] Taking a "subjective approach,"[5] these reports employ an understanding of race as an identity marker. While they attempt to move beyond the idea of race as "constituting only genetic traits,"[6] their acceptance of the notion of "racial groups" and their focus on qualifying Palestinians as a racial group demonstrate a view of race as a natural category, rather than one that is politically mobilized and engineered in the service of colonial domination.

The reports determine that Palestinians can be viewed as a racial group based on their ethnicity and nationality because Israel itself conceives of Jews and Palestinians as two distinct national, and thus racial, groups. In doing so, race is perceived in the reports in terms of identity and as synonymous with ethnicity, nationalism, and culture. The Human Rights Watch report, for example, states that "international human rights law had clearly defined racial discrimination to include differences of ethnicity, descent, and national origin," reflecting "a broader conception of race."[7] It finds that "in the local context, Jewish Israelis and Palestinians are regarded as separate identity groups that fall within the broad understanding of 'racial group' under international human rights law.... Even within Israel where both Jews and Palestinians are citizens, authorities classify Jews and Palestinians as belonging to different 'nationalities.'"[8] Likewise, the report by the UN special rapporteur proposes that "in the context of Israel's actions towards the Palestinians living in the occupied territory, Jewish Israelis and Palestinian Arabs may be understood as distinct racial groups distinguished by their nationality, ethnicity, religion, ancestry and descent."[9] And Amnesty International notes that "the State of Israel perceives Palestinians as 'different and ... inferior ... on account of particular ... cultural attributes.'"[10] The use of race as exchangeable with nationality, ethnicity, and religion, John Reynolds argues in his chapter on the apartheid reports, produces, in effect, a reading of apartheid "without race itself." Addressing this conflation, he writes that "it is important to insist on the importance of race qua race."[11]

The focus on nationality as the basis for racial discrimination is not without logic (the problem is more with how the relationship between nationality and race is approached in these reports through a positivist focus on "racial groups" as the basis for their analysis). In Israel, Saree Makdisi argues, "the categories of race and nation are collapsed into one another. For, according to the Israeli state and its juridical apparatuses, there is no such thing as an Israeli nation in a secular or nonracial sense."[12] Under "nationality," Israeli citizens are defined on Israeli identity cards and in official statistics as belonging to different ethnic and religious groups (Jewish, Arab, Druze, Bedouin, or Christian), but there is only one category that matters: Jewish.[13]

The category "Jewish" functions as a racial category that defines the nation, itself racially construed. To read race and nationality in Israel is also to read religion as a marker and maker of race. Religion determines national difference, and both operate, in effect, as racial difference. Israel is defined as the nation-state of the Jewish people, and the right to self-determination is an exclusive right of the Jewish people, as explicitly articulated in the 2018 Basic Law: Israel—The Nation-State of the Jewish People. Religious mythologies are used to justify racial laws that produce the Jewish people as an indigenous population returning to its ancestral lands and the Palestinians as foreign invaders. Racial hierarchies are codified and instituted through religious-qua-genealogical belonging, with the 1950 Law of Return—which provides Jews with the entitlement to immigrate to Israel and to be automatically naturalized, while preventing the Palestinians who actually lived in Palestine from returning to their homeland—being but one example. In Israel, it is religion—as a signifier of race and of the nation—that determines the extent of the rights and freedoms one enjoys, as well as one's political and legal status and access to land and property.

This book begins with the apartheid reports because they offer a roadmap to the different conceptions (and misreadings) of race that are at play in conversations on race and Palestine, including biological, genetic, ethnic, and subjective. The reports reflect not only the limitations of the interpretation of race in international law and in academic and political discourse, but, more notably, a wider lack in racial literacy[14] that extends also to scholarly work and activist conversations on Palestine. As put by Loubna Qutami, "Popular political discourses on Palestine suffer from an anemic racial lexicon."[15] It is not uncommon to hear the claim that race is an irrelevant category in understanding the question of Palestine. While the liberal and conservative positions insist that the colonization of Palestine is essentially a national conflict between rival groups, on the critical end there is also objection to understanding Palestine in terms of race, insisting instead that it is a colonial, not a colonial-racial, question (even though, as I discuss in the next section, Palestinians and other anticolonial scholars and activists have long argued that the colonial project is always also racial).

This discomfort, particularly in critical circles, demonstrates what is at stake when we either neglect race altogether or use it interchangeably with ethnic, cultural, or national identity, and as disconnected from theorizations of race both in Palestinian intellectual and political legacy and in race critical theory—as do the apartheid reports.[16] Palestinians have warned, and rightly so, against examining Palestine exclusively through a lens of race that is disassociated from settler colonialism and a critique of Zionism because it results in a liberal and limited reading of race in terms of equality and discrimination.[17] Such a reading risks reconfiguring Palestine from a colonial question into a liberal one.[18] Understanding Palestine through a liberal antiracist framework implies that Israel's racial and colonial rule could be remedied merely by extending citizenship and political rights to all Palestinians, rather than requiring an anticolonial (and antiracist) commitment to decolonization that centers liberation and the dismantling of settler colonialism, racial capitalism, and heteropatriarchy.

The apartheid reports and the reservations about the use of race demonstrate the need for a more nuanced conversation about race and Palestine. It is important to note that the use of race as an analytical framework has a long and rich history in Palestine studies. Early work, especially in the 1960s and 1970s, read race and racism as intrinsic features of the Zionist settler-colonial project in Palestine.[19] However, since the 1980s, as work on Palestine has shifted its focus away from settler colonialism and liberation and toward occupation, state building, and liberal peace,[20] race and racism have largely fallen out of use. Even though scholars such as Joseph Massad, Nadia Abu

El-Haj, and Elia Zureik sustained a race-informed focus on Zionism and set-tler colonialism, race and settler colonialism were replaced with ethnicity and ethnonational frameworks, with Israel conceptualized as an ethnic state and as an ethnocratic regime characterized by ethnic privilege and ethnona-tional and cultural difference.[21] Israel has accordingly been portrayed as a multiethnic state marked by a rift between Israeli Jews and Palestinians as "ethnic-national" groups, not as a racial-colonial project premised on the racialization of Palestinians, racial distinctions, and racial hierarchies that place Jews (both those who reside in Israel and those outside it) as superior to Indigenous Palestinians.[22]

The turn to settler-colonial analysis of Palestine in the 2010s, following the consolidation of settler-colonial studies as a distinct field, did not alter this trend much; instead, much of the work retained a commitment to eth-nicity and ethnonationalism, overlooking the role of race, racialization, and racism in shaping Zionist settler colonialism.[23] That said, recent years have seen a growing interest, in both scholarly and activist circles, in thinking about Palestine (and the Middle East more generally) through the prism of race, with new work emerging that addresses race, security, and surveil-lance; racial capitalism; law, race, and property; the racialization of Israeli settler colonialism; citizenship and race; Black-Palestinian solidarity; the imperial politics of race; race and labor; anti-Palestinian racism; gender and race; refugees and race; and health and race.[24]

*Race and the Question of Palestine* centers race in the study of Palestine, building on this renewed interest. The question, I maintain, is not merely whether race is a productive lens, but rather what kinds of theories and conceptualizations of race are relevant. The book is concerned with how to understand and analyze race in Palestine—not as a prescriptive question, but as an analytical and political one. I argue for an analysis of race that situates Palestine within the global histories, legacies, and present politics of imperialism, colonialism and settler colonialism, capitalism, and hetero-patriarchy, and that centers the racialization of Palestine and Palestinians. Through such analysis, the book demonstrates that the study of Palestine not only benefits from the integration of race critical theory but also contrib-utes more generally to an understanding of how race works. I further argue for an analysis of race that considers the specificities of the Palestinian case and that recognizes and builds on long-standing Palestinian theorizations of race that critique Zionism and Israel as a settler-colonial racial project. Engagement with Palestinian critique and critical theorizations of race that account for the colonial genealogy of race can help challenge the exceptionalism of the Palestinian case and the conceptualizations of race in terms of skin color, identity, ethnicity, and culture, and of race as a fixed category. Such engagement, I propose, helps explicate the political work of race in facilitating, sustaining, and justifying the Zionist settler-colonial project in Palestine and enriches our understanding of the global history of race and settler colonialism.

I follow Rana Barakat's important call for "a reading of settler colonialism *within* a Palestinian narrative."[25] Like Barakat, I stress the need for a reading of race within a Palestinian narrative. This entails a reading of race, racialization, anti-Palestinian racism, and antiracism from within Palestinian experiences and knowledges. It requires a consideration of the fragmentation of the Palestinian people and the multiple racialization regimes to which different Palestinian groups are subjected and their resistance to them, both within historic Palestine and in the diaspora, as well as the intersectionality of race with ethnicity, religion, class, gender, sexuality, age, and dis/ability. Likewise, the recognition that race and racism are core to Zionism and the architecture of the Israeli state also invites thinking about how the Palestinian struggle for liberation is both "anticolonialist and antiracist,"[26] and how Palestine activism involves the ongoing rearticulation of the relationship between anticolonialism and antiracism. That said, and although this book focuses on race and settler colonialism, I also caution against limiting the study of race in relation to Zionist colonization. This means attending to race formations and race regimes in Palestine prior to Zionist colonization and in relation to the global histories of race and race politics in the Middle East—concerns that are overlooked in Palestine studies and yet are critical to understanding racism, anti-Blackness, and class relations in Palestinian society.

Speaking of race in the context of Palestine, readers may ask why use "race" instead of "ethnicity," "people," or "nation," and what analytical and explanatory work "race" does that "ethnicity" or "nationality" does not. This also raises the question of how to theorize and understand the concept of race itself. Although categories such as "ethnicity" and "nation" intersect with "race" and operate as markers of race—Stuart Hall referred to the three of them as the "Fateful Triangle"[27]—their use alone without race analysis, I suggest, not only fails to capture the work of race, racialization, and racism as constitutive of colonial projects, but also conceals it. The apartheid reports, mentioned above, provide an example—one of many—of such concealment through their failure to recognize settler colonialism and race as the defining features of Israeli apartheid or to account for Zionism as the racial ideology that drives Israeli-Zionist colonization.[28]

Privileging ethnicity allows speaking about the hierarchy in Zionism and the Israeli state between Jews and Palestinians without acknowledging race and the practices of racialization that allow racial distinction to occur in the first place. Ethnicity, in this respect, functions as a category that is "race-free" and "raceless," a nonracial neutral and descriptive category of difference (although, in practice, one that is deeply racialized)—and a category that also treats Jews and Palestinians as homogenous groups, overlooking their ethnic heterogeneity.[29] The favoring of ethnic-centered paradigms, Nahla Abdo argues, is less because of their theoretical validity and more because they "provide softer, less politically charged concepts to describe what are basically racist policies and practices embedded in the Zionist ideology on which Israel has been—and continues to be—founded."[30]

The colonization of Palestine—like other imperial, colonial, and settler-colonial projects—cannot be understood outside the grammar of race. Concepts such as ethnicity and nationality do not capture the history or the political work of race as a project of colonial distinction that rationalizes dispossession and domination,[31] nor are they capable of accounting for racialization and dehumanization as central to the colonial project. The colonial quest to eliminate, contain, assimilate, exploit, and replace Indigenous peoples depends on the hierarchical classification of peoples and nations according to a civilizational value, as deemed by the European colonists. As Patrick Wolfe writes, race is "colonialism speaking."[32] Likewise, race itself needs to be understood in relation to its *colonial constitution*," argues Barnor Hesse. Race, he points out, "is an inherited western, modern-colonial practice of violence, assemblage, superordination, exploitation and segregation."[33] The modern history of racial classification systems emerged in relation to colonialism and in the encounter between European settlers and Indigenous peoples in what was called the "New World" (a racial term in its own right).[34] In the nineteenth century, race became "the organizing grammar of an imperial order in which modernity, the civilizing mission and the 'measure of man' were framed."[35] Zionism, as the next section elaborates, emerged as part of this imperial, colonial, and racial history, speaking to imperial order and aspirations and building on nineteenth-century European conceptions of race.

The question of the human is central to the operation of race and settler colonialism. As Alexander Weheliye argues, "race and racism shape the modern idea of the human"[36] through practices of differentiation that arrange "Homo sapiens species into humans, not-quite-humans, and nonhumans."[37] The regulation of humanness, its attribution and denial, Samera Esmeir argues, is a "technology of colonial rule."[38] The arrangement of the human across a spectrum, Hortense Spillers reminds us, cannot be separated from colonialism and settler colonialism, from enslavement, and from the creation of the "New World" and its sociopolitical, economic, and legal order—an order that "represents for its African and indigenous peoples a scene of actual mutilation, dismemberment, and exile."[39] Addressing societal orders, Sylvia Wynter suggests, requires attending to the sociogenic principle[40]—a concept she borrows and develops from the work of Frantz Fanon, who insisted that the human is to be understood not only through phylogeny and ontogeny, but also, and primarily, through sociogeny and the centering of Black and colonized people's experiences of racism, hierarchization, and dehumanization. Society, Fanon notes, "cannot escape human influences. Man is what brings society into being."[41] Importantly, while both Wynter's and Fanon's analyses speak to processes and practices of dehumanization, their centering of the colonized and the racialized also leads them to assert that their humanity is always there,[42] and for Wynter this acknowledgment asks that we think about being "human" not as a noun but as a praxis.[43]

In Palestine, the expulsion of the majority of Palestinians from their land; the refusal to allow refugees to return to their homeland; the ongoing Nakba (the catastrophe); the occupation of the West Bank, Jerusalem, and Gaza in 1967; the siege of Gaza since 2006 and the 2023 genocide; the oppression of, and discrimination against, Palestinians with Israeli citizenship, who comprise one-fifth of Israel's citizenry; the routine killing of Palestinians; settler violence; land dispossession and house demolition; the entrenched system of checkpoints and segregated roads; the exploitation of Palestinian labor; the use of Palestinians for the testing of new weapons and security technologies; and the mass incarceration of Palestinians all rely on the racialization of Palestinians as less than human and nonhuman, rather than on "ethnic" or "national" difference.

A proper engagement with race requires us to move beyond the inquiry into whether Jews and Palestinians are "races." Race critical scholars have emphasized time and again that race is not an identity; it is, in the words of Azfar Shafi and Ilyas Nagdee, "a social system" that shapes "the structural relationships of certain social groups to power . . . something one is subject to rather than something one possesses."[44] Put differently, race is "a process, not an ontology."[45] Stuart Hall regards race as a "sliding signifier," alluding to its dynamic and ever-changing nature, rather than a stable category with a fixed meaning. Its power lies in its function as a meaning-making discourse that establishes itself as a "regime of truth."[46] Recognizing that it is not fixed, Alana Lentin proposes that race is better understood in terms of what it does rather than what it is, and as a technology of power and "a technology for the management of human difference."[47]

When it comes to Palestine, there is a strong reluctance in scholarship and in public discourse to speak about race, even though Palestinians have been doing so for decades. While there has been a growing willingness, especially in some liberal circles, to describe Israeli laws, policies, institutions, and public discourse as racist toward Palestinians, there remains a refusal to acknowledge race as a relevant category, reducing racism to a set of practices and policies and to individual behavior.[48] The preference of racism over race is not unique to the Palestinian case. For many, speaking about racism is safer and less threatening than speaking about race, precisely because of its use in the public domain to confer a moral judgment or to indicate personal aberrations.[49] Moreover, the treatment of race and racism as separate implies "that 'race' is fundamentally a neutral category that is merely disfigured by acts of racism."[50] Such treatment overlooks that there is no racism without race—something that Palestinian scholarship has long acknowledged. The refusal to mention race, Ronit Lentin argues, is connected to the prevalent view of Israel as a safe haven for Jews from antisemitism. The history of the Holocaust categorically renders Israel and Zionism immune from a conversation on their racial foundations—a logic that is, in her words, a "trace of racial exception."[51]

*Race and the Question of Palestine* offers new directions in thinking about race in Palestine, with chapters by scholars from diverse disciplines including history, cultural studies, politics and international studies, law, race critical theory, and Middle East studies. The chapters cover themes such as Zionism and race; race and international law; the racialization of Palestinian refugees; imperial constructions of race; gender and racialized sexual politics; antiracism and antisemitism; race, land, and labor; racial capitalism and militarized accumulation; and Black-Palestinian solidarity. All chapters highlight that the colonization of Palestine could not have taken place—and cannot be effectively sustained—without the racialization of Palestinians.

This introduction to the book is composed of four sections that address key themes and concepts, as well as highlighting gaps in the literature on race and Palestine and potential directions for future research. The first section focuses on the relationship between Zionism, race, and settler colonialism. It shows that Palestinian critics have long developed theorizations of race that position Palestine within the wider context of global racial politics of imperialism, colonialism, and settler colonialism, while considering the specificities of the Palestinian case but without exceptionalizing it. Further, it highlights the importance of Palestinian tradition as a foundation on which to build and expand. The second section focuses on racial capitalism and settler colonialism in Palestine, and more specifically on the relationship between racial capitalism, land, and labor. It proposes that the study of Palestine could benefit from the emerging interest in racial capitalism in settler-colonial studies and Indigenous studies. At the same time, it points out the need to consider also the multiple histories of racial capitalism in Palestine, some of which predate British imperialism and Zionism. The third section focuses on race formation, racism, Blackness, and anti-Blackness in Palestinian society. While there is a rich conversation on anti-Palestinian racism and on Black-Palestinian solidarity, there is a significant gap, admittedly also in this book, when it comes to exploring racism and antiracism and Blackness and anti-Blackness in Palestinian society. Tackling these difficult and confronting issues is necessary for the pursuit of an antiracist, anticolonial liberationist project. Palestine studies, it is further suggested, can contribute to and benefit from the emerging conversation in Middle East studies on how to theorize race in ways that attend to the specificities of the region and to the differences within and across it. The fourth section outlines the structure of the book.

## ZIONISM, RACE, AND SETTLER COLONIALISM

Race analysis by Palestinians has stressed critiques of Zionism as a racial settler-colonial ideology and movement and of Israel as a racial settler-colonial regime. Palestinian scholars have highlighted that the Nakba—which has involved the Zionist destruction of hundreds of Palestinian cities and villages, the transformation of the majority of Palestinians into refugees, and the mass dispossession of land and property—is racially inflected and motivated and can only take place in a racialized world order in which the division of nations and peoples into a hierarchy of races is deemed acceptable. They have asserted that "colonialism is the context,"[52] but also that the colonial and the racial are intertwined. As Joseph Massad remarks, "Zionism as a colonial movement is constituted in ideology and practice by a religio-racial epistemology through which it apprehends itself and the world around it. This religio-racial grid informs and is informed by its colonial-settler venture."[53]

Palestinians have also acknowledged—in an analysis that aligned with Third World thought—that colonialism is always also racial and racist. As Ibrahim Abu-Lughod and Baha Abu-Laban wrote in their book from 1974 on settler regimes in Africa and the Arab world, a comparative lens exposes "the role of belief in racial superiority and manifest destiny in the colonial condition."[54] Likewise, in their political mobilization Palestinians have stressed the racial dimensions of Zionist settler colonialism. In his famous "the gun and the olive branch" speech to the UN General Assembly in 1974, Yasser Arafat, chairman of the Palestinian Liberation Organization, referred to Zionism as an "ideology that is imperialist, colonialist, racist" and to Israel as a "racist entity, founded on the imperialist-colonialist concept." He articulated the Palestinian struggle in anticolonial, anti-imperialist, and antiracist terms: "Our resolve to build a new world is fortified—a world free of colonialism, imperialism, neo-colonialism and racism in each of its instances, including zionism."[55] And, in a major achievement for Palestinians in the United Nations, the UN General Assembly adopted in 1975 Resolution 3379, which determined that "zionism is a form of racism and racial discrimination."[56] As Noura Erakat argues in her chapter on its history, the resolution is a clear articulation of the Palestinian anticolonial struggle in antiracist terms.[57]

Racism, Palestinian critique highlights, is inherent in Israel's laws and legal system, its land and property regimes, and its refusal to respect the Palestinian right of return, as well as in the unconditional support of Israel by the West and the denial of Palestinian rights. Importantly, when Palestinians spoke of the racism inherent to Zionism, they did not read racism as a category free of race, or as "race without racism." Rather, their analysis revealed the political and systemic work of race, the discursive and material practices of racialization, and the processes of racial classification, distinction, and categorization that allow, facilitate, and sustain the Zionist colonization of Palestine. They located Palestinian experience in relation to the experiences of Black Americans, Native Americans, and colonized peoples in the Americas, Asia, and Africa. This not only prompted Third World and Fourth World solidarity[58] but it also informed a political understanding of race that considers its function as a colonial technology of domination while recognizing that regimes of race and practices of racialization can take diverse forms and be informed by distinctive racial logics in different contexts.[59]

Critiques of Zionism in racial terms shaped Palestinian writing and political mobilization. In 1965, Fayez Sayegh's "Zionist Colonialism in Palestine"—a foundational essay on race and settler colonialism—was published. In that essay, Sayegh argues that race is inherent to Zionist ideology and the colonization of Palestine: "Racism is not an acquired trait of the Zionist settler-state. Nor is it an accidental, passing feature of the Israeli scene. It is congenial, essential and permanent. For it is inherent in the very ideology of Zionism and in the basic motivation for Zionist colonisation and statehood." Zionism, he suggests, is premised on *"racial self-segregation, racial exclusiveness*, and *racial supremacy"* and on a commitment to racial purity.[60] Attentive to the specificities of the Palestinian case, Sayegh differentiates between the racial logics that have shaped colonialism in Asia and Africa and settler colonialism in Palestine. The former, he notes, has been based on the exploitation of the native. While *"race-supremacist European settlers* . . . found it possible to express their 'supremacy' over the other strands of 'lesser people' and 'inferior races' within the framework of 'hierarchical racial coexistence,'" Palestine was different.[61] He writes: "If *racial discrimination* against the 'inferior natives' was the motto of race-supremacist European settler-regimes in Asia and Africa, the motto of the race-supremacist Zionist settler-regime in Palestine was *racial elimination*."[62]

Sayegh's notion of "racial elimination," which is central to settler-colonial regimes,[63] captures that the quest of white settler-states to eliminate Indigenous peoples is racial. Elimination, Sayegh recognized, is contingent on the creation of racial categories of difference that position white European settlers as possessing greater civilizational value than do natives and therefore as being worthy of land, sovereignty, and self-determination, and on practices of racialization that render the natives inferior, dispensable, and expellable. While European Jews may not have been considered "white" in Europe, they were white Europeanized Jews in Palestine and employed a racial-colonial discourse that portrayed them to be developmentally more advanced and civilized than Palestinians.

Two years after Sayegh's essay, Ghassan Kanafani wrote *On Zionist Literature*, which offers a race analysis of Zionism's mobilization of literature to justify settler colonialism in Palestine. In this text, Kanafani theorizes political Zionism as a racist movement premised on principles of racial superiority and domination and on the mixing of "religion and race under the banner of the national homeland." It is, however, also a racist colonial movement that portrays itself as one against racism and antisemitism.[64] Such representation, Kanafani notes, "conceals the essence of Zionism, which counters racist oppression with racism."[65]

In his essay "Zionism from the Standpoint of Its Victims," Edward Said addresses the essence of Zionism. He writes:

> effective political ideas like Zionism need to be examined historically in two ways: (1) *genealogically*, in order that their provenance, their kinship and descent, their affiliation both with other ideas and with political institutions may be demonstrated; (2) as practical systems for *accumulation* (of power, land, ideological legitimacy) and *displacement* (of people, other ideas, prior legitimacy).[66]

Tracing the genealogy of Zionism, Said, in line with other Palestinian theorizations, argues that Zionism has its origins in Western imperialism, orientalism, colonialism, racism, and capitalism. "Imperialism was the theory, colonialism the practice," he points out.[67] Western imperialism and racism rendered territories and lands belonging to nonwhite peoples, including Palestinians, available for invasion, exploitation, and settlement. Zionist leaders themselves described the movement as one of colonial settlement, an extension of European imperialism, bringing civilization and modernization to the Orient—or, as put by Theodor Herzl, the Jewish state was to be "an outpost of civilization as opposed to barbarism."[68] Racialization was thus inherent to Zionist thinking, producing what David Theo Goldberg calls "racial Palestinianization," which involved the treatment of Palestinians as a "subjugated race."[69] The Zionist movement, Shira Robinson notes, "portrayed Palestinians as a 'mixture of races and types,' a 'multitude' distinguished not by their shared history or national character but by their inferior human 'quality.'"[70]

Not unlike other European imperialists, Zionists mobilized race to rationalize imperial expansion and domination.[71] Race was treated as a biological category. Nations were classified into superior and inferior races, civilized and uncivilized, and "lesser races were put in direct use in the Empire."[72] Those "lesser races"—including Palestinians—were portrayed, in line with liberal imperialist thinking, as primitive and insufficiently civilized to self-govern, control their lands and natural resources, or possess sovereignty. In the international political context of the early twentieth century, Palestine, along with Syria, Iraq, and Lebanon, was classified under the Covenant of the League of Nations as an "A" territory, meaning that it held the potential for independence.[73] Palestine and Palestinians occupied a "semi-civilized" status (not quite civilized and not entirely primitive).[74] Palestine, however, was different from other "A" territories because the Mandate in Palestine was "the only case in which the Permanent Mandates Commission endorsed settler colonialism."[75] The 1917 Balfour Declaration, a British imperial promise to establish a national home for the Jewish people in Palestine, represented this commitment to settler colonialism. It recognized Jews as a people with national and political rights, while referring to the Arab majority—who comprised 95 percent of the population in Mandatory Palestine—as "non-Jewish communities," granting them only religious and civil rights, not political rights or national recognition. The Balfour Declaration, suggests Rashid Khalidi, was premised on "the idea that the Palestinians simply do not exist."[76] It constituted, according to Sherene Seikaly, the erasure of Palestinians and was based on a racial distinction between those deserving and those undeserving of self-determination.[77]

While Palestine and Palestinians were not at the bottom of this imperial racial categorization (which was based on skin color), they were nonetheless considered as civilizationally inferior to Jews, with this racist view guiding the British governance of Palestine.[78] The Peel Commission in 1937, for example, referred to Jews as "a highly intelligent and enterprising *race* backed by large financial resources" and to Palestinians as "a comparatively poor, indigenous community, *on a different cultural level.*"[79] Accordingly, the commission recommended the partition of Palestine, with a Jewish state in approximately 17 percent of the land of Palestine and the expulsion of more than two hundred thousand Palestinians from that territory, and with the rest of the territory remaining under the control of the British.[80] A decade later, the 1947 Partition Plan suggested the division of Palestine along racial lines into a Jewish state and an Arab state and promised the Zionist movement more than half of Palestine in what has been described as an anti-Arab and anti-Palestinian proposal.[81]

As opposed to the view of Zionism in the West as an anticolonial and antiracist national liberation movement, Palestinian critique has shown that Zionism was not antagonistic to colonialism, nor to the idea of race itself; on the contrary, Zionists built on and benefited from both. Race was central to the Zionist mission of establishing Jews as a nation and a people, not just a religious group. While, in Zionism, religion is a signifier of race, religion alone was not enough to substantiate the claim that Jews were a nation.[82] Beginning in the late nineteenth century, Jewish social scientists mobilized race science to show that Jews had a shared ancient, and biologically distinguishable, origin in Palestine: in other words, as a race.[83] Even today, the search for "Jewish DNA" persists. The rabbinical courts, for example, have been encouraging Israeli migrants from the former Soviet Union whom the rabbinate does not recognize as Jews to undergo a genetic test to prove their Jewishness, with Israel's Supreme Court affirming the legality of DNA testing to establish such claims.[84]

In her book *The Genealogical Science*, Nadia Abu El-Haj shows that race science was central to the making of Jewish peoplehood and nationhood and was used "to articulate a secular conception of Jewishness."[85] It was also part of nation-building efforts that continued well after the establishment of the Israeli state, seeking to establish "biological unity—a shared origin—among the Jewish migrant communities."[86] Work in Israeli population genetics, she argues, reflects two settler anxieties. The first is among "Israel's Ashkenazi elite about whether or not *these* Jews—oriental Jews, that is—could *really be* national kin." The second is related to processes of settler indigenization and the quest of settlers to appear natural to the land, which, in the case of Jewish settlers, is manifested in the quest to prove Near Eastern origins. Abu El-Haj writes: "For a state in which the Ashkenazi (European) Jew was the normative citizen, the search for their biological origins in the ancient Near East was crucial. What evidence was there that European Jews were actually *of* the Middle East?"[87]

The Zionist and Israeli conception of Jews as a "blood community"[88] also came to mean that "bloodlines" are uncrossable (Zionism never pursued assimilation as a technology of elimination in the way that other white settler colonies did). Sarah Ihmoud demonstrates that the quest for racial purity has also taken gendered forms through the advancement of anti-miscegenation policies and programs—funded and implemented by the government, local municipalities, and the third sector—that aim to protect Jewish women from Palestinian men, who are racialized as hypersexualized predators. Referring to these projects as "policing the intimate," she suggests that gendered racial policing aims to create "racialized boundaries between Palestinian and Jewish subjects" that enable "both Jewish men and women to achieve a sense of gendered racial superiority."[89] Racialized boundaries are so rigid that even in the very rare cases in which Palestinians choose to convert to Judaism, they are not accepted as Jews by the public or by the relevant religious authorities, even when they endorse Zionism.[90] In fact, the Israeli government's Conversion Authority automatically and categorically rejects all Palestinian requests to convert to Judaism,[91] reflecting that "birth (that is, blood)" is "the sole path to membership in the settler community."[92]

Zionism's preoccupation with, and pursuit of, racial purity and "regeneration" informs the specific forms that Jewish supremacy takes and its intersection with whiteness and white supremacy. The prevalence of whiteness is rooted in the emergence of Zionism as a European Ashkenazi movement. The Zionist movement did not merely endeavor to create a "Jewish state"; it sought to create a Jewish Ashkenazi state that excluded Mizrahi (oriental) Jews, who it considered to be primitive Arabs, intellectually inferior, and less civilized.[93] While some Mizrahi immigration, such as that of the Yemenite Jews, was recorded prior to the establishment of the Israeli state, it was only in the aftermath of the Holocaust, and following the refusal of the Soviet Union to allow Jews to migrate to Palestine, that Zionists resorted, reluctantly, to bringing oriental Jews in their masses to Palestine (sometimes against their will) in order to ensure the demographic advantage of Jews over Palestinians and to provide cheap labor.[94]

No doubt, intra-Jewish racialization of Mizrahi and Ethiopian Jews by Ashkenazi Jews complicates the way we think about the relationship between Jewish supremacy and white supremacy, especially given that nonwhite Jews are integral to Jewish supremacy while being subject to Ashkenazi white supremacy.[95] These groups have come to occupy an ambivalent position in the racial hierarchy of Zionism, racialized upwardly as Jews (with Jewishness providing proximity to whiteness) and racialized downwardly as nonwhite by Ashkenazi Jews. This has meant that even though the Mizrahim and Ethiopians are racialized (albeit in different ways, since Ethiopians also face anti-Blackness), both groups are, in effect, part of the Zionist project and play an active role in the colonization of Palestine and the racialization and dispossession of Palestinians.[96]

When it comes to exploration of the nexus between Jewish supremacy and white supremacy, there is a tendency to focus on nonwhite Jews and intra-Jewish racialization, often at the exclusion of the Palestinian experience. However, once Palestinians (rather than settlers, even if racialized) are centered, the inextricable relationship between settler colonialism, whiteness, and Jewish racial superiority becomes visible. Even though Jews in Israel are a heterogeneous group composed of white and nonwhite Jews, the racial category of Jews under Zionism plays a similar epistemological role to that of whiteness, with Jewish supremacy assuming similar functions to white supremacy. After all, as Charles Mills notes, *"Whiteness is not really a color at all, but a set of power relations,"*[97] and Israelis, Goldberg points out, "occupy the structural positions of whiteness in the racial hierarchy of the Middle East."[98] In Israel, Jews, including nonwhite Jews, are akin to the "white race." Commenting on African Muslims seeking asylum in Israel, former minister Eli Yishai of the Sephardic party Shas said, "Muslims that arrive here do not even believe that this country belongs to us, to the white man."[99] In this regard, the Zionist project has succeeded in foregrounding Jewish supremacy as white supremacy and Israel as a white-like supremacist state, despite the ethnic diversity of its Jewish citizenry.

## RACIAL CAPITALISM AND SETTLER COLONIALISM IN PALESTINE

Race, capitalism, and settler colonialism are intimately linked. Yet the relationship between the three has received limited attention in the context of Palestine, although new work on race, land, labor, securitization, and development is emerging.[100] This gap is not unique to the Palestinian case and extends to other settler-colonial contexts. The growing recognition of racial capitalism in critical analysis has prompted an interest in the concept in settler-colonial studies and Indigenous studies. Commenting on the relevance of racial capitalism to settler colonialism, scholars have pointed out that "dispossessive regimes of accumulation through differentiation, elimination, expropriation, enslavement, and incarceration have themselves always been settler colonialist."[101] At the same time, scholars have also warned against applying the concept of racial capitalism without addressing precolonial histories, the particularities of settler colonialism, and the specific forms that the relationship between capital accumulation, land, and labor takes in and across settler-colonial contexts.[102]

The concept of racial capitalism is mostly associated with Cedric Robinson, who examined the history of modern capitalism and showed that capitalism is always racial.[103] The term, however, originated in the context of settler-colonial apartheid South Africa during the 1970s. It was used by intellectuals and activists to frame the apartheid colonial regime not only as a political system of discrimination but also as a system of capitalist domination.[104] The term came to capture the relationship between settler colonialism, white supremacy, anti-Blackness, imperialism, and capitalism,[105] and to bear on the question of decolonization, with South African activ- ists affirming that the end of apartheid "depends on the eradication of the system of racial capitalism," as put in the Azanian Manifesto.[106] In their book *Colonial Racial Capitalism*, Susan Koshy et al. argue that to further the an- alytical specificity of the concept of racial capitalism to settler colonialism requires an understanding of capitalism as a colonial relation and to "push Robinson's analytic of racial capitalism back to the significance of the term's South African settler colonialist origins to examine how Indigenous dispos- session is not the precondition for racial capitalism to emerge but always has been part of its very structure." As they put it: "Racial capitalism *is* colonial capitalism."[107] Returning to the roots of the concept in South Africa and ap- plying it to Palestine, Andy Clarno suggests that the relationship between racial capitalism and settler colonialism is more constitutive than often rec- ognized. As he writes, "forcible dispossession is not merely a settler-colonial strategy but also a racialized process of capital accumulation."[108]

The study of Palestine could be enriched by examining how capitalism and settler colonialism are structured by race. This raises the questions of how to read racial capitalism in Palestine and how to advance a Palestin- ian theorization of racial capitalism. Ruth Wilson Gilmore points out that "if we seriously want to enliven, and make useful, and keep useful the con- cept of racial capitalism, we have to get over thinking that what it's about is white-people capitalism. There *is* white-people capitalism, but that's not all of capitalism."[109] In bringing the concept of racial capitalism to bear on Pal- estine, there is a risk of seeing Palestinians merely as victims of capitalism or through an essentialist lens that constructs and fetishizes them as an Indig- enous people who are inherently anticapitalist.[110] Considering Palestinian agency requires accounting for the multiple histories and present workings of racial capitalism, class formation, and class relations in Palestine and for Palestinian engagement with, and against, capitalist structures.

Overall, there has been "a resounding silence on Arab capitalist practice" in the literature on Palestine, with a tendency to focus on contrasting the Palestinian economy, depicted mostly in civilizationally inferior terms, with the Zionist economy, seen as modern and advanced.[111] Capitalist transfor- mations in Palestine, however, predate Zionist settler colonialism and are rooted in regional and global developments. As Beshara Doumani shows in his work on Jabal Nablus between the seventeenth and nineteenth centuries, Palestine was integrated into the global capitalist economy and had exhibited capitalist features, such as "commercial agriculture, a money economy in the rural areas, differentiation within the peasantry, commoditization of land, and ties to the world market," since before British colonialism or 1882, when the first Zionist settlers immigrated to Palestine.[112] The coastal cities of Jaffa, Haifa, and Acre and the interior city of Nablus were trade and manufacturing centers exporting cotton, olive oil, sesame, soap, citrus fruit, wheat, barley, and other crops to Europe, Egypt, and northern Syria.[113] Capitalist transformations in Palestine shaped social structures and relations, social status, and land ownership patterns, informing the creation of new middle-class and capitalist elites, among other developments.[114]

In the exploration of race and capitalism in Palestine, it is likewise important to engage with critiques of capitalism and its interrelation with racism, imperialism, Zionist settler colonialism, and patriarchy. These are part of the history and present of Palestinian leftist, Marxist, and radical feminist politics and mobilization. Although not necessarily always conceived through anticapitalist commitments, the Palestinian struggle for liberation has involved boycotts, general strikes, and the boosting of Palestinian goods, agricultural cooperatives, and economic solidarity, from the 1936 General Strike through to the first and second Intifadas, the May 2021 Unity Intifada, and the global Boycott, Divestment, Sanctions movement. Moreover, groups such as Palestine Action, which is active against the Israeli arms manufacturer Elbit Systems, and the feminist group Who Profits, a research center that tracks the involvement of corporations in the Israeli occupation industry, are pushing the boundaries of racial capitalist analysis by examining how settler accumulation operates on local and global scales, informing also the oppression of other racialized and Indigenous communities worldwide. Such groups, Keiron Turner argues in his chapter, push the boundaries of what constitutes anticolonial solidarity by articulating it also as anticapitalist resistance.

Despite Zionist claims to socialist commitments, Zionist settler colonialism in Palestine has involved several aspects of racial capitalism, including but not limited to the colonization of Palestinian lands by the Zionist movement since the early twentieth century; the segmentation of labor and the Zionist Conquest of (Hebrew) Labor policy; the reliance on cheap and dispensable Palestinian labor, especially after the establishment of the Israeli state and up to the 1990s; and, finally, the recently booming Israeli arms, security, and intelligence industry, which relies on the testing of arms and new technologies on Palestinians.[115]

The dispossession of Palestinian land has been central to Zionist settler capital accumulation. This is not unique to the Palestinian case, since in settler colonialism "capitalism exploits and expropriates not only labor but also land."[116] To Zionists, the land is a racial God-given entitlement of the Jewish people, and Zionism's guiding principle has been to gain control of as much land as possible with as few Palestinians as possible. As Neve Gordon and Yinon Cohen show in their chapter, this involves a process of racializing the land as Jewish and the Palestinians as expellable.

Prior to 1948, Zionists colonized land by purchasing it from Palestinians. In 1899, the World Zionist Organization established the Jewish Colonial Trust, and in 1901 it founded the Jewish National Fund to extend Jewish land ownership in Palestine, with the first land purchases taking place in 1905.[117] Zionists purchased land mostly from absentee landowners, which led to the displacement of thousands of peasants.[118] The crisis of the absentee landholding class was not unique to Palestine and extended to other parts of the Middle East. It was a product of Ottoman land reforms and the introduction of the 1858 Land Code and the 1859 Tapu (Land Registry) Law, which were designed to tighten the empire's control of land and grow revenues. These reforms, which also included the privatization of land, resulted in "a new class of absentee landlords."[119] Zionists, Munir Fakher Eldin notes, saw in this an opportunity for settler-colonial accumulation. But the story of land in Palestine, he reminds us, also extends to local middle-class owners who struggled to develop and keep their land in the face of British and Zionist pressure and violence. The experiences of Palestinian middle-class landowners in the Beisan valley, a key development area in the 1930s and 1940s, demonstrate, Fakher Eldin argues, that the history of private property in Palestine has been one of double loss, "of Indigenous land relations and ecologies to capitalist developments" and "of territory to the settlers."[120] Despite the economic constraints, many Palestinian landowners—who saw in themselves a force of national development—did not sell their land and were dispossessed of it and forcibly displaced in the aftermath of the Nakba.[121]

Notwithstanding Zionist efforts to secure land by purchase, by the end of 1947 Jewish landholding in Palestine had reached only 6.95 percent.[122] During the Nakba and after the establishment of Israel, Zionist militias and the Israeli state shifted to obtaining land through military conquest, with law becoming the main instrument for the mass transfer of Palestinian land into Jewish and state ownership via the Jewish National Fund and the Israel Land Administration. Most Palestinians—peasants, middle class, and capitalist elites—lost their land, demonstrating that a major effect of colonial racial capitalism is denying, prohibiting, and limiting Palestinian ownership and access to their land.

With its establishment, the Israeli state, Noura Erakat argues, "ascribed new value onto Jewish nationality relative to the Arab other." It did so through its legal system, its racialized citizenship regime, and the application of discriminatory laws.[123] The legislation of the 1950 Law of Return (which provides automatic citizenship to Jews) and the 1952 Citizenship Law (which governs the citizenship of Palestinians) effectively operated as a mechanism for the expulsion of Palestinians from their homeland and as an instrument of settler capital accumulation.[124] Through this racial bifurcation, Erakat suggests, "Israel both achieved the supremacy of Jewish nationality as refracted through a lens of European white supremacy and facilitated the dispossession, displacement, and containment of Palestinian natives."[125] In 2018, Israel further constitutionally consolidated the superior value of Jewish nationality through the enactment of the Basic Law: Israel—The Nation-State of the Jewish People, which defines "the Land of Israel" as "the historical homeland of the Jewish people," requiring the state to advance "the development of Jewish settlement as a national value."[126]

In her work on whiteness as property, Cheryl Harris shows how whiteness "evolved into a form of property, historically and presently acknowledged and protected in American law," with this evolution having its origins in the domination of Native Americans and Black Americans.[127] Bringing Harris's work to bear on Palestine highlights the need to consider dispossession and racialized property relations in relation to both whiteness and Jewish superiority. In Israel, Jewishness evolved into a form of property, a process contingent on the dispossession of Palestinians and codified in Israeli law.[128] Indeed, all Jewish settlers, white and nonwhite, benefit from access to stolen land and property.

At the same time, Ashkenazi Jews have accumulated more capital than non-white Jews and they benefit more from Palestinian dispossession, demonstrating the intricacies of the relationship between Jewishness, whiteness, and settler colonialism.[129] This illuminates, as Brenna Bhandar shows, the ways in which property law, a crucial mechanism for the colonial accumulation of capital, and racial subjectivity developed in relation to one another.[130]

One of the first acts to solidify Jewishness as property in Israeli law was the 1950 Absentee Property Law, which enabled the State of Israel via the Custodian of Absentee Property to expropriate land, houses, and bank accounts belonging to Palestinians expelled after November 29, 1947, with the law applying also to '48 Palestinians (known also as Palestinians with Israeli citizenship).[131] Other property-related laws include the State Property Law of 1951, the Land Acquisition Law of 1953, and the Law for the Requisitioning of Property in Time of Emergency of 1949.[132] As a result, Palestinian refugees were robbed of all their land and property and '48 Palestinians lost most of their land during the military regime imposed by Israel between 1948 and 1966. For example, Israel left Umm al-Fahm, a Palestinian village in the Triangle, with just 15,000 of its original 140,000 *dunums*.[133]

Codified by race, the effects of Jewishness as property are apparent across historic Palestine. Between 600,000 and 750,000 Israeli settlers live in hundreds of illegal settlements in the West Bank and occupied East Jerusalem in violation of international law.[134] And, within the "Green Line," Israel has legalized admission committees that are designed to limit the ability of Palestinians to live in Jewish towns on racist grounds of "social suitability." The effects are also evident in the continual demolition of Palestinian homes and schools, the destruction of Bedouin villages, and the paucity of building permits granted to Jerusalem's Palestinian residents and to Palestinians in Area C of the West Bank.[135] Like other settler-colonial regimes, Israel produced "racial regimes of ownership," based on a hierarchy of Indigenous ownership regimes, considered premodern and inferior, and modern Western property law, with the latter relying on land registry and the (modern) use of land (for example, showing modern forms of land cultivation) as core principles in the regulation of land ownership.[136] Israel used this logic to categorically deny the Palestinian Bedouin of the Naqab ownership of their land, claiming that the Bedouin are nomads and classifying their land as *mawat*—literally, dead land, the equivalent of *terra nullius*. This paved the way for Israel's mass takeover of Bedouin land.[137] Meeting the requirements of modern property law, however, has not helped other Palestinians, since the land itself is seen as exclusive Jewish property that is for the Jewish people alone.

Alongside land, labor was the second significant pillar of racial capitalism. Zionists adopted the policy of the "conquest of labor"—a racially "split labor market"—with the aim of developing a strong Jewish economic sector independent of Palestinian labor and dispossessing Palestinians of their economic relevance.[138] The hebraization of labor was in line with the creation of the "new Jew" (a masculine version who would differ from both the diasporic antecedent, perceived as weak and submissive, and the Palestinian Native), and it also served as a means for the indigenization of settlers in the attempt to foster rootedness in and connection with the land through labor.[139] Since the ultimate goal was to displace Palestinians, Zionists did their best to minimize dependency on Palestinian labor and to ensure the dispensability of Palestinians. In the words of the Zionist labor organization, the Histadrut, "to allow Arabs to penetrate the Jewish labour market meant that the influx of Jewish capital would be employed to service Arab development, which is contrary to Zionist objectives."[140] Accordingly, the immigration of oriental Jews was intended not only to advance demographic superiority but also to supply the Zionist project with the Jewish proletariat it needed.[141]

In *The 1936–39 Revolt in Palestine*, Ghassan Kanafani describes the impact of the Jewish-labor-only policy on Palestinians, from the destruction of local industries such as the pearl industry and the closing of soap factories, through to wage gaps, the locking of Palestinian workers out of the labor market, and the eviction of peasants from their lands.[142] The concentration of European Jewish capital in Palestine, the creation of a labor surplus among Palestinians, and the British government support of Zionist industrialization through tax policies and the allotment of concessions led, according to Kanafani, to "an almost total collapse of the Arab economy in Palestine."[143] At the same time, the Great Revolt also informed cross-class commitment among Palestinian peasants, small landowners, and urban middle bourgeoisie to national liberation and the struggle against Zionist colonization, and prompted mass mobilization and the creation of popular institutions and movements rooted in projects "of state formation from below," of which capitalist elites were part.[144]

The Nakba left Palestinian refugees dispossessed of their land and property, and '48 Palestinians lost most of their land and were proletarianized as low-wage laborers in the service and construction industries.[145] In 1967, Israel occupied more Palestinian and Arab lands. The occupation resulted in an inflow of tens of thousands of Palestinians into the Israeli labor market, increased Israel's reliance on cheap Palestinian labor, and made Palestinians dependent on Israel for their livelihoods. Israel's control of Palestinian borders also meant that the West Bank and Gaza effectively became captive economies for Israeli goods, producing significant profits for Israeli companies.

The 1993 Oslo Accords and the neoliberalization of racial capitalism and settler colonialism transformed patterns of labor exploitation. Liberal Zionists became more committed to a separation between Israelis and Palestinians and intensified strategies of securitization while reducing the dependency on cheap Palestinian labor.[146] The neoliberalization of the Israeli economy and its further integration into the global labor market allowed Israel to import a large foreign migrant workforce to replace, as much as possible, Palestinian labor.[147] Israel, however, Nadia Abu El-Haj reminds us, is not only a neoliberal state but also a colonial state. This means that while Israel employs neoliberalism in the service of the colonial project, it is also dependent on state intervention that does not necessarily take neoliberal forms—such as subsidizing settlements and providing tax breaks to settlers in the West Bank to advance the de facto annexation of the West Bank.[148]

At the same time that transformations in its racialized labor regimes were taking place, Israel's arms, security, and intelligence industries began to play a larger global role. Israeli companies became a leading force in developing and marketing weapons, surveillance technologies, and advanced security equipment first tested on Palestinians in the West Bank and Gaza.[149] Israel became more dependent on advanced strategies of securitization,[150] and capital accumulation began to take a different shape: less reliance on Palestinian labor and more reliance on the necropolitical use of Palestinians and their bodies as a testing ground for Israel's arms and security industries. This has created a paradoxical condition whereby Palestinians became racialized as both dispensable and indispensable, subjected to exploitation while exposed to "premature death, abandonment, or elimination."[151]

After 1993, and with the creation of the Palestinian Authority (PA), the West Bank has also undergone a process of neoliberalization.[152] Kareem Rabie traces how the PA's shift toward a neoliberal economy, with the guidance of international financial institutions and Western governments, was advanced within the national aims of state building while in practice sustaining and entrenching Israeli settler colonialism and occupation. The PA, scholars have demonstrated, has created a new economic elite that is benefiting from "processes of racial capitalism and settler colonialism."[153] Engaging in a comparative analysis of post-Oslo Palestine and postapartheid South Africa, Andy Clarno shows that the dynamics of racial capitalism and settler colonialism produce conditions that inhibit decolonization.[154] Learning from the South African experience—traditionally seen by Palestinians as a successful model of decolonization—Palestinian activists have been recognizing that they "must more seriously account for racial capitalism and social liberation as part of their struggle"; otherwise, inequalities, labor exploitation, land dispossession, and patriarchy will persist.[155]

## RACE AND RACISM IN PALESTINIAN SOCIETY

Recent years have seen growing use of the term "anti-Palestinian racism" by activists, scholars, and civil society organizations.[156] The concept has been conceived in intersectional, rather than exceptionalist, terms, recognizing its entwinement with anti-Arab racism and Islamophobia. It has gained momentum with the Black Lives Matter movement and in view of the intersection of state violence with imperialism, colonialism, capitalism, and white supremacy. Anti-Palestinian racism emerged to identify, capture, and name the forms of racism that Palestinians experience *as* Palestinians, the hostility they face, and the denial of their histories, oppression, and rights that is so prevalent in the West and in liberal circles.[157] Mezna Qato defines "Anti-Palestinianism (noun)" as "Prejudice, hostility or discrimination against Palestinians. Denial of the Nakba. Accusing a Palestinian of 'latent' racism(s) without cause. Allowing Palestinian exception to all other held liberal or left values/politics."[158] Scholars have also conceptualized anti-Palestinian racism as a form of racial gaslighting that works "epistemically to deny and blur" Palestinian experiences of settler colonialism and racism[159] and to racialize Palestinians and Palestinian critique as antisemitic.[160] As the concept of anti-Palestinian racism continues to gain traction in academic work and in activism, it is important to consider how different social groups within Palestine and the diaspora experience anti-Palestinian racism in ways that are specific to their geographic location, and along the intersectionality of ethnicity, class, gender, and sexuality.[161]

Speaking of anti-Palestinianism, however, is not entirely new. In the 1970s, the *Journal of Palestine Studies*, for example, published an essay by Mahmoud Darwish that "described the atmosphere of anti-Palestinian prejudice" in Europe.[162] Darwish writes, "In Europe the atmosphere, always ready to explode against the Arabs, was full of Zionist agitation against Palestinians in particular." He further notes the hypocrisy of the European left, which had lent support to the antiapartheid struggle in South Africa and the anticolonial struggle in Algeria but remained sympathetic to Zionism, refusing to extend similar support to Palestinians.[163]

Anti-Palestinian racism cannot be understood without the powerful hold of antisemitism as an "exceptional racism."[164] The view of Zionism, especially in the West, as the sacrosanct remedy to antisemitism has prompted a conflation between anti-Zionism and antisemitism, which Israel has been actively invested in producing and advancing for decades to shield itself from criticism and accountability.[165] The two, however, as noted by Palestinians, antizionist Jews, and allies, are not the same. Nadia Abu El-Haj explains:[166]

> Anti-Semitism, Islamophobia, and anti-Palestinian racism are directed against persons for *who they are*—or, perhaps more accurately, for who they are assumed to be. As speech acts, they constitute racist and hate speech. Anti-Zionism, by way of contrast, is directed at a state-building project and a political regime. To render anti-Zionism equivalent to the first three is to commit a fundamental category mistake that is not sustainable on any serious intellectual grounds.

In fact, the labeling of anti-Zionism as antisemitic is itself an act of racism against Palestinians, the victims of Zionism. And yet often the existence of anti-Palestinian racism is denied, and Palestinians are not recognized as subjects who face racism; instead, they are constructed as the producers of antisemitism—that is, the producers of what is considered in the West as the worst type of racism.

While there is growing attention to how racism against Palestinians operates, less consideration is given to questions of race formation and racism in Palestinian society—including in this volume, indicating a significant lacuna. Susan Beckerleg, one of the few scholars who have written on Palestinians of African origins, and Darryl Li, who has written about the Bushnaqs, a Muslim community decedent of what is now Bosnia-Herzegovina, both note that the reluctance to deal with these issues in Palestine studies stems out of fear that dealing with race and migration would play into the Zionist agenda, especially in light of Zionist claims that Palestinians are latecomers to Palestine and Zionist denial of Palestinian peoplehood, nationhood, and indigeneity.[167] The dominance of masculinized nationalism has also played a role in suppressing engagement with difference and shying away from exploring race and racism within Palestinian society.

One area that has received attention in relation to race—including in this volume, in the chapters by Michael R. Fischbach and David Palumbo-Liu—is the solidarity between Black Americans and Palestinians. In 2014, a series of events—the onslaught on Gaza, the rise of the Black Lives Matter movement, and the protests against police brutality and for justice in Ferguson, Missouri, following the killings of Michael Brown, Eric Garner, and Tamir Rice— prompted Black-Palestinian camaraderie, building on a history of solidarity between the two groups. At the same time, these events drew attention to issues of racism and anti-Blackness in Arab and Palestinian communities inside and outside the Middle East.[168] In response, scholars and activists began to open the conversation on these issues, convening webinars and roundtables aiming "to better understand what a commitment to anti-blackness should look like in the Palestinian solidarity movement and among Black-Palestinian solidarity efforts."[169] Growing calls to consider anti-Blackness in Middle East studies also emerged.[170]

These emerging discussions stress the importance of locating Black-Palestinian relations not only in relation to solidarity but also within the broader racial and imperial history that shapes the ambivalent relationship of Palestinians with Blackness. In Palestine, the construction of "whiteness" and "Blackness" has been informed by several factors including imperial racial classifications, settler colonialism as a white supremacist and anti-Black and anti-Native project, and the history of slavery and race formation in the Middle East and North Africa.[171] As Sherene Seikaly's article "The Matter of Time" demonstrates, when taken together, these factors illustrate that race and racialization are neither fixed nor stable but rather context specific and, in the case of Palestine, they also operate in the service of imperial and colonial interests and are shaped in relation to broader capitalist transformations. In her article, Seikaly traces, through the story of her great-grandfather Naim Cotran, the multiple racial subject positions that Palestinians had occupied within the British imperial racial taxonomy. Cotran was a Palestinian Christian doctor stationed in Sudan in the early twentieth century as part of the British colonial administration. In Sudan, he was white adjacent, inferior to the white British but superior to the local Black population. Upon his return to Palestine, then under the British Mandate, he found himself racialized as an inferior native, ending up a refugee in Lebanon in the aftermath of the Nakba. Cotran's story illustrates the complex historical relationship of Palestinians with "whiteness" and "Blackness"—a history relevant for considering racism and anti-Blackness in Palestine and among Palestinians today.

In recent years, there has been growing interest in Black Palestinians and their experience of settler colonialism and anti-Blackness. Palestinians of African origins reside in different parts of Palestine including Jerusalem, the Naqab, Jericho, Kafr Kassem, and Gaza, and they have a rich history of resistance to Israeli settler colonialism.[172] They are not a homogenous group. For example, some Afro-Palestinians arrived in Palestine as pilgrims, some came during the 1947–48 war to support the fighting against Zionist colonizers, and some arrived as part of the Indian Ocean slave trade. Their distinct histories shape their different experiences of Israeli colonial violence, their relationship to Palestinian nationalism and Pan-Africanism, and their racialized social place in Palestinian society.

One of the most widely known Afro-Palestinian communities comprises the Afro-Palestinian Jerusalemites who descended from Nigeria, Senegal, Sudan, and Chad and arrived in Palestine as Muslim pilgrims in the nineteenth and twentieth centuries.[173] Known as the guardians of Al-Aqsa, they live close to the Al-Aqsa compound and between two checkpoints. This has made them especially vulnerable to Israeli colonial violence, which targets them both as Palestinian and as Black.[174] This experience has informed how they conceive of and narrate their identity. While Afro-Palestinian Jerusalemites acknowledge their African origins, they identify first and foremost as Palestinians and center Israeli settler colonialism and Israeli anti-Blackness as the source of their oppression and the target of their resistance.[175] As put by Mahmoud, an Afro-Palestinian activist: "*Our* history does not allow us to be African. We are, most importantly, Palestinian first."[176] This calls attention to the importance of reading race, Blackness, and anti-Blackness from within Palestinian experience and without imposing conceptions of race that might be foreign to the Palestinian context. Marc Lamont Hill notes that one of the lessons he learned from Afro-Palestinians is not to impose "a rigid conception of 'shared Blackness'" that could "fetishize 'sameness' in ways that obscured key contextual differences." Reflecting on how he and fellow Black American comrades responded to the existence of Afro-Palestinians during a solidarity visit to Palestine, Lamont Hill noted that "rather than understanding Afro-Palestinian racial politics and its relationship to the Palestinian freedom struggle, we ultimately framed their political struggle on our terms rather than theirs."[177]

The experience of Black Bedouin in the Naqab is different from that of Afro-Palestinians in Jerusalem. Unlike Jerusalemite Afro-Palestinians, who arrived in Palestine as free people, Black Bedouin were forcibly brought for select Bedouin tribes as part of the Indian Ocean slave trade. It is important to note that slavery in Palestine was not confined to the Bedouin and extended also to other segments of the population. But while there is growing literature on slavery in the Middle East and North Africa, the history of slavery in Palestine remains untold.[178] The very little that we do know about slavery and its legacies in Palestine is about the Black Bedouin, in part because they are the largest known surviving Black community in Palestine with a legacy of slavery.

The Bedouin occupy a specific place in the Palestinian racial hierarchy. While admired for their struggle for land justice, the Bedouin are also racialized by other Palestinians as less civilized and modern, a primitive-like population. At the same time, Bedouin society itself is marked by a racial social structure that is based on a hierarchy between the *samran*, the superior "original" and "true" Bedouin (landowners); the *hamran/falaheen* (the peasants), who are inferior to the *samran*; at the bottom are the Black Bedouin, who served as slaves. Strict (and gendered) racial rules govern the interaction between the different groups in areas such as marriage (a Black Bedouin man cannot marry a *samran* Bedouin), blood feuds (Black men do not count), and land (Black Bedouin are landless). Importantly, the legacy of slavery determines access and claims to land. Having no right to land under the Bedouin property regime and under Israeli colonial law, the Black Bedouin are more vulnerable targets for displacement. As a result, most Black Bedouin had little choice but to move to the townships that Israel has designated for the Bedouin since the 1970s. It is estimated that in Rahat, the largest Bedouin township, one-third of the residents are Black Bedouin who live in their own neighborhoods.[179]

The experiences of different Black Palestinian communities raise important questions: What does it mean to be a Black Palestinian in a settler state committed to white supremacy? What forms do "whiteness" and "Blackness" and anti-Black racism take in Palestinian society and how are they linked to race formation in the Middle East, settler colonialism, and global color lines? Why do legacies of slavery (or their absence) matter? How do these legacies shape social status and access to land and property? And what do these legacies mean for decolonization, deracialization, and antiracism in Palestinian society?

Importantly, there is a need for wider engagement with difference in Palestine studies. Scholarly attention to communities such as Afro-Palestinians, Armenians, Bedouin, Bukharis, Bushnaqs, Circassians, Dom (Romani), and Druze can enrich our understanding of Palestinian nation making and of racial hierarchies in Palestinian society and how they are shaped by ethnicity, religion, class, skin color, and global politics of race.[180]

## STRUCTURE OF THE BOOK

The chapters in this book focus on different aspects of how race functions as a colonial project, a political and economic structure, a set of legal and discursive practices, and a classificatory technology. They demonstrate the constitutive role of race in shaping the Zionist movement, the architecture of the Israeli state, and the colonization of Palestine. They also illuminate how the Palestinian struggle and solidarity with Palestine have been shaped through anticolonial and antiracist discourse and praxis.

The book opens with Neve Gordon and Yinon Cohen's chapter, "Race and Space in Israel/Palestine," which examines the relationship between race and land— a central pillar of Zionist settler colonialism. It shows that the biospatial scaffolding that underlies Israel's colonial project has deployed strategies of dispossession and settling across the entire territory of historic Palestine. Israeli colonization, the authors argue, relies on the constitution of space and land as a racialized category. Seeking to delineate Israel's efforts to racialize the appropriated space, the chapter identifies a boomerang trajectory, beginning with the massive confiscation and Judaization of Palestinian land after the Nakba, the duplication of many of the practices originally developed inside Israel and their extension to the West Bank and Gaza, and, finally, the turn inward to solidify the racialization of land within Israel.

The book then turns to John Reynolds's "Apartheid without Race" and Noura Erakat's "Zionism as a Form of Racism." These two chapters focus on how Palestinians have analyzed, understood, and theorized race in their struggle for liberation, their writing on the question of Palestine, and their mobilization of international law. They trace the Palestinian intellectual legacy of race analysis and invite us to consider the Palestinian struggle in antiracist terms. In his chapter, Reynolds examines the reports by Israeli and international human rights organizations that characterize the Israeli regime as apartheid. He shows that their conceptualization of apartheid has produced a reading of apartheid without race. This, he shows, stands in stark contradiction to the Palestinian tradition, which read apartheid as inseparable from a critique of Zionism as a settler-colonial and racial project.

Erakat's chapter sheds light on how Palestinians sought to enshrine international recognition of Zionism as a racist project. It traces the history of UN General Assembly Resolution 3379, which determined that Zionism is a form of racism, and explores how the resolution, led by Fayez Sayegh, shaped a racial theory of Zionist settler colonization. She revisits the diplomatic and intellectual history of the resolution as a way of considering an alternative trajectory for the Palestinian anticolonial freedom struggle as one that is also against racism.

The next three chapters—Seraj Assi's "The Invention of the 'Bedouin Race,'" Zvi Ben-Dor Benite's "Proletarianization of the Mizrahim," and Abigail

B. Bakan and Yasmeen Abu-Laban's "The Racial Hierarchy of Refugees"—
examine racialization and racial distinction in Palestine, focusing on three
subjugated groups: the Palestinian Bedouin, the Mizrahim (oriental Jews),
and Palestinian refugees. They illuminate the importance of paying close
attention to regimes of race and how they shape context-specific forms and
practices of racialization. Assi's chapter explores the symbiotic relationship
between race and empire in British ethnographic discourse on the Arabs of
Palestine. It shows that in British imperial racial taxonomy, the Palestinian
Bedouin came to be viewed as a separate race within a hierarchy of Arab
races, and that within this racial reconfiguration the Bedouin embodied not
only an ideal model of racial purity but also a racial archetype according
to which Arabness itself was measured, codified, and reproduced. The racialization of the Bedouin, Assi observes, continued unabated well into the
Mandate period and was carried forward by Zionists as they advanced their
vision of nationhood and state building.

Ben-Dor Benite explores Zionist racialization of Mizrahi labor, drawing
on a newly discovered report from 1920 on labor conditions among Yemeni
workers. Written by Ashkenazi Zionist-socialist leaders, the report offered a
shocking account of Yemeni Jews working for Zionist planters and outlined
what it called a "satanic plan." The intersection of Mizrahi labor, Palestinian
workers, and Zionism, Ben-Dor Benite argues, was characterized by "capitalist" Zionist settlements in Palestine, but it also governed the dynamics in socialist ones and in the entire Zionist project, with the socialists believing that
they could proletarianize Middle Eastern Jews better and more effectively.

In their chapter, Bakan and Abu-Laban focus on the racialization of Palestinian refugees both by Israeli settler colonialism and in the international
refugee regime. The chapter suggests that the abandonment of Palestinian
refugees has been shaped by "a racial hierarchy of refugees" between Jewish
and Palestinian refugees, and by the inferior position that Palestinian refugees occupy in the global refugee regime and via the existence of the UN
Relief and Works Agency for Palestine. This racial hierarchy, the authors suggest, results in the denial of the rights of Palestinian refugees, including their
right of return.

The last set of chapters bring to the fore transnational connections that
shape racial structures of domination, as well as solidarity and antiracist

alliances. Michael R. Fischbach's chapter, "Black-Palestinian Solidarity and the Global Color Line," engages the rich history of Black-Palestinian solidarity and traces the origins and development of Black Power support for Palestinians as a kindred people of color fighting for freedom during a tumultuous period of American history. The chapter pays attention to the explosion of Black American attacks on Israel and statements of solidarity with the Palestinian resistance movement following Israel's victory in the 1967 war. Fischbach details how their understandings of the racial dimension of the Arab-Israeli conflict affected the struggle of Black Americans at home, particularly in terms of how Black Power activists suffered from the hostile reactions to their stances on the question of Palestine that emanated from pro-Israeli figures within the mainstream Black civil rights movement and from whites, notably Jews.

Next, the book turns turn to Kieron Turner's chapter, "Racial Capitalism and Militarized Accumulation," which focuses on Israel's arms industry, exploring the relationship between racial capitalism and settler colonialism. The chapter looks at Israeli arms and drone manufacturer Elbit Systems and the activist group Palestine Action, a British-based direct-action network, and its campaign to shut down Elbit's operations. Tracing the supply chain of Elbit's "combat-proven" weaponry and technology, Turner considers the role of Elbit Systems in the colonization of Palestine and in global proliferations of militarized accumulation. Importantly, the chapter draws on the experience of Palestine Action to explicate the ways in which transnational anticolonial resistance constitutes political intimacies that can generate decolonial praxis and global solidarities that disrupt both settler colonialism in Palestine and the global relations of racial capitalism that sustain it.

Ronit Lentin's chapter, "Zionist Racialized Sexual Politics and Palestinian Refusal," centers gender and racialized sexual politics and examines how "playing gender" works to enable and justify the project of racializing Palestine. Lentin uses the discourse of refusal in juxtaposing the case of the Israeli Eurovision winner Netta Barzilai, who refuses to abide by patriarchal conventions, with Israel's rape culture to argue that Israel's refusal to honor international law and morality enables it to consolidate its racialization of Palestinians. This refusal is facilitated by Israel declaring itself, paradoxically, a gay haven, weaponizing pinkwashing and rape culture to justify its colonization of Palestine—and doing so in an increasingly nationalistic Jewish state in which women's rights and LGBTQI+ rights are under attack, more so with the sharp turn to the right in Netanyahu's government.

Alana Lentin's chapter, "Antisemitism and the Proxification of Antiracism," turns to examine racialization in relation to the broader conversation on antiracism and on antisemitism as exceptional racism. It argues that to be against antisemitism today is variably to uphold racial rule and to undermine it, and that sorting out these strands can shed light on how antisemitism coheres with other forms of racism, particularly Islamophobia. Confronting the weaponization of antisemitism by Zionist apologists, Lentin argues that a challenge to antisemitism that is attentive to the role it plays in racial rule points toward productive ways to decolonize and politicize antiracism in critical times.

The book concludes with David Palumbo-Liu's chapter, "Martin Luther King and the Struggle for Palestinian Rights." Exploring the possibilities for radical antiracism, the chapter addresses the vexed issue of Martin Luther King Jr.'s stance on Israel and the Palestinian question, especially since supporters of Israel have been using King's words to endorse Israel and its settler-colonial racial project in Palestine. In examining his legacy, Palumbo-Liu argues that although King issued no definitive statement, there is enough evidence in the historical record to believe that his antiracist ethics and politics would have led him to support the Palestinian cause had he lived even a few years beyond his untimely death.

*One*

# RACE AND SPACE IN ISRAEL/PALESTINE

NEVE GORDON AND YINON COHEN

NOT LONG AFTER THE JUNE 1967 WAR, AT A MEETING OF THE LABOR
Party, Golda Meir turned to Prime Minister Levi Eshkol and asked: "What
are we going to do with a million Arabs?" Eshkol paused for a moment and
then answered: "I get it," he said. "You want the dowry, but you don't like the
bride!"[1]

This anecdote underscores that in the immediate aftermath of the 1967
war, Israel made a clear distinction between the land it had occupied—the
dowry—and the Palestinians who inhabited it—the bride. While the distinction between the people and their land swiftly became the overarching
logic informing the structure of Israel's colonial project in the Occupied Palestinian Territories, it also informed Israel's land policies within the pre-1967
borders. Indeed, the liberal Zionist notion that there are "two Israels"—the
virtuous liberal democracy west of the "Green Line," or the 1949 armistice
agreement border, and the iniquitous colonial regime within the territories
that Israel occupied in 1967—conceals the intricate links between the racialization of people and the racialization of space as it has been produced by the
Jewish state. This "good Israel"/"bad Israel" framing does not hold water once

one acknowledges that the racialization of Palestinians and the Judaization of land has been a prime objective of every government since Israel's establishment in 1948, and that the modes of Palestinian dispossession on both sides of the Green Line have been uncannily similar.

Alongside efforts to empty the land of its Palestinian Indigenous inhabitants, Jewish civilians were relocated to the land seized and deployed within the broader architecture of control as an integral part of the process of racializing space and rendering it "Jewish." This process has depended on a strict bifurcation between Jews and Palestinians produced over time through racialized forms of governance that introduced a variety of mechanisms, including practices of demographic classification.

Applying Israel's land-grabbing practices and demographic classifications as a conceptual lens, this chapter makes two claims: the first concerns *biospatial* strategies, including the construction of people and space as racialized categories; the second is *historical*, and shows the continuity of the expropriation of Palestinian land from 1948 until today. We derive the term "biospatial" from Michel Foucault's notions of biopolitics and biopower. Biopolitics focuses on the administration of life and populations, while biopower is the way in which biopolitics is put to work in society.[2] Biopower uses statistical devices and scientific methods, as well as mechanisms of surveillance, to measure and intervene in a set of processes designed to administer, optimize, and multiply the population's productive capacities and at times to repress and subjugate the people through different forms of governance. As opposed to *discipline*, however, these biotechnologies operate on the level of the population as a whole, rather than the individual. The term "biospatial" denotes the deployment of such biotechnologies to demarcate, control, manage, shape, and ascribe signification to people and space. Here, we invoke the term to describe the diverse mechanisms and processes by which space is constituted as racialized or in racialized terms.

Even as the vast majority of the literature on Israel/Palestine has focused on national, religious, and ethnic differences, we maintain that Jewish nationality is also informed and even determined by race. Edward Said, for example, mentions the Emergency Defense Regulations originally devised and implemented in Palestine by the British to be used against the Jews and Arabs. When Israel retained these regulations after 1948, it used them in a racialized way to control only the Palestinians, limiting their right of movement, their right to purchase land, their right to settle, and so forth.[3] In the Israeli context, then, race pervades nationalism and religion and helps explain the state's land-grabbing policies.

We accordingly show that the particular biospatial scaffolding underlying Israel's colonial project has deployed two major strategies—namely, legal-bureaucratic mechanisms of dispossession, followed by the movement of Jewish civilians to settle Palestinian land across the entire territory located between the Jordan Valley and the Mediterranean Sea—in order to grab and control as much land as possible.[4] We go on to draw a connection between these strategies and the statistical classifications and techniques of enumeration of people that Israel has adopted in order to delineate how the racialization of people is tied to the racialization of space, and how the link between the two serves the project of spatial expropriation. The constitution of the land as Jewish allows Israel to cast the Indigenous Palestinians as "invaders," people whose race does not match the race ascribed to the land. These classifications and forms of enumeration at times not only defy international standards of statistical reporting[5] but also are deployed either to cement or to sever the connection between people and space. Historically, we identify a boomerang trajectory, beginning with the massive confiscation and Judaization of Palestinian land in the wake of the 1948 war, then duplicating many of the practices originally developed inside Israel and extending them to the West Bank and Gaza Strip in 1967, and finally turning back inward to solidify the Judaization of land within Israel. When we consider that settler colonialism, as Patrick Wolfe has shown,[6] is a structure and not an event, this recoiling movement across space and time is neither surprising nor unexpected. Later in the chapter, we draw some connections between our analysis and Israel's response to the Hamas attack on October 7, 2023, claiming that the way Palestinians have been racialized as lesser human beings for many decades helps explain Israel's horrific military campaign in Gaza.

## THE RACIAL-SPATIAL LOGIC

Before the 1948 war, there were nearly three hundred Jewish and over six hundred Palestinian villages and towns in the territory that would later become Israel. During and after the war, Palestinian cities were depopulated and about five hundred Palestinian villages were destroyed, while most of their inhabitants either fled or were expelled across international borders, becoming refugees in neighboring countries. In total, about 750,000 Palestinians were displaced in what Fayez Sayegh called "racial elimination"[7] and today would be characterized as ethnic cleansing,[8] replacing, as it were, race with ethnicity—a term considered less offensive in the aftermath of World War II and the Nazi crimes.[9] As part of what Palestinians have called the Nakba (catastrophe) and Israel the War of Independence, thousands of Palestinians were also internally displaced within the nascent Jewish state.[10] By 1951, the Palestinians who had become refugees had been "replaced" by a similar number of Jewish immigrants, both Holocaust survivors from Europe and Mizrahi Jews from Arab countries, thus transforming the state's racial composition without altering its overall population size.[11]

The Zionist claims to Jewish indigeneity and the depiction of the Zionist project as a "return" to ancestral lands, alongside the racialization of Palestinians as backward and lacking connection to the land, served as justification for expelling the Palestinians and expropriating their land. To achieve this goal, soon after the war Israel introduced a series of administrative and legal mechanisms to seize Palestinian land.[12] It classified property belonging to Palestinian refugees first as "abandoned" and then as "absentee property" and quickly appropriated it, while also confiscating much of the land owned by the Palestinians residing in the villages that survived the war. The establishment of a military government (1948–66) responsible for governing the Palestinian citizens within the fledgling state facilitated this massive confiscation of land.[13] A twofold strategy was adopted: Israel confined the estimated 160,000 Palestinians who had remained in the Jewish state to their villages and towns and simultaneously converted Palestinian land into closed military zones and nature reserves, confiscated what it defined as absentee property, and restricted the cultivation of Palestinian agricultural plots, all the while registering Palestinian estates as "state land."[14] As early as 1951, the state effectively owned over 90 percent of the land within its territory, up from 13.5 percent in 1948.[15]

Seizing land alone, however, does not guarantee effective control or the racialization of space as Jewish. Using the rhetoric of "population dispersal," Israel consequently established new Jewish towns in areas still populated by Palestinians and created agricultural settlements to ensure control over large swaths of Palestinian land. Of the 370 new Jewish settlements established soon after 1948, 350 were built on or in proximity to Palestinian villages that had been destroyed.[16] While Jews of all stripes and classes settled on confiscated Palestinian land, the state sent mostly new Mizrahi immigrants—a weakened and racialized group that came from Arab and Muslim countries[17]—to Israel's periphery, especially to the frontiers along its borders.[18]

In later years, middle- and upper-middle-class Jews were offered incentives to relocate to the Galilee to live in hilltop communities overlooking Palestinian villages. As Alexander Kedar and Oren Yiftachel explain,[19] the Palestinian settlement map was "frozen" in 1948 by prohibiting the establishment of new Palestinian villages and towns and arresting the development of those still intact after the war by confiscating most of their land reserves, preventing any construction outside the already developed area, and surrounding these villages with Jewish settlements. In this way, Israel created a "geography of enclaves" of non-Judaized space in which the majority of Israel's Palestinian citizens remain to this day—even as their population has increased tenfold. These policies maintained and reproduced extreme residential segregation between Jews and Palestinians.

Residential segregation along racial lines—characterized by acute disparity in the state's investment in infrastructure and social services—is arguably the most salient feature informing the organization of Israeli space, with nearly all localities defined as either Jewish or non-Jewish by the Israeli Central Bureau of Statistics (CBS). To create and maintain such segregation, Israel adopted a variety of biopolitical technologies while harnessing statistical tools to produce and reproduce a series of classifications that create a clear racial demarcation between Jews and Palestinians; it did so by homogenizing the Jewish group and fragmenting the Palestinian one. From the outset, the CBS adopted religion as the population's primary classification, using Jewish identity to constitute migrants coming from different historical, social, cultural, and linguistic backgrounds as a unified group. The term "Jew" in this context is just as much a marker of race as it is of religion, while the statistical reports frame Jews as the norm and contrast them with all "non-Jews." Echoing processes of settler-colonial erasures,[20] to this day the word "Palestinian" does not appear in Israel's statistical abstracts, while only in 1995 did the word "Arab" finally emerge after decades in which Palestinians were referred to as "non-Jews," reminiscent of the "judicial erasure" carried out in the Balfour Declaration and the 1922 British Mandate for Palestine.[21] The racialization and erasure of the natives facilitates processes used to transfer their land to settlers and to legitimize these processes.

Moreover, to determine their "origin," the CBS classifies Jews according to their (or their father's) country of birth. Possible "origins" do not include Mizrahi or Arab Jews (presumably because these terms are considered divisive) but only continents of birth, such as Europe, Asia, and Africa.[22] If, however, both individual Jews and their fathers were born in Israel (or Palestine, before 1948), they are assigned an "Israeli origin." Kenneth Prewitt, a former director of the United States Census Bureau, calls this "Israel's policy of ethnic erasure," explaining that it was "designed to solve any problem of [Jewish] ethnic cleavage."[23] One of its outcomes was the rapid erasure of the Arab origin of Mizrahim, about half the Jewish population, thus contributing to the "cleansing," in Ella Shohat's words, of their Arabness, while ensuring that Arab Jews would swiftly become "Israeli."[24] By contrast, Palestinians have never been able to attain the status of "Israeli origin," irrespective of how many generations their ancestors had resided in Palestine or Israel.[25] In fact, they have no "origin," only religion. In other words, according to Israel's official statistics, all Jews ultimately become "Israeli" within the span of two generations, and no Palestinian can ever become "Israeli." This produces a bifurcated racial reality where Jewishness trumps all other categories of identification.[26]

A case in point is nationality. The word "nationality" has never appeared in CBS statistical abstracts, probably because adding nationality would undo the strict racial division between Jews and Palestinians. Nationality, however, is recorded in the state's population registry, which has a list of 137 acceptable nationalities—yet "Israeli" is not one of them. Common nationalities of Israeli citizens are Jewish, Arab (for Muslims and "Arab Christians"), and Druze. A 2008 petition filed by citizens of different registered nationalities, including Jewish, Arab, Buddhist, and Druze, asked the Jerusalem District Court to compel the state to register their nationality as "Israeli." The Court rejected the petition, ruling that such a change has "far reaching implications for the State of Israel's identity," while accepting in part the government's claim that an Israeli nationality would "undermine the foundation of the State of Israel."[27] In 2013, Israel's Supreme Court upheld this decision.

The statistical acrobatics carried out following the mass migration from the former Soviet Union in the 1990s underscores the steps the CBS has been willing to take in order to consolidate the strict Jewish/Palestinian divide: adding non-Jews to the Jewish group as long as they are not Palestinians.[28] Of an estimated one million immigrants who arrived on Israel's shores, approximately 250,000 had Jewish relatives but were themselves either Christian or had no religious affiliation. As part of its efforts to recreate the racial divide between Jews and Arabs, the CBS decided to alter the way it classifies the entire population. It labeled the new non-Jewish immigrants as "others," uniting them with Jews in a group called "Jews and others." This group is contrasted with the newly created group designated "Arab population," which includes Muslims, Druze, and Christians. Thus, since the mid-1990s, according to the CBS, there are two kinds of Christians in Israel: "Arab Christians" and "non-Arab Christians." The algorithm developed by the CBS to distinguish between these two groups is based in part on where they live, namely, in a "Jewish locality" or a "non-Jewish" one. This suggests that race and space are mutually constitutive in such a way that biotechnologies are used to produce a population's racial (and other) identity and in this way to racialize the inhabited space, while space itself helps determine the population's identity.

Over the years, Israel has continuously monitored the changing proportions of Jews and Palestinians, not only at the national level but also in each region, as it attempts to guarantee, in David Sibley's words, the "purification of space."[29] Israel's demographic anxiety has manifested itself prominently in the state's spatial policies in the northern district, especially in the Galilee, where nearly two-thirds of the population after the 1948 war were Palestinians. What has been seen by the state as demographic imbalance led it to devote massive resources to Judaize the land, and, after decades of investment in the northern district, the proportion of the Palestinian population was reduced to 54 percent.[30] As a consequence of the state's policy of halting all Palestinian development, Palestinians in northern Israel currently reside in 78 localities, all of which existed before 1948, while Jews reside in 307 localities, mostly established since 1948. Even though Israel did not succeed in creating a Jewish majority in this district, the size of the Jewish population relocated to the area has been sufficient to advance three major objectives. First, the establishment of Jewish towns and farming communities has helped restrict Palestinian development, transforming Palestinian villages into enclaves. Second, it has enabled Jews to exercise effective control over the land confiscated after the 1948 war and thus fulfill the plan to Judaize it. This was particularly important in the Galilee, parts of which had been allotted to the Palestinian state in the 1947 UN Partition Plan. Israel's Labor-led government believed that if Palestinian development were left unchecked in the Galilee, it could potentially lead to demands for Palestinian autonomy or even Palestinian independence, a concern that has also informed the West Bank settlement project.[31] Third, the Jewish civilians who were relocated to these areas served, wittingly or not, as a vital component in the state's apparatus of ethnic policing and surveillance (more on this below).

The biospatial strategies adopted in the south, which is Israel's largest geographical region, known in Hebrew as the Negev and in Arabic as the Naqab, are particularly pronounced. An estimated ninety thousand Palestinian Bedouin inhabited the region in 1947, but only eleven thousand remained following the state's establishment, the rest having been pushed across the borders.[32] After the 1948 war, Israel concentrated the majority of the remaining Palestinian Bedouin population into a restricted, 1,500-square-kilometer area known as al-Siyaj (meaning "fence" in Arabic), located in the northeastern Negev/Naqab, the region's least arable land. After the military governorate ended, forced urbanization of the Bedouin community began.[33]

For Israel, concentrating the Bedouin in urban areas meant that it could seize almost all of the Negev/Naqab's land while concomitantly consolidating its control over the population. After 1969, the state established seven Bedouin-only towns within the Siyaj area—the only Palestinian communities that have been established since 1948—touting them as paradigms of modernity.[34] The allocation of plots of land within these hastily fabricated towns was, however, contingent on the Bedouin surrendering at least some of their land claims, which drove almost half of the population to refuse to move into the designated towns.[35] A significant portion of the Bedouin population remains in villages unrecognized by the state. The CBS does not include these Bedouin villages in the count of localities and asks the people inhabiting them to indicate the name of their tribe instead of an address, thus revealing, yet again, the CBS's power of interpellation: namely, the imposition of categories and classifications that constitute people as socially recognizable subjects. This is how the CBS severs a group that it racializes—in this case, the Palestinian Bedouin—from space, a process that facilitates, as we show below, their constitution as "infiltrators" on their ancestral land.

## TERRITORIAL EXPANSION

On June 27, 1967, the day East Jerusalem was annexed by Israel, a group of Israeli archaeologists was appointed as supervisors of the archaeological and historical sites in the West Bank. In a press release issued by the military, these sites were defined as Israel's "national and cultural property."[36] The sites were rapidly incorporated within the overall research agenda of Israel's archaeological establishment and were excavated, according to Nadia Abu El-Haj, in an effort to reveal their "national origins," which were "believed to be contained within the remains of specific ethnic or racial groups visible in the archaeological record."[37] Hence, archaeologists were tasked to create a link between the Jewish race and space. This act reveals that the ideology of a Greater Israel—namely, that the West Bank was part of the biblical land of Israel and, as "Jewish land," should be integrated into the state—informed Israel's policies from the moment it occupied these territories. Alongside this messianic ideology, a militaristic ideology that considered the West Bank to be a defensive corridor against invasion from the east also gained ground after the fighting had subsided.

Israel, however, annexed more than what had been Jordanian Jerusalem, the main city in the West Bank, but also an area eleven times larger, including twenty-eight adjacent Palestinian villages with a total population of nearly seventy thousand. The "united" city's post-1967 borders were drawn according to a racial-spatial logic in order to maximize its urban territory while integrating the smallest possible number of Palestinians. Nonetheless, the city's ethnic makeup was transformed overnight, from 98 percent Jewish to 74 percent Jewish and 26 percent Palestinian.[38] These Palestinians were not granted citizenship but rather were classified as Israeli "residents," thus enhancing Palestinian fragmentation by distinguishing them from the Palestinian citizens of Israel and from the noncitizens in the West Bank and Gaza.[39]

Following the annexation, Israel once again adopted a two-pronged approach of confiscating the newly captured land and sending civilian emis-
saries to settle it. Imposing its own legal system on the city's eastern part,
Israel applied land-use codes, building restrictions, and regulations on infrastructure distribution in order to expropriate Palestinian land, prevent
the development of Palestinian neighborhoods and disrupt their urban con-
tinuum, and transform them into enclaves by building new Jewish neighborhoods. These colonial policies blurred the lines dividing West and East
Jerusalem, creating an urban fabric that, on the one hand, is geographically
interwoven, yet, on the other hand, preserves a strict segregation between
the city's Jewish and Palestinian areas.

Moreover, the satellite "neighborhoods" nearly tripled the city's Jewish
population, even though, thanks to higher Palestinian natural growth, in the
fifty-five years since 1967 the share of Jews in the city has actually declined
from 74 to 61 percent.[40] The rising proportion of Palestinians in Jerusalem,
viewed as a strategic threat, led Israel to implement a "quiet deportation"
policy,[41] whereby legal-bureaucratic mechanisms have been used to strip
thousands of Palestinians of their residency rights. More recently, the politics of space and race has moved up yet another notch, with the government contemplating ways to redraw the city's municipal boundaries, either
to include more Jews from neighboring settlements within its borders or to
reduce the municipality's size by transposing 140,000 Palestinian residents
of Jerusalem to the rest of the West Bank.[42]

Israel took over East Jerusalem in one fell swoop through the de jure annexation and the application of Israeli laws to the area. By contrast, in the
West Bank, it carried out the confiscation piecemeal by utilizing a mixture
of Ottoman and British Mandatory law, regulations from the Jordanian legal
systems, and orders issued by Israeli military commanders. Before the 1967
war, the West Bank contained about 800,000 Palestinians living in 12 urban
centers and 527 rural communities, including 19 refugee camps. During the
war, the Jordan Valley (excluding Jericho) was partially cleansed of its population because Israel wanted to secure the border with Jordan.[43] Similarly,
the Latrun enclave was depopulated of Palestinians because their villages
overlooked the highway leading from Tel-Aviv to Jerusalem, and the Israeli
military destroyed them as part of what Defense Minister Moshe Dayan

called the "complex framework of the unpleasant and unpopular aspects of fulfilling Zionism."[44]

Demolitions were part of a broader policy aimed at clearing part of the area adjacent to the West Bank's western border—where, for example, more than 40 percent of the dwellings in the border town Qalqilyah were demolished—as well as the entire Magharbia Quarter located in Jerusalem's old city in front of the Haram al-Sharif and the Wailing Wall.[45] All in all, about two hundred thousand people, or 25 percent of the West Bank's inhabitants, fled to Jordan during the war and its direct aftermath.[46] Similar to the policies within the Green Line, Palestinians have been allowed to build only one new town in the West Bank over the course of the fifty-eight-year occupation, even as the population has grown fivefold since 1967.[47]

Similar processes of land confiscation and Jewish settlement unfolded in the Gaza Strip. When Israel occupied it in 1967, at least 385,000 Palestinians lived there, of whom around 70 percent were refugees, having fled or been expelled from their homes in 1948.[48] Israel considered these refugees, who were living not far from their ancestral lands, a threat. Over a decade before the 1967 war, Moshe Dayan eulogized Roi Rutenberg, who had been killed by Palestinian fedayeen in the agricultural fields of kibbutz Nahal Oz: "Let us not cast the blame on the murderers today," Dayan averred. "Why should we declare their burning hatred for us? For eight years they have been sitting in the refugee camps in Gaza, and before their eyes we have been transforming the lands and the villages, where they and their fathers dwelt, into our estate."[49]

In both the West Bank and Gaza, Israel used complementary methods that were first developed within the pre-1967 borders to seize Palestinian land. These included declaring land absentee property; transforming swathes of land into nature reserves; claiming that land had been left uncultivated for many years; or, alternatively, simply declaring that a particular area of land was needed for military or public use, where "public" denotes Jewish.[50] Under Labor-led governments, Israel Judaized land by establishing military bases in the region immediately following the war, and then gradually converting some of them into civilian settlements, while also establishing civilian settlements from scratch. Once the right-wing Likud Party assumed power in 1977 (following twenty-nine years of Labor coalitions), the cooperation between the government and the settler leadership—Jewish fundamentalists with clear goals and astute political skills—became more intimate, and, as a result, settlement construction was accelerated. Nineteen of the twenty-one Jewish settlements that existed in the Gaza Strip before their evacuation in 2005 were established by right-wing governments, which used these settlements to control most of the seashore and to create a wedge between the northern and southern parts of the Strip.[51] In the West Bank, between 1978 and 1984, the Likud government established sixty-three new settlements—many of them in close proximity to the Green Line. The Likud's goal was to Judaize the entire "Land of Israel" and prevent the establishment of a Palestinian state, an option that had seemed viable following Israel's 1979 peace treaty with Egypt.

By 1987, Israel had managed to restrict Palestinians to 50 percent of the West Bank's land and 60 percent of the land in the Gaza Strip.[52] This de jure land grab has translated into de facto annexation through the establishment of Jewish settlements, the construction of bypass roads, and, eventually, the erection of the separation barrier in the West Bank. Composed of a series of electronic fences, deep trenches, wide patrol roads, and, in certain places, nine-meter-high concrete slabs, the separation barrier—also variously called the Separation Wall, Security Fence, and Apartheid Wall—runs over six hundred kilometers, almost double the length of the Green Line, with 80 percent inside the West Bank, further expropriating Palestinian land.[53]

From the very beginning, settlements were established not only according to a military-strategic logic but also according to a national-religious one. Not unlike Jewish citizens in the Galilee, the settlers and settlements, which in the West Bank are usually located on hilltops overlooking Palestinian villages, serve as a means of social control. Not only do they restrict Palestinian development and movement, they also serve as mechanisms of civilian surveillance and racial policing. Eyal Weizman cites a Supreme Court ruling dealing with the security function of the settlements: "Terrorist elements," wrote Justice Vitkon in that case, "operate more easily in territory occupied exclusively by a population that is indifferent or sympathetic to the enemy than in a territory in which there are also persons liable to *monitor* them and *inform* the authorities of any suspicious movement."[54] This kind of racial policing has become increasingly violent over the years, and in February 2023 it took the form of a settler pogrom in the village of Hawara, with settler violence in the West Bank intensifying since October 7, 2023.

Under the 1993 Oslo Accords, all the civil institutions used to manage the population in the West Bank and Gaza were transferred to the Palestinian Authority and the West Bank was divided into Areas A, B, and C, which were drawn according to a biospatial logic. In Areas A and B, which were more densely populated with Palestinians, the Palestinian Authority was given more responsibilities, while in Area C, which contained almost 60 percent of the land, all the Jewish settlements (reaching, at the time of writing, 146 settlements and 191 outposts, excluding those in Hebron and East Jerusalem), and only a minority of the Palestinian population, Israel retained full control of security and public order, as well as civil issues relating to territory, such as planning and zoning.[55] Oslo reveals that the biospatial logic underlying Israeli settler colonialism not only racializes space but also divides and organizes it, thereby determining, in this case, forms of racialized governance that extend their control also through the dissection of space. Because Areas A and B were densely populated by Palestinians, they were divided into 131 clusters, scattered like an archipelago across the terrain and separated by strategic corridors that facilitated Israeli control, whereas Area C remained contiguous. It is also in the context of such biospatial strategies that one needs to understand the 191 Jewish outposts that have been erected in the West Bank since 1996. Of these, 40 new West Bank outposts were established during 2023–24, in a period spanning less than 18 months. These outposts, populated by relatively few Jews, were built with government assistance but labeled "unauthorized" because Israel had promised the US administration that it would not establish new settlements.[56]

The way Israel enumerates its population bolsters this biospatial logic. Since the 1967 war, the state includes in its population count all the people residing within the pre-1967 borders and annexed East Jerusalem, but in the West Bank it includes only those residing in Jewish settlements, leaving out the Indigenous population in what Lana Tatour has called "statistical elimination."[57] Statistical virtuosities of this kind—counting Jewish residents, while ignoring millions of Palestinians within the same region—provide a distorted picture of reality. These practices reflect a settler-colonial logic of erasure and help reproduce the de facto annexation by engendering a link between Jews and the land, while severing the Palestinians' connection to it.

Simultaneously, Israel completed the process of caging Gaza's population in the Strip. In 1989, it introduced a policy that only people with "magnetic cards"—which contained coded information about each person's "security background," taxes, and electricity and water bills—could exit the region and, in 1991, following the US-Iraq war, it implemented the first "hermetic closure," which sealed off the Gaza Strip for long periods. Only a very small number of Palestinian political leaders and businessmen whom Israel wanted to support and promote received permits to travel during the closures. And then, in the midst of the Oslo process, Israel built a fence around the Gaza Strip. Within a relatively short period, a patrol road and a series of fences fifty-four kilometers long closed off the border between the Strip and Israel, leaving only four passageways connecting the two regions (two of which operate in one direction only, from Israel to Gaza) and one more connecting Gaza with Egypt. The Green Line was accordingly converted from a "normally open" border into a "normally closed" one.[58]

In 2004, Prime Minister Ariel Sharon decided that it was no longer feasible to deploy hundreds of Israeli soldiers to secure the eight thousand Jewish settlers in the Strip and decided to withdraw Israeli troops. Sharon thought that by implementing a unilateral "disengagement plan," Israel could present itself as having deoccupied Gaza. That, in turn, would help separate Gaza from the West Bank in the public imagination and allow Israel to fortify its West Bank settlements and entrench its control of the land. Accordingly, in 2005, the Israeli government dismantled the Jewish settlements in Gaza and redeployed its troops to the border. Israel intensified its control of the enclave from a distance—in part, following rocket attacks from Gaza—building military bases just outside the Strip, setting up remotely controlled machine guns on watchtowers, increasing the use of drones, and establishing a buffer zone 150 to 500 meters wide that eats up agricultural land and mandates that farmers limit themselves to short leafy crops such as spinach, radish, and lettuce, presumably to avoid blocking the soldiers' views.[59] Two years after the 2005 withdrawal, Hamas became the governing party in the Gaza Strip. In response, Israel implemented a permanent military blockade on Gaza, cordoning the population in what many commentators have described as an "open air prison," while transforming Gaza into a ghettoized frontier.

## THE COLONIAL LEVIATHAN RECOILS

Having succeeded in Judaizing large parts of the West Bank, Israel has in recent years turned back inward. In a boomerang-like trajectory, it is now completing the project it left unfinished in the Negev/Naqab.[60] Approximately 807,000 people currently live in the Negev/Naqab, which contains about 60 percent of the country's land but is home to only 8.5 percent of its population. Of this population, 37 percent are Palestinians, the vast majority of them Bedouin, whose number has grown from about 11,000 in 1948 to about 300,000 in 2021, thanks to their high fertility rate (which was similar to that of ultra-Orthodox Jews until the new millennium but has since decreased from seven births per woman in 1995 to five births per woman in 2013).[61] Nonetheless, only 18 localities of the 144 in the region are designated for the Bedouin community, while about 65,000 Bedouin citizens reside in 35 villages classified as "unrecognized" by the Israeli government.[62] These Bedouin are prohibited from connecting their houses to the electricity grid or the water and sewerage systems. Construction regulations are strictly enforced, with 5,584 Bedouin homes and animal pens demolished in 2021 and 2022.[63]

No paved roads lead to the villages, and signposts on main roads indicating their location are prohibited. Moreover, the villages do not appear on maps. As a matter of official policy, these localities do not exist. Demographically, their inhabitants (who are Israeli citizens) are linked to tribes rather than to a locality, thus officially erasing their connection to their land. This, as Brenna Bhandar shows, is part of the settler-colonial strategy that casts Bedouins as nomads who have no rights to the land.[64] Indeed, three of the eighteen Bedouin localities that were recently recognized by the state were considered "places" rather than "localities" in the state registry because, according to the official records, they were deemed empty. Informed by biotechnologies that racialize this group differently from the Palestinians in the north, Israel uses the specificity of their racialization to further sever the Bedouin from their land. The particular way the biotechnologies are put to use alongside government statements and policies indicates that Israel plans to demolish most of the unrecognized villages and to relocate at least thirty thousand inhabitants into already established Bedouin towns.

While the confiscation of the Negev/Naqab's land was accomplished in the state's early years, in the wake of the new millennium the government has intensified its attempts to strengthen its effective control of this area and to Judaize it fully. In addition to its draconian policy of home demolitions, until 2007 Israel sprayed agricultural plots with herbicides.[65] Instructed by the Supreme Court in 2007 to stop the sprayings due to collateral damage, the state began instead to plow over the plots.[66] Simultaneously, the Israeli government has been reinforcing the Jewish presence on the ground, establishing new Jewish settlements and encouraging Jews to move to the region, while planting thousands of "Jewish trees" provided by the Jewish National Fund on large strips of Bedouin land.[67] The use of nonnative trees to cover up the remains of destroyed villages like Al-Araqib should also be understood as an integral part of Israel's effort to racialize the land as Jewish.[68]

In addition, in the early 2000s, the government decided to allocate plots of land to some sixty Jewish families, scattering farms across the Negev/Naqab terrain in order to restrict and circumscribe the space that its non-Jewish citizens could occupy. What is unique about these farms is that they connect existing strategies of Judaizing the land with neoliberal entrepreneurship projects. The new farms stifle Bedouin expansion as they prosper from boutique guesthouses and homemade wine and cheese, catering to the bourgeois tastes of Tel Aviv tourists. Thus, space not only becomes increasingly Jewish, but it also acquires a specific entrepreneurial valence. This is all part of "Blueprint Negev," a Jewish National Fund flagship project that aims to attract five hundred thousand Jews to the Negev/Naqab in the coming years,[69] and indeed in 2022 the government approved the establishment of four new Jewish settlements in the region so as to consolidate the Judaization of the land.[70]

An illustration of how the colonial leviathan is turning back inward is perhaps most obvious in Umm al-Hiran, a village of about 350 Bedouin citizens that was destroyed in 2018 and will be replaced by a Jewish settlement called Dror.[71] Just a few kilometers away from this Bedouin village, about thirty religious Jewish families have been living in a makeshift gated community, waiting patiently for the government to expel the Bedouin families from their homes. Ironically, the people who are destined to dispossess the residents of Umm al-Hiran are West Bank settlers who made an ideological decision to return to the pre-1967 borders to "redeem Jewish land" from "Bedouin invaders." Because the land itself is constituted as Jewish, the Bedouin who have inhabited it for decades are criminalized as "invaders," thus revealing not only the classic colonial inversion between the colonizer and the colonized, but also how the spatial-racial nexus produces the biocriminal—the person who is deemed a felon due to the racial status ascribed to him or her. In Israel, Foucault's[72] notion of the biocriminal is further developed since space itself is racialized and the racial mismatch between space and Palestinians is sufficient to transform the latter into criminals. This type of racial mismatch is even more apparent when considering the treatment of Palestinians from the West Bank and Gaza, who are ignored—as part of their statistical elimination—in hundreds of CBS Tables of the Statistical Abstracts of Israel, with the exception of one table that presents data on convicted persons who are not residents of Israel.[73] In 2015, 94 percent of the total of 7,693 convicted persons were Palestinian residents of the occupied West Bank and Gaza, and nearly half of them were "unauthorized" stayers in Israel. They were defined as criminals for "infiltrating" Jewish space.

## GAZA AFTER OCTOBER 7, 2023

The Israeli occupation of Gaza is, in many respects, related to the biospatial logic we discuss in this chapter. Since 1967, Israeli politicians have routinely wished for the Strip's complete cleansing. In the months following the war, Israel contemplated plans to transfer Gaza's population to Al-Arish, to the West Bank, to Iraq, and to several countries in Latin America.[74] Prime Minister Levi Eshkol was clear: "I want them all to go, even if they go to the moon."[75] Many Israelis held on to the fantasy that Gaza would somehow disappear. In 1992 Prime Minister Yitzhak Rabin asserted: "I wish I could wake up one day and find that Gaza has sunk into the sea."[76] Over the years, other leading politicians have made similar remarks.

Following the withdrawal of its troops in 2005, Israel's policy was to maintain control over Gaza by "mowing the grass," a phrase that denotes the periodic deployment of lethal military violence to maintain a certain level of control over the area without committing to a long-term political solution. In four major military campaigns from 2008 until 2021, Israel killed 5,196 Palestinians in Gaza, of whom 1,182 were minors and 496 were women.[77]

This was the backdrop to the October 7, 2023, Hamas attacks on military bases, kibbutzim, towns, and the Nova music festival. Palestinian fighters massacred 815 civilians, among them 36 children, killed close to 400 members of the security forces, and abducted 251 people (mostly civilians) and took them to Gaza.[78] The scale of the attack—in particular, the number killed and abducted in a single day—was unprecedent in Israel's history. Most Jewish Israelis—stunned, afraid, and humiliated by the high number of casualties, the inability of the Israeli military to defend civilians, and the atrocities committed by Hamas and Islamic Jihad fighters—were instantly united by the desire for revenge. The Israeli media became saturated with calls to destroy the population, in whole or in part: to "erase" Gaza, "flatten" it, turn it "into Dresden." And, when Israel's defense minister characterized the population in Gaza as "human animals" and its president claimed that there are "no uninvolved" civilians there,[79] large parts of Israel's population were unfazed. Undoubtedly, the decades-long racialization of Palestinians as lesser human beings contributed to the frenzy.

At the time of writing (July 2024), the Israeli military has bombed entire neighborhoods, killing over 38,000 Palestinians, of whom more than 15,000 are children (these numbers do not include thousands of Palestinians estimated to be lost under the rubble).[80] More than 80,000 residents have been injured. Seventy percent of civilian infrastructure has been destroyed or damaged, leaving many areas uninhabitable. About 75 percent of Gaza's population, some 1.7 million people, have fled their homes; many have been forced to move repeatedly. Israel has also carried out almost 500 attacks on Gaza's healthcare facilities, in what can be characterized as *medicide*.[81] Several thousand civilians have been killed and injured in these attacks, among them doctors, nurses, medics, and ambulance drivers. About two-thirds of the hospitals are no longer running, and those that remain open operate in limited capacity due to lack of fuel, medicine, medical equipment, and food.[82] Concurrently, about 90 percent of Gaza's 737 schools, and all of its universities and colleges, have been destroyed or damaged and about 100 professors have been killed, including three university presidents.[83]

As part of this violence, Israel also destroyed more than one-third of Gaza's agricultural land, more than one-fifth of its greenhouses, and one-third of its irrigation infrastructure. Large swaths of that land were razed by soldiers using D9 bulldozers and explosives to expand the "buffer zone" on Gaza's side of the border from three hundred meters to an estimated eight hundred meters, reducing the Strip's area by 16 percent (in comparison, 8 percent of the West Bank's land was expropriated by the separation barrier). Forensic Architecture argues that "the destruction of agricultural land and infrastructure in Gaza is a deliberate act of ecocide."[84] The effect of these actions is clear. Since December 2023, aid agencies have warned that Palestinians in Gaza are at risk of famine.[85]

As the violence unfolded, Israeli Jewish society was divided about whether and how to end the military campaign. Substantial segments of the population associated with the messianic political right consider Hamas's attack as an opportunity to resettle the Gaza Strip and Judaize the land. Simultaneously, under the cover of Israel's violence in the Gaza Strip and with the support of the military and police, settlers belonging to this political camp have been attacking and expelling Palestinian communities in the West Bank. Between October 2023 and June 2024, eighteen Palestinian herding communities have been uprooted from their homes, with the residents now living in makeshift dwellings on the outskirts of other villages.[86] The racialization of space, its constitution as purely Jewish, and the racialization of Palestinians as "human animals" or subhumans enable Israel to follow policies whereby the lives of Palestinians do not matter. Even the International Court of Justice, the highest court in the land, found that "at least some of the rights claimed by South Africa under the Genocide Convention and for which it was seeking protection were plausible."[87]

## CONCLUSION

One obvious conclusion when examining the political ecology of the Jewish state is that the common tendency to single out Israel's policies in occupied Gaza, the West Bank, and East Jerusalem as representing an epiphenomenon or some kind of deviation from the pre-1967 "good Israel" is misguided. In her work, Suhad Bishara has examined all the Supreme Court rulings relating to the expropriation of land, revealing how regardless of whether the court is operating under administrative law inside the pre-1967 borders or international humanitarian law in the occupied West Bank, the rulings are uncannily similar, almost always favoring the state over Indigenous Palestinians.[88]

This underscores the extent to which race permeates the court's interpretation of the law, and how its rulings assume the existence of a natural link between the space that has been constituted as Jewish and Israel's Jewish citizenry. The judges, in other words, interpret both administrative and humanitarian legal regimes using a racialized biospatial lens and have done so uniformly and consistently over the years.

Since 1948, four related strategies have governed Israel's preoccupation with biospatial policies with remarkable regularity and little change. First, Israel has adopted biotechnologies to help constitute Jews as a homogenous group while distinguishing them from Palestinians, who are constituted as heterogeneous Muslims, Bedouins, Druze, Christians, and so on. The second strategy—even if only partially achieved—has aimed to create and maintain a solid Jewish majority, not only in the entire territory between the Jordan River and the Mediterranean Sea but also in each and every district (except Area A in the West Bank). The third has been the country's extreme residential segregation, where over 99 percent of the 1,214 localities listed by the CBS are exclusively either Jewish or Palestinian. This racialized segregation is crucial to the state's biospatial project, since it not only encourages the Jewish localities to expand across space while stifling the development of the Palestinian localities but also helps to ascribe and inscribe Jewishness to and in space. These three strategies inform and are informed by the fourth, namely, the quest to Judaize the land.

There are, of course, differences between the demographic and spatial strategies introduced on either side of the Green Line. Even though land has been seized using very similar mechanisms, Jews and Palestinians are segregated differently in each region. Due to these differences, the efforts to Judaize the land are beginning to produce contradictions within the pre-1967 borders that have yet to materialize in the West Bank. Consider Nazrat Ilit (literally, "Upper Nazareth"), a Jewish town that was built in 1957 on a hilltop overlooking Palestinian Nazareth and recently renamed Nof HaGalil (Hebrew for "Galil's landscape") to render it more attractive to Jewish citizens. Notwithstanding the Jewish town's role in the Judaization of the Galilee, the acute housing shortage—propelled by restrictions on the expansion of Palestinian municipal boundaries and on housing construction within Nazareth and nearby villages—has led middle-class Palestinians to move to

Nazrat Ilit. Despite the fierce opposition of many of its Jewish residents and their elected officials, by the end of 2021 Palestinians made up 29 percent of Nazrat Ilit's population of over forty thousand. The significant point is that the movement of Palestinian citizens to Jewish cities is seen to "contaminate" the purity of the Jewish city[89] and, in doing so, undermines, even if very gradually, the biospatial link and the construction of space as Jewish. The strict segregation in the West Bank does not allow for such "spatial miscegenation" processes.

It is precisely in this context that one should understand the July 2018 legislation of the Basic Law: Israel—The Nation-State of the Jewish People.[90] Until 2018, Israel's mistreatment of Palestinians inside the pre-1967 borders, including the dispossession of their lands, was rarely achieved by introducing laws that explicitly favored Jews.[91] Rather, as we have seen above, for many years Israeli settlement policies have been implemented using seemingly racially neutral laws that nevertheless enabled the transfer of land from Palestinian to Jewish ownership and control. The nationality law has changed this. Section 7 of the new law is not much more than a description of Israel's actions and policies since 1948: "The State views the development of *Jewish* settlement as a national value, and shall act to encourage and promote its establishment and consolidation."[92] Clearly, what Israel has done informally for seventy years is now the law of the land. Perhaps this is why liberal Zionists criticized this law first and foremost as "unnecessary" and "provocative"—for, in the past, this policy of favoring Jews over Palestinians was achieved without the introduction of blatant racial language within the law. Hence, the law is deemed superfluous, not because it will lead to dramatic changes on the ground, but because it uncovers the true nature of the State of Israel.

By way of conclusion, it may be important to state the obvious. Historically, states have frequently connected the *bio* with the *spatial* since at least the eighteenth century, at times with horrific consequences. Contemporary manifestations also abound, ranging from the biospatial strategies that Europe has been implementing to deal with the massive refugee crisis, through President Donald Trump's Muslim ban and asylum policies in the United States, and all the way to Myanmar, where Rohingya Muslims are being racially cleansed from Rakhine State. Nonetheless, excavating the specificities of each case remains vital. Before Israel's establishment, for instance, the 1937 Peel Commission and the 1947 UN Partition Plan clearly based their recommendations on a biospatial logic, dividing the territory according to racialized classifications of the population produced by the colonial power. The difference between these partition plans and the Oslo archipelago is instructive, however, since in the latter case the biospatial logic was used not to harness and maximize the population's demographic and economic potential or to enable self-determination, but rather to guarantee the ongoing subjugation of the colonized Palestinians. Notwithstanding this difference, both the long history of biotechnologies and the different geographical settings in which they are currently being mobilized suggest that Israel is not really an innovator. The uniqueness of Israeli colonialism is that for decades it has received the unconditional support of almost all liberal democracies, a striking phenomenon in the postcolonial era that is due in part to these countries' perception of Israel as a democracy. The tragic irony is that Israel's biospatial politics have given birth to a reality of a single apartheid state.

*Two*

# APARTHEID WITHOUT RACE

JOHN REYNOLDS

"REALITY HAS CHANGED"; "THE SITUATION HAS CHANGED." THIS WAS the explanation given by the Israeli human rights group B'Tselem as to why the organization decided, in 2021, to characterize the Israeli regime—whose laws and practices of domination over Palestinians it had already been painstakingly documenting for three decades—as one of apartheid from the river to the sea.[1] Here, B'Tselem was following the lead of Yesh Din: Volunteers for Human Rights, who some months earlier had published a report accusing the Israeli state of perpetrating the crime of apartheid—though with its focus limited to the West Bank only.[2] These organizations garnered widespread international attention and plaudits for doing so, paving the way for Human Rights Watch, one of the world's largest human rights organizations, to follow suit.[3] This was a significant step toward mainstream consensus on the structural reality of the oppression of Palestinians. We can also understand it as significant in two other, somewhat more troubling, ways.

The first is as a moment of clarification in which long-standing epistemic exclusion of Palestinian thought and knowledge is brought back into stark light. When the analysis is presented by Israeli or international organizations, it gains legitimacy across circles that have not heard (or have not wanted to listen to) the critiques that have been coming from Palestinian activists, organizations, and scholars for decades. The second and more substantive way is that the Yesh Din, B'Tselem, and Human Rights Watch positions articulate a certain *version* of Israeli apartheid that delinks apartheid from its own structural underpinnings of settler colonialism and its racial structures. My argument here is that these two phenomena cannot be separated. They are, indeed, intimately related.

The epistemic exclusion is not simply an issue of representation or the politics of citation; it has a substantive bearing on interpretive nuances and tensions over how apartheid is understood. I will refer broadly to a general distinction between *liberal* and *radical* critiques of Israeli apartheid.[4] The first section of this chapter traces liberal critiques of Israeli apartheid, their limitations, and the role of international law in consolidating such limited critiques over time. The liberal reading of apartheid by some lawyers and legal organizations is itself enabled only by omitting or glossing over more radical readings of apartheid from a Palestinian liberation perspective, which is the focus of the second section of the chapter. That liberation perspective has insisted on the racial dynamics of Zionism as a colonial project, and on the nexus of race, apartheid, and settler colonialism. It has stressed an understanding of apartheid in its context of conquest and territorial expansion, and as baked into the state's constitution and land policies of accumulation by dispossession. It is not just apartheid, but *colonial apartheid*. This conceptualization has been articulated in Palestinian political thought since the 1960s, but also even within some of the more legalistic Palestinian iterations of Israeli apartheid since the 1990s, which have remained conscious of keeping an analytic connection to colonialism.

In contrast, B'Tselem, Yesh Din, and Human Rights Watch do not make reference to settler colonialism or Zionism, or to the constitution of the state as such as an apartheid entity from its formation. Their interventions are framed more around a narrative of relatively recent "changes" to the reality in law and fact. These changes are cast as *exceptionally* right wing, even by Israel's standards. Indeed, *unexceptionally* right-wing Israeli leaders, from Yitzhak Rabin in the 1970s to Ehud Barak in the 2010s, have made a continual pretense of warning that if Israel fails to soften its oppressive excesses, it will risk *becoming* an apartheid state. The Yesh Din, B'Tselem, and Human Rights Watch studies replicate this narrative, with the kicker that the tipping point has now been reached: certain developments and accumulations have pushed Israel across the apartheid Rubicon. It is now *A Threshold Crossed*, as the title of the Human Rights Watch report puts it. The 2018 Nation-State Law and subsequent Israeli government articulations of more explicit plans for formal annexation of large swathes of the (already effectively annexed) West Bank are cited as examples of such phenomena. The reality, of course, is that these developments are less anomaly and aberration, more continuation and codification. But framing them as a new departure, somewhat independent of underlying structures or colonial ideology, makes possible a narrative that Israeli apartheid has emerged through excess over time, "without being founded on racist ideology."[5] The third section of the chapter argues for the need to reinscribe conceptions of apartheid with a proper understanding of race in its colonial context.

## ISRAELI APARTHEID, LIBERAL CRITIQUE

The idea of apartheid without racist ideology—that is, without race itself— is in no small part the result of how international law, for its part, has defined and dealt with apartheid over time. Since the 1960s, international law has essentially conceptualized apartheid along two parallel lines: as the denial of a collective right to self-determination in a colonial context by an oppressive regime of racial domination; and as systemic discrimination within a state's legal system against individuals from a particular racial group. It also implies culpability on two registers: state responsibility for the imposition of the overall apartheid regime of racial domination as an unlawful and illegitimate regime (rooted in the experiences of the colonial-apartheid regimes in southern Africa); and individual criminal responsibility for specific inhumane acts perpetrated as part of an apartheid system. The international legal provisions remain somewhat vague on what is meant by "regime," "domination," and even "race" and "racial group."

From the formal onset of apartheid in South Africa in 1948, African intellectuals, political leaders, and legal scholars understood it very clearly as a legal-political architecture of colonialism, not something new or separate from it. After 1960, when the Third World bloc became the majority in the

United Nations, General Assembly resolutions began to employ consistently the language of self-determination and ending colonialism in all its forms and manifestations. They repeatedly condemned apartheid as a regime of racial domination that amounted to an inherent violation of self-determination.[6] Apartheid was understood very much in the same bracket as colonial rule and foreign occupation, necessitating the same remedy: collective liberation and *land back*.[7] In time, with the decline of more radical streams of the Third World liberation project by the early 1980s, the individualizing logics of human rights law and international criminal law asserted precedence over the anti-imperial politics that had briefly threatened to transform international law in the 1960s and 1970s. With that, the anticolonial essence and implications of the apartheid prohibition have faded into the background somewhat. Apartheid as "colonialism of a special type," in the phrase famously coined by the South African Communist Party,[8] has been recast as (or reduced to) something more approximate to "racial discrimination of a special type."

International human rights law operates through this rubric of racial discrimination. It conceives of race primarily as an internal and often individualized issue focused on nondiscrimination and status equality before the law within a state, rather than as an international issue aimed at pursuing material inequality or facilitating transnational redistribution or reparations. Racism has increasingly been localized as internal racism in a way that obscures the history and legacies of colonial racism and brackets discussion of white supremacy as a phenomenon that continues to structure the global order.

This is part of a broader dynamic at play in international law whereby race is "depoliticized, dehistoricized, and domesticated,"[9] and a focus on procedural equality serves to water down the structural claims of racial justice movements. This has allowed, for example, settler-colonial states to treat Indigenous rights and resistance as domestic affairs within the framework of cultural rights, rather than as international relations defined by conquest, racial domination, and the imperatives of decolonization.[10] International law's articulation of "racial discrimination" also casts a wide conceptual net, one that is not tied to the specific historical material impositions of race. This is international law's fudge, in that it does not define race (or racism) as such. The core definition in the 1965 International Convention on the Elimination of Racial Discrimination (ICERD) includes race as one among five group categories in setting out that "'racial discrimination' shall mean any distinction, exclusion, restriction or preference based on *race, colour, descent, or national or ethnic* origin."[11] This percolates through to international law's subsequent definitions of apartheid, which refer to domination by one racial group over another—again, without delineating what constitutes a racial group. It can be assumed in one reading, then, that for the purposes of defining apartheid in international law, the "racial" in racial group covers a similarly broad range of categories as that in ICERD's racial discrimination. This can be useful from a doctrinal and tactical point of view in establishing that Israeli apartheid exists in breach of international law[12]—based on a pragmatic understanding of racial groups as straddling elements of nationality, ethnicity, and descent—without having to spend much time grappling with the question of race itself.

Thinking primarily in terms of a particular liberal-legal frame, however, means that the full character of Israeli apartheid may not be captured. Liberal legalism does not deal well with race. Race is clearly an ambiguous and unwieldy category—socially constructed, scientifically debunked, economically embedded, politically pervasive, and now cynically misrepresented in the right-wing culture war crusades. There is, naturally, discomfort with thinking of Palestine through the lens of race, given all the overlapping and competing nuances, textures, and manifestations of race within and between Jewish-Israeli and Palestinian communities. But with colonialism, settler colonialism, and race long understood as interlinked, including within the Palestinian radical intellectual traditions, what the frame of race does provide is a distinct historical material and analytic connection back to colonialism. And apartheid itself in southern Africa could not have crystallized without the particular dynamics of European settler colonialism on those lands. So Lana Tatour is right to say that "we should be cautious of liberal readings of Israeli apartheid."[13] The 1973 UN Apartheid Convention,[14] formulated in the context of Third World agitation, includes distinctly colonial elements in its definition of apartheid: the expropriation of land, the creation of separate reserves and ghettos, the exploitation of the labor of the subjugated racial group, and the obstruction of social and economic development (as well as physical violence, murder, torture, and other human rights abuses). The years that followed were marked by the West's counterrevolutionary tactics at the United Nations, the end of the Cold War, and the predominance of a liberal politics of human rights. This created the conditions in which the International Criminal Court's 1998 definition of apartheid would embed a more liberal universalist type of reading against which Tatour cautions. That definition still characterizes apartheid as institutionalized racial domination, but ties it more narrowly to the physical atrocity of crimes against humanity and strips away the settler-colonial-oriented elements of land, territory, labor, and exploitation.

International law generally has indeed tended to elide or overgeneralize race as substitutable by other group categorizations. This means that we lose some of the specificity of the European colonial project's intimate connections with, and reliance on, race thinking. It means that we lose something of the very material essence of apartheid as a particular manifestation and medium of settler colonialism. Apartheid instead becomes an aggravated version of group-based discrimination that can emerge in any state, regardless of historical context. It can exist without any connection to conquest, land, or territory, and in theory can likewise be perpetrated by natives against settlers.

What all of this has produced is a scenario in which the crime of apartheid, though "historically linked to the racist regime in South Africa," is now an independent concept "with a life of its own, which can exist without being founded on racist ideology."[15] B'Tselem argues that while "the division in South Africa was based on race . . . in Israel it is based on nationality and ethnicity."[16] B'Tselem avoids mentioning race or racial group anywhere in its position paper. Where it refers to "Jewish supremacy from the Jordan River to the Mediterranean Sea" or echoes the language of the legal definitions of apartheid, B'Tselem sticks to describing dominance by "one group over another"—never referring to "*racial* groups" as such.

This notion of apartheid without race/racism may appear implausible, but it draws on the particular interpretation of international law I have alluded to that universalizes apartheid to such an extent that it becomes any form of institutional domestic discrimination and is distanced from its distinctly settler-colonial origins. It is understandable and perhaps inevitable, then, that human rights organizations have utilized the less contentious, narrower version of apartheid offered to them by international law. This enables them to apply an apartheid framework to situations of systemic discrimination in their reporting and analysis, without having to reckon with the material imperatives of decolonization in the face of a colonial state carrying out an ongoing settler-colonial project. This more liberal, criminal law–oriented understanding of apartheid can potentially be remedied by formal equality rights, without necessarily having to directly confront the colonial conquest and political economy dynamics that the apartheid regime has consolidated. The consequence of this in Palestine would be to delink Israeli apartheid from Israeli settler colonialism and the Nakba. Apartheid can be ended, in that sense, without decolonization, reparations, or redistribution. In South Africa, this has produced a form of "neo-apartheid"[17] or "neoliberal apartheid."[18] In the context of Palestine, then, it is imperative that antiapartheid analysis and activism avoid falling into a similar trap. A good place to start, with this in mind, is to revisit earlier manifestations of Palestinian radical and antiracist thought.

## ISRAELI APARTHEID, ANTICOLONIAL CRITIQUE

In contrast to the narrative of Israeli apartheid as a line lately crossed, Palestinians will maintain that little, in fact, has substantively changed. Indeed, what is in some respects more striking than the relatively recent liberal epiphanies on Israeli apartheid is the consistency of Palestinian analysis of, and reference to, Israeli apartheid over several decades prior, and the contextualization of that apartheid as a structure of conquest, colonization, and settler sovereignty.

Many Palestinians have indeed characterized Israel as an apartheid regime since well before B'Tselem, Yesh Din, or Human Rights Watch existed. From the mid-1960s, Fayez Sayegh and other scholar-activists associated with the Palestine Research Center founded by the Palestinian Liberation Organization (PLO) were intent on internationalizing the Palestinian struggle "by theorizing the particular and connected forms of racism animating Zionist settler colonialism."[19] In his canonical 1965 text *Zionist Colonialism in Palestine*, Sayegh wrote:

In fact, in its practice of racial discrimination against the vestiges of Palestinian Arabs, the Zionist settler-state has learned all the lessons which the various discriminatory regimes of white settler-states in Asia and Africa can teach it. And it has proved itself in this endeavor an ardent and apt pupil, not incapable of surpassing its teachers. For, whereas the Afrikaner apostles of *apartheid* in South Africa, for example, brazenly proclaim their sin, the Zionist practitioners of *apartheid* in Palestine beguilingly protest their innocence![20]

Sayegh theorizes the nature of the Zionist state-building project and the enactment of racial hierarchy in Israeli law not just as indicative of discrimination or domination, but as premised on the colonial "elimination" of Palestinians.[21] In Palestine, this manifests most viscerally in the violence and dislocation of the Nakba. But settler colonialism also underpins Israel's default imposition from 1948 onward of an apartheid system over "those *remnants* of the Palestinian Arab people who have stubbornly stayed behind in their homeland in spite of all efforts to dispossess and evict them, . . . who have continued to live in the Zionist settler-state since 1948 [and] have their own 'Bantustans,' their 'native reserves,' their 'Ghettoes.'"[22] Settler colonialism and apartheid are tied together as such. Sayegh insists on the centrality of race and racial ideology: "Racism is not an acquired trait of the Zionist settler-state. Nor is it an accidental, passing feature of the Israeli scene. . . . It is inherent in the very ideology of Zionism and in the basic motivation for Zionist colonization and statehood."[23]

In this reading, apartheid is not an acquired deviation; it is not a situation changed; it is not a threshold recently crossed. It is inherent from the inception of Zionism's particular state project on a particular land, with particular implications for the people of that land. And so, while Sayegh may not have had a fully rounded and wholly consistent theory of race in the context of Palestine[24]—if such a thing would even be possible—it is striking that Palestinian intellectuals like him in the 1960s had a more sophisticated engagement with race and racialization than many liberals and lawyers do sixty years on.

Hasan Sa'b, adding to Sayegh's analysis that same year, likewise made clear the juridically racial character of the Israeli state and emphasized that the domination was both national *and* racial. It was, significantly, not a case of nationality in place of race: Israel discriminates among its citizens "on racial and national grounds. . . . Israel has one law for its Jewish citizens and another law for its Arab citizens."[25] *The Arabs in Israel*, by lawyer-scholar-activist Sabri Jiryis, first published in Hebrew and Arabic in 1966, is another crucial pre-1967 analysis of Israel as a structurally racial regime. It is further testament to the argument that the subjugation of Palestinians inside Israel cannot be viewed or resolved in isolation from the situation of Palestine as a whole.[26]

Israeli apartheid in the light of these analyses was not an accumulation of the worst excesses of the post-1967 conquests and occupation. It predated that expansion and was rooted from the outset in the very constitution of the settler state. Palestinian sociologist Elia Zureik would write of Israel's "internal colonialism" within the 1948 territory as a form of "national apartheid"—in which race relations converged with class and political economy dynamics, and "manifested in segregation in housing, land ownership, education, interpersonal contact, modes of political organization and occupational distribution, not to mention the area of marriage."[27] For Zureik, the settler-colonial state was constituted and developed from 1948 as a site of apartheid. This is the background against which Palestinian intellectuals would continue to articulate and escalate the charge of apartheid after the 1967 Naksa.

From the early 1970s, *Al-Hadaf*, the weekly magazine of the Popular Front for the Liberation of Palestine (PFLP) (with Ghassan Kanafani as editor-in-chief, until his assassination), and the PLO periodical *Shu'un Filastiniya* published examinations of Israel through the apartheid rubric. They characterized, for example, Israel and apartheid South Africa as "parallel racist entities"[28] and as similarly neoimperial apartheid regimes.[29] They also specifically highlighted the similarities between South Africa's Bantustan policy and Israel's concerted fragmentation of the Palestinian territories with proposed autonomy in limited enclaves—described in one critique as "Palestine-stans."[30] The PFLP sustained this analysis in its English-language publications as well. A 1980 text, for instance, castigated apartheid South Africa as a colonial hub of white supremacy, Western imperialism, and extractive capitalism, before drawing its parallels to Palestine: "The Palestinian and South African struggles have historical and contemporary links. The peoples of both countries are confronting racist, settler colonial regimes that are supported by the full weight of imperialism."[31]

The *Journal of Palestine Studies*, from its inception in the early 1970s, likewise included consistent critique of Israeli apartheid: "Israeli kibbutzim are apartheid institutions with regard to Israeli non-Jews"; Jewish settlements in the occupied territories, "from their very nature, constitute a dispossession, a discrimination and a system of apartheid."[32] The journal also covered the "economic apartheid practiced by Zionist organizations,"[33] as well as the "South African parallels" inherent in "the nature of the state of Israel [as] a settler colony" and its "assertion of a special superiority over the native."[34] Rashid Khalidi argued that Israel had imposed an unsustainable reality of "apartheid and Bantustans."[35] Haydar 'Abd Al-Shafi also made the case in the journal that in the occupied territories, in particular, the "two separate administrations, two separate judicial systems," constituted "a kind of apartheid."[36]

The Palestinian analysis of race and apartheid in the early 1970s had indeed been significant enough to raise concerns in Washington. The 1972 Report of the Attorney General to the Congress of the United States on the Administration of the Foreign Agents Registration Act, for instance, flagged up pamphlets published by Sayegh and the PLO because of their focus on "Zionism with its racial connotations, its inherent political chauvinism ."[37] The Palestine Research Center continued its analysis unfazed, and in 1975 published *Israeli Racism*, a text describing "the full extent of Israeli racism" as embedded in its juridical order: "All non-Jews living in Israel are by definition second-class citizens. This element of racism which is contained in the ideological foundations of the State—as expressed, for example, in the Law of Return—receives numerous other concrete expressions."[38] In addition to the citizenship and immigration laws, the text pinpoints the role of the Zionist land acquisition funds and parastate institutions in expropriating Palestinian land. It also highlights Israel's systemic use of emergency law[39] as an instrument of racial domination (a pervasive feature of colonial governance generally[40]). *Israeli Racism* contains some insightful commentary on social-racial hierarchies in Israel between European and non-European Jews within the state apparatus, while noting that the material and ideological discrimination against the Palestinian population of Israel is distinctly linked to the nature of the state itself: "The racism against Arabs is in some sense the inevitable yet peculiar product of their status as a non-Jewish minority in a Jewish State."[41] From the Palestinian perspective, structural racism in Israel "has its roots deep in the ideology of Zionism," as well as "Israel's organic relationship with western imperialism." The upshot is that at that particular moment, Israel and South Africa "share similarities in historical development and contemporary structure" as settler states, while anticolonial resistance "is the inevitable result of Israeli, and South African, racism."[42]

All this research and analysis on race and apartheid fed into the developments that followed. These included, most famously, the 1975 UN General Assembly Resolution 3379 on Zionism as a form of racism, which Noura Erakat vividly revisits and unpacks.[43] They also included the founding, by Palestinian legal scholar Anis Al-Qasem, of the International Organization for the Elimination of All Forms of Racial Discrimination and its inaugural symposium in 1976. The proceedings of that symposium characterized Zionism and apartheid as "two sides of the same coin."[44] In a striking essay included in that collection, Edward Said traces the common intellectual origins of European imperialism and Zionism, emphasizing the centrality of scientific racism to colonial consolidation, expansion, and legitimization from the nineteenth century onward. For Said, "It is in the history of 19th-century European intellectual culture that one finds the common origins of imperialism and Zionism."[45] This intellectual culture would underpin the general colonial pillars of territorial conquest and domination, and the colonial-apartheid facades of racial and juridical classification, segregation, and domination. Said notes that "Jewish rights in Palestine were formulated in the juridical and even metaphysical language of a powerful European imperialism." He argues that in its racial and juridical rationalizations, the Zionist idea of a "separate European enclave in Asia is exactly analogous with Leopold de Saussure's theses on the necessity of maintaining separate European and native structures in newly acquired territory. The concept of an unlimited Law of Return for Jews and none for non-Jews is based on the same thing to be found in every white colony."[46]

Throughout his relentless writings on Palestine over the decades that followed, Said refers explicitly and repeatedly to Israel's apartheid as a racial,
colonial project. Israeli rule over the Palestinians is "a specific, continuing
process of dispossession, displacement, and colonial de facto apartheid,"[47]
which Said roots in its underlying conquest and racial ideology, "from the
wholesale dispossession of the 'non-Jews,' to the minute details of apartheid
on the West Bank . . . all of it coming from the essentially racialist difference between Jew and non-Jew."[48] Through all his analysis, the implications
are clear: Zionism, as a settler-colonial project, cannot but manifest itself
in apartheid anatomies. Jewish-Israeli domination in Palestine, like colonial-apartheid domination elsewhere, must be resisted as such. The core of
the issue, as Said puts it, "is intellectual truth and the need to combat any
sort of apartheid and racial discrimination. . . . We should concentrate our
resistance on combatting Israeli settlement . . . and on fully confronting the
apartheid provisions inherent in Zionism."[49] This reality of apartheid as intrinsic to Zionism has been clear to Said and countless other Palestinian and
anticolonial thinkers and activists from the outset. It underlines the nexus
between apartheid and settler colonialism, and the need to situate race in
that context. It also demonstrates that the liberal (Zionist) narratives of "democracy" inside the 1948 lines and of "occupation-turned-apartheid" in the
1967 territories are defective and deceptive.

Since the turn of the century and Said's passing, Palestinian scholars
and thinkers have only furthered the interrogation of Israeli apartheid. Ali
Abunimah wrote of the "similarities between the ideologies of Afrikan-
erdom and Zionism," noting that "Israel, like apartheid-era South Africa,
grants rights to individuals based not on their citizenship, but rather on
their membership in a specific ethnic group."[50] Azmi Bishara's essay "A Short
History of Apartheid" characterized Israeli apartheid as a particular form
of demographic separation that has continued to define the ongoing Nakba
and Zionism's approach to the question of land and people: "The uprooting
of Palestinians in 1948 was an exercise in demographic separation through
displacement."[51] The dynamics of race and colonization combine through
conquest of the land on classic civilizational grounds and segregation of
the population on racial lines. For Bishara, Zionist colonialism inhabits the
space between South African apartheid and French-style settler colonialism

à la Algeria. It is "a distillation of the worst in each" that produces a "unique type of colonialism," defined by multiple layers of racial segregation linked to the territorial fragmentation: "Separation, within separation, is the logic of Zionist colonialism."[52]

Political scientist Leila Farsakh has been another Palestinian intellectual persistently examining Israeli apartheid and, again, situating it in the context of settler colonialism. In texts published in 2003 and 2005, Farsakh emphasizes that while Israel's regime is distinct in certain ways from South African apartheid, the first and most important element of apartheid itself "is the historical colonialist foundation" upon which it is built: "White settlers in South Africa, like Zionist pioneers, colonized a land already inhabited."[53] From that colonization flowed dispossession of native land and homes, and legal segregation. White domination in southern Africa was based primarily on segregation and exploitation, whereas Zionist domination in Palestine has also involved mass external expulsion and a logic of elimination. But both regimes are defined by conquest, supremacy, and domination. So, while Farsakh is unsure about the full precision of the apartheid framework in all its elements, she concludes that certainly in its post-1993 consolidations of fragmentation, closures, and permits, Palestine looked ever more similar to apartheid South Africa. She also flags Ariel Sharon's well-known fixation with the Bantustan system as an ideal blueprint to impose on the Palestinians, showing that Oslo was pivotal to locking in the "Bantustanization" of Palestine through its economic and labor aspects and its territorial and legal facets.[54] More recently, a chapter by Farsakh in Ilan Pappé's collection *Israel and South Africa: The Many Faces of Apartheid* again insists that

> what has made the comparison between Apartheid South Africa and Israel attractive is the colonial foundation of both states. Both Apartheid South Africa and the Zionist project in Palestine were concerned with land expropriation and exclusive territorial control. Both were based on European settlers appropriating already inhabited land, expelling the indigenous population, and depriving them of equal political rights within their polity.[55]

The other Palestinian featured in Pappé's collection is Amneh Badran, whose own book, *Zionist Israel and Apartheid South Africa*,[56] explores questions around social movements and internal dissent in the two similar apartheid states. The list goes on and on.[57] I cannot do justice here to the wealth of all this literature. The point by now, I hope, is clear. Reality has not changed as of 2018 or 2021 or 2023. Palestinians have been conceptualizing and critiquing Israeli apartheid for the last six decades, and have insisted on understanding it as colonial apartheid. Critical and anti-Zionist Israeli and international scholars have followed their lead, and prominent South African antiapartheid figures have lined up to denounce Israeli apartheid after seeing it for themselves in Palestine.

And yet there has been a marked lack of mainstream recognition of this Palestinian scholarship and thinking across a range of disciplines. B'Tselem's eight-page position paper alone garnered more attention and coverage in many Western institutional and media spaces than had decades of sustained Palestinian research and activism. Even when it is recognized in solidarity, this work is cast as peripheral: "For years, the discourse around apartheid in the Israeli context was the purview of relatively marginal, and extremely radical circles in international civil society and in Palestinian society."[58] Yesh Din's acknowledgment of the analysis on Israeli apartheid that existed before its own 2020 study asserted that it "relied on intuitive analogies to Apartheid South Africa and remained in the political-public realm." Specifically, it "rarely included legal analyses."[59] This depiction again somewhat diminishes the analytic voice of Palestinian legal activist-researchers and legal scholars, and downplays the fact that they (and others) had been producing legal analyses of apartheid for decades.

Through this period, a host of Palestinian legal scholars advanced their own varying deconstructions of Israeli law and policy with reference to the international legal prohibition of apartheid and the crime against humanity of apartheid.[60] Some of these legal arguments have focused on the situation within Israel's 1948 borders in Palestine, some on the situation only in the 1967 occupied territory, and others on the singular Israeli regime over Palestinians as a whole. Some emphasize links to colonialism and unpack race and "racial groups" more than others. But the claim that this array of scholarship can be cast as barely existent does a disservice to Palestinian legal research and knowledge production. Perhaps even more relevant in the context of the work of human rights organizations is the identification and analysis of Israeli apartheid produced by equivalent Palestinian legal advocacy and human rights groups over the years and decades prior.[61] Even in this more legalistic iteration of Palestinian antiapartheid discourse—and even where it ultimately relies on a tactically broad conception of "racial group" as the path of least resistance in demonstrating Israeli apartheid—there is an understanding of apartheid beyond its narrow legal confines. And certainly in the work of some of these organizations and in the new generations of Palestinian activism, we hear the more radical and unapologetic language of Palestinian liberation that emphasizes Zionism as a settler-colonial structure with a racial logic expressed through apartheid laws and institutions.

## REINSCRIBING RACE

In 2004, Raef Zreik argued that we should be cautious in applying the apartheid framework in Palestine. While accepting that the analogy can be a powerful window into the reality of Israel's architecture of "institutionalized, legalized discrimination on ethnic and racial grounds," Zreik worried that it might obscure other less analogous elements. His particular concern revolved around "the tendency of the rights discourse, with its view of law as universal, to ignore historical context."[62] Zreik acknowledged that the real focus of his essay was on rights discourse, and a particular human rights and nondiscrimination response to apartheid, rather than apartheid itself. There are certainly elements in the content and presentation of liberal critiques of Israeli apartheid that bear out Zreik's concerns. The broad universalist human rights and International Criminal Court definitions of apartheid can work to render it as simply an aggravated version of (all too) standard state discrimination. Insisting instead on the more radical critique of apartheid (as colonial apartheid) interrupts the suspension of disbelief in which apartheid exists without racialization, and brings us back to Third Worldist bottom lines: colonialism and apartheid in southern Africa and Palestine "have a common imperialist origin"[63] and are part of the "same racial fascism institutionalized . . . to the misfortune of the Palestinian people."[64]

An understanding of Zionism as colonialism and as a form of racism continues to underpin the Palestinian critiques of Israeli apartheid. These critiques, however, have not always explicitly addressed race itself. Here, Noura Erakat does important work in unpacking the racializing dynamics of the Israeli legal system in transforming Jews of various backgrounds into a homogenous category that is granted specific legal privileges: "In so doing, Israel both achieved the supremacy of Jewish nationality as refracted through a lens of European white supremacy and facilitated the dispossession, displacement, and containment of Palestinian natives."[65] The fact that there is no such legal thing as Israeli nationality is key here. There are instead multiple (racially inflected) nationalities that have been granted recognition in Israeli law, but with Jewish nationality having a unique value, analogous to whiteness in apartheid South Africa.[66] These dynamics are deeply entangled with property and capitalist social relations, and underpin analyses of "whiteness as property in Israel"[67] and "Jewishness as property under Israeli law."[68] This reminds us that while race may be a "floating signifier,"[69] it is one that is ultimately and specifically rooted in the colonial context: "Race is colonialism speaking, in idioms whose diversity reflects the variety of unequal relationships into which Europeans have co-opted conquered populations."[70] Understanding the particularities of race and racial groups in that context of colonial history is therefore crucial to understanding apartheid and its material relationship to land, property, and territory.

In this sense, it is important to insist on the importance of race qua race, not simply through the medium of nationality, ethnicity, or religion. There are, of course, multiple layers of overlap. But the fundamentally settler-colonial nature of Zionism and its place in the landscape of empire requires us to think in terms of race. Palestinians were racialized by a colonization project seeking to displace and replace them. This was situated in a broader racial-imperial politics in which Zionism's founder, Theodore Herzl, could forthrightly argue the merits of a Zionist state project in Palestine as "a rampart of Europe against Asia, an outpost of civilization as opposed to barbarism,"[71] and Israel's first prime minister, David Ben-Gurion, could speak of Israel as a European entity in a non-European region: "Our regime, our culture, our relations, are not the fruit of this region."[72] Notions of European supremacism and imperial conquest continue to underpin Israeli sovereignty and settlement doctrines. The layers of "internal" racial hierarchy that stratify Jewish communities in Israel (as well as non-Jewish migrants and refugees) have persisted and indeed proliferated since 1948, but the Palestinians as a racial group across historic Palestine and in exile continue to be oppressed in a specific and systemic way. The premise of Israel as a state of the Jewish people only—openly and explicitly *not* a state of all its citizens—is dependent on maintaining multiple elements of an apartheid regime over Palestinians: domination and discrimination; displacement, segregation, and fragmentation; exclusion and repressive inclusion.

In this light, there are particular dynamics of Israeli apartheid that render it colonial, that stress the connections between race and colonization, and that show Israeli apartheid to be colonial apartheid. Palestinians have long stressed the links between colonialism and racism, and the commonalities of British imperialist and Zionist visions of Palestinians: both visions "belong fundamentally to the ethos of a European *mission civilisatrice*—nineteenth-century, colonialist, racist."[73] Palestinians, in response, "are clearly anticolonialist and antiracist in our struggle."[74] There is an important point here about the forming and forging of language, analysis, and theory in struggle, in the process of "decolonization from the bottom up."[75] Ultimately, Palestinian communities and movements have understood and articulated their subjugation as a form of apartheid, and one that is based on racial ideology. It is not the same as the anti-Blackness that dominated apartheid in southern Africa, but it does have certain common colonial characteristics, and the reality of race is that it moves and speaks in different guises. It can be reshaped and retooled in different contexts by its particular relationship to the given system of political power. And while it emanates from the expansion of European capital and empire, it can also be conceptualized and theorized from the bottom up, through the conditions and traditions of the oppressed in their local arenas of struggle. Palestinians intuitively and intimately understand the modes of domination and segregation that have been imposed on them—legally, spatially, and racially. The core demands of Palestinian activism—as amplified most recently in the Unity Intifada of 2021 and the mass mobilizations against the Gaza genocide through 2023 and 2024—are not just for an end to the 1967 occupation, but for the right of return for Palestinian refugees and an end to the Israeli state's racial regime. This puts the settler-colonial and apartheid essence of the state itself as the locus of the freedom struggle and makes clear that it is an antiracist struggle as well as, and as part of, a national liberation struggle.

## CONCLUSION

To conclude, I want to stress that this idea of the Palestinian struggle as simultaneously and innately anticolonial and antiracist, linked to global struggles but standing on its own merits and specificities, is the legacy of the work started by the Palestine Research Center all those decades ago. In 1969, Jibran Majdalany argued "the necessity for an anti-racialist solution to the Palestine conflict," making clear that racial ideology did underpin the structures and must be confronted and dismantled as such: "The taking of a stand is a sort of praxis in which the ideological option materialises into a political attitude; for the condemnation of particular ideologies must lead to a condemnation of the regimes and the political structures to which they give rise."[76] In this analysis, "there is no other course but to refuse and to combat the structure of a state which is based on this form of discrimination."[77] Thus, "the beginnings of an anti-racialist solution are to be found in a clear formulation of the conception of the state.... There can be no compatibility between anti-racialism and the constitutionalisation of the privileges of a race."[78] Majdalany put forward an antiracial formula as essential to the decolonization of Palestine. It seems clear that there can be no meaningful material antiapartheid transformation without dismantling apartheid's racial structures and privileges and redistributing the land and resources that have been expropriated and extracted.

In this light, the current conjuncture in Palestine—in which 2021 was characterized as "the year of Israeli apartheid"[79] and 2023 brought the escalation of Israel's eliminationist violence and ethnic cleansing in Gaza—is a pivotal moment. There now is a growing consensus on Israeli apartheid existing as a discriminatory system. If the role of race and racial-colonial structures was not sufficiently addressed in the human rights reports on Israeli apartheid, the Gaza genocide has changed prevailing popular conceptions of this element of Zionism quite fundamentally. The implications here for possible futures are profound: rather than liberal hope for reform within colonial structures, we see a radical insistence that apartheid does not exist without racial ideology, that it is entwined with settler colonialism, and that it can only be properly dismantled as part of a process of decolonization and redistribution.

*Three*
# ZIONISM AS A FORM OF RACISM

NOURA ERAKAT

ON NOVEMBER 10, 1975, THE UN GENERAL ASSEMBLY VOTED FOR Resolution 3379, declaring Zionism a form of racism and racial discrimination.[1] The resolution, part of the UN Decade for Action to Combat Racism and Racial Discrimination (Decade against Racism), condemned Zionism as a racialized and illegitimate form of governance alongside colonialism, racism, and apartheid. It was a hard-won victory that caused tremendous uproar among Global North countries that felt that the resolution was incendiary and counterproductive to the nascent Middle East Peace Process. The Third World, constituting an automatic majority within the General Assembly, celebrated it as a victory against Western imperialism and enduring domination, more generally.

Several vectors led to Resolution 3379. One is the intellectual work within the Palestinian Liberation Organization (PLO) developed primarily by individuals. Palestinian scholar-activist Fayez Sayegh guided the drafting effort within the Third Committee and later the advocacy effort within the General Assembly plenary in his capacity as a representative of the Kuwaiti mission to the United Nations. The work of Sayegh and other leading Palestinian thinkers, such as Hasan Sa'b, constitutes a robust racial analysis of Zionism and Zionist settler colonialism that bridges Afro-Asiatic struggles in the spirit of Third World upheaval characteristic of the time. This intellectual work featured prominently in the drafting history of the resolution and underscored its success. Another vector of the resolution is its diplomatic history within the United Nations.

Resolution 3379 was an amendment to a broader initiative launching the Decade against Racism aimed primarily at the South African apartheid regime. A coalition of states introduced the amendment in the Third Committee after a failed attempt to unseat Israel from the General Assembly. Upon the introduction of the resolution, Western states made clear that they would withdraw their support for the entire Decade if it was not rescinded. The threat diminished support among African states that considered it strategically shortsighted to dilute consensus opposition to apartheid and preferred to advance a Palestine-related resolution separately. Despite procedural maneuvering and outright threats by the initiative's opponents, it ultimately passed with a solid majority.

Sixteen years later, in 1991, the PLO agreed to rescind Resolution 3379 as a precondition for entering into the Oslo peace agreement.[2] The US-led bilateral agreement reframed the Palestinian freedom movement from a struggle against Zionist settler-colonial "racial elimination" and territorial expansion to a conflict between two warring peoples. The shift obscured the power imbalance that subjects the Palestinian people to conditions of unfreedom and supplanted critical protest against Israel with entreaties for dialogue and compromise. The Oslo Accords have proven to be a sovereignty trap for Palestinians: a political arrangement of derivative sovereignty featuring native collaboration with settler-colonial and imperial powers, whereby good native behavior is rewarded with limited autonomy and perpetual subjugation.

This untenable status quo began to unravel when the peace process crumbled in 2000, leading to the Second Palestinian Intifada and, ultimately, a tectonic shift from Israeli military occupation to all-out warfare against stateless Palestinians.[3] Critical scholars and activists produced analyses highlighting Israel's settler-colonial and racial nature, declaring the condition tantamount to apartheid. The summer of 2014 marked another momentous juncture when the concurrent bombardment of Gaza and the occupation of Ferguson, Missouri, by the US Army National Guard during protests catalyzed renewals of Black-Palestinian solidarity and provoked an analytical return to understanding racism and colonialism as co-constitutive structures of domination.[4]

The steady and unequivocal unraveling of the peace process, together with a resurgent transnational solidarity movement, has compelled increasing examination of the Palestinian condition through a racial framework. The drafting and intellectual history of Resolution 3379 offers tremendous insight for this inquiry. Using the works of Palestinian intellectuals, the 1975 Third Committee deliberations, and the transcripts of the thirtieth session of the UN General Assembly, this chapter seeks to reconstruct the history of Resolution 3379 as a way of considering an alternative trajectory of the Palestinian freedom struggle as one against racism.

The chapter begins by exploring the geopolitical context from which Resolution 3379 emerged, namely, the Third World revolt against imperialism, as well as the Middle East Peace Process initiated in the aftermath of the October 1973 war. It then traces how the expulsion of South Africa from the United Nations in 1974 helped shape the PLO's diplomatic strategy and ultimately led it to introduce the resolution condemning Zionism at the United Nations. The following section examines racial theories advanced throughout the contentious UN proceedings. The chapter then unpacks the procedural maneuvers to defeat the resolution and concludes with thoughts on outstanding questions and challenges in establishing the Palestinian liberation movement as an antiracist struggle.

## THE PLO DECLARES ARMED STRUGGLE UNTIL LIBERATION AND JOINS THE THIRD WORLD STRUGGLE

By the close of the 1967 war, Israel occupied the Egyptian Sinai Peninsula and the Syrian Golan Heights, as well as the West Bank and Gaza Strip. Not only did Israel's occupation further normalize its conquest of Palestinian lands since 1948, the nineteen-year-old state also became an imperial power. For five months following the cessation of hostilities, Arab states and their allies urged the UN General Assembly and the Security Council to declare Israel's use of force initiating the war as illegitimate, making its withdrawal from Arab lands imperative. Their efforts failed, and the Security Council unanimously passed Resolution 242 establishing a quid pro quo arrangement whereby Israel would return the Arab territories in exchange for permanent peace.[5]

Palestinians saw Resolution 242 as an instrument of defeat. It ensured Israel's presence and failed to recognize the Palestinian right to self-determination, referring to Palestinians as merely a "refugee problem."[6] The Arab defeat catalyzed the takeover of the PLO by Palestinian militant factions. Under the helm of Yasser Arafat, the organization committed itself to revolution through popular armed struggle for the sake of liberating the "Arab Palestinian" homeland, returning to that homeland, and exercising "their right to self-determination and sovereignty over it." The PLO's declaration of national liberation warfare against Israel, which described Israel as "the instrument of the Zionist movement" and a "geographical base for world imperialism," further aligned it with the broader Third World movement.[7]

The self-identified Third World sought to chart a historical trajectory distinct from the two offered by the opposing poles in the Cold War.[8] Initially congealed in Bandung in 1955 and later conceptualized as the Non-Aligned Movement (NAM) in Cairo in 1961, this nonaligned bloc sought to upend Western imperialism and usher in a new world order.[9] The liberation of Palestine was central to this agenda. The NAM considered the denial of Arab Palestinian sovereignty, like the denial of sovereignty to all colonized peoples, a racial matter. The League of Nations Mandate System, established after World War I, had predicated eligibility for sovereignty on proximity to European models of government and society.[10]

In observation of the subjugation of colonized peoples throughout the 1930s, including the League of Nations' role in sustaining it, Black anglophone revolutionary scholars theorized that colonialism reflected a "dual structure" of enslavement and international racial hierarchy.[11] W. E. B. Du Bois explained that this racial-capitalist structure subjected colonized peoples to conditions of unfreedom for "the benefit of the 'white people of the world.'"[12] In 1960, in its capacity as an automatic majority at the United Nations, the nonaligned bloc successfully condemned colonialism as an illegitimate system of governance and established that self-determination was tantamount to national independence.[13]

Third World nations and nation-states also considered Israel's establishment as an imperial imposition that effectively divided the African and Asian continents from one another.[14] This analysis crystallized further as Israel aligned itself with other imperial powers, particularly with South Africa. While the international community steadily isolated and condemned the apartheid regime, Israel maintained its economic and trade relations with South Africa, thereby enabling it to withstand the international sanctions. This led the General Assembly to condemn "the unholy alliance between Portuguese colonialism, South African racism, Zionism and Israeli imperialism" in December 1973.[15]

That same year, in October, Egypt and Syria had launched a surprise attack against Israel. Though they ultimately lost the war, they successfully altered the balance of power in their favor. Despite the binding nature of Resolution 242, for six years there was no political will to initiate negotiations between Israel and the aggrieved Arab parties. The October 1973 war mobilized the international community to act. Security Council Resolution 338[16] mandated the commencement of negotiations, thus ushering in the Middle East Peace Process. Henry Kissinger, then US secretary of state, led the effort with the primary intention of diminishing Soviet influence in the Middle East.[17] He disaggregated the "Arab-Israeli conflict" and insisted upon bilateral negotiations between Israel, Egypt, Syria, and Jordan respectively to enhance Israel's negotiating leverage. The United States unequivocally refused to recognize the PLO or involve it in the peace process.

Notwithstanding the exclusion of the Palestinians, the October 1973 war made imaginable the first political opportunities for Palestinians to negotiate a diplomatic solution for their self-determination.[18] Mindful that Egypt and Syria had no intention of waging a war of liberation against Israel and unable to overcome the PLO's exclusion from the regional peace process, PLO chairman Yasser Arafat sought entry into the United Nations as another site of battle. By the end of 1974, the PLO had become a nonmember observer entity at the United Nations, established the juridical status of the Palestinian people,[19] and created an alternative legal framework to Resolution 242 for the sake of achieving Palestinian self-determination through negotiations.[20] Following its momentous achievements, the PLO pursued a multifaceted strategy that sustained its revolutionary commitments and paved a path to diplomatic negotiations. These efforts included a campaign to expel Israel from the United Nations based on the South African model.

## À LA SOUTH AFRICA

The situation in South Africa had been a focal point at the United Nations at least since 1960, when police officers opened submachine gunfire on unarmed Black protestors in Sharpeville, killing sixty-nine and wounding nearly two hundred. Within two years of the massacre, the General Assembly condemned apartheid and called on member states to end all economic and military relations with South Africa as a means of coercion.[21] By 1973, the General Assembly had developed the Apartheid Convention, declaring apartheid a crime against humanity and ascribing criminal liability to individuals who perpetuate, aid, or abet it.[22] The body also recognized that the authentic representatives of the South African people were liberation movements recognized by the Organization of African Unity (OAU).[23]

During this period, African members and their allies sought to expel South Africa from the United Nations, but failed to overcome British, French, and American opposition within the Security Council, which exercises exclusive purview over UN membership.[24] Upon his assumption of the General Assembly presidency in 1974, Algeria's Abdelaziz Bouteflika overcame Western opposition by creating a new rule that empowered the General Assembly to suspend or expel a state without a Security Council recommendation. He thereby enabled the General Assembly to unseat the apartheid regime.[25] Inspired by the Third World's fortitude and success, the PLO initiated a similar campaign to expel Israel. To develop momentum, the PLO sought endorsement from multiple regional and political meetings throughout the summer of 1975, beginning with the World Conference of the International Women's Year convened in Mexico City.

The final Declaration of the World Conference on Women mentioned Zionism twice in the preambular text. The first time, it expressed that women participate equally in the struggles against "imperialism, colonialism, neo-colonialism, foreign occupation, zionism, alien domination, racism and apartheid." In the second iteration, the conference recognized that all women, regardless of their differences, suffer equally under "colonialism, neo-colonialism, zionism, racial discrimination, and apartheid."[26] In two of its operative articles, the conference decided to "eliminate" Zionism along-side other illegitimate forms of governance.[27] The conference also passed a specialized resolution regarding Palestinian and Arab women, whereby it similarly condemned Zionism, this time alongside fascism, and appealed to the international community to provide Palestinians "moral and material" assistance to achieve their right to return and self-determination.[28] Israel, which participated in the proceedings, objected to the preambular and op-erative paragraphs and moved to strike "Zionism" from the text in the four places in which it appeared. Israel's motion was deftly defeated in a vote of 61–23, with 21 abstentions.[29]

The PLO then attended the Islamic Conference of Foreign Ministers in Jeddah, where the convening thirty-nine ministers endorsed Israel's expul-sion.[30] This would be its only successful endorsement. At the OAU Summit held in Kampala, the initiative failed. Egypt, eager to enhance its relation-ship with the United States for the sake of recouping the Sinai Peninsula, diluted the PLO demand, while Uganda explicitly blocked it.[31] The reason for Uganda's opposition is unclear, especially as it would condemn Zionism at the 1975 African Unity Summit and, later, at the United Nations.

The OAU Summit passed a resolution endorsing Afro-Arab cooperation.[32] It also decried Zionism as "a danger to world peace" and as a "racist regime," noting that the racist regime in Palestine and the "racist regimes in Zimba-bwe and South Africa have a common imperialist origin, forming a whole and having the same racist structure and being organically linked in their policy aimed at repression of the dignity and integrity of the human being."[33] The OAU affirmed "the cause of Palestine as an African cause," and called upon states to "sever political, economic, and cultural relations with Israel."[34] Finally, as a compromise position with the PLO, the OAU called upon all its member states "to take all appropriate measures to intensify pressure against Israel at the United Nations and the other Agencies, including *the possibility of eventually depriving it of its status as a Member* of these Agencies."[35]

Israel's expulsion remained a real possibility as PLO representatives traveled to Lima for the NAM conference. The NAM's eighty members em-braced the PLO enthusiastically as they granted it full membership, thus altering its observer status extended in 1973, and welcomed it onto the Coordinating Committee. The NAM also endorsed the right of Palestinian

self-determination and condemned Zionism as a racist ideology that threat-
ens world peace and security.[36] However, as in Kampala, Egypt emerged as
a primary force of opposition, compounded by internal conflicts within the
NAM, and the PLO failed to achieve a resolution endorsing the expulsion of
Israel from the United Nations.[37]

In addition to its failed effort to curry support for the removal of Israel,
the peace process continued apace as Egypt and Israel neared an agreement.
To recalibrate the balance of power, the PLO mobilized the nonaligned bloc
when the UN General Assembly reconvened in September 1975. The thirtieth
session of the General Assembly successfully passed Resolution 3375, calling
for the PLO's inclusion in the Middle East Peace Process on terms established
by the legal corrective to Resolution 242.[38] The General Assembly also established the Committee on the Inalienable Rights of the Palestinian People,
similar to the standing committees on ending apartheid in South Africa and
ushering in independence for Namibia. Finally, the PLO's allies took advantage of ongoing proceedings within the UN's Third Committee to introduce
a resolution declaring Zionism as a form of racism and racial discrimination.

## THE UNITED NATIONS DEBATES RACIAL THEORY

The Third Committee—responsible for social, humanitarian, and cultural
issues—was continuing its work on the Decade against Racism.[39] African
states initiated the Decade and the General Assembly endorsed it in 1972 for
the sake of targeting apartheid South Africa. Participating states, however,
expressed the Decade's goals more broadly as eliminating "racism, *apartheid*, racial discrimination and the liberation of peoples under colonial domination and alien subjugation."[40]

In this context, on October 3, 1975, Somalia, on behalf of a coalition of
states, introduced an amendment to the Decade against Racism. Resolution
2157 proposed that the word "Zionism" be inserted into the Decade wherever
"apartheid," "colonialism," and "racial discrimination" appeared.[41] Approximately two weeks later, Somalia moved to withdraw the amendment and
replace it with a new draft resolution. Resolution 2159 expanded the preambular text to reflect the sense of the Global South—established throughout
the summer of 1975 in Mexico City, Jeddah, Kampala, and Lima—that Zionism was a form of racism and racial discrimination.[42]

The nonaligned effort on behalf of Palestinians seemed to be an alternative to the primary goal of unseating Israel from the United Nations. Anis Al Qasem—at the time, a leading Palestinian jurist and PLO legal adviser—explains that Palestinians "turned to racism as a framework because during this time, racism became an international crime." He notes that "African nations and organizations were more active than Arab ones."[43] While Palestinians were certainly taking advantage of the political moment, their efforts were sincere and reflected ongoing efforts to provide a racial theory of Zionism.

Fayez Sayegh, director of the PLO's Palestine Research Center and the primary architect and engine of Resolution 3379,[44] had developed a racial theory for Zionism, as well as a legal analysis demonstrating the applicability of the International Convention on the Elimination of All Forms of Racial Discrimination (ICERD)[45] to Israeli policies.[46] In 1965, inspired by the civil rights movement in the United States, Sayegh published a pamphlet titled *Zionist Colonialism in Palestine*, in which he provides both a settler-colonial and a racial theory of the Zionist ideology and movement.[47] Zionism, he explains, was the instrument of nation building rather than a by-product of a preexisting nationalism, thus distinguishing it from European colonial efforts that sought to expand their territorial holdings beyond their borders.[48] Zionist nationalism is incommensurable with a Palestinian nation. Unlike other forms of European colonization, which are predicated on racial domination, Zionist colonization is predicated on the "racial elimination" of Palestinians through destruction and erasure in order to take their place.[49] In its effort to build the Jewish-Zionist nation, Zionist colonization features unrelenting Jewish-Zionist settlement, territorial expansion, and Palestinian removal.

Sayegh is careful to show that Zionist ideology, beyond its colonial practice, is by definition racist. The Zionist belief that Jews constitute a race and a singular people, irrespective of religious piety or ethnic heterogeneity, produces "three corollaries: racial self-segregation, racial exclusiveness, and racial supremacy."[50] Sayegh points to the writings of leading Zionists to illuminate how self-segregation within an exclusive Jewish state is an aversion to assimilation within non-Jewish societies. He then demonstrates how racial exclusivity—which he also calls "racial purity"—is the force that propels Palestinian removal and precludes cohabitation with them. Finally, Sayegh concludes, segregation and exclusivity make possible the manifestation of a "Jewish superiority," fundamentally rooted in the belief that Jews are God's "chosen people."[51]

Sayegh and his peers were well aware that the concept of a Jewish race is a cornerstone of secular European antisemitism. Europe's racialized exclusion of Jews was predicated on orientalist conceptions of Jews as backward, dirty, religious, and unfit for modernity.[52] It is precisely what led to Nazi insistence that, for example, Jews cannot be integrated into national society, thus rendering them ineligible for whiteness and exogenous by definition.[53] As Edward Said would put it, "the militant concept of a Jewish 'race' derived itself not simply from the age-old persecution of Jews in Christian Europe, but from the racial typologies of Gobineau, Stewart Chamberlain, and Renan."[54]

In a companion pamphlet, Palestinian scholar Hasan Sa'b critiques Eastern European Zionists for seeking "the revival of a Jewish nation" rather than "the defense of the rights of individual Jews" in response to antisemitism.[55] He dismisses the Zionist concept of a Jewish race as a myth on par with the mythology of a German race conceived by Nazi ideology.[56] Sa'b highlights how racial consciousness led both ideologies to believe in a "special historic destiny," and although "the deadly struggle between Zionism and Nazism should have made such similarities unthinkable," antisemitism, Zionism, and Nazism were varying forms of nationalism and racism nurtured in a similar geography and "in the same intellectual climate."[57] Hence, and ironically, he highlights, both antisemites and Zionists believe that Jewish integration is an impossibility, and Jews must have a state of their own.[58]

In the Third Committee, and later in the General Assembly, it is this uncomfortable and disturbing connection that made the claim that Zionism is racism so controversial. Even among the resolution's most fervent proponents, support for it reflected a belief that Zionism is a bedfellow of imperialism and/or that Palestinians endured discrimination at the hands of Israel, but the flashpoint remained whether Zionism was indeed a form of racism.

The then US ambassador to the United Nations, Daniel Patrick Moynihan, summed up this dissonance when he stated, in the General Assembly plenary, that "whatever else zionism may be, it is not and cannot be 'a form of racism.'"[59] Moynihan cites the Oxford English and Webster's Third New International Dictionaries to define racism as a biological distinction that stratifies humanity and affords a particular group superior status with the right to dominate others. He then goes on to show that Zionism is a "strictly political movement" born in the late nineteenth century in the context of the upsurge of nationalism, which thus gave birth to the Jewish "national liberation movement," the members of which are defined by "belief" rather than by birth.[60] Zionists, Moynihan explains, are Jews, self-defined as "anyone born of a Jewish mother or—and this is the absolutely crucial fact—anyone who converted to Judaism."[61] Moynihan's emphasis on Jewish conversion is meant to show that, unlike other categories enumerated in ICERD, Jewish identity is not a biological category. He goes on to highlight the "racial stocks"—that is, Middle Eastern and Black Jews—to demonstrate Israel's racial diversity, thus negating the idea of a singular Jewish race.[62]

Moynihan's reference to ICERD is pertinent because its content and drafting history are a source of the controversy surrounding Zionism. Drafted in 1965, ICERD is the first international human rights treaty. It did not come into force until 1969, due to aversion among states that shunned scrutiny of their racial regimes (the United States did not ratify it until 1994). Notably, ICERD does not define race or racism. Instead, it defines "racial discrimination" as

> any distinction, exclusion, restriction or preference based on race, colour, descent, or national or ethnic origin which has the purpose or effect of nullifying or impairing the recognition, enjoyment or exercise, on an equal footing, of human rights and fundamental freedoms in the political, economic, social, cultural or any other field of public life.[63]

The definition compounds the ambiguity over the meaning of race, first by distinguishing it from other immutable categories—color, descent, and national or ethnic origin—and second by suggesting that a state can racially discriminate on a basis other than race.

ICERD deliberately does not enumerate any particular forms of racism, with the singular exception of apartheid, although its impetus was an outbreak of attacks on Jewish cemeteries and synagogues in Germany in 1960.[64] Fearing the rise of neo-Nazism, the international community responded in

the UN Sub-Commission for the Prevention and Discrimination of Minorities, which ultimately led to a proposal for an international instrument on
the matter. In 1962, the issue reached the Third Committee, which did not
agree on naming antisemitism as a form of racism.[65]

There existed general consensus that antisemitism was a form of racism
but controversies that involved whether to name antisemitism in the pream-
ble or in the operative articles; whether it should be listed alongside apartheid and racial discrimination or in its own article; whether to refer to it as
"antisemitism" or "anti-Judaism," since "Semites" referred to a much broader
ethnic category; whether to also name Nazism and neo-Nazism in the same
article; and whether to name Zionism as a form of racism as well. Significantly, the concern of Arab states that condemnation of antisemitism would
be interpreted as endorsement of Israel's establishment underpinned much
of the political controversy. Eagerness among the Afro-Arab bloc to develop
an instrument to help further its struggle against colonialism and apartheid
also formatively shaped the document's political character.[66] Ultimately, the
Third Committee decided to draft two conventions: one on racial discrimination and a second on religious intolerance.[67] The final convention on racial
discrimination did not name Nazism or antisemitism, and the international
community categorized the latter as a matter of religious intolerance.[68]

The lack of a definition of race or racism created significant room for
political maneuvering, as well as genuine confusion, during the UN deliberations. In his capacity as the representative of Kuwait, Sayegh repeatedly
and tirelessly made the case against Zionism. He rejected Moynihan's definition of racism as a biological category by pointing to ICERD's expansive
definition, which includes discrimination based on descent as well as ethnic
and national origin.[69] Sayegh explained that Zionist ideology is racist for insisting that Jews are united not merely by faith but by membership in an
"ethnic community" that had the right to create an exclusive state in the
place of another people. He surmised that "if it could not be demonstrated
that zionism considered being a Jew as a matter of race, it was impossible to
speak of racism."[70] He then met his own challenge by referencing the works
of Theodor Herzl, the founder of political Zionism, to show that the Zionist
conception of Jewishness "had nothing to do with religion; it was the racial
link that made a Jew a Jew."[71] As for diverse "racial stocks" in Israel, Sayegh

explained that racism is like a "cancer" that "defies containment" and, once Zionism had racialized non-Jews in Palestine, it "soon came to draw a color-line or a racial line among the Jews themselves."[72] Far from establishing racial diversity, as argued by Moynihan, the subjugation of oriental and Black Jews exposed the Zionist myth of "one Jewish people" and demonstrated the supremacy of the "White Jewish Establishment."[73] Sayegh did not, however, explain the relationship between white supremacy in Europe and its Zionist manifestation in Palestine. He seemed to consider the color line a derivative of Zionism, rather than one of its constitutive features.[74]

Significantly, Sayegh emphasized that, unlike antisemitism, political Zionism refers to juridical policy embodied by an actual state. Indeed, while all states may practice racism, Israel was among a minority that defined itself upon that basis. In his appeals, Sayegh persistently moved to a level of abstraction and asked the multilateral body to apply the law of ICERD to the facts of the Zionist movement, as well as the Israeli state, and to "act logically" by opposing racism in this instance as it had opposed racism elsewhere.[75] Western powers and a handful of Latin American and Caribbean countries—including Uruguay, Haiti, El Salvador, and Costa Rica—remained unmoved.

In response to intransigent opposition, the Indian delegate appealed to the body to consider the impact of Zionism, if not its actual character. Mr. Jaipal argued:

> It was not necessary for the Third Committee to attempt to define in scientific terms what zionism was, or to go into its legendary origins. What was important, however, was to consider what zionism had come to mean in actuality. . . . It was surely understandable that the victims of zionism should regard it as a form of racial discrimination and it was therefore proper for the General Assembly also to recognize it as such. By equating zionism with racism, one was anti-racist but certainly not anti-Semitic. To condone the evil effects of zionism would be giving the green light to various other forms of racism endemic in human societies.[76]

This seemed to be of no avail among the Western powers that refused to consider any dimension of Zionism's racial character. They insisted that the mistreatment of Arab Palestinians reflected a contest over sovereignty and was thus, squarely, a political matter to be resolved by the Middle East Peace Process.

## PROCEDURAL MANEUVERS: LAST-DITCH EFFORTS TO KILL THE RESOLUTION

On October 17, 1975, the Third Committee deliberated on whether to adopt Resolution 2159 and make the condemnation of Zionism part of the Decade against Racism. The resolution would be the last in a three-part series constituting the Decade: part I was the Programme of Action that condemned the South African apartheid regime, and part II was the endorsement of a World Conference against Racism to be convened in Ghana. This sequence would become consequential. Led by the US delegation, Western states that had pledged their support for parts I and II of the Decade threatened to vote against the entire Programme of Action should the Third Committee adopt Resolution 2159. Procedurally, this was not necessary. Framing the different parts as "inseparably linked" was a tactical maneuver to defeat the effort to condemn Zionism.[77]

Aware that the procedural maneuver was a loaded threat to sacrifice the entire Decade against Racism in order to defeat the resolution, several African states began to urge the nonaligned bloc to retract the resolution. Sierra Leone proposed postponing its consideration until the next General Assembly session, thus removing it from the Decade. The Third Committee defeated Sierra Leone's proposal in a vote of 68–45, with 16 abstentions.

As the debate continued, and fearing that opponents of the resolution on Zionism were trying to filibuster the proceedings, Libya moved to close the debate and called for an immediate vote.[78] In response, the United States condemned what it saw as a "procedural maneuver" and moved to adjourn the meeting altogether to defer a vote on the resolution.[79] The Third Committee rejected the US motion 65–40, with 21 abstentions. It adopted the motion to close the debate by 66–29, with 32 abstentions. Despite the adoption of Libya's motion, the committee chair invited representatives to explain their vote but "to be as brief as possible."[80]

In this context, Liberia and Ethiopia expressed strong opposition to the draft resolution on Zionism. Liberia opposed the equation of apartheid and Zionism and insisted that the OAU position on the matter did not reflect a consensus among African states.[81] Ethiopia urged deferment of the resolution's consideration, stating that its delegation would otherwise vote against it.[82] The Ghanaian representative supported the spirit of the text, explaining that "obviously Israel was guilty of an injustice in continuing to occupy certain Arab territories and denying the Palestinian Arabs the right to their homeland," but noted that, on "instructions from its Government," his delegation would abstain on the vote.[83]

Ultimately, the Third Committee adopted the full draft resolution by a vote of 70–29, with 27 abstentions. Liberia was the only African state to vote against it. The resolution concerning Zionism would be considered a constitutive part of the Decade against Racism to be deliberated at the UN General Assembly only a few weeks later. Those proceedings would be similarly contentious.

When the Decade against Racism reached plenary proceedings on November 10, 1975, it included two additional parts: one affirming the Apartheid Convention and a second affirming ICERD and encouraging its ratification. Upon introduction of the five-part program, Belgium immediately motioned to defer voting on the resolution concerning Zionism—literally the same proposal that Sierra Leone had made and lost in the Third Committee. The motion to postpone was defeated by 67–55, with 15 abstentions. The Belgian delegation then made another motion to vote on part III of the Decade, before voting on parts I and II for the explicit purpose of "mak[ing] one last effort" to adopt those two parts of the initiative by consensus to demonstrate robust global support against apartheid.[84] Until the introduction of the Zionism resolution, decisions on the Decade against Racism had been achieved by consensus.

Sayegh deftly responded by illuminating the hypocrisy of the Belgian delegation, as well as the European Economic Community (EEC) on whose behalf it spoke. He suggested that, were it not for opposition to the Zionism resolution, the EEC group of countries would not have opposed racism in South Africa at all. They all maintained trade relations with the apartheid regime, they all opposed the rejection of its credentials, and they all opposed its expulsion from the United Nations. Sayegh concluded that the only thing the EEC countries promised was verbal consensus, with no action making their "ultimatum" on the Decade against Racism "irrelevant."[85] The second Belgian motion was defeated by 74–36, with 26 abstentions.

Other efforts to defeat the resolution included unabashed political co-ercion.[86] Black African states remained split on the issue. Most opposing states condemned Zionism but believed that the resolution undermined the Decade against Racism and should be considered separately.[87] Liberia was exceptional in that it did not believe Zionism was racism because it insisted that racism was a colorist ideology that did not prevail in Israel.[88]

Several supporters of Palestinian freedom did not necessarily object to Israel's establishment. Yugoslavia, for example, endorsed the resolution on Zionism and simultaneously expressed support for a negotiated peace.[89] The Yugoslav position illuminated that endorsement of Zionism as a form of racism was not necessarily at odds with the recognition of Israel along the 1967 borders. In contrast, Germany supported "the right of the Palestinian people to express its national identity," as well as Israel's withdrawal from all Arab lands occupied since 1967. However, it would vote against the res-olution on Zionism in order to increase the chances of a negotiated peace.[90]

For its part, the Israeli delegation denounced the proceedings as categor-ically antisemitic and particularly noxious for taking place on the same date that, thirty-seven years prior, had seen Kristallnacht (the "Night of Broken Glass"), when Hitler's stormtroopers ransacked Jewish homes, temples, and establishments across Germany.[91] Chaim Herzog, the Israeli ambassador to the United Nations, emphasized that Zionism represented a Jewish national liberation movement and the return to the Jewish homeland as designated by the Bible. Herzog mentioned the Bible no less than five times in his ad-dress, emphasizing the religious nature of Judaism in a deliberate attempt to obscure the distinction between Jewish religious faith and Jewish-Zionist nationalism.[92] The Brazilian delegation tackled this issue head-on by empha-sizing that "not all members of the Jewish community have accepted Zionist ideas," and those who repudiate Zionism do not lose "their religious or ethnic condition as Jews." Thus, the "alleged identification of anti-Zionism with an-tisemitism," continued the Brazilian delegation, "cannot be accepted."[93]

When the Declaration for Action finally came to a vote, the General As-sembly considered each of the five parts separately. Parts I, II, IV, and V were adopted by a minimum of 112 votes and as many as 131 votes. The resolution declaring Zionism as a form of racism and racial discrimination also passed, but by a much smaller margin of 72–35, with 32 abstentions. Of the 38 Black African UN member states, 5 opposed the resolution and 12 abstained.

The UN proceedings on Zionism illuminate that what was at stake was not merely a proper definition of the Zionist ideology and movement. The controversies were also political and strategic. In their interventions, delegates weighed in on the optimal pathways to a resolution of the Palestinian question. Western states insisted that this was a matter for political negotiations and hid behind liberal aversion to racial critiques of Zionism, even as they continued to protect the South African apartheid regime in practice. For the majority of the Third World movement, the denunciation of Zionism reflected an anti-imperial politics that considered the Zionist project as part of a broader effort to subvert Brown and Black self-determination. Finally, opposition among Black African allies reflected strategic concern with the timing of the resolution and the risks posed by its association with the Decade against Racism, rather than an issue with casting Zionism as racism. The overwhelming condemnation of Zionism in the conferences across Mexico City, Jeddah, Kampala, and Lima, leading to the thirtieth session of the General Assembly, demonstrates as much. The voting record was therefore mixed and was not definitive regarding the precise contours, or condemnation, of Zionism's racial character. The resolution on Zionism was a hard-won victory, but, examined in its geopolitical context, it reveals a much more complicated story about Afro-Arab unity, Third World movement strategies against imperial domination, and fraught understandings of racism and racial discrimination.

## CONCLUSION

The drafting history of Resolution 3379 indicates that inclusion of the resolution on Zionism in the Decade against Racism was, at best, a strategically haphazard intervention. Initiated on the heels of an unsuccessful effort to expel Israel from the United Nations, the resolution seemed to be a last-minute—and suboptimal—choice for the liberation movement. The fact that the PLO did not formally discuss amending the Decade against Racism in the regional and organizational meetings throughout the summer of 1975, where it sought endorsement for Israel's expulsion, underscores this point. This does not suggest a lack of sincerity on the part of the PLO or put into question its commitment to combat racism. It does, however, raise questions regarding the PLO's racial analysis—assuming that we can understand the intellectual contributions of individuals as representing the institutional position. The drafting history leads to questioning whether the Palestinian liberation movement considered racism as a structure, or saw it as a derivative manifestation of, and secondary to, the colonial structure.

Following the UN proceedings in 1975, Anis Al-Qasem, the PLO jurist who supported the passage of Resolution 3379, established the International Organization for the Elimination of All Forms of Racial Discrimination specifically to support and strengthen the antiracist agenda established at the United Nations. In recalling the Palestinian initiative, he explained, "Palestinians had never thought of their condition as a racial one. They saw their condition as a national occupation. If they overcome [Zionist] occupation they will end their subjugated condition." When pressed on the racial nature of Zionist domination, Al-Qasem replied that if a one-state reality prevailed, then the Palestinian struggle becomes a "struggle against racism." However, he continued,

> if you do protect the nation, these issues are trivial. Every day, Israel is removing Palestinians from their homes to build a settlement. Racism doesn't capture that this is a national struggle. Because of this, I deal with deeper issues because Zionist colonialism is erasing the presence of the Palestinian nation and asserting that it is the only nation that exists.[94]

Al-Qasem echoes Sayegh's formulation of Zionist "racial elimination," but believes that the racial dimension of the Palestinian freedom struggle is subsumed within the national quest for sovereignty in response to settler invasion. His analysis suggests that antiracism is a bid for inclusion and equality while anticolonialism is a bid for national independence, thus indicating two distinct liberation strategies. Hence, the Palestinian struggle becomes explicitly antiracist in a one-state reality but, in the case of national independence, the racial question becomes "trivial." Indeed, Indigenous nations have long considered assimilation as an instrument of genocide and have sought sovereignty as a pathway to freedom, as opposed to equality, highlighting that Palestinians are not unique in centering their quest for national sovereignty. However, what may be missing is an understanding of how racism is inscribed into the colonial structure as one of its predicate elements, rather than manifesting only in practice as one of its outcomes. Taken at face value, then, did the PLO consider racism redundant in a settler-colonial setting like Palestine, or, as put by Patrick Wolfe, is racism simply "colonialism speaking"?[95]

The record examined in this chapter does not shed adequate light on the Palestinian intellectual history regarding racism and is therefore insufficient to answer that question. For example, what were the intellectual legacies that preceded and/or complemented Sayegh's and Sa'b's interventions in 1965? Did the 1975 resolution catalyze further introspection within Palestinian society? Or was this racial analysis restricted to an anti-imperial understanding that condemned the denial of national sovereignty but did not reach the interior of national societies? How committed was the PLO to Resolution 3379 before rescinding it became a condition for entering into a peace agreement with Israel in 1991? These are among many outstanding questions yet to be addressed.

Part of the challenge in pursuing this inquiry is rooted in the disparate approaches to understanding racism. For example, during the 1975 UN proceedings, there existed at least three different analytical strands: racism as an imperial logic that denied sovereignty to colonized peoples; racism as a state practice of differentiation and domination; and racism as an ideology predicated on the righteous and timeless superiority of one group. While these strands have been clearly reinforcing, they also led to controversy within the multilateral body. The fact that Israel was seen as an extension and expression of European imperialism made this controversy less pronounced in 1975 than it is today, thus explaining the successful passage of Resolution 3379.

In the direct aftermath of the collapse of the peace process in 2000, the analysis of Israel as a singular apartheid regime crystallized among Palestinians. The following year, Palestinian advocates and their allies would make Israel's racial regime a central issue at the Durban Review Conference, convened to continue the work begun in the Decade against Racism.[96] Similar to the 1975 proceedings, the racial critique of Israel and Zionism became a flashpoint and the United States and Israel withdrew in protest, undermining the entire global initiative.[97] Despite this reactionary performance, racial analyses have continued to develop and flourish with equal parts of controversy and ambiguity.

In 2012, the Committee on the Elimination of Racial Discrimination established that Israel's maintenance of "Jewish and non-Jewish sectors" within its borders evidences "segregation" and thus triggers the Apartheid Convention's Article 3, prohibiting racism and apartheid.[98] The committee's emphasis on segregation further distinguished Israel's discriminatory regime from other states where racism exists. The committee did not, however, describe Jews or Palestinians as racial groups, instead referring to them as distinct "sectors" and "communities." The committee's finding was based in part on its 1995 General Comment concluding that apartheid is not particular to South Africa but applies to "all forms of segregation in all countries," thereby emphasizing the spatial and juridical nature of apartheid.[99]

Five years later, in 2017, another UN body, the Economic and Social Commission for Western Asia, released a report concluding that Israel practiced apartheid against all Palestinians without distinction of geography or legal jurisdiction. Significantly, the report drew on the ICERD definition of racial discrimination to describe Jews and Palestinians as distinct "racial groups."[100] Backlash, again among Western countries, forced the United Nations to shelve the report.[101]

When, in 2021, the Israeli human rights organization B'Tselem released its report concluding that Israel is an apartheid regime, it explicitly refrained from describing the situation in racial terms at all. B'Tselem drew the comparison to South Africa but insisted that whereas "the division in South Africa was based on race and skin color . . . in Israel it is based on nationality and ethnicity."[102] B'Tselem went on to describe the discriminatory regime as practiced for the benefit of "Jewish supremacy."[103] The organization thus suggested that, firstly, race is synonymous with color and, secondly, that racism is not a predicate element of apartheid. The avoidance indicates that the invocation of racism remains an incendiary topic among Jewish Zionists.

Contemporary renewals of Black-Palestinian solidarity[104] have helped propel these analyses still further by illuminating the antiracist nature of the Palestinian liberation struggle and, inversely, the anticolonial nature of the Black liberation struggle.[105] These renewals have also raised pressing questions and some controversy, including with regard to the prevalence of anti-Blackness in Palestinian society,[106] as well as the limits of a racial analysis in understanding the Palestinian condition.[107] Moving forward, perhaps one should also ask whether we should adopt a more complex and variegated understanding of racism that defies universal definition, in ICERD or otherwise, and is instead historically contingent on place and time.[108] Further to this point, what happens when we do not impose a theory on Palestine but allow Palestinian experience to provide a theory for us? What would be gained and what would be lost in that practice? The only thing we can tell for certain is that understanding the racial dimension of the Palestinian struggle for freedom, including that Zionism is a form of racism and racial discrimination, is work that is still ongoing, on the ground and in scholarship; it remains our unfinished business.

*Four*
# THE INVENTION OF THE "BEDOUIN RACE"

IN 1957, FORTY YEARS AFTER THE BALFOUR DECLARATION, JOHN
Bagot Glubb, also known as Glubb Pasha, set out to write his memoir, an
unorthodox autobiographical account he flamboyantly titled *A Soldier with
the Arabs*—in reference to his role as commander of the Arab Legion, a British-led army of tribesmen in Transjordan, which later became the Royal
Jordanian Army. Writing from his quiet retirement in Mayfield, Sussex, the
legendary British commander had a rare confession to make, a belated reali-
zation of sorts: "A further illusion prevailed, arising from indiscriminate use
of the word 'Arab,' that the non-Jewish inhabitants of Palestine were nomads
from the desert. 'Why cannot the Arabs return to their desert?' was a question which used frequently to be asked."[1]

It is quite uncanny to hear such a statement from the founder of the
Desert Patrol, the British-led paramilitary force of Transjordan, and the
man who had presided over the Arab Legion for nearly two decades and
for whom such "illusion" had been the winning formula of colonial rule—
namely, sorting out the Bedouin as a "warlike race" as a way to integrate
Bedouin forces into the Arab Legion. This sort of racialized discourse

enabled colonial administrators in Mandate Palestine to depict the Bedouin as a separate race that belonged in the desert, a stateless people devoid of the national aspirations that are often attributed to settled populations. Ultimately, hailing the Bedouin as the "original Arabs" allowed British administrators to view the Bedouin, and Arabs more broadly, as foreign invaders in Palestine. It is the depiction of the Bedouin as the "original Arabs" that would later enable British colonial administrators to exclude the Arabs from their ethnonational visions for Palestine. The perception made it easy for British colonialists and Zionists alike to argue that the Arabs were a nomadic people who belonged in the desert, or "Arabia," and hence were not entitled to the national rights that are often preserved for settled populations. In other words, depicting Bedouin and Arabs as a nomadic race enabled Zionists to claim that Palestine was empty in the national sense—it was a "land without a people."

The racial classification of the Bedouin, however, did not start with the Mandate; rather, it has deeper roots in British colonial discourse on Palestine. Writing nearly a century before Glubb, British explorers in late Ottoman Palestine believed that they had sorted out the "Bedouin race." In racializing the Bedouin, they were guided by three ethnographic axioms. The first is the primacy of racial classification—a new scientific dogma sparked by the need to manage differences overseas. The origins of racial classification in modern European thought can be traced back to the debate between monogenists and polygenists in the early decades of the eighteenth century. These two groups sought to map the origins of human race(s) by charting differences in external appearance among present and past populations. While monogenism espoused a single origin of humanity, as envisioned in the biblical narrative, polygenism maintained that human races originated in separate racial lineages with varying qualities, and hence represented a hierarchy. Polygenism rested on the assumption that external appearance—including physical, biological, social, linguistic, and cultural traits—corresponded to distinct racial strata. Ultimately, it was the seemingly secular polygenists who began advocating the existence of racial supremacy among humans. Polygenism proved especially appealing to Europeans in the age of overseas adventure, trade, exploration, and discovery. In the course of nineteenth-century European colonial expansion—which involved the accumulation of new ethnographic, anthropological, linguistic, and biological knowledge—polygenism prevailed, becoming the intellectual hallmark of European racial thinking.[2] Because it offered a new way of dividing and ruling native populations, racial classification would become a distinctive feature of European colonial enterprise.[3]

In Palestine, this way of imagining human relations was undertaken by a new breed of British explorers whose interest in the Bedouin went far beyond the romantic legacy of the eighteenth century, which consisted mainly of ethnographies that depicted the Bedouin as a living vestige of biblical life.[4] The race-oriented shift was undertaken by a new generation of British explorers in Palestine, notably Richard Burton, Edward Palmer, Charles Warren, Horatio Kitchener, Charles Wilson, and C. R. Conder. These men were writing at the peak of scientific racism in England, British nationalism, and imperial expansion. Working under the auspices of the Palestine Exploration Fund Society, they embarked on imperial careers that reflected the strong nexus of knowledge and power underpinning British policy in Palestine. Their legacy culminated in a new racial taxonomy that, by simply sorting out the physical and social peculiarities of the local population, insisted on viewing its demographic strata as belonging to different races. As a result, three "Arab races" were identified: the Bedouin, the fellahin, and the townspeople. Only the Bedouin, however, were labeled "true Arabs."

The second axiom is the dialectical relationship between race and nomadism. In a remarkably deterministic view, British ethnographers in Palestine, notably Burton and Conder, singled out the Bedouin as a pure race *because* they are Bedouin: thanks to a unique value system and mode of life, the Bedouin managed to survive the vicissitudes of time, preserve their racial purity, and survive as the "original Arab race." According to this view, the Bedouin are also a mobile, evasive, and fugitive people whose inherent character is averse to modern civilization. They live deeper in the desert, on the fringe of the country, where the tempo of life never changes, as a homogeneous, archaic, and primordial people in a pristine state free of foreign influence. They maintain a strict system of intermarriage and a deep-rooted tradition of blood relation and noble descent. They originate in the cradle of the Arab race, the Arabian Peninsula, and speak pure Arabic. In short, this view maintained that if there existed an Arab race, then, inherently, it must be Bedouin-nomadic.

The third axiom is the inherent opposition between nomadism and autochthony. Locking their tribal subjects into a state of perpetual mobility, British ethnographers viewed the Bedouin as a race of stateless, unsettled, and rootless nomads. As the descendants of the original Arab tribes who invaded Palestine in the seventh century, they represent a foreign race that, immune to racial assimilation, remade the country in its own image as a barren land. They are a race of conquerors responsible for the destruction of what was once the fertile granary of Roman Palestine. They are lawless intruders, enemies of the state, and barbarians at the gate. They are anathema to history, progress, and state building. They live on primitive modes of production devoid of labor, property, and land cultivation. The Bedouin, in this view, stand at the opposite end of European conceptions of belonging, autochthony, and nationhood.

This chapter explores racial views of the Bedouin in the writings of British explorers and ethnographers, and how those views informed the British colonial legacy in Palestine. It focuses on how racialized views of the Bedouin enabled British colonialists to exclude the Bedouin, and the Arabs in general, from their nation-state visions for the future of Palestine. As the chapter shows, it was the well-established link between race and nomadism, embodied in the identification of Arabness with tribalism and conquest, that ultimately enabled the British ethnographers to reinforce the image of Arabs, as a whole, as a foreign race in Palestine. The Bedouin are not inherently nomadic, but treating them as such enabled the British to view tribal formations as the antipode of rootedness, belonging, and—most importantly—state building and nation building. Racializing nomadism, or nomadizing Arabs, meant that Palestine, where the Bedouin constituted a tiny minority of the population, was not "purely Arab," as one official document put it,[5] and hence belonged not to the Arabs, but rather to the Jews, as the Balfour Declaration would have it. It was thus assumed that the Arabs of Palestine, being direct descendants of Bedouin tribes, belonged to Arabia, "the cradle of the Arab race, where Bedouin blood is still accounted the purest."[6] During the British Mandate period, this view would culminate in one of the most enduring and widespread myths about the Bedouin of Palestine in British ethnographic discourse: the clearly ideological construct that they were the "original Arabs."

Historians of the British Empire tend to agree that racial thinking emerged in British literature and the British popular imagination in the late eighteenth century.[7] Their scholarship, however, tends to focus on manifestations of racial thinking in this discourse, paying little attention to its colonial origins.[8] Yet there is sufficient textual evidence to suggest that British racial thinking was born in the encounter with natives through the uneasy marriage between race and ethnography. A notable case is British India. Historians of the British Raj have recently examined the rise of scientific racism in colonial India, and how modern theories of racial hierarchy guided nineteenth-century British encounters with Indian society.[9] Ottoman Palestine was yet another stage for this kind of encounter. By the close of the nineteenth century, British explorers such as Richard Burton and Charles Tyrwhitt Drake had already turned Ottoman Syria into a laboratory for experimentation in scientific racism. It was left to their successors at the Palestine Exploration Fund Society to implement their doctrine on the population of Palestine, a process that culminated in a new taxonomy of racial classification.

Tracing the roots of British racialized discourse on the Bedouin in Mandate Palestine, the chapter focuses on Burton's legacy. Burton was a colonial authority on the Arabs and the Bedouin and has had an unmatched impact on British discourse on the Bedouin. His research and explorations in Ottoman Palestine were funded by the state-sponsored Palestine Exploration Fund. Burton held several official and colonial posts, starting as a British consul in Damascus. He cofounded the Anthropological Society of London, which sponsored numerous publications that advocated the doctrine of racial hierarchy, propagated the superiority of European races, and championed British imperial paternalism. In this sense, Burton embodies the strong nexus of power and ethnographic racism in British colonial policy on the Bedouin. He was an influential figure whose ethnographic legacy shaped British colonial discourse on the Bedouin. Indeed, Burton's British successors in Mandate and Ottoman Palestine, including Conder, all show their debt to his work. In brief, we are dealing with a network of British colonial agents whose influence on British policy on the Bedouin of Palestine is undeniable.

THE INVENTION OF THE "BEDOUIN RACE"    103

## THE DISCOVERY OF THE "BEDOUIN RACE"

In 1869, after a long journey that took him from West Africa to the Americas, Richard Burton landed in Syria to assume his new post as British consul in Damascus, which he would hold until 1871. Taking on an official position did not end his passion for exploration in a country that he still considered terra incognita, as he recalled upon his return to London in 1872.[10] Sponsored by the newly founded Palestine Exploration Fund, Burton documented in detail his explorations in Syria and Palestine in his largely overlooked collection *Unexplored Syria*, written jointly with his fellow traveler Charles Tyrwhitt Drake.[11] Burton and Drake presented part of their findings in Palestine in a separate paper at the meeting of the Anthropological Institute on November 20, 1871.[12] The paper, entitled "The Anthropological Collection from the Holy Land," examines an exhaustive list of skeletons, fossils, skulls, bones, and other human remains gathered by the two explorers during their expedition in the country. They sorted, compared, and classified these specimens into distinct racial types, origins, and survival capacities. In one instance, they asked members of the institute to determine whether the extreme length of a given skull typified a race or an individual character. Matching the skull to its corresponding racial type, the members labeled it as "Syrian." In another instance, they classified a large jaw as corresponding to racial characters of "the Badawi Arabs."[13]

*Unexplored Syria* marks Burton's interest in phrenology as the locus of ethnographic classification. The book, mostly neglected by the existing research on British orientalist and colonial discourse on the Bedouin, was the culmination of two decades of radicalization in his racial thinking following the scientific revolution wrought by the publication of Charles Darwin's *On the Origin of Species* in 1859, described by Burton as "the best and wisest book of this, or perhaps, of any age."[14] Taken by the spread of scientific racism, Burton sought to build his theories into an institution. In 1863, he collaborated with James Hunt to establish the Anthropological Society of London as a breakaway from the London Ethnological Society. The Anthropological Society distinguished itself from its predecessor by advocating the doctrine of polygenesis as the basis of racial classification, abandoning the philological approach to ethnographic research, and denying the influence of climate on physical appearances. Emerging as the hallmark of scientific racism in

Britain, the new society embraced a strict biological approach to ethnographic classification, one involving the application of the phrenological and
craniological anatomy of the human body—such as skull size, body shape,
and skin texture and color.[15] Within a few years of its inception, the Anthropological Society had sponsored numerous publications that advocated the
doctrine of racial hierarchy, propagated the superiority of European races,
and championed British imperial paternalism over the "lower races" of Asia
and Africa.[16] Burton, who served as the first vice president of the new society and chaired its inaugural meeting in London, embodied the scientific
dogmatism that characterized its doctrine. Nowhere is this dogmatism more
manifest than in his phrenological description of Bedouin-like skulls: "The
bones vary from the very massive to the remarkably thin, and the first points
which struck me were the shortness of the lower bi-temporal diameter, the
long square face, and the flatness or compression of the parietes, which every
traveller remarks in the Bedawin, the flower of the Semitic race."[17]

Burton was far ahead of his Victorian contemporaries and his racial
legacy reshaped the ethnographic thinking of his time. To him, anthropology was no longer concerned with human societies but with human races.
His travel literature was equally racialized. Whereas, for European travelers
in the early nineteenth century, exploration was primarily associated with
the discovery of hitherto uncharted lands, Burton linked exploration to the
discovery, if not the invention, of human races. His passion for race knew no
limits and it characterized both his research and his personal life. Burton
was so enchanted with the "Arab race" that he ordered a tomb for himself in
the shape of a Bedouin tent and even suspected that he had Arab blood in his
veins. An obituary reprinted by his wife, Isabel Burton, suggested that there
might have been "a tinge of Arab, or, perhaps, of Gypsy blood in Burton's
race."[18] Writing within the fast-growing tradition of raciology, and at a time
when Englishness itself was being restructured into new racial taxonomies,
Burton sought to create the Bedouin in his own image: an ideal archetype of
racial purity.

To be sure, Burton did share with his British peers, notably his fellow traveler in Palestine, Edward Palmer, the view of the Bedouin as noble savages—
even, as he put it, "a nuisance to be abated by civilisation."[19] Yet he diverged
from this view by maintaining that the Bedouin could be managed, if not

used for genetic replication: "The race has high and noble qualities which, as the old phrase is, the world would not willingly see die; and perhaps the pure blood of the wilderness may be infused to good purpose into burgher-men, as into their horses."[20] Burton's views also diverged from those of his peers around the notion of the racial superiority of the Bedouin, which he linked to the capacity for survival characteristic of life in the desert. In his early travelogue *Personal Narrative of a Pilgrimage to Al-Madinah and Meccah* (1855), he even anticipates Darwin by viewing Bedouin society as one in which only the fittest could survive and flourish: "In the first place, it is a kind of *société léonine*, in which the fiercest, the strongest, and the craftiest obtains complete mastery over his fellows."[21] For Burton, the ethnologist, it is this racial quality that ultimately enabled the Bedouin to survive as the pure Arab race.

Burton divided the Arabs into three racial stocks—Caucasian, sub-Caucasian, and pure Arabian—a classification that agrees with "the observations of modern physiologists."[22] He viewed the Arabs as a mixture of disparate races, and their racial disparity to be attested by the Bedouin, who demonstrate "strong evidence in favour of variety in the Arabian family."[23] His view rests on the easy assumption that the Bedouin serve as a model of racial purity because they live in a state of being where physical and social differences are absolute. Three observations appear to have guided this conclusion. First, unlike the settled population, the Bedouin exhibit unchangeable, homogeneous expressions: "There is not much difference in this point between men of the same tribe, who have similar pursuits which engender similar passions."[24] Whereas "expression is the grand diversifier of appearance among civilised people," Burton asserted that "in the Desert it knows few varieties."[25] Second, the Bedouin inhabit the desert, and "they who know how immutable is race in the Desert, will scarcely doubt that the Badawi of Al-Hijaz preserves in purity the blood transmitted to him by his ancestors."[26] Third, tribal society is adverse to interracial marriage, and hence condemned to absolute racial purity: "Such is the Badawi, and such he has been for ages. The national type has been preserved by systematic intermarriage."[27] It should come as no surprise, then, that the later Burton would view the racial disparity between the Bedouin and the settled fellahin as unbridgeable.[28]

Like many of his contemporaries, Burton offered his services to the empire. He advised the British Foreign Office on how to subdue the unruly

Bedouin effectively should England annex the Arabian Peninsula to its imperial domains:

> By a proper use of the blood feud; by vigorously supporting the weaker against the stronger classes; by regularly defeating every Badawi who earns a name for himself; and, above all, by the exercise of unsparing, unflinching justice, the few thousands of half-naked bandits, who now make the land a fighting field, would soon sink into utter insignificance.[29]

In anticipation of the "martial race" doctrine, which assumed that certain ethnic or caste groups possessed a more masculine character and therefore were uniquely fit for military service, Burton deemed tribal qualities especially manageable and useful in wartime, for "should we find it necessary to raise regiments of these men, nothing would be easier." He advised his fellow Englishmen to "pay them regularly, arm them well, work them hard, and treat them with even-handed justice—there is nothing else to do." Burton even took pains to enumerate those tribal qualities he deemed vital to the British takeover of Palestine.[30] His ethnographic corpus is replete with suggestions that the British must manage the Arabs in the same way that they had been managing Indians in the Sind, where "military government is the only form of legislature precisely adapted to these countries."[31] He also suggested implementing in Ottoman Palestine "the Roman system of garrisoning the forts and outposts to the east and south of Syria."[32]

Burton left his imprint on fellow British ethnographers of the time.[33] His racial legacy, while largely devoted to the Bedouin of Arabia, would color British policies and attitudes towards the Bedouin of Palestine. By the time of his death in 1890, England had already occupied Egypt and further extended its influence in the Levant, where the Ottoman Empire desperately struggled to come to terms with growing ethnic and national sentiments in its Arab provinces. By the close of the century, England had been battling imperialist rivals such as France and tsarist Russia to gain a permanent toehold in the Levant. British officials began to recognize the political importance of Palestine, its strategic location as a major juncture between competing empires, and the benefits of integrating it into the global market.[34] This period was also a time of growing missionary activity in Palestine. England's interest in the Bible was revived by its explorers in the Holy

Land. British missionaries joined American missions in Jerusalem, and the idea of Jewish return to Palestine began to gain currency in Britain, where imperial policy joined forces with Christian evangelism in championing England's paternalistic claims to protect religious minorities abroad.[35] British fascination with the "Arab race" lost none of its force in this period. On the contrary, the British realized that, in order to hasten the end of the Ottoman Empire, England had to ally itself with, mobilize, and—most importantly—gain knowledge of the native Arab population by studying its racial and ethnic composition.

## EXPLORING THE ARABS: THE BRITISH ETHNOGRAPHIC LEGACY IN PALESTINE

In 1865, nearly two years after the establishment of the Anthropological Society, the Palestine Exploration Fund was founded in London with the aim of carrying out surveys on the topography, ethnography, and anthropology of Ottoman Palestine. At its first official meeting, held at the Jerusalem Chamber of Westminster Abbey, William Thompson, the archbishop of York, summed up the scholarly objectives outlined in the new society's original prospectus as an attempt "to apply the rules of science . . . to an investigation into the facts concerning the Holy Land." One of those objectives also involved "bringing to light the remains of so many races and generations which must lie concealed under the accumulation of rubbish and ruins on which those villages stand."[36]

Yet, as we shall see, this seemingly scientific vision of the new society was challenged by two factors: first, the inherent tension between the biblical source and the findings of modern science, which was often resolved in favor of the biblical interpretation; and second, the uneasy ties between the Palestine Exploration Fund and the British imperial enterprise in Palestine. This imperial link became all the more apparent as the new society, in part due to its complex relationship with the Corps of Royal Engineers, rapidly abandoned its original objectives and embarked on military intelligence gathering and conducting reports on how to manage the local population effectively. This strong nexus between knowledge and empire was also largely embodied in the imperial careers of prominent Palestine Exploration Fund personages, such as Edward Palmer, Charles Warren, Horatio Kitchener, Charles Wilson, T. E. Lawrence, and C. R. Conder.

British explorers who visited Palestine on behalf of the Palestine Exploration Fund fell under the same racialist outlook that had attracted Richard
Burton and his longtime partner, Charles Drake. Nowhere was the influence
of these two men more manifest than in the writing and activity of Colonel
Claude Reignier Conder, the British explorer whose legacy would color the
ethnographic debate in Palestine for decades to come. Conder was educated
at University College London before earning a degree from the Royal Military
Academy at Woolwich and, in 1870, a commission in the Royal Engineers.
Two years later, he was selected by the Royal Engineers to undertake a grand
survey in Western Palestine, where he joined Drake and his team in mapping
the topography of the land, exploring its archaeological sites, and studying
the ethnography of its population. By 1875, Conder had completed the greater
part of his survey but fell ill and was taken back to London.[37] The expedition
resulted in a landmark topographical survey of Western Palestine, from the
Litani River in the north to Beer al-Sabe'/Beersheba in the south, and the 1881
publication of the monumental *Survey of Western Palestine*, which included
a "Great Map of Western Palestine," printed in twenty-six sheets on a scale
of one inch to one mile.[38] The impact of Conder's survey, undertaken with
Drake, can hardly be exaggerated. The project sparked flames of anticipation
in England. As a review of Condor's earlier book, *Tent Work in Palestine*,[39] put
it: "For the first time then, and as the reward of these efforts, Palestine is
brought home to England." Conder was celebrated in London as the man who
"placed Palestine vividly before the reader."[40]

In 1882, the year after the *Survey of Western Palestine* was published,
Conder returned to Palestine to supervise a new grand survey in the eastern part of the country (in present-day Jordan), before the project was tem-
porarily halted within a year by the Ottoman authorities.[41] The results of
this expedition appeared in Conder's second landmark survey, *The Survey
of Eastern Palestine*, published in 1889.[42] Both expeditions were carried out
under the auspices of the Palestine Exploration Fund. In the words of David
M. Jacobson, honorary secretary of the fund, "this substantial legacy provided the foundations for the survey work done during the period of the British Mandate."[43]

Like Burton, Conder found in Palestine the kind of intellectual freedom
cherished by European explorers and travelers abroad. For the most part,

the country remained largely a terra incognita to him. Palestine also presented Conder with "a chance of studying the archaic manners of the peasantry and the natural condition of the nomadic Arabs."[44] The two groups, by virtue of being largely untouched by foreign influence, presented him with carte blanche to conduct his ethnographic research: "I have attempted to give some idea of the country as it was in the last years of its truly Oriental condition, with a peasantry as yet hardly quite tamed by the Turk, and regions as yet hardly traversed by the European explorer."[45]

Conder's ethnographic corpus also includes *Tent Work in Palestine* (1878) and *Palestine* (1889). *Palestine*, fashioned after *Unexplored Syria*, attests to his intellectual devotion to Burton and Drake. It is a classic example of the tendency, established by Burton, to group ethnography and raciology into a single taxonomy, and to read ethnography through the lens of race by fitting physical and social differences into distinct racial categories. *Tent Work* follows the same methodological pattern. That book, which summarizes Conder's first ethnographic survey in the country, tends to fuse race with ethnography by viewing Arab Palestine as a mishmash of pure and mixed races.

Initially, Conder divided the "present races of Palestine" into three original stocks: Semitic, Turanian, and Aryan. Like Burton, he employed phrenology as a key criterion for matching each of these stocks with its respective race within the population: "If peasants are to be asked to have their heads measured, we must know something of their genealogies also. If skulls are to be collected, we must find out what skulls they are."[46] Linking race to genealogy, Conder, who appears to have examined the skulls gathered and brought to London by Burton and Drake, further remarked: "I have known the skulls of peasants recently murdered to be sent home as types of the ancient population of the country."[47]

Cultural traits provided Conder with another key criterion for racial classification. Thus, for example, he contended that the Semitic origin of the Arabs and the Jews is attested by their common distaste for the arts: "The distinction is, however, one of race, for the Arab hates carved images as much as did the Jew, while the Turanian Canaanites were fond of such arts."[48] Conder also offered a warning: "In considering the character and manners of the natives of Palestine, there is one circumstance which must always be kept in sight—we are dealing with a Semitic, not with an Aryan, people, and they must be judged from a Semitic point of view."[49] This "Semitic point of view" entailed the "faults and virtues of the Semitic races [which] are so distinct and peculiar, that it is not easy for a European to judge of them fairly."[50] In other words, the Semitic race is not merely the sum of its physical and phrenological traits, but also the product of cultural and social peculiarities that include "ideas of right and wrong, of the beautiful and the praiseworthy, of religion and morality"—in short, ideas that had ultimately rendered the Semites "*essentially* different" from us.[51]

After establishing its Semitic origin, Conder divided the local Arab population of Palestine into three distinct races: the Bedouin, the fellahin, and the townspeople. The racial distinction between the Bedouin and the fellahin was translated by Conder into one of national difference: "The peasantry must not be confounded with the Bedawin or nomadic tribes, living in the uncultivated districts; *for the two nations are quite separate branches of the Semitic people*, and they themselves acknowledge the distinction."[52] To the British observer, the racial disparity between the Bedouin and the fellahin was largely an outcome of their common aversion to "interracial" marriage: "The Badawi speaks with the greatest contempt of the Fellah, and rarely, if ever, do intermarriages occur, as both sides would consider themselves degraded by the alliance."[53] Racializing Bedouin "contempt" for the fellahin is a governing theme in Conder's writings, where the presumed, if not projected, traditional enmity among the local population is almost habitually reconstructed into well-defined racial strata. Ultimately, and upon consulting a host of biblical passages, Conder asserted the "time-honoured conflict between two races" as a matter of well-established historical fact.[54]

Conder had little to say about the townspeople Arabs. Instead, he referred the reader to the work of his fellow British orientalist Edward Lane, whose "wonderful account . . . of the life of townsmen in Egypt, would apply almost equally well to the middle classes in Damascus and Jerusalem."[55] The reason for Conder's omission of this "third race" from his ethnographic narrative, we are told, is to draw more attention to the life and manners of the Bedouin and the fellahin, which are "far more valuable in illustration of the Bible narrative than are those of the townsmen."[56] Compared with the townspeople, the other two races are more ancient, archaic, and pristine. They serve not only as human relics of a sacred history, but also as agents of historical return to a lost biblical time. For Conder, the Bedouin are most interesting to the study of early Jewish history because "if among the peasantry we find a vivid picture of the life and customs of the later period, it is from the Bedawin that we learn most that can throw light on the Patriarchal times, and the life of Abraham and his immediate descendants."[57]

Not that the Christian explorer viewed the fellahin to be of less biblical value than the Bedouin. On the contrary, "it appears in short that in the Fellahin, as descendants of the old inhabitants of Palestine, we find a people whose habits and customs are well worthy of study, because we should naturally expect them to throw much light on the Bible narrative."[58] The fellahin, in fact, represented a race many centuries more ancient than the Bedouin, whom Conder viewed as a horde of recent invaders. This last observation is attested to by a host of linguistic and cultural differences that "tend rather to confirm the views already expressed as to the antiquity of the Fellah race, contrasted with the more modern settlers who have encroached on their territory."[59] One could hardly overlook the irony of dubbing the nomadic Bedouin "modern settlers."

Conder constantly contrasted the perception of the Bedouin as a foreign race with the autochthony of the fellahin. By introducing the conquest paradigm, he rendered absolute the disparity between the two "races." This presumed disparity perhaps explains Conder's main conclusion that the present fellahin of Palestine are none other than the descendants of the ancient Canaanites: "The resemblance is equally striking when they are compared with the earlier inhabitants of the land, from the days of Samuel downwards; and the parallel is so remarkable that it seems justifiable to dub the Fellahin by the simple title of 'modern Canaanites.'"[60] As the descendants of the old inhabitants of Palestine, and hence the true sons of the land, the fellahin are labeled "the Syrians, for want of a better title."[61] For Conder, the fellahin constituted, along with the Arabs (Bedouin) and the Jews, the fabric of the Semitic race in Palestine, joined by an admixture of foreign races—such as the Germans, the Turks, and the mongrel Levantines. The fellahin, therefore, represent a single nation by virtue of their "character, language, and religion, which are the three fundamental questions regarding any nation."[62]

Like Burton before him, Conder put his expertise in the service of the
empire. His imperial scheme for Syria and Palestine was outlined in a lecture delivered for the Palestine Exploration Fund in 1892 and reprinted in
the sixth edition of *Tent Work*.[63] The lecture, aptly entitled "The Future of
Palestine," reads more like an imperialistic manifesto than ethnographic research. It addresses, with an air of urgency, questions of a political nature,
notably the colonization of Palestine and "the acceleration of the return of
the Jews."[64] Most importantly, it attempts to account for the emergence of
Palestine on the British imperial stage as a strategic juncture in the Levant.
With Conder, Palestine is no longer seen merely as the locus of biblical revival, but also as a country with "immense military value" to England. For
example, Conder was quick to realize the centrality of Palestine to British
imperial interests following the acquisition of Cyprus in 1878, which enabled
England to secure a military base for future operations on the Levantine
coast and in the event of any struggle on the Indian borders.

Conder proves most valuable to empire-building efforts in his area of expertise—namely, race. In 1882, he joined the British expedition to Egypt as
a general officer in the intelligence department, where he collaborated with
Edward Palmer in his efforts to mobilize the Bedouin tribes against a nationalist uprising led by 'Urabi Pasha. Conder would make his name in happier
times as a leading expert on Palestine, where his ethnographic surveys on
the local population, along with his topographic mappings of the country,
would offer a recipe for effective British administration. As early as 1892, in
his lecture to the Palestine Exploration Fund, Conder was already presenting himself as an astute observer of the racial dynamics in the country. Like
Burton, he advised his government to follow the example of India, where "we
have a living witness of the fact, that to some Western nations, and to England pre-eminently, is given the capability of governing the Oriental races
with benefit to both the ruler and the subject."[65]

Echoing his British predecessors, Conder tended to exaggerate the
enmity between the Arabs and the Turks. In his repeated claims to speak
on behalf of the local population, a paternalistic terminology creeps in.
Thus, for example, he informed his fellow Englishmen that the native population "lay the blame of their misery on the shoulders of their rulers, and
are only too anxious to pass into other hands."[66] Conder, who spent the bulk

of his survey in Palestine among the peasant population, further asserted that "there is a very general belief that the land is destined to become once more the property of the Christians, and the Fellahin often inquire of visitors when this time is to come."[67] For Conder, that the fellahin "declare a preference for an English occupation of the country" is not a matter of dispute. Rather, it "shows clearly the high esteem in which our Englishmen stand, and reflects the highest credit on our Consuls, and on others, who, by their probity and energy, have created this high public opinion of a nation which is represented by so few individuals."[68]

In a revealing statement that meshes his strategic vision with the grandiose rhetoric of a civilizing mission, Conder reassured his audience that "the happiest future which could befall Palestine seems to me to be its occupation by some strong European power, which might recognise the value of [its] natural resources."[69] He noted efforts "to deck the figure of Oriental despotism with the garb of Western constitutional government, to impose the ideas, the laws, the customs, and the government of European Christianity on people to whom the motives and the methods of such a condition of society were naturally repugnant."[70] Conder had a canny talent for imperial governance. His corpus is permeated by a tendency to weave his racial dogma into the fabric of empire. In both his lectures and his articles, Conder underscored the benefits of Arab unity against the Turks, which perhaps explains why his interracial divisions of the Arab population rapidly recede into the broader division of Semites versus Turanians. Oftentimes, the racial disparity of the Arabs gets lost in an imperialist propaganda that swirls around his hostility to the Turks, on the one hand, and his blind devotion to the British Empire, on the other. When contrasted with the Turks, the Arab race emerges superior. "The history of the Turks has been that of an uncivilised, a cruel, and a rapacious race, whose transitory conquests were due to the decay of a superior civilisation, and whose literature, religion, and law have all been stolen from the conquered Arab." In contrast, "the history of the Arab race has been that of a progressive and intelligent people of peculiar genius, whose civilisation is founded on the most ancient civilisation of Asia."[71]

Race was at the root of Conder's vision for the future of Palestine. The only conceivable policy for the British in the country, he concluded in his Palestine Exploration Fund lecture, is to forge alliances along existing racial lines, and to utilize the innate qualities of each race in a way that helps realize its best potential. "Among the sturdy peasantry and warlike nomads of Palestine and the desert, she [England] might find allies of extreme value," he affirmed, drawing on a common binary.[72] Finally, the audience was given, with an air of obligation that both echoed Rudyard Kipling and anticipated T. E. Lawrence, a picture of what rests on England's shoulders in the Near East: because "the nationalities once conquered by the Turks [are] recovering their freedom and the right of self-government," England should lead "the emancipation of Semitic nationalities" by helping "the Arab and the Syrian alike to shake off the hated yoke of their Turanian masters."[73]

In his racialized views of the Arabs, Conder inherited the tension between knowledge and power underpinning British colonial discourse, which had characterized the imperial legacy of his predecessors. From his post in the Colonial Office, he, too, struggled to reconcile the twin doctrine of racial demarcation and imperial integration. On the one hand, the Arabs represented a race that was pure and singular, primordial and unchangeable. On the other, they were to be ruled by a superior power bent on managing, if not civilizing, the backward races under its dominion. Like Burton before him, Conder seemed barely troubled by the internal contradiction in his scheme to manage what he himself deemed an inherently unruly race.

## CONCLUSION

Burton and Conder spent two decades (1870–90) producing British ethnographic writing on the Arabs. For British ethnographers, late Ottoman Palestine provided a fertile ground for racial thinking and imagination. As this chapter has shown, in both discourse and praxis, race and empire went hand in hand, recasting British perceptions of the Arabs into new ethnographic configurations. In the second part of the nineteenth century, men such as Conder, Burton, and Drake turned Ottoman Palestine into a laboratory for their experiments in scientific racism. Theories of racial purity and hybridity shaped, and were shaped by, the uneasy encounters between these explorers and the native Arab population. This culminated in a new taxonomy of racial classification, mediated by the growing tendency to translate spatial categories into fixed racial hierarchies. For members of the Palestine Exploration Fund, the Bedouin served merely as a passive agent of this "scientific revolution." In this reconfiguration of human reality, nomadism marked no longer simply a demographic or socioeconomic category but a form of met-anarrative that generated a ready set of racial, ethnographic, and anthropological assumptions about the Arabs.

By the early twentieth century, it had become customary among British ethnographers to speak of the Bedouin as the "original Arabs." To their British observers, the Bedouin continued to perform not only as the pure Arab race, but also as a racial archetype on which Arabness itself was measured and codified. In this view, Bedouin, fellahin, and townspeople represented discrete racial elements with separate and disconnected national trajectories. This classification ultimately enabled British ethnographers to sort out the Bedouin, indeed the Arabs, as a destructive race in Palestine.

The construction of the Bedouin as a distinct nomadic race served later to deny Palestinians their national aspirations. This fact was laid bare by the infamous Balfour Declaration, which promised British support for the establishment in Palestine of a national home for the Jewish people. In this sense, the Balfour Declaration was more a negation of Arab rights, than an affirmation of Jewish rights, to Palestine—a negation that had its roots in British racialized views of the Bedouin and the Arabs described above.

The perception of the Bedouin as the "original Arabs" would continue to dominate ethnographic discourse in Palestine into the Mandate period. Ironically, it was around this perception that the ethnographic views of Arab nationalists, Zionist pioneers, and British administrators would ultimately converge: the Arabs because they sought to integrate the Bedouin into the fabric of the Arab nation, the Zionists because it suited their settler-colonial scheme to identify the Arabs with nomadism and conquest, and the British because it fit well into their divide-and-conquer policy.[74] Even Arab nationalists beyond Palestine seemingly embraced the narrative of the racial purity of the Bedouin. One need not go beyond the writings of Arab historians from that period to grasp the irony.[75] In fact, if we were to believe the firsthand testimonies provided by desert administrators in tribal Palestine, the Bedouin themselves would concede to this romanticized image, yet not in the racial sense, and that is precisely what British ethnographers in Palestine had done: racialize Arabness.

Importantly, hailing the Bedouin as the "original Arabs" enabled Zionist leaders like David Ben-Gurion to view the Bedouin, and Arabs more broadly, as foreign invaders in Palestine.[76] The colonial daily destruction of Bedouin villages and the dispossession of Bedouin land by Israel today are predicated on the time-honored notion that the Bedouin of Palestine are not indigenous to the land. This racial exclusion and the racialization of the Bedouin as a distinct race explain the specific forms of colonial violence that the Naqab Bedouin endure by the Israeli state.[77]

*Five*

# PROLETARIANIZATION OF THE MIZRAHIM

ZVI BEN-DOR BENITE

AS IN SOME OTHER CASES IN THE HISTORY OF ZIONISM, THIS STORY BEGINS
with the moment it was erased. In 1920, a committee of the Po'ale Tsion
party came to Palestine to inquire about labor conditions in the Yishuv (the
Jewish community in prestate Palestine). The committee visited cities, all
*moshavot* (settlements of privately owned property), and all *kvutzot* (settlements of collectively owned property that would become kibbutzim). The
delegates met with workers, gathered information, and composed a lengthy
report in Yiddish that was promptly distributed in two thousand copies. A
larger forum discussed the report over many meetings that produced two
volumes of protocols.[1] Soon after its completion, major portions of this work
were translated into Hebrew and published in a special issue of the leading
socialist journal *Ha-Adama*.[2] The editor of *Ha-Adama*, Hayyim Brenner, was
known to be a "big fan of the truth."[3] But, in 1920, he omitted some passages
from a specific section of the original Yiddish version of the report that he
translated. The erasure comprised specific passages in a special section of
the report dedicated to Yemeni labor. The author of these passages was the
final editor of the original report in Yiddish, Zalman Rubashov—better

117

known as Zalman Shazar, the future third president of Israel—who was then a young socialist.

Tellingly, the essential details in Shazar's text were known in the Yishuv. Brenner's *Ha-Adama* had published a lengthy report with similar information a year earlier.[4] Thus, the details were not the issue, and Brenner did not remove similar information from the new report he published in 1920. What he omitted was Shazar's commentary and analysis of these details. Shazar's omitted text remained hidden until the whole report was published fully in Hebrew in 1989 by Yad Tabenkin, an institute dedicated to the history of socialist Zionism. It was only then that the previously hidden section caught the eye of Shlomo Tivoni, a prolific amateur historian of Yemeni background, a kibbutz member, and a socialist Zionist activist. Without Tivoni, we would probably have missed the whole story. Tivoni published the omission with hardly any commentary in a semi-samizdat book of historical sources on Yemeni Jewish migrations to Palestine. He made only one short critical comment on the text. In what follows, I use that story to revisit the question of Mizrahim—oriental Jews, Jews of Middle Eastern/North African origins[5]—and racialization in Israeli society. I argue here that Shazar's assessment of the problem of Zionism with Mizrahi labor at the time provides an essential insight concerning how socialist Zionism was coming to understand the "question" of Mizrahim and why, eventually, it would racialize them.

Why start in 1920, when it is well known that the overwhelming majority of the Mizrahim arrived in Israel after 1948? Since the literature on anti-Mizrahi racism in Israel is vast, why bother with this old story? Why do that, when one can quickly and simply turn to the writings of the founding Zionist thinkers and pick some racist comments about the Orient or about Middle Eastern Jews? Theodor Herzl famously said that the future Jewish state would be "a rampart of Europe against Asia, an outpost of civilization as opposed to barbarism."[6] Wouldn't it suffice to say that intra-Jewish racist attitudes are simply a derivative of such statements? Middle Eastern Jews are "Orientals" like the rest of the "barbarians." Recent histories of Zionist thought have exposed plenty of similar statements made by leading early Zionist thinkers. For instance, Arthur Ruppin has emerged as a master generator of some of the nastiest ideas about oriental Jews.[7] These ideas belong squarely in the rich culture of early modern and modern European thinking about race, eugenics, biology, and hygiene. So, in this regard, we cannot say that they have much to do with the *realities* in Israel itself. There is still a long, concrete road between the fantasies of early-twentieth-century German Jewish thinkers like Ruppin and the persistent social gaps between Mizrahim and Ashkenazim in contemporary Israel.[8] Yet, recent Mizrahi writings on intra-Jewish conflicts in Israel tend to begin with such statements and follow with a history of anti-Mizrahi practices and attitudes that are understood as derived from them. Since no one could, would, or should deny that early Zionist thinkers were European racists, there is, in effect, little discussion about race.[9] Race remains almost undiscussed precisely because it is accepted as a given derivative of "old-style" European racism. When race is—rarely—discussed in terms of racialization at the society level, this is done, perhaps not surprisingly, by an anthropologist.[10]

Ronit Lentin has recently critiqued contemporary Israeli studies on racism, including anti-Mizrahi racism, for their "tendency to occlude race in favor of racism." Scholars still describe Israeli society as a site where racism exists, but without race.[11] The result, a tedious historian would say, is an unhistoricized circuitous conversation about racism that goes like this: the social gaps are "proof" of the racist nature of the society; the racism is the evidence of the social gaps in it. Instead of searching for an unhistorical category of "race" that produces racism in Israeli society, Lentin proposes focusing on *racialization*. Racialization is not a single uniform process that begins with the premise that race exists. Lentin reminds us that "racialized assemblages" construct race "not as biological or cultural but rather as sociopolitical processes of differentiation and hierarchization."[12] Insisting on racialization is helpful, indeed necessary, when we come to discuss race questions in an intra-Jewish context. Zionism holds that the Jews are one nation, implicitly one "race."[13] If so, from where does the "racism" among different Jewish groups come? The historical road to "racism" must have been paved with acts of racialization. These insights are critical for my present discussion. Borrowing from Lentin, I look for "traces of race" far "below" the shining stars of European racist thought á la Herzl and Ruppin. Here, I present and discuss observations and discourses produced by Zionist socialists at a time when a distinct sphere of labor was being created on the ground in Palestine itself as part of the Zionist project. I call this sphere the "theater of labor," appropriating the seventeenth-century term "theater of war" (*theatrum belli*). The Zionist theater of labor is an arena of conflict. In this charged space, different types of workers and owners contended: Ashkenazi landowners, Ashkenazi Zionist workers, oriental Jewish workers, and Palestinians. The theater is there where Mizrahi labor, and consequently the Mizrahim, became racialized through the discourses it produced.

Why labor and race in this context? Patrick Wolfe maintains that race in the Israeli context must be discussed within a colonial/postcolonial framework and a settler-colonial setting. Drawing on a wealth of contemporary scholarship and emphasizing the relationship between colonialism and exclusion, Wolfe locates the racialization of the "Jew" within a series of exclusions and erasures—beginning with the category "Arab"—practiced by the Israeli state. These exclusions have roots in Zionist ideology itself and have historically forced Mizrahim to make a "cultural choice" between "Arab" and "Jew."[14] Bringing in labor, Wolfe considers the Mizrahim as a labor force "that is racialized in contradistinction to their Ashkenazi superiors."[15] This insight concerning a racialized labor force is critical to what I present here. But, within the history that Wolfe narrates,[16] this contradistinction is already a given reality. The question of *how* the racialization of labor itself came to be is left undiscussed. More importantly, it is unclear how the Mizrahi predicament of having to choose between two cultural (in this context) categories—"Jew" and "Arab"—is related to racialized labor. One still must examine how this labor force became racialized. That gap is precisely where this chapter comes to intervene, demonstrating how racialization of Mizrahim is generated within a concrete context of a Zionist labor project and with Ashkenazim, Mizrahim, and Palestinians playing an active role in it.

## THE "PROBLEM" OF MIZRAHI LABOR

In the 1920s, Po'ale Tsion was becoming the dominant socialist party and an emerging Zionist force. Its rise would ultimately mark the transition of power from earlier nonsocialist forms of Zionism to socialist ones. Almost all future socialist Zionist parties would emerge from this organization. Indeed, socialist Zionism would continuously lead Zionist politics and the State of Israel until 1977. In hindsight, the 1920 delegation, charged with the mission of inquiring about labor in Palestine, was crucial. It was meant to provide the necessary information so that the party could reform its plans concerning the future of Zionism. The Po'ale-Tsion Commission in Palestine of the World Socialist Union of Jewish Workers—the Erets-Yisroel-arbayter-komisye, as it was known in Yiddish—included intellectuals such as Nahman Syrkin, Yitzhak Ben-Zvi, David Ben-Gurion, Zalman Rubashov (Shazar), Yitzhak Tabenkin, and Shmuel Yavnieli. Crucially, some of these people would eventually become top Israeli leaders. The "question of labor" was a critical issue on the committee's agenda, the second item in the order of things in its protocols after the top issue—"the land question." The combined enterprise of the "conquest of the land" and the "conquest of labor" was becoming, at that point, the driving principle behind Zionist settlement in Palestine. Briefly put, the dual dynamics of the "two conquests" meant acquiring as much land as possible with as few Palestinians as possible on it as laborers.[17] That meant first pushing Arab labor out of the acquired land. That is why, for me, the theater of labor is a charged arena. Indeed, the "question of labor" on the committee's agenda is explained as "the problem of workers: the question of wages in the city and the rural areas." The subtitle of this item is even more telling: "the competition of the Arabs, minimum wages and their effective use, the question of wages, social policy, the problem of skills."[18]

One of the "problems" discussed in the report is Yemeni labor. Shazar opens his text with praise for Yemeni Jewry—a "Jewish tribe [that] protected, with awesome persistence, its autonomous Jewish existence in the diaspora." The Yemenis were "used to hard labor from childhood" and were blessed with "ancient love" for the Land of Israel.[19] In 1910, "under the guidance of a young worker from the Land of Israel," several hundred families left Yemen for Palestine. They joined their Ashkenazi brethren in "carrying the burden of work, suffering, and building a new Jewish homeland." The "young worker from Eretz Yisrael" whom Shazar mentions, who "guided" the Yemenis to Palestine, was Shmuel Yavnieli, a future member of the aforementioned committee. Famously, Yavnieli played a vital role in the story Shazar tells. In an essay he wrote in 1910, "Avodat Ha-Tehiyya ve-Yehudei Ha-Mizrah" (On the labor of revival and the Jews of the Orient), he urged that Middle Eastern Jews be brought to the Zionist settlements and stressed their potential as laborers.[20] Yavnieli placed great importance on bringing "hundreds of thousands" of Middle Eastern Jews to Palestine, where they would join the great

project of the national revival of the Jewish people after years of exile. Labor
('avoda) would be the crucial element in this project.

Yavnieli's mission to Yemen was a scouting expedition, and he kept a detailed
and informed journal of his mission. He later published the journal as a book
with related correspondence and additional reflections.[21] The mission was the
subject of an occasional heated debate concerning its impact on Yemeni Jewry.
Israeli historians, mostly of Yemeni descent, tend to downplay Yavnieli's role in
causing the migration of Yemeni Jews to Palestine in 1912, arguing that Zionist
sentiment was already there, not "waiting" for Ashkenazi intervention. Other
historians of Zionism, mostly of Ashkenazi background, claim the opposite.[22]
The question, however, is not who is the bigger Zionist here, but rather what
Yavnieli's journal says about labor. Labor, the possibilities of its transformation,
and their limits are central themes in the journal. Yavnieli repeatedly writes
that the "redemption" (ge'ulah) of the Yemenis and all the Middle Eastern Jews
will come not merely through returning to the holy land, which will stop the
process of "national degeneration." Labor, he insists, and not just immigrating
to Palestine, would be their "true" redemption (ge'ulatam tihiye ba'avoda).[23]

In other words, the "revival" of oriental Jews would entail their transformation into laborers. But one must be clear here: laborers in the Zionist sense
of the word, which was different from their originary conditions in Yemen.
Upon his arrival in Yemen, Yavnieli realized that, like many other Jews in
the Middle East at the time, Yemeni Jews worked as artisans, craftsmen, and
traders, as well as in other services. These occupations did not constitute the
type of labor that he was seeking to find.[24] Yavnieli spent a good part of his
journal meticulously detailing their crafts and occupations in every locale
he visited, noting that there were no Jewish farmers and only a few landowners.[25] Furthermore, Yavnieli's overview states explicitly that the entire
Yemeni economy, including the Yemeni Jewish economy, was highly dependent on the "spinning factories in England and India." That makes sense,
given Yemen's location between the Indian Ocean and the Mediterranean
Sea.[26] As Yavnieli tells us, "massive amounts of cotton" come to the ports of
Hodeida and 'Aden, from where they are "carried on camels" to all regions of
the country. Many of the Jews work as spinners or weavers, just like many
non-Jews. In fact, "the entire land" is full of weavers and spinners.[27] Yavnieli
keeps reiterating this point throughout.

As is well known, by that time, the global textile industry had already profoundly changed many economies and societies across the globe.[28] But, despite its exposure to massive amounts of cotton, Yavnieli mentions that this was not the case in Yemen. The Yemeni economy, certainly the Jewish one, remained "traditional"—better yet, precapitalist. The cotton is moved inside the land on camels, not by faster or larger modern means. Yavnieli points out that weaving is done with "primitive" machinery. He also points out that there is "hardly any hired labor" in the Yemeni textile industry. Most weavers and spinners work at home.[29] That is a significant point to note: Yavnieli is telling us that, even when the Yemeni economy is exposed to the forces of capitalism through the "massive amounts" of cotton that the British Empire moves between India and Europe, it remains "primitive" and traditional. Another concern he raises is that Jewish blacksmiths have been declining in numbers. Evidently, Yavnieli asked his local interlocutors specific questions about this aspect of their economic life and was quite scrupulous about the issue. The attention he pays to such questions suggests, strongly, that he was very concerned with the possibility of *transforming* Yemeni Jewish labor into something that would be more suitable to what Zionism in Palestine needed with regards to Middle Eastern Jewish labor. This insight leads me to depart from earlier assessments of this episode. Earlier accounts emphasized the perception, on the part of the Zionist establishment, that Middle Eastern Jews were "natural workers," as opposed to "idealistic"—read Ashkenazi—workers, and that they were needed to help drive away Arab labor.[30] The latter part is (always) true. The former, however, is not.

## THE "THEATER OF LABOR" IN PALESTINE

Ze'ev Smilanski, a prominent Zionist socialist intellectual, had articulated his views on what I call the "theater of labor" already in 1908. His "Hebrew or Arab Workers," a hitherto unstudied essay that was declared at the time to be "extremely important," is a unique portrayal of the theater that captures the sense of conflict within it.[31] The Jewish landowners, he explained, "prefer" the Arab worker for the following reasons:

1. The Arab settles for fewer wages; 2. The Arab is not yet as civilized [*kulturi*] as the Jew and has no complaints and demands. 3. The newly arrived [Jewish] workers are more dedicated to work, but the landowners

do not like their behavior, and sometimes they even consider them dangerous and suspicious.[32]

There is more: despite being cheap, Arab workers are a liability. They are lazy, they cannot learn "new skills," and they are "untrustworthy." Sometimes they even "sabotage work deliberately."[33] Worse, "even when it comes to jobs that pay little and require physical strength and perseverance, it is often the case that the Hebrew worker is better than the Arab one because he is more civilized and developed and therefore more honest and loyal." The "Arab, who is natural [ben ha-Teva'] and half-savage, does not refrain from stealing from his employer," and that cancels the benefit of cheap labor.[34] Finally, "the Arabs, whose savagery comes before their humanity, excel in their cruelty to animals." Here, we see an early instance of racialized articulation of the "Arab problem," specifically in the context of labor.

Conversely, the "more civilized" Jewish workers ensure that the animals eat on time.[35] Having "finished" with the Arabs, Smilanski turns his attention to Jewish (Ashkenazi Zionist) workers: they are trustworthy. But the problem with them is that the landowners see them as too "Zionistic" (tsionistich) and too "socialistic" (sotsialistich).[36] Smilanski's use of these two strange words, instead of "Zionist" and "socialist," suggests that he does not locate the problem in Zionist ideology itself. Rather, the peculiar "behavioral" traits of the young Zionist workers conflict with the landowners. Jewish workers were not only more costly and "annoying," they were also too mobile. They were leaving their jobs after a short while. For the landowners, this was too much, so they continued preferring Arab workers. Moreover, Smilanski reports that the number of Arab workers is much greater, sometimes hundreds of percentage points more, than that of Jewish workers.[37] Strangely enough, despite his ideological leanings, Smilanski seems to be sympathetic to the landowners' predicament with the Jewish workers. In some places, he even justifies their "habit" (hergel) of hiring Arab workers.[38]

At this point, Smilanski turns to ponder the possibility of employing "our brethren the residents (toshavim) of Eretz Yisrael," the "maghribis, Persians, Yemenis, and the poor Sephardim." We "have done some statistics," he says, and "realized that many of them would agree to work for low wages, and one has to note that females do household work [in the landowners' homes] and that they are better than the Arabs." Somewhat surprised, he mentions that during the grapevine-harvesting season, "when only Jews are hired" because of Kosher issues, they "do a good job." In fact, "some of them are really strong." In a winepress in Rehovot, he says, "I have seen two Ashkenazi workers pushing the wheel [of the press], but one Persian Jew was pushing it alone, taking turns with another Persian Jew." Baskets full of grapes "that require two Ashkenazi workers" were carried by "one Jew from Aleppo." It also turned out that work that hurt Ashkenazi workers "hardly affects the Jews of the East."[39]

Oriental Jews were considered to be better workers than the Arabs, but there were also problems with them. Even when poor oriental Jews worked, it was only seasonal labor. Once the season was over, they returned to their "poor homes" in the cities. Also, they "cannot be trusted, and they steal." Indeed, honesty and theft among Jews were racialized categories for Smilanski. It is "true," he admits, that there are landowners who "prove" that the oriental Jews are "not as honest as the Ashkenazim." But "all agree that they are more honest than the Arabs." Smilanski adds that oriental Jews usually prefer to beg for money and not to work. Indeed, this was something to which "all seem to have been accustomed."[40] Tellingly, Smilanski admits that Ashkenazi workers at the Rothschild wineries also steal. Still, that type of stealing is "different" because Ashkenazi workers see unwatched tools and "think it is ok" to take them because no one is using them.[41] Mizrahi workers, apparently, just steal. As if it is their nature to do so.

Far closer to earth than the heights of Herzl's and Ruppin's European thought and its racist baggage, Smilanski gives us an eyewitness account, replete with racialized language, from the "theater of labor" in the early Zionist Yishuv in which he participated as a keen observer. Smilanski seemingly provides an empirical, almost neutral, description of labor conditions, but *explains* the whole situation in racial terms. When he addresses the gaps between workers, he does so in racial terms—the Arabs are "natural" and "savages," the oriental Jews are slightly "better." However, they are still lazy and untrustworthy, and, because of that, they lack the necessary skills. Moreover, Smilanski's text reminds us that it was not only profit that played a role in this theater. Zionist objectives, the Jewish conquest of land and labor, also play a role, and they sometimes conflict with the desire to maximize profit. Smilanski paints and rationalizes a

hierarchized picture of labor life, with Ashkenazi landowners and Ashkenazi workers at the top and Palestinians at the bottom. Oriental Jews,
as seasonal workers or as people who "prefer" not to work, are occasional
actors in the theater. Since they are not a fixed category, it is unclear
"where" they are in this schema. But that problem has nothing to do with
the everyday labor life of the Mizrahi. It stems from the fact that their work
habits do not fit Zionist plans.

Smilanski reflects well the socialist Zionist mood concerning Mizrahi
labor. I surveyed 180 notices and articles about Yemenis and Mizrahim that
appeared in the socialist press (most notably, *Hapo'el Ha-tsa'ir*) between 1907
and 1925. Labor, particularly among the Mizrahi poor, whom the Zionists
hoped to employ, was the primary concern. Lamentations concerning lack of
skill or ideological "drive" to join the new Zionist workforce appear repeatedly. Many of the articles are replete with complaints about laziness, lack of
physical strength, and adherence to "old practices" and "old crafts." Finally,
when it comes to organizing and cooperating, local oriental Jews were seen
as simply too "difficult."[42]

Therefore, the problem behind employing more Mizrahi workers was
not, as Shafir analyzed, the lack of a (Jewish) human supply for work, or
the behavior of idealistic workers.[43] The problem was the limitations concerning their entrance into the theater of Zionist labor—their racialization.
Racialization emerges in Smilanski's text about the *possibility* of transforming oriental Jews into workers. Smilanski notes that all the above problems
with oriental Jews could be "corrected through education" (Arabs cannot be
"amended"). But there was one insurmountable problem that made it impossible to turn them into permanent workers. Unlike Arab workers, who live
in villages near where they work, oriental Jews do not. Oriental Jews who
work in the summer live in tents and temporary housing. When the harvest
ends, they go back home. It is a pity, laments Smilanski, that the landowners
do not arrange homes in their settlements for these workers.[44] And, finally,
there is the attitude of the Ashkenazi landowners themselves, who "treat the
Sephardim and the Jews of the rest of the Orient" as "strangers."[45] Concerning
the relationship between the landowners and their employees, he mentions
that the relationship between the two populations is close in the Galilee.

There, "the landowner works together with his workers in the field, and they sit and eat together." However, in "Judea," referring to the Judean foothills in the south, "where the conditions are different, and labor is more capitalist in shape, there is no such close relationship as in the Galilee."[46] Smilanski's comment is revealing. In characterizing labor in the southern territories of Palestine as more "capitalist," he means, in the context of the relationship between workers and employers, that it is more alienated. In the south, unlike in the more "traditional" Galilee, where people break bread together, there is a real gap between employers and workers. We shall see soon that this hint of alienation, mixed with the landowners' view of oriental Jews as strangers, and their desire to get labor that was cheaper than Arab labor, would become deadly.

## CAPITALISM BETRAYS ZIONISM

With Smilanski in mind, we can now better understand why Yavnieli came up with the idea of "importing" oriental Jews from elsewhere in the Middle East and why others supported him. The importees would have all the "positive" traits of the local oriental Jews, but, since they would come under Zionist auspices (and control), they would not present the same problems. As "Zionist immigrants," they would be easier to "train." Thus, the solution is bringing "new" oriental Jews and *proletarianizing* them. And so, in 1912, several hundred Jewish families left Yemen and came to Palestine. In 1913, the number of Yemeni workers emerging from these families stood at 328. Though this number seems small, it comprised no less than 41 percent of the Jewish workforce at the time.[47] We must remember that, unlike the "old" oriental Jewish population of the Yishuv, these "new" Yemenis made the *first* Mizrahi group that came to Palestine in the context of the Zionist project as it was taking shape.

We now turn again to Shazar to see how they were received. Having summarized the basic facts of the story, and telling us that the Yemenis arrived in the wake of Yavnieli's mission, Shazar asks: "What an opportunity . . . to show that we are unifying as a nation?" And he proceeds immediately with another rhetorical question: "And what did the Yishuv in Eretz Israel do regarding this opportunity presented by Jewish history?" Shazar quickly provides the answer:

First, the landowners immediately sensed the smell of poverty enfolding those returning brothers, and instantaneously a rumor was spread that these Yemenis did not need much to survive. And so, a satanic conspiracy was born to keep them in their misery and turn them into an object of exploitation as a cheap labor force that would satisfy the appetite and lifestyles of the landowners who had exploited the Bedouins and the Arab Falaheen for years.[48]

The landowners and the Zionist establishment hatched a "satanic plan." "This was the dream," thunders Shazar, "the landowner will be happy, he will not have to change his lifestyle or lose money, and the Zionist ideal will be well-preserved and stay clean without stain: Eretz Israel will be built by Jews, and the Arab danger will disappear."[49]

It is clear how Shazar understands the "satanic plan" and the roles "assigned" to each group. The Arab "danger" should "disappear," the Yemenis will work for lower wages, and the landowners will stay rich. Most importantly, Zionism will remain untainted. Shazar explains the logic behind the plan:

> The Zionist leaders dedicated all their managerial skills and authority to the realization of this dream. Everything was done so that the Yemenis *would indeed fulfill the satanic role ordained for them in the name of Zionism* and the [idea of] settling of the Land of Israel. The Jewish Yishuv was never so petty, inhumane, and antinational. The Zionist leaders were never so alienated from the primary sense of the nation [*regesh le'umi*] as in this story of the Yemeni settlement. A Yemeni family with five children received only 1,000 square meters of land, 300 times less than any Ashkenazi settler! And all of this was done so that the Yemenis would be forced into the trap that the landowners had prepared for them.[50]

Indeed, the Yishuv was "never so petty, inhumane, and antinational." Shazar spares no imagery in describing this conspiracy. He invokes the biblical story of the Levite's concubine, in which a war between two Israelite tribes resulted in a terrible organized massacre of one of them by the other.[51] The details Shazar provides when telling us about the consequences of this conspiracy justify his harsh tone: "Once the Yemenis began looking for jobs," they "received less than the daily pay of an Arab laborer." That made them "slaves to slaves." In many places, they were housed in stables, chicken houses, or small shacks where they suffered both in the winter and in the summer. They were forced to walk for miles to get water. In some instances, they were deliberately given land in disease-stricken areas. They had no civic rights in any *moshava*. The results amounted to a massacre: "Out of 237 Yemenis in the Moshava of Rehovot, 110 died within six years. . . . In Mahane Yosef, there is a death in every Yemeni home." Elsewhere, it was the same: "Out of 300 people who lived in Nahaliel, 154 passed away. All the children born in Yemeni homes during these years, about 50, passed away. There is no medical help. And on and on. . . . When they protest, the landowners beat them."

Shazar concludes: "This is how the Zionist ideal was being realized, through exploitation and cheap labor!"[52] Indeed, a horrible story. Note that details of this story were known in real time in the Yishuv. The press was full of stories about dying starved Yemenis. What is significant in Shazar's treatment of it here is his analysis: it was a conspiracy, a "satanic plot" to drive people to starvation and death so that they would work for lower wages than Arabs. All to protect the Zionist tale about peaceful conquest of land and labor. That is why Brenner retained the details but consciously omitted these specific passages. What he expunged was not the facts. It was the scathing judgment.

The number of dying people and how Shazar places them in his report exposes another logic behind the reality it describes. As I have shown above, socialist Zionists were concerned about oriental Jews, in Palestine or elsewhere in the Middle East (Yemen, in this context), and with what they saw as traditional artisans and craftsmen. That is evident in Yavnieli's investigations about Jewish labor in Yemen and his statements concerning the fact that it does not transform into something more modern, even when the scales of material and wealth around it—in the Indian Ocean and the Gulf of Aden—dramatically increase. Rosa Luxemburg once explained what happens to people in such conditions. In "Introduction to Political Economy," she speaks of the "crusade against the human maintenance of the workers [that] began in England—along with capitalist industry." It was a "crusade by capital against any trace of luxury, comfort and convenience in the life of the worker, as he was accustomed to in the earlier period of handicrafts and peasant economy."[53] That is what proletarianization means, and workers are forced to accept it. If they do not, the consequences are dire. Using the example of the traditional shoemaker, Luxemburg explains that the craftsperson

> can produce the best commodity, but if other shoemakers have suffi-ciently met the demand, his commodity is superfluous. If this happens repeatedly, he has to abandon his trade. The redundant shoemaker is ex-pelled from society in the same mechanical way as superfluous material is expelled from the animal body. Since his work is not accepted as social labor, he is en route to extinction.[54]

Simply put, the process of mass production of (in this case) shoes tells the craftsperson that "society has no need of you, my friend, your labor was just not necessary, you are a superfluous person and can happily go and hang yourself."[55]

Luxemburg's insights are apt and pertinent if we apply them to a set-tler-colonial setting. The Jews who left Yemen were not supposed to come to Palestine and join their "lazy" oriental brethren there. They were supposed to enter an economy that was building capitalism in a settler-colonial con-text. Enhanced by the logic of the need to drive Arab labor and the Pales-tinians out, this Luxemburgian story became deadly. First, the landowners made sure that they could not become independent farmers and drove them to starvation. Then they said, "Work for us for low wages, and if not, you can happily go and hang yourself." Shazar's socialism explains the harsh words against the landowners. But we cannot forget his Zionism. He understands that capitalism—the same alienated capitalism that Smilanski identified more than a decade before him—defeats the Zionist cause because it kills people, or at least drives them away. Now "socialism" comes in. The inclusion of this specific document on Yemeni labor was prepared as part of the Po'ale Tsion's effort to persuade the Jewish world that socialist Zionism—and not capitalist Zionism—was the only path to national salvation in Eretz-Yisrael. The implication, I would contend, is that socialist Zionism would, presum-ably, come up with a more humane way of proletarianizing people without defeating the Zionist cause.

But this is not a tale of socialist innocence, as Tivoni, a later member of Shazar's same socialist movement, reminded us in 1993. In the one snide comment beneath the report that he exposed, he writes: "Only one question I have in respect of the Po'ale Tsion Committee, why did they forget to write, even one word, about the Yemenis of Kinneret?"[56] Tivoni's comment refers to another terrible reality that is somehow not mentioned in Shazar's report. Although a harsh critic when it comes to capitalism, Shazar neglects to say that, at the very same time that Yemeni workers were being starved and beaten by capitalist landowners, Yemenis who had settled in the socialist settlement Kinneret were being treated almost as badly by their socialist Ashkenazi brethren. Historian Yehuda Nini described in 1996 how ten Yemeni families who came in 1912 to the then four-year-old socialist settlement were abused.[57] The Yemenis were, in fact, the constant presence in Kinneret, while "idealist" workers from Europe came and left. But they were treated terribly, housed in dreadful conditions, and suffered greatly. In 1932, when Kinneret was a more robust settlement, they were expelled. The leadership of the socialist *kvutza* declared them "unsuitable" and they were "forced" to move to a small Yemeni town near Rehovot.[58] Rehovot was the site where, as Shazar tells in the extract above, 110 Yemenis had died within six years of their arrival in 1912. The Kinneret story remains a matter of debate concerning how "racist" the Ashkenazi settlers in Kinneret were.[59]

Here we come across another erasure that was hiding in the report all along. Whereas Brenner erased Shazar's harsh judgments about capitalist Zionism, Shazar himself erased the realities of Yemeni life in the socialist settlements. Shazar and the committee must have been fully aware of the goings-on in Kinneret. They visited the place, as mentioned many times in their report. Shoddier still, during the deliberations about the report, Kinneret is discussed and, in this context, Yemeni families are also mentioned. Still, not a word is uttered about how they were treated.[60] That is the socialist way of keeping Zionism untainted. Moreover, we can still see the differences between capitalist Zionism and its socialist counterpart. The socialists do "better" than the capitalists. Whereas the latter starve Yemenis and deliberately drive them to poverty, the former "only" mistreat them and, more importantly, segregate them. For me, the moment of declaring the Yemenis "unsuitable" by the leaders of Kinneret is critical. When it comes to oriental Jews, capitalist Zionists simply proletarianize them through presenting a choice between labor and the condition of superfluousness: work for us or "happily go and hang yourself." Zionist socialists are more sophisticated. They racialize. Whereas the Zionist project brings Ashkenazim and Mizrahim together, the need to proletarianize the latter produces racialization. Racialization—creating hierarchies and generating discourses justifying them—accompanies the making of the Mizrahi proletariat in socialist Zionist thought and practice.

## LESSONS OF 1920: PROLETARIANIZATION AND RACIALIZATION

Can this insight about proletarianization and racialization tell us anything about post-1948 realities concerning Mizrahim and Ashkenazim? I would say yes. Take note of the key word in the Kinneret story: "unsuitable." It tells us nothing in terms of what was "wrong" with the Yemenis. But precisely because of its vagueness, it was so valuable in the process of expelling them. Anyone familiar with discourses of exclusion of Mizrahim from a broad spectrum of (mostly socialist or "progressive") communal settlements in Israel after 1948 will recall that "unsuitability" is a racializing marker that Ashkenazim used—and continue to use—to maintain segregation between the two populations. The same tool was also used to hierarchize, and preserve the gaps in housing, health, education, and the military. The Kinneret story was probably where Mizrahi "unsuitability" was born as a potent tool of exclusion and racialization. The history of this tool after 1948 is the history of making it more sophisticated, applying to every sphere of social life.

In 1958, Abraham Abbas, a Syrian-born member of Knesset, published a first-of-its-kind report on "The Communal Problem in Israel."[61] That was a decade after hundreds of thousands of Palestinians were deported or forced to leave the land because they were non-Jewish Arabs, and hundreds of thousands of Arabs were brought to the land because they were Jews (as one brilliantly elegant phrase put it[62]). Abbas's report concerned all social aspects of life in the young Israel, primarily the social division of labor and its causes. It was the first thorough analysis of how the gaps that existed between two populations—the Ashkenazi and the Mizrahi citizens of Israel—came into being after 1948. Like Shazar, Abbas was a Zionist-socialist leader and a member of the more socialist wing of Mappai, the Ahdut Ha'avoda Party. He was also a member of the executive committee of the Histadrut, the General Organization of Workers in Israel, and oversaw the monitoring of Mizrahi labor. He thus had unique access to labor-related issues, numbers, and fig-ures, which he provided and analyzed in his report. The report stated that Israel had created a divided labor force within less than ten years, with Ash-kenazim at the top and Mizrahim at the bottom as underpaid workers per-forming menial labor. (The Palestinians in Israel, then a crushed minority under severely restricting martial law, were not yet part of such studies.)

Regarding the Jewish workforce, the report showed that inequality within it was the fruit of *deliberate* policies. Abbas was a party apparatchik and a good Zionist with a perfect record in the prestate days. He was a leader in several kibbutzim and an organizer of illegal immigration to Palestine by Jews from Syria, his birthplace, and from Lebanon. But what he saw in nearly ten years of service in the Histadrut pushed him over the edge. In his concluding remarks, Abbas was harsh: "Most of the oriental Jews have been *cruelly* and *bitterly* disappointed, and they have ceased to have any faith in the public declarations of party leaders about true equality for all the citi-zens of Israel."[63] Just as Shazar had used harsh words about Zionist capital-ism in 1920, Abbas used similarly powerful words about Zionist socialism in 1958. Both men, each in his turn, lamented the betrayal of Mizrahi Jews by Zionism.

## CONCLUSION

Lamentations aside, the fact that Israel created, within less than a decade, such a hierarchized and divided labor force with persistent gaps is sugges-tive. Did the founding fathers of Zionism "plan" to create a racialized Jewish society? Is this condition the product of late-nineteenth-century European racism? Again, I would say yes. But plans and ideas are not enough. We must consider the concrete realities in Palestine and the region regarding how the settlers grappled with them instead of just blaming the racist ideas of the founding Zionist thinkers. In other words, the decisive factor in igniting the process of the racialization of the Mizrahim was the concrete intersec-tion between capitalism, labor, and the Zionist pressure to dispossess the Palestinians. These conditions mandated a process of coerced, even brutal, proletarianization that entailed, in turn, racialization.

The real lessons from past experiences in attempting to proletarian-ize oriental Jews in the Yishuv and the racializing effects they produced beginning in 1920 were at work here. The story told in this chapter shows that the goal of turning the Mizrahim into a Zionist proletariat was already on the table in 1920, and perhaps even in 1910. It also shows that Zionist leaders were already struggling with the question of how to attain it without hurting the Zionist cause itself—particularly after they realized that the Zionist capitalist way of achieving that goal was too brutal. The practices of racialization, exclusion, and erasure were much more effective. The founding fathers of the Jewish state in 1948 encountered, in this regard, the same dilemmas that the early Zionists had faced in the 1910s—only this time, on a much larger scale. The continuity at work here was not just abstract but also very real. The same people who staffed the committee in 1920 were Israel's leaders in the 1950s and later. What was hidden in early Zionist socialist discourses, and only implied in Shazar's report, was the possibility of a "better" way to proletarianize the Mizrahim. After 1948—when Zionist socialism became the state—the possibility became a reality. That proletarianization did not entail deliberately starving anyone. But it entailed the racialization of the labor force and, consequently, of all other aspects of social life.

*Six*

# THE RACIAL HIERARCHY OF REFUGEES

ABIGAIL B. BAKAN AND YASMEEN ABU-LABAN

WELL BEFORE ISRAEL'S 2023 GENOCIDAL WAR ON GAZA, PALESTINIANS constituted one of the world's largest refugee and stateless populations. The recent events in the region have both exposed and amplified this reality, displacing an estimated 1.7 million persons (over 75 percent of the population of Gaza)—most of whom have experienced displacement multiple times.[1] There is legitimate sorrow in the West and elsewhere for the loss of innocent lives in Israel on October 7, 2023. However, the lack of similar empathy by many Western politicians and publics speaks to the inherent inequality of human rights for what is estimated at the time of the writing (December 2024) to be nearly 46,000 (and some reporting as high as 186,000) Palestinians, most of them women and children, who have lost their lives.[2] The International Court of Justice has identified Israel's military assault on the people of Gaza as plausible genocide.[3] Similarly, Francesca Albanese, the UN special rapporteur on the situation of human rights in the Palestinian territories occupied since 1967, concluded that "there are reasonable grounds to believe that the threshold indicating Israel's commission of genocide is met."[4] Still, there is a lack of political will among Western global powers to force Israel to adhere to even basic norms under international law. The marginalization of Palestinians from the framework of international human rights is rendered painfully visible, we suggest, from long-standing patterns associated with refugees, generating recent genocidal conditions that can be understood both as a continuation of the first Nakba and as the production of a second one.

The *Nakba* is the term used to reference over 750,000 Palestinians—estimated to be 80 percent of Palestine's population at the time—being expelled or forced to flee violence in 1948 and becoming stateless refugees within and outside of historic Palestine.[5] Palestinians constitute one of the world's largest refugee and stateless populations. The abandonment of Palestinian refugees by the international community is indicated not only by their historic and ongoing dispossession, but also by what we term a racial hierarchy of refugees that operates on both a regional and a global scale. This involves an enduring racialized hierarchy of rights between Jewish refugees and Palestinian refugees, as well as the subordinated position of Palestinian refugee status in the international refugee rights regime, rendering Palestinian refugees systematically and comparatively marginalized in a world composed of states.

While there was a global Western abandonment of Jewish refugees during and after World War II, this has been seemingly atoned for by support of Israel and through Israel's Law of Return of 1950, which allows Jews from anywhere in the world to immigrate and automatically become Israeli citizens. Palestinians, however, have been displaced and dispossessed, becoming permanent refugees and denied the right of return—a right recognized in international law. The Law of Return was accompanied by Israel's Absentee Property Law of 1950, which was the main legal instrument among a series of laws that transferred the homes and property of Palestinian refugees to the newly declared State of Israel in an act of colonial theft and ethnic cleansing.[6] Israel's use of violent and repressive measures to prevent the return of Palestinian refugees from neighboring countries such as Lebanon, Syria, and Jordan—along with the use of a military government regime, forced transfer, and the expulsion of Palestinians who remained—laid the groundwork for continued settler-colonial territorial expansion through the 1950s and 1960s.[7] Israel further entrenched its settler colonial project following the 1967 war through occupation and the building of Jewish settlements. Despite the recognition of the Palestinian right of return in the 1948 UN General Assembly Resolution 194,[8] Israel faced no sanctions for its ongoing refusal to allow Palestinian refugees to return.[9] Such racialized exclusion, accepted by the world's most powerful states, helps account for why the Nakba presents an ongoing process and an intergenerational trauma for Palestinians.[10]

In addition to Israel's refusal to allow Palestinian refugees to return to their land, the racial hierarchy of refugees is also demonstrated by the exclusion of Palestinian refugees from the limited rights afforded to other displaced populations through the institutional UN structures. This is symbolized and enforced by the placement of Palestinian refugees under the United Nations Relief and Works Agency for Palestinian Refugees in the Near East (UNRWA), established in 1949. However, Palestinian refugees were excluded from the mandate of the United Nations Office of the High Commissioner for Refugees (UNHCR), established in 1950, as well as from the 1951 Convention Relating to the Status of Refugees.[11] This separation in UN infrastructure was intentional, resulting from decisions in the international community regarding the Refugee Convention, the UNHCR Statute,[12] and, as Rashid Khalidi summarizes, "a balance of forces massively favourable to Israel."[13] While the Refugee Convention was initially limited in geographic scope to protecting some forty million European refugees displaced prior to 1951, the 1967 Protocol removed that geographic and temporal specificity.[14] Yet Palestinian refugees continued to be largely excluded from its scope.

Moreover, the legitimacy—and even the existence—of the UNRWA is continually contested by Israel, and longtime Western supporters have increasingly cut funding, putting the future of the organization in jeopardy.[15] This reached unprecedented proportions in 2024, when Israel accused UNRWA employees of participating in the October 7, 2023, attacks. Although those claims remained unsubstantiated months later, the agency lost over US$450 million at the moment of heightened humanitarian need as Gazans faced famine, dislocation, and the destruction of civilian infrastructure as a result of Israel's bombardment.[16] Here, it can also be noted that between October 7, 2023, and May 2024, it was reported that at least 430 displaced Palestinians sheltering in UNRWA buildings had been killed and 1,442 had been injured, while 189 UNRWA staff had been killed.[17]

Significantly, in many scholarly accounts, the idea of the "international refugee regime" erases Palestinians from discussions pertaining to refugees more generally.[18] This erasure means that the way Palestinian refugees experience the racial hierarchy of refugees often goes unnoticed. There are, of course, many displaced persons and refugees who suffer serious discrimination. The Palestinian refugee experience, however, is notably unique in its institutionalization in the United Nations, and in the associated longevity of historic injustice amplified by ongoing displacement. Palestinians, and Palestinian refugees specifically, have also been subjected to anti-Palestinian, anti-Arab, and anti-Muslim racism, where border regulations, state violence, and related stereotypes are institutionalized; moreover, these forms of racism have increased over time, particularly since 9/11.[19]

This chapter examines the racialization of Palestinian refugees in the context of Israel's colonization of Palestine. We argue that understanding the issues pertaining to refugees in the Israel/Palestine context would be advanced by considering displacement in relation to power and race and by attending to the role of states as a primary source of power in the global context. While, at times, some refugees are given solace and granted legal immigration status, at no point have refugees universally been treated equally to citizens, despite claims of universal human rights. Instead, states aggressively police their borders, sharply delineating insiders from outsiders and ensuring conditionalities on those permitted entry.[20] In our joint work as scholars drawing from the Palestinian (Abu-Laban) and Jewish (Bakan) diasporic and cultural experiences, we link issues of race to an analytic lens attentive to political, economic, and social power.

In our view, the racial hierarchy of refugees in the context of Israel/Palestine must start from the recognition that the Jewish population of Israel—and particularly the Ashkenazi, or European Jewish, population—has been constructed as more deserving of rights and privileges by complex and interacting racial processes. We understand Israel as a settler-colonial state[21] and as a state meeting the internationally recognized definition of apartheid under international law.[22] At the same time, in the Israeli state's foundational narrative and in the eyes of many power holders in Western countries, Israel presents itself as a state of refuge for the world's Jewish population, historically racialized by antisemitism (understood as anti-Jewish racism).[23] This allows discursive space for Israeli officials to reject the label of apartheid, even as racialized policies are aggressively advanced.

The invisibility of Palestinian refugees is consistent with the discrepancy between the demands of stateless Palestinians and the general rejection of those demands by powerful states. In illuminating and forwarding this argument, the chapter proceeds in three parts. First, we address the hierarchy of refugees in international law and politics and its impact on the epistemic framing of rights and justice in relation to Palestinian refugees. Second, we address how the right of return of Palestinian refugees has been curtailed by Israel's policy responses and an international system that fails to hold Israel accountable for refusing to allow the return of Palestinian refugees. Third, we consider how Israel's epistemic recognition of the rights of Jewish refugees fleeing Nazi persecution reveals the contradictions of an exclusivist relationship to European whiteness, where Ashkenazi Jews have been privy to a conditional whiteness while antisemitism remains an issue in the West. We conclude the chapter by briefly considering the implications of this comparative perspective.

## THE STATE OF ISRAEL'S RACIAL HIERARCHY OF REFUGEES

While Israel has defined its mission as a refuge for Jews persecuted due to antisemitism, it is a state built on Indigenous Palestinian land. It has been established through war and occupation, producing an international refugee population that is among the largest in the world and has experienced one of the longest periods of displacement.[24] The conditions that created the Palestinian refugee population date back to the 1948 Nakba and persist into the present time, as Jewish settlements continue to expand on Palestinian land occupied by Israel in 1967. The displacement of Palestinians following the 2023 war on Gaza has been extreme, extending this pattern into the twenty-first century. But in this case, there is also ample evidence that even the option to flee the territory and seek refuge has been eliminated in the face of continual military attacks, the limitation of food and water, the forced closure of borders, and the threat of starvation.[25] While the Nakba was a pivotal moment, the colonization of Palestine and the racism toward Palestinians did not begin in 1948. As Khalidi encapsulates: "The modern history of Palestine can best be understood in these terms: as a colonial war waged against the indigenous population, by a variety of parties, to force them to relinquish their homeland to another people against their will."[26]

These conditions of ethnic cleansing and forced displacement have rendered the Palestinian population racialized, stateless, and without the ability to return to their homes, despite repeated recognition of that right in international law.[27] Our analysis draws from and is inspired by Charles Mills's notion of the racial contract,[28] as well as the lived realities and experiences of Palestinian displacement.[29] From this vantage point, the concept of a global racial hierarchy of refugees—where Palestinians are denied not only rights but also the right to claim rights—refers to the widespread, unspoken, and hegemonic acceptance of white supremacy and the oppression of racialized minorities embedded in contemporary liberal discourse, policy, and practice. For Mills, the racial contract is a philosophical concept similar to the social contract. However, rather than positing equality among all people, the racial contract indicates how equality is applied only to those who count, or matter. When the concept of the racial contract is applied to specific national and international experiences, it sheds light on the painful normalcy of a hierarchy of differentiated rights among refugees.

Applied to Israel/Palestine, there are both international and local elements that sustain racial inequalities. Ashkenazi Jews have moved in an historically unprecedented shift in the West from a position, during World War II, of being the most despised to one of "whiteness by permission,"[30] while an anti-Arab racism against Palestinians has intensified. The international dimension of Israel/Palestine has transformed two refugee populations, Jews and Palestinians, in divergent ways since 1948, in a racialized process. In the context of international racism, Jewish refugees fleeing Nazi persecution were denied entry to all major Western countries before and during World War II. However, the establishment of the State of Israel in 1948 served to transform Ashkenazi (European) Jewish refugees and their descendants into the ideal settlers and citizens of a new state strategically located in the Middle East. Significantly, as Patrick Wolfe has argued, because the State of Israel was constructed as a space of "return," there was a "particularly rigorous settler colonialism that comprehensively excluded non-Jews," and therefore differed from other settler colonies in rejecting the colonial logic of Indigenous assimilation.[31]

The Ashkenazi Jewish population, which in Christian liberal democracies had historically been seen as disposable, now became sufficiently white as colonial settlers to become agents of the European displacement of Palestinians. As a political ideology and a movement for settlement, "really existing Zionism," a term used to refer to the present reality of Israel as a state based on Zionist political ideology,[32] was aided and supported by European and Western imperialism and racism. Given that Palestinians experienced settler colonization and dispossession in an age that also came to be identified with the "human rights revolution" following the 1948 Universal Declaration of Human Rights,[33] discussions of Israel and Palestine take place through exceptionally coded discursive racial claims. These coded claims draw upon material distortions,[34] biblical mythology,[35] and complex historical elisions and evasions.[36]

The failure of the United Nations to implement measures to support the rights of Palestinians is extensively documented over decades of investigations and reports.[37] The UNRWA exclusively provides assistance to 5.5 million registered Palestinian refugees.[38] The agency was launched in 1949, in the aftermath of the 1948 war, to attend to emergency relief for Palestinian refugees, replacing organizations such as the International Committee of the Red Cross, the League of Red Cross Societies, and the American Friends Service Committee.[39] The ongoing work of the UNRWA indicates the intractable condition of Palestinian refugees and the failure of the United Nations to enforce lasting policies for redress. Among various services, the organization assists refugees with access to health care and schooling and provides emergency response support to those further displaced by state violence, including Palestinian refugees in Syria affected by the ongoing civil war who have again been forced into displacement.

The lack of enforcement of the human rights of Palestinian refugees, and of other Palestinians, is rooted in Israel's investment in producing a racial hierarchy of refugees locally and internationally. The Palestinian right of return, as recognized in UN General Assembly Resolution 194, was a precondition of Israel's admission into the United Nations in May 1949, yet the resolution has never been enforced.[40] Instead, Israel has used violent measures to block the return of Palestinian refugees and further the project of settler colonization.[41] While the apartheid state of South Africa (1948–94), led by the National Party, offered an overt defense of white supremacy, all the major political parties in Israel insist on the state's unique "Jewish" character through a Zionist political discourse. This discourse asserts that Israel is representative of all Jews internationally, but in fact it stands for a specific and racial political project that denies Palestinian rights and claims and even denies the presence of Palestinians. As a political ideology, Zionism is the core foundational narrative and political structure of the Israeli state and is widely accepted among Israel's powerful global political allies. The assumption that the survival of Jewish refugees fleeing an antisemitic genocide—particularly during the period of Nazism in Europe—is dependent upon the existence of Israel as a Jewish state, and the dispossession of the Indigenous population of Palestine, leads to Palestinian refugees facing permanent exile and related inequities.

## PALESTINIANS AND THE HIERARCHY OF REFUGEES

There are multiple ways in which the racialized characteristics of the Israel/Palestine context play out in the question of Palestinian refugees. While refugee policies internationally are inherently racialized, delineating outsiders beyond the realm of citizenship in sovereign states, Palestinians face additional discriminatory patterns, indicated in UN structures and policies. The UNRWA's mandate intentionally excludes repatriation and is limited to service provision. These limitations are further reinforced by the fact that even with its functions narrowed to address only some critical services, the agency has been a lightning rod for ideological attacks. Well before the events of October 7, 2023, the UNRWA was accused of employing or benefiting "terrorists"; promoting hatred, in particular of Zionism, Israel, or Jews, in textbooks used in UNRWA schools; and inappropriately increasing the numbers of refugees eligible for services.[42] These attacks build on the racialized nature of the label "terrorist," which has been applied distinctly to Palestinians since the 1960s and more broadly to Arabs and Muslims since 9/11.[43] Not least, these charges fail to acknowledge that in any protracted refugee situation, "refugeehood" becomes intergenerational and reliance on international aid is cemented.[44]

It also must be noted that the UNRWA counts as "Palestine refugees" only those who have registered in jurisdictions where the organization operates.

For example, the BADIL Resource Center for Palestinian Residency and Refugee Rights observes that, of the 6.7 million 1948 refugees and their descendants, 5.5 million Palestinian refugees are overseen by the UNRWA, but another 1.16 million refugees were displaced in 1948 but are not eligible to apply for UNRWA assistance. In addition, there are 1.24 million 1967 Palestinian refugees and their descendants, 415,876 internally displaced Palestinians in Israel, and 344,599 internally displaced Palestinians in the Occupied Palestinian Territory.[45] Far from overrepresenting refugees and displaced Palestinians, the UNRWA's numbers are actually underrepresentative.

Nonetheless, ideological attacks have made the UNRWA—and, by extension, the Palestinian refugees it oversees—especially vulnerable to sudden withdrawals of funding, including from key donors. Former US president Donald Trump broke with all other post–World War II presidents when, in 2018, his administration withdrew aid to the UNRWA—aid that President Joe Biden restored.[46] In 2024, the United States again withdrew funding following Israel's accusations that UNRWA staff had participated in the October 7 attacks, this time with no indication that the funding would be restored before at least 2025.[47] There was and remains no evidence to support these accusations, even after extensive investigations.[48] Such unfounded claims of impropriety against the agency by the Israeli state, however, are not a recent invention. Efforts to discredit and dismantle the UNRWA date back to the earliest days of its establishment, as the UNRWA serves both to document and to humanize Palestinian refugees and also stands as a reminder of the UN-recognized right of return. Denial of such basic rights is long standing, and the UNRWA is the only refugee body that explicitly addresses Palestinians and their key needs.[49]

The relatively weak position of the UNRWA, the nature of the ideological attacks, and the ease with which some states have withdrawn funds from a vulnerable stateless population need to be seen in relation to the international Israel/Palestine racial contract, which renders Palestinians as nonwhites and subjects them to repression, oppression, and statelessness. However, these factors also need to be seen in relation to the role played by Israeli state policy and discourse in racializing, dehumanizing, and erasing Palestinian refugees. This has been achieved by what Nur Masalha[50] has aptly called a "politics of denial," which involves Israel's rejection and deflection of responsibility for the creation of Palestinian refugees and its continued denial of the right of return. In Masalha's words: "Since 1949 Israel has consistently . . . refused to accept responsibility for the refugees and views them as the responsibility of the Arab countries in which they reside."[51]

The continued permutations of the racial hierarchy of refugees mitigate just solutions to the Palestinian refugee issue in the current global configuration. This was evident, for example, in the US "deal of the century" released by Trump in January 2020.[52] That plan rejected outright any of the tenets of UN General Assembly Resolution 194, claiming that the UN endorsement of the Palestinian right of return has never been "realistic." This level of recurring global international refusal to enforce the Palestinian right of return is an example of institutionalized racialized violence. It draws on the continual Israeli reference to Palestinians as a "demographic threat," an overtly racialized discourse of erasure and exclusion.[53] Building on the work of Edward Said, Muhannad Ayyash notes how Israel's institutional structures produce "violences of expulsion [that] are 'over there,'" and, while persistent and endemic to the state and civil society, are also rendered invisible.[54]

## JEWISH SETTLEMENT AND THE RACIAL HIERARCHY OF REFUGEES

The racial hierarchy of refugees is further illuminated in the dramatic change of status of Ashkenazi Jews in Israel following the establishment of the state in 1948. While the West frames European Jews as "refugees fleeing the Nazis and the subsequent horrors of post-Holocaust Europe," as Joseph Massad notes, upon arrival in Palestine, these refugees became settlers and "armed colons committing massacres" in a manner consistent with settler colonialism in other countries.[55] In addition to taking part in the expulsion of Palestinians, "many Holocaust survivors were, as a matter of government policy, settled in evacuated Palestinian homes in Arab towns like Jaffa, Haifa, Lod and Ramla, thus forcibly grafting the memory of the Holocaust onto Palestinian national memory," as argued by Yosefa Loshitzky.[56] Even those who resisted complicity with the atrocities lived as part of this colonial project and "were normalized into its ranks."[57]

The State of Israel was and is imagined as a uniquely Western European enclave in the Middle East. The genocidal antisemitism cruelly expressed in the Nazi Holocaust is embedded in centuries of Western thought and practice in many states besides Germany.[58] While an extensive discussion of antisemitism goes beyond the scope of this chapter,[59] it is important to note that Jews in North America, the vast majority of whom are Ashkenazi, transitioned after World War II from a people despised—racialized as "less than white"[60] or "off-white"[61]—to one integrated into the dominant "Judeo-Christian" tradition. Moreover, as the Jewish population was gradually incorporated into citizenship in liberal Western democracies, Jews were no longer refugees. However, the idea of Israel as a state grounded in both refuge and return is central to the Zionist settler-colonial project. The Zionist ideology was of a suffering people whose survival depended upon constructing, as Wolfe summarizes, "a pre-existent Jewish nation that had been marking time in the wings of history pending reunion with its ancestral territory."[62] While Ashkenazi Jews moved from a place in the refugee hierarchy to a place of citizenship, they are still considered to have a kind of permanent refugee status with rights to Israeli citizenship—"a constant reminder of the 'refugee' status the dominant discourse has accorded them."[63] In short, the State of Israel's material interests and imperial links cannot be understood without considering the Zionist settler-colonial project, the related whitening of Ashkenazi Jews,[64] and the orientalist, anti-Muslim, and anti-Arab racialization of the Palestinian population.

Ideological tropes of the Israeli state, associated with its "really existing Zionism,"[65] are racialized and contradictory. Specifically, Israel defines itself not as a nation of citizens[66] but as the homeland of all the world's "Jews." With the emergence of the citizenship infrastructure of the Israeli state between 1948 and 1952, as Lana Tatour demonstrates, Jewish immigration from any country in the world was favored while Indigenous Palestinians were dispossessed and expelled.[67] In practice, Ashkenazi Jews have consistently been considered a privileged stratum among the Jewish settler citizenry, enjoying "greater political power, income, and occupational and educational attainment" than Jewish immigrants from non-European countries.[68] As Wolfe notes, the regulatory processes of who is, and who is not, considered to belong to the politically defined "Jewish" ethno-state also involve some specific epistemic constructions of Ashkenazi whiteness. This applies, for example, to Jews who are not actually arriving from outside but have epistemic privileges through the application of the Law of Return, ensuring that, in Israel,

> there could hardly be a clearer example of settler colonialism's replacement of Natives by immigrants. Under this foundational provision, the conferral of racial privilege on Palestine-born Jews was achieved by means of a poker-faced contrivance of converting them into honorary immigrants . . . "returning" to somewhere they had never left.[69]

Importantly, however, there is no evidence for the claim that this elite status of Ashkenazi Jews has solved, or even offered redress for, antisemitism internationally. Clearly, antisemitism continues to exist and has periodically been amplified in the post-1948 era. This is painfully exemplified in the armed attack that killed eleven and injured six at the Tree of Life synagogue in Pittsburgh in October 2018[70] and in the growth of white nationalism over the past decade. Moreover, discourses regarding redress or challenges to antisemitism—including Holocaust memory, antiracism, and solidarity— have commonly become confounded by Zionist assertions. The core claim of such a confounding is the dangerous and false equating of antisemitism with criticisms of Zionism and Israel's violation of human rights.[71]

Ashkenazi Jewish identity in Israel closely aligns with Christian and Western European hegemonic concepts of white supremacy.[72] Ashkenazi Jews hold a place closest to the Western construction of "whiteness"[73] within Israeli society, affording them a level of influence, power, and cultural capital. Even though demographic data analysis among Jews is skewed by an "ethos of unity that emphasizes shared ancestry of all Jews and their collective stake in the nation-building project,"[74] evidence shows that Arab and North African Jews—the Mizrahim (Hebrew for "Easterners")—have suffered from long-standing racial discrimination relative to Ashkenazi Jews.[75] Ashkenazi Jews, as opposed to other Jewish groups, enjoy exceptional epistemic privileging as almost permanent refugees, fostering a narrative of Israeli victimhood.

The 1990s witnessed a series of changes in the composition of the Israeli population that exposed the racial hierarchy between European and non-European Jews. Massive immigration from the former Soviet Union complicated the racial hierarchy dividing white European Israelis. Jewish migrants from the former Soviet Union, many of whom were not Jewish according to strict rabbinical interpretation (*halacha*), were welcomed to settle in Israel if they could show Jewish ancestry, following a 1991 amendment to the Law of Return.[76] Those who were non-Jewish "were admitted mainly because they were not Arabs and they were deemed as a demographic antidote to the Palestinian society inside and outside the 1967 border."[77] However, Russian and Eastern European settlers were soon othered by barriers associated with Hebrew language fluency and by an unstable relationship to national belonging, with Israel presented mainly as a means of exiting the former Soviet Union.[78] This added further differentiation around who was "Jewish," complicating the hierarchy among Israeli Jews.

Immigrants from the former Soviet Union and Ethiopia were welcomed, albeit in different ways, within a common racialized colonial logic where the "need to reduce the proportion of Palestinians trumped the desire to build an exclusively Jewish state."[79] The immigration of Ethiopian Jews to Israel also fed into existing racial hierarchies among Jews in Israel. While the Ethiopian Jewish community had anticipated being welcomed to Israel as a "Jewish state," as Black African Jews they faced racism, rejection, and impoverishment.[80] The presence of Ethiopian Jews, who first arrived in the mid-1970s but whose numbers dramatically increased in the 1990s, further revealed the anti-Blackness rooted in Zionism. The structural racism embedded in Israel as a settler-colonial state is also evident, for example, in the treatment of non-Jewish, primarily African, refugees seeking asylum in Israel. Strict controls on who is, or is not, allowed to enter are part of the racialized refugee regime. This extends to border controls generally, exemplified in the detention of over 13,000 Sudanese and Eritrean asylum seekers in Israel between 2013 and 2018.[81]

The epistemic primacy of Ashkenazi Jewish migration and settlement is an echo of the original foundational narrative of the State of Israel as a state of refuge for Jewish people facing genocide, particularly in Western and Eastern Europe, but also of an international refusal to welcome Jewish refugees seeking safe haven. By contrast, Palestinians, who are present-day displaced refugees, continue to be denied the right of return to their native land, demonstrating that anti-Palestinian racism is central to the Zionist and Israeli nation-building project. In fact, the racist anxiety regarding the "demographic threat" posed by Palestinians is persistent and has arguably increased over time. The seemingly permanent abandonment of Palestinian refugees by the international community underscores the epistemic and material relegation of Palestinians to the bottom of a racial hierarchy of refugees, especially notable in a state that has normatively embraced the image of a refugee homeland.

## CONCLUSION

As the genocide in Gaza confirms, the time has come to look at Israel, the question of Palestine, and refugees through a lens that focuses on racialized exclusion, power, and privilege. Naming the current assault on the Palestinian population of Gaza as genocide, and identifying the war crimes associated with the State of Israel, are important in this context, as the slaughter has continued under the eyes of both mainstream and social media without effect.[82] The concept of a hierarchy of refugees, suggested in this chapter, may go some distance toward advancing the thinking about refugees in Palestine and Israel and the racialization and denial of the rights of Palestinian refugees. Such analysis also demonstrates the highly inequitable reality that is a product of racialized structures, practices, and policies that demand analytic attention be paid to race and racism.

There is a mythic idea that Israel is a nation-state without international comparators, and this purported exceptionalism is advanced from several perspectives. Israeli state actors claim that Israel is a "Jewish" state, unique on the world stage. It is also a state lacking universally recognized borders, functioning more as a colonial outpost than a bordered territorial state. Furthermore, Israel claims to be distinctly "modern" and "democratic" in the Middle East region, while being simultaneously ideologically grounded in mythical biblical history.[83] However, it is important that the particularities of the State of Israel not be used to avoid comparison as there is much that Israel has in common with other settler-colonial and apartheid states.[84]

The claimed exceptionalism of Israel, however, has not been without consequences. Palestinian refugees have been treated as distinct in the global refugee regime, falling outside the UNHCR purview. Palestinian refugees are also commonly invisibilized in migration scholarship.[85] And, in the epistemic privileging of the Ashkenazi Jewish population, Palestinian refugees have been racialized through a coded language of false charges of antisemitism and security threats.

This exceptionalism is supported internationally as a system that continually reproduces Palestinian refugees while simultaneously abandoning claims to their right to return, relegating their basic needs to the UNRWA. But here, even minimal supports to Palestinian refugees are consistently threatened, a feature not confined to the 2023 war on Gaza. Consider that in 2019 Israel announced plans to close UNRWA-directed schools for Palestinian children in occupied East Jerusalem, a plan consistent with colonial claims that Palestinian East Jerusalem is part of Israel's undivided capital. In keeping with the invisibilization of Palestinian refugees, according to former Jerusalem mayor Nir Barkat: "There are no refugees in Jerusalem, only residents."[86]

*Seven*
# BLACK-PALESTINIAN SOLIDARITY AND THE GLOBAL COLOR LINE

MICHAEL R. FISCHBACH

ON FEBRUARY 4, 1899, THE ENGLISH POET RUDYARD KIPLING published his famous poem "The White Man's Burden," originally subtitled "The United States and the Philippine Islands." In it, he not only urged the United States to take over the Philippines and "serve your captives' need" but clearly delineated a global racial divide: a noble enlightened white world on one side, facing a much larger nonwhite world replete with "terror," "Sloth," and "Folly" and full of "silent, sullen peoples" on the other.[1] Almost exactly four years later, the Black American scholar W. E. B. Du Bois also referenced a racial divide in the world when, on February 1, 1903, he wrote that "the problem of the Twentieth Century is the problem of the color line."[2] Over five decades after that, Du Bois made it clear that this global color line divided the Middle East and that Israel and the Arab world lay at opposite ends of it. In a poem entitled "Suez," which he wrote in late 1956, after Britain, France, and Israel had invaded Egypt, he called the Israelis "the shock troops of two knaves / Who steal the dark men's land" and advised the West, "beware, white world, that great black hand / Which Nasser's power waves."[3]

Du Bois's racial analysis of the Arab-Israeli conflict was soon shared by many other American Blacks who not only situated themselves on the same side of the global color line as the Arabs, notably the Palestinians, but who also began publicly championing their cause and claiming it as their own. Beginning in the 1960s, Black Power activists in the United States based their transnational support for the Palestinians on a combination of revolutionary anti-imperialism and a sense of kindred peoples of color struggling together against a racialized system of global oppression. As such, they viewed Israel as the oppressor of the Palestinians and as an extension of the very force that was oppressing them—namely, racialized American imperialism.[4]

This chapter details Black Power support for the Palestinians as fellow people of color fighting for freedom during a tumultuous period of American history, the 1960s and 1970s. It pays attention to the explosion of Black American attacks on Israel and statements of solidarity with the Palestinian resistance movement following Israel's victory in the June 1967 war. It further examines how Blacks' understandings of the racial dimension of the Arab-Israeli conflict symbiotically affected their struggle at home, particularly in terms of how they suffered from the hostile reactions to their stances on the conflict emanating from whites, notably Jews. Finally, it notes how American Blacks' racialized understandings of power and oppression spread to the Middle East, where they impacted not so much the Palestinians but, perhaps ironically, Mizrahi Jewish activists in Israel. As self-described Black Israelis, they were demanding social and political power in a racialized power structure dominated by the Ashkenazi elite. They directly copied the language, tactics, and iconography of the American Black Power movement and formed the Israeli Black Panthers in 1971. The chapter concludes by noting that because Black support for the Palestinians continues to manifest itself decades later, in the United States and elsewhere, Israel advocates today are using the language of race and color to reshape Jews as "nonwhite" in order to deflect intersectional support for the Palestinians.

## BLACK POWER AND THE COLOR LINE

The figure who best articulated the transnational vision of Black American solidarity with Third World peoples and their struggles in the early 1960s was Malcolm X. Malcolm X was a trailblazer in the Black Power movement, which, in contrast to the civil rights movement, sought not mere integration with whites but instead real political, economic, and cultural power for American Blacks. Malcolm X analyzed the oppression of Blacks along not just racial lines but anticolonial lines as well. He considered African Americans an internal Black colony in the United States, stating in April 1964: "America is a colonial power. She has colonized 22 million Afro-Americans by depriving us of first-class citizenship, by depriving us of civil rights, actually by depriving us of human rights." To break free from their colonial status, Malcolm X called on Blacks to rise and be part and parcel of the wider anti-imperialist struggles then being waged by colonized peoples of color abroad. He noted:

> What happens to a black man in America today happens to the black man in Africa. What happens to a black man in America and Africa happens to the black man in Asia and to the man down in Latin America. What happens to one of us today happens to all of us. . . .
>
> 1964 will see the Negro revolt evolve and merge into the world-wide black revolution that has been taking place on this earth since 1945. The so-called revolt will become a real black revolution.[5]

Because Malcolm X viewed oppression overseas as an extension of the exploitation of Blacks in the United States, he felt that it was their duty to support Third World revolutions as part of their own struggle to be free—particularly because they were winning: "The dark people are waking up. They're losing their fear of the white man. No place where he's fighting right now is he winning. Everywhere he's fighting, he's fighting someone your and my complexion."[6]

It is important to note that Malcolm X's vision of a Black revolution was not based on a literal phenotype of Blackness. He stated that this revolution included all peoples on one side of the color line who had been colonized by the white West: "When I say black, I mean non-white—black, brown, red or yellow."[7] This definition included Arabs: "The people of Arabia are just like our people in America," Malcolm X wrote in 1959. "None are white. It is safe to say that 99 per cent of them would be jim-crowed in the United States of America."[8] Malcolm X particularly identified with the Palestinians' struggle against Israel. He argued that "the Jews, with the help of Christians in America and Europe, drove our Muslim brothers ... out of their homeland, where they had been settled for centuries, and took over the land for themselves."[9] He was moved to visit Palestine twice, once for a brief trip to East Jerusalem in July 1959 and a second time for a two-day stay in Gaza in September 1964. Also in 1964, he met Palestinian leaders such as the preeminent politician of the pre-1948 era, al-Hajj Amin al-Husayni, and Ahmad Shuqayri, chair of the newly established Palestine Liberation Organization (PLO). Shortly after meeting the latter at a PLO press conference in Cairo in September 1964, Malcolm X published "Zionist Logic," a harsh critique of Israel and Zionism, in an English-language Egyptian newspaper. In that essay, he wrote:

> These Israeli Zionists religiously believe their Jewish God has chosen them to replace the outdated European colonialism with a new form of colonialism. ....
>
> Did the Zionists have the legal or moral right to invade Arab Palestine, uproot its Arab citizens from their homes and seize all Arab property for themselves just based on the "religious" claim that their forefathers lived there thousands of years ago?[10]

Malcolm X was murdered in February 1965, but his support for the Palestinians lived on. Indeed, Black Power stances on the Palestinian struggle skyrocketed into public consciousness in the United States shortly after Israel's victory in the June 1967 Arab-Israeli War, when the Student Nonviolent Coordinating Committee (SNCC) roundly condemned Israel.

## BLACK SUPPORT FOR PALESTINE
Established in 1960, SNCC developed from a civil rights group into a Black Power organization in 1966, when it was headed by the Trinidad-born Stokely Carmichael. Carmichael and other SNCC activists had read not only Malcolm X, but other Black nationalists—such as the Martinican intellectual Frantz Fanon—as well. Like Malcolm X, Fanon supported Arab liberation struggles. He wrote of "negroes and Arabs" fighting together and called on American Blacks to decolonize their minds and assert their Black identity—what his fellow Martinican writer Aimé Césaire earlier had called "négritude"—in the way that Arabs were doing: "The poets of negritude will not stop at the

limits of the continent. From America, black voices will take up the hymn with fuller unison. . . . The example of the Arab world might equally well be quoted here."[11]

Carmichael and other SNCC activists, such as Ethel Minor and H. Rap Brown, were well aware of Arab and Palestinian struggles, even forming a book club in Alabama in the mid-1960s in order to read one book a month on Israel and the Palestinians.[12] Leading SNCC figure James Forman also knew about the Middle East, writing as the 1967 war was underway that "actually Israel represents an extension of United States foreign policy as well as an attempt by the Zionists to create a homeland for the Jews."[13]

It was two months after Israel's victory in the 1967 war that SNCC's stance on the Arab-Israeli conflict was made public, when an article Minor wrote appeared in August in the *SNCC Newsletter*. Besides harshly attacking Zionism for "sending Jewish immigrants from Europe into Palestine (the heart of the Arab world) to take over land and homes belonging to the Arabs," the article voiced SNCC transnationalism by linking American Blacks to the Palestinians and others on the one side of the global color line. Blacks were "an integral part of the Third World" who deserved to know what "our brothers are doing in their homelands."[14] Several weeks later, another SNCC publication proclaimed that "SNCC clearly supports the revolutionary aspirations of the Third World: and Israel, as characterized by the actions of its statesmen and military men, is opposed to these aspirations."[15]

Although SNCC's fortunes waned after 1967, figures who had been associated with it maintained their support for the Palestinian cause. Carmichael continued to view Israel's struggle with the Palestinians in racial terms. He traveled to Egypt and Syria in September 1967 and, in the latter, visited a Palestinian refugee camp. While touring there, he was accompanied by Randa Khalidi al-Fattal, a Lebanese-Palestinian scholar and writer who worked with the Arab League's Arab Information Office in New York. Expanding on his belief that Blacks and Palestinians stood on the same side of the global color line, Carmichael jokingly told al-Fattal—whose complexion was very fair—"Sister Randa, you don't know it, but you are blacker than I am."[16] In December 1968, he emphasized this again when he said: "It is important because the so-called State of Israel was set up by white people who took it from the Arabs."[17] Earlier that year, he asserted the commonality of the Palestinian and Black struggle when he proclaimed:

> Now we in this country, as a gesture of solidarity with our brothers in the Arab world, intend to deal with the Zionists for several reasons. *One reason is, the same Zionists that exploit the Arabs also exploit us in this country. That is a fact. And that is not anti-Semitic. . . .*
>
> Our eyes are now open: we have begun to see this trickery of Zionism; we have begun to see the evil of Zionism, and we will fight to wipe it out wherever it exists, in the Middle East or in the ghetto of the United States.[18]

Finally, Carmichael's racial worldview affected his view of Israel's conflict with other Arab states as well. Addressing a rally in February 1968, he implored Blacks to make the particular link between Israeli attacks on Egypt and their own African heritage: "Not only that: [Zionists are] moving to take over Egypt. Egypt is our Motherland—it's in Africa! . . . Egypt belongs to us."[19]

Expressions of support from SNCC activists for the Palestinians as a people of color similarly fighting against racism were some of the first to emerge publicly within the Black Power movement, but they were not the only ones. Others also saw the racial dimensions of the Arab-Israeli conflict and viewed themselves and the Palestinians as standing on the same side of Du Bois's global color divide. The third National Conference on Black Power, held in Philadelphia in late August and early September 1968, for example, produced a minority report describing Zionism as a racist threat not only to Palestinians but to Black Americans as well. It stated: "The Black Power Conference recognizes that the Zionist Movement is a threat to the internal and external security of the Black people in America and in Africa. It is further recognized that the Zionist ideology is a force for colonialism, racism, and western imperialism, therefore, a threat to world peace."[20]

In November 1970, a group called the Committee of Black Americans for Truth about the Middle East placed an advertisement in the *New York Times* in response to an earlier advertisement in the same paper by a group of pro-Israeli Blacks. Called "An Appeal by Black Americans against United

States Support of the Zionist Government of Israel," it too denounced imperialism and invoked the global color line:

> We, the Black American signatories of this advertisement, are in complete solidarity with our Palestinian brothers and sisters, who like us, are struggling for self-determination and an end to racist oppression. . . .
> Zionism is a reactionary racist ideology that justifies the expulsion of the Palestinian people from their homes and lands. . . .
> WE STATE that Israel, Rhodesia, and South Africa are three privileged white settler-states that came into existence by displacing indigenous peoples from their lands.[21]

Fifty-six individuals signed the advertisement.

Building on the legacy of Malcolm X and SNCC, the Black Panther Party (BPP) became the force within the Black Power movement that exerted the greatest efforts in the late 1960s and early 1970s to support and publicize the Palestinian struggle as part of a global fight against racialized imperialism.

## ARMED STRUGGLE

The BPP emerged in October 1966 as an armed self-defense force to protect the Black community of Oakland, California, yet it also developed a sophisticated revolutionary ideology that put it on the same side of the global color line as the Palestinians. The BPP minister of information, Eldridge Cleaver, noted, in 1968, that

> the link between America's undercover support of colonialism abroad and the bondage of the Negro at home becomes increasingly clear. Those who are primarily concerned with improving the Negro's condition recognize, as do proponents of the liquidation of America's neo-colonial network, that their fight is one and the same. . . .
> It is at this point, at the juncture of foreign policy and domestic policy, that the Negro revolution becomes one with the world revolution.[22]

The Panthers' conceptualization of the interconnectedness between their struggle against racism and that of the Palestinians became a theme that they often stressed. A torrent of stories about the Palestinian struggle appeared in the BPP's newspaper, the *Black Panther*. Indeed, of the forty-three issues of the paper that appeared from June 1, 1969, to March 28, 1970, alone, the party ran thirty-three articles or other items supporting the Arabs and/or attacking Israel.[23] The BPP minister of education, Raymond "Masai" Hewitt, made clear that the Palestinian struggle mirrored that of US Blacks and that both struggles were part of a wider global conflict against racism and imperialism. In August 1969, he stated: "We recognize that our oppression takes different forms—Zionism in Palestine and fascism here in America—but the cause is the same: it's US imperialism."[24] In February 1970, the *Black Panther* quoted the BPP chief of staff, David Hilliard: "We want to make it very clear that we support all those who are actively engaged in the struggle against US Imperialism and Zionism, which means to us racial supremacy."[25] In September 1970, the BPP's international section in Algiers, where Cleaver and some other Panthers were living in exile, issued a statement noting: "The struggle of the Palestinian people for their freedom and liberation from US imperialism and its lackeys is also our struggle. We recognize that if the Palestinian people cannot get their freedom and liberation, neither can we."[26]

For their part, Palestinian guerrilla groups like Fatah encouraged the feeling of international solidarity between Palestinians and Blacks, including those in the BPP. Even though Fatah was not an African organization, its cadre were present at the July 1969 Pan-African Cultural Festival in Algiers, which was attended by Hilliard; Cleaver and his wife, Kathleen Neal Cleaver; and the BPP minister of culture, Emory Douglas. Fatah representatives made a statement that they also printed as an English-language pamphlet titled *To Our African Brothers*. The statement linked the Palestinians with Africa by asserting that even though the Palestinians and their struggle were not part of "Africa the continent," they *were* part of "Africa the cause." There was a *geographic* map of the world, Fatah asserted, that showed the divide between racism, colonialism, and repression versus revolution, rebellion, and freedom.[27] A few months later, the *Black Panther* quoted Yassir Arafat, chair of both Fatah and the PLO, saying: "The Palestinian Liberation Movement considers itself a part of the people's struggle against international imperialism. We are fighting the same enemy. The mask may differ, but the face remains the same."[28] The Palestinians also understood the global color line.

## ONE STRUGGLE, MANY FRONTS

The embrace by Black Power advocates of the racial dimension of the Arab-Israeli conflict symbiotically affected their struggle at home. Activists suffered from the hostile reactions to their stances on the conflict that emanated from whites, notably Jews. Jews had been prominent among white supporters of the civil rights movement, and many of them were stunned and angry to see Blacks denounce Israel and champion the Palestinians. Vociferous attacks were levied against SNCC, the BPP, and others for denouncing Israel as racist and for embracing the Palestinian struggle. For example, in 1969, Jay Kaufman, executive vice president of B'nai B'rith,[29] dismissed transnational Black American Third Worldism as thinly disguised antiwhite, anti-Jewish racism, ironically agreeing with Du Bois's notion of an international color line:

> Black racists . . . augment this age-old brand of anti-Semitism with a new "Third World" ideology which is essentially a pitting of the black against the white world, a code word for the world of color's racist hatred of whites. . . . They have gone further and successfully depicted the white Arab people as blacks and the Israelis as oppressive whites.[30]

Reactions like these further convinced Black Power militants that their analyses were correct: that they and the Palestinians stood on the same side of the global color line, and both were fighting against the same enemy: racialized American imperialism and its allies—in this case, Israel. This, in turn, stiffened the resolve of Black Power activists in SNCC, the BPP, and other groups to take stances against Israel and its American supporters because the struggle was the same. Decades later, SNCC activist Courtland Cox noted: "Palestine was another example of what was happening to us. It was happening to us, and it was the same people involved in our oppression who were involved in their oppression over there. People saw people in like situations."[31]

The negative reaction that Black Power advocates received from whites—even liberal and radical allies—also convinced many that whites cynically thought that Blacks were welcome to talk about domestic race relations at home but not to take stances on foreign policy issues like the Arab-Israeli conflict. For example, a few months after the newsletter article attacking Israel had generated harsh criticism, another SNCC publication reasserted that Blacks and Israel and its supporters stood on opposite sides of the global color line: "SNCC clearly supports the revolutionary aspirations of the Third World: and Israel, as characterized by the actions of its statesmen and military men, is opposed to these aspirations."[32] SNCC figures challenged white allies to check their privilege at the door. In speaking of liberal Jews in particular, an article in the September–October 1967 issue of the *SNCC Newsletter* conceded that SNCC's liberal Jewish allies could not be expected to back SNCC's stance alongside Third World revolutionaries like the Palestinians: "Perhaps we have taken the liberal Jewish community or certain segments of it as far as it can go. . . . Our message to conscious people everywhere is 'Don't get caught on the wrong side of the revolution.'"[33]

The BPP also stridently defended itself after receiving criticism from white comrades in the New Left, including some in Students for a Democratic Society (SDS) over its attacks on Israel. To the Panthers, this smacked of racism: whites telling Blacks who their friends and allies should be. Masai Hewitt bristled in response. He noted, in August 1969, that "the white left gets uptight because we dig Al Fatah."[34] At about the same time, David Hilliard attacked what he called "little bourgeois, snooty nose motherfucking S.D.S.'s" and complained that "we don't see S.D.S. as being so revolutionary. . . . S.D.S. had better get their politics straight." For his part, BPP chairman Bobby Seale asserted: "We want to make it clear to all the S.D.S.'s . . . that we have a mind of our own, and yes we support Al-Fath [*sic*] in the Palestinian struggle. And that we make our decisions, and we support who we want to support, and that we're here to make revolution."[35] BPP international coordinator Connie Matthews was even blunter, pointing out that Jews were prominent among those leftists who criticized the Panthers over their stance on the Middle East:

> The White Left in the U.S.A. is comprised of a large percentage of the Jewish population. . . . However, since our stand [on the Arab-Israeli conflict] the White Left started floundering and became undecided. This leaves us with no alternative than to believe that a large portion of these people are Zionists and are therefore racists.[36]

The Black Panthers also used Palestinian-themed art and sloganeering not only to generate support for the Palestinians but also to bolster the domestic revolutionary image they were creating for themselves as armed revolutionaries. They were not alone in using the arts to create a new Black culture, or to link Black aspirations with those of the Palestinians. They were Black men and women of letters.

## THE LANGUAGE OF LIBERATION

The Black Arts Movement has been described as the cultural wing of the Black Power movement and refers to a series of persons and cultural fora that witnessed a new expression of Black pride and cultural production in the 1960s. One of its pioneers was Harold Cruse, who, like political Black Power militants, also understood the Zionist movement that created Israel out of a predominantly Arab part of the Middle East as an example of white European colonialism. "The European experience also shows that European imperialism was not exclusively a Christian affair," he wrote in 1967. "Witness the international machinations that brought about the State of Israel."[37] He, too, saw the transnational connection between American Blacks and the Arab-Israeli conflict: "Black Nationalism, Zionism, African affairs, and Negro Civil Rights organizations are intimately interlocked on the political, cultural, economic and international fronts, whether Negro intellectuals care to acknowledge it or not."[38]

Amiri Baraka (born Everett LeRoi Jones) was another pioneering figure in the Black Arts Movement. An activist as well as a poet, Baraka frequently denounced Zionism as a form of racism and colonialism. So did Askia Muhammad Touré, another poet who linked the Black struggle with that of the Palestinians. In 1970, he wrote a poem that specifically compared the Black struggle against racism in Harlem with that being waged by Palestinian guerrillas:

> Black, Brown, Red, Yellow Brothers starving
>     in the streets of Calcutta, dying on
>     the reservations, nodding in the Harlems,
>     napalmed in Vietnam, or marching with
>     the people's armies down the streets
>     of PEKING/GUINEA/TANZANIA/PALESTINE GUERILLA [sic]
>     armies marching. . . .[39]

Finally, Don Lee, who later adopted the name Haki R. Madhubuti, wrote a poem that same year dedicated to the famous Palestinian poet

Mahmud Darwish. In that poem, he evoked the commonality of the exile of Palestinian refugees and that faced by American Blacks who had been wrenched from Africa. Part of the poem noted, "Our enemies eat the same bread."[40]

Those in the Black Arts Movement were not the only Black writers to understand the racial context of the Palestinian fight with Israel. So too did intellectuals and journalists. W. E. B. Du Bois's widow, Shirley Graham Du Bois, applied her late husband's color line to the Arab-Israeli conflict in a fiery article published in the influential journal the *Black Scholar* the month after the 1973 Arab-Israeli War. Graham Du Bois clearly viewed Israel's struggle with Egypt and the Arabs in racial terms: "It is 'colored folk' battling with the 'white folk' of Israel! . . . Surrounded as they are by an ocean of suntanned peoples, Israel has repeatedly, defiantly and arrogantly asserted its superior 'whiteness.' . . . Nobody was allowed to forget that the State of Israel belonged to the dominant, 'enlightened' *white* world."[41] Continuing, she hailed the pan-African support extended to Egypt during the war, writing that Israel and other "white folks" were surprised that all of Africa stood up and stood by their fellow African state:

> Israel had no idea that when Egypt's Anwar el Sadat lifted his hand sig-
> naling, *now is the time* and dark-skinned troops crossed to the occupied
> east bank of the Suez Canal throwing themselves against the "invincible"
> invaders, with their mighty US armaments, dug deep in African soil—no
> white folks dreamed that all Africa would get the message and line up! . . .
> He knew thtt [sic] the world's majority peoples were behind him—that
> dark-skinned majority ingenuously referred to as the Third World.[42]

The celebrated author James Baldwin also linked the Black freedom struggle with Western colonialism and the conflict in the Middle East. He visited Israel in 1961 and, nine years later, referred to *The Fire Next Time*, his famous 1963 book about race in America, when he said: "But to me it was obvious why the Western world created the state of Israel. . . . They created the state as a European pawn." Baldwin added, "I don't believe they [Zionists] had the right, after 3,000 years, to reclaim the land with Western bombs and guns on biblical injunction. When I was in Israel it was as though I was in the middle of *The Fire Next Time*."[43]

Black Power's transnational linkage with the Palestinian cause was part of what Malcolm X had called a "world-wide black revolution." Indeed, there was a significant cross-cultural mixing of ideas and information among people who found themselves on the same side of the color line during what some have called the "Global 1960s." A fascinating aspect of this is that Black American stances on Israel and Palestine played a symbiotic role; they not only mirrored and amplified their own attitudes toward race and identity but also affected Middle Easterners' own concepts of Blackness. The best example of this was the emergence of the Israeli Black Panthers.

## BLACK POWER IN ISRAEL

American Blacks' racialized understanding of power and oppression spread to Israel, where self-identified "Black" Jewish activists demanding social and political power vis-à-vis the "white" ruling elite directly copied the name and tactics of Black Panthers to form the Israeli Black Panthers in 1971. Zionism developed and grew as a movement of Ashkenazi (Central and Eastern European) Jews, who created and later ruled Israel along European political and sociocultural lines. During and after 1948, Israel absorbed large numbers of Mizrahi Jews of color from the Middle East and North Africa, who often faced discrimination.

Indeed, Ashkenazim looked down on these Jews as primitive and derided what they called their "Arab," "Levantine," and "Third World" way of living.[44] At times, they overtly racialized these sentiments: some Ashkenazi Jews called the new immigrants *shvartze hayes*—Yiddish for "black animals."[45] Israel's first prime minister, David Ben-Gurion, compared them to the Africans brought to America as slaves.[46] Henriette Dahan Kalev has written that "the Ashkenazi (East Europeans) have set up white skin tone as the 'zero point of reference'" in a post-1948 Israel marked by a "skin tone discourse [that] was still implicit but potent."[47] Orna Sasson-Levy has noted that "among the Jewish population of Israel, however, the social category of 'Ashkenaziness' can be deemed white, as it has many features in common with whiteness in the United States: both categories are associated with European ancestry [and] both are identified with power structures."[48] In this sense, whiteness is a "tangible good" that is "malleable and functions as a gateway to other forms of ownership, privileges, and access."[49]

The founders of the Israeli Black Panthers—such as the Moroccan immigrants Charlie Biton, Robert Reuven Abergel, and Sa'adya Marciano, and
the Iraqi-born Kochavi Shemesh—tapped into the discontent felt by many
Mizrahi Jews and expressed it back to the Ashkenazi elite in racial terms,
images, and actions directly copied from their American namesakes. "We
hunted around for a name which would attract attention, which would help
to get our problem into the headlines," Shemesh said. "We have no connection with them [the BPP]. But the name caused a stir, and that is what we
wanted."[50] They shared the American Black Power movement's idiom of
dispossession and rebellion: "The Blacks are being screwed," "white power,"
"masters and slaves," "police state," "brothers," "equal rights," and other slo-
gans.[51] They called the Musrara neighborhood in Jerusalem, where many of
them lived, "Harlem," employed the clenched-fist image made famous by
American Blacks, and staged spirited demonstrations in Jerusalem and elsewhere for several years, starting in early 1971.

The Israeli Black Panthers demanded economic and social justice for
Mizrahim. They absorbed left-wing ideological formulations from, among
others, activists from groups such as SIAH (the Israeli New Left) and the anti-Zionist Matzpen, and even criticized Zionism as something that had not
solved the problems in their lives as it seemed to have done for Ashkenazi
immigrants from Europe. Yet, for all their criticisms of Israeli society and
government, they never really broke with Zionism, speaking of "social revolution" more than the revolutionary transformation of Israel.[52] Some, like
Marciano, even entered electoral politics in 1973, a move opposed by Abergel
and other Panthers.

Like the American Panthers, some Israeli Black Panthers saw themselves on the same side of the color line as the Palestinians and spoke of
joint action with them. At a gathering in April 1972, Shemesh articulated
the Israeli Panthers' vision of a new society built in cooperation with the
Palestinians:

> We intend to initiate in this country a social revolution. . . . We must
> reach a situation in which we shall fight together with the "fucking"
> Arabs against the establishment. We are the only ones who can consti-
> tute a bridge of peace with the Arabs in the context of a struggle against
> the establishment.[53]

In a country whose dominant ideology was the unity of the Jewish people, many Israelis were astonished to see self-described Black Jews in Israel identifying more with American Blacks than with Ashkenazi American or Israeli Jews—as well as identifying more with the Palestinians than with them. "Reality shows, at least to me, that there is no difference between the Arabs and me," Shemesh stated. "The only difference is in the religious origins."[54]

## RACE AND IDENTITY IN TWENTY-FIRST-CENTURY ISRAEL

The Black Power movement in the United States had largely disappeared by the end of the 1970s, a victim of factors such as changing times and state repression. Yet the example it set continues to affect Black Americans' support for the Palestinians, which has continued to grow—notably, in the first two decades of the twenty-first century. This coincides with the rise of a global discourse of a powerful colonial Israel oppressing a weaker colonized people of color, the Palestinians. This more recent phenomenon has been the result of several factors, including the collapse of the Israeli-Palestinian peace process; the rise of the Boycott, Divestment, Sanctions movement in 2005; periodic Israeli assaults on Gaza; and the 2018 Israeli Nation-State Law, which codified Israel as the nation-state of the Jewish people.

Alongside those factors was the rise of the Black Lives Matter (BLM) movement in the United States in the wake of the August 2014 shooting of Michael Brown, a young Black man killed by a white police officer in the town of Ferguson, Missouri. Palestinian and BLM activists began visiting one another thereafter, comparing notes on how people of color could resist the powerful security forces that attacked them during protests. More than 1,100 people signed the 2015 Black Solidarity Statement on Palestine, among them noted activist Angela Davis.[55] The discourse of intersectionality has provided some theoretical underpinnings for BLM and other marginalized groups that are drawn to the Palestinian cause, leading to rising intersectional support for the Palestinians—not just from Blacks but also from LGBTQ people, women, Indigenous peoples, and others. The 2016 election of Donald Trump accelerated this growing coalition against racism, sexism, imperialism, homophobia, and Islamophobia. This was exemplified by the fact that Linda Sarsour, a Palestinian-American activist, was one of the two cochairs of the 2017 Women's March—a demonstration against Trump's inauguration that has been described as the largest one-day protest in American history.

Israel advocates were alarmed at this growing intersectional global solidarity with the Palestinians as an oppressed people. Two nongovernmental organizations, the Reut Group based in Israel and the Anti-Defamation League based in the United States, issued a report in 2010 that laid Israel's image problem—the perception that it is a powerful state oppressing a weaker people of color—at the feet of intersectionality, which it saw as part of a campaign to delegitimize Israel: "Because of a discourse of intersectionality, the delegitimization movement has successfully been able to frame the Palestinian struggle against Israel as part of the struggle of other disempowered minorities, such as African-Americans and the LGBTQ community."[56] Israel advocates began fighting back against this phenomenon. One way was to drum up public Black support for Israel in the United States. In 2013, Dumisani Washington, a Black American Christian clergyman, founded a strongly pro-Israel group called the Institute for Black Solidarity with Israel. He was also active with the powerful evangelical group Christians United for Israel, serving as its "diversity outreach coordinator."

Another way Israel advocates have fought against intersectional support for the Palestinians has been by attempting to rebrand the country: changing the perception of Israelis as powerful, privileged white oppressors and portraying them instead in a more sympathetic way, one worthy of intersectional support from progressive activists. This has included global public relations efforts to define Israeli Jews, both Ashkenazi and Mizrahi, as not white but "of color," albeit in different ways.[57] As David Schraub has noted, by "contesting their Whiteness," some Jews felt that they could help "elide Jewish enjoyment of White privilege."[58]

One of the leading voices in this effort at colorizing Jews has been Hen Mazzig, an Israeli Jew who is quick to point out his own Middle Eastern and North African Jewish heritage as proof that he is nonwhite. In 2019, he wrote:

> Along with resurgent identity politics in the United States and Europe, there is a growing inclination to frame the Israeli-Palestinian conflict in terms of race. According to this narrative, Israel was established as a refuge for oppressed white European Jews who in turn became oppressors of people of color, the Palestinians.[59]

Mazzig therefore excoriated pro-Palestinian Black American activists like Tamika Mallory and Marc Lamont Hill, claiming: "I believe their misrepresentations are part of a strategic campaign to taint Israel as an extension of privileged and powerful white Europe, thereby justifying any and all attacks on it."[60]

This campaign is ongoing and is likely to fail, even among Jews themselves. Identifications by color are not permanent, and self-definitions often involve negotiations over social and political currency. One of the pioneers in the field of whiteness studies, Ruth Frankenberg, expressed this succinctly by noting: "Whiteness changes over time and space and is in no way a transhistorical essence. . . . It is a complexly constructed product of local, regional, national, and global relations, past and present."[61] Not all Israeli Jews, therefore, are likely to accept the new colorized vision of Jewishness. Mizrahim, in particular, may object to this new colorizing discourse positing that Ashkenazim are not white. For decades, they have felt like second-class citizens of color in a white Ashkenazi-dominated society. Watching Ashkenazi Jews suddenly claiming to be of color no doubt will strike them as an example of white privilege: using the privilege of being part of a white power structure to deny being part of that very structure. Others, however, have been outspoken in insisting that Israeli Jews *are*, in fact, white. In June 2012, Interior Minister Eli Yishai—who, ironically, is Mizrahi, of Tunisian heritage—complained about the influx of Black Muslim African migrants into Israel by stating, "Muslims that arrive here do not even believe that this country belongs to us, to the white man."[62]

### CONCLUSION

Notions of race, color, identity, and oppression that emerged in the 1960s and 1970s among Black Americans, notions that led them to side with the Palestinians, still factor into how they and other actors around the world view the Arab-Israeli conflict. While certainly bolstered by anti-imperialist and anti-capitalist theoretical underpinnings, the idea that they and the Palestinians are standing together on one side of the color line—a line separating the oppressed on one side from an armed, global gated community of privilege on the other—continues to animate the support given by Black Americans, and others, to the Palestinian cause.

Nowhere has this been better seen in the twenty-first century than through the vocal support of African Americans for the Palestinians in Gaza who were subject to Israel's devastating, brutal war that began in October 2023. Blacks were prominent among pro-Palestinian demonstrations at universities and elsewhere in the United States and some directly linked their participation with the BLM movement. One commentator noted: "It's bringing about a kind [of] solidarity that I don't think we've seen since the George Floyd demonstrations"[63] (Floyd was a Black man killed by a police officer kneeling on his neck in Minneapolis in May 2020). For her part, Cori Bush, a Black Democratic Party member of the House of Representatives, told her colleagues in Congress shortly after the Gaza war started: "Let me be clear: The collective punishment of Palestinians in Gaza is a war crime."[64] The Movement for Black Lives issued a statement proclaiming:

> For people of African descent in the global diaspora, the scars of colonization, occupation, and racial terror are etched deep. However, it is not our suffering that binds us to the Palestinian people, but the spirit and will to remain resilient in the face of brutality. Our history compels us to act. We will not remain silent in the face of this full military assault against Gaza. Hear us now: End the occupation of Palestine, and the violent harassment and blacklisting of allies who believe that Palestinians deserve true freedom.[65]

Nor was it just students and politicians who expressed public support for beleaguered Palestinians in Gaza. Religious figures like the Reverend Stephen A. Green, founder of Faith for Black Lives, did as well. He organized a "Peace Pilgrimage" from Philadelphia to Washington, DC, in February 2024. Green later stated:

> We walked 150 miles to push the Biden administration to demand a ceasefire to protect the lives of all precious Palestinians and to pursue the beloved community. The Black prophetic tradition calls me to do justice, love mercy and walk humbly with God as we speak out against genocide, occupation and war.[66]

Black support for Palestine in the United States is ongoing and shows no sign of waning, particularly as Generation Z and Generation Alpha youth mature into adults and begin to alter American politics. As the song goes, "For the times they are a-changin.'"[67]

*Eight*

# RACIAL CAPITALISM AND MILITARIZED ACCUMULATION

KIERON TURNER

IN JANUARY 2022, AFTER EIGHTEEN MONTHS OF SUSTAINED DIRECT action and local community mobilization, Elbit Systems UK declared that it was restructuring its company strategy in Britain and had sold its subsidiary, Ferranti Technologies, which was based in Oldham, a small town outside Manchester. Elbit is an Israeli private arms and drone manufacturer that has gained international recognition as a pioneer in "combat proven" military technologies, tested on Palestinians. It is the main supplier of drones, weapons, and military technologies to Israel. The development was in response to a campaign led by the British-based network Palestine Action—a group committed to the Palestinian people's struggle for liberation that has been active since the summer of 2020—against Elbit and its production sites and offices across Britain. The campaign is based on direct action activism, including activists occupying and blockading Elbit's factories, throwing red paint on factory windows and walls, disrupting the company's production of specialist military technologies for Israel's fleet of combat drones, and holding weekly community protests. Sustained protest made Elbit's operations untenable and led the company to shut down the Oldham factory.[1] To date (January 2025), Palestine Action has targeted Elbit's sites across the country hundreds of times, preventing the production of military technologies for more than one hundred days during 2021 and costing the company millions of pounds in damages. The sale of the Oldham site marked the first major victory for the group's efforts to end Britain's complicity with Israeli settler colonialism and apartheid. This achievement provides momentum to Palestine Action's ongoing national campaign against Elbit and charts new pathways for the Palestinian Boycott, Divestment, Sanctions (BDS) movement by articulating the struggle against settler colonialism in Palestine as also a struggle against global racial capitalism, a system that facilitates and sustains settler colonization.

The case of Elbit Systems reveals the close entwinement of settler colonialism and racial capitalism, which remains significantly understudied in the Palestinian case. Work on racial capitalism has articulated the histories of capitalist social and economic relations as racial histories by which racial regimes are constructed both to rationalize domination and to reproduce capitalist accumulation patterns through processes of racial differentiation.[2] As put by Cedric Robinson, racial capitalism works "not to homogenize but to differentiate."[3] These processes of differentiation include the making of differentiated forms of labor, classes, and populations, designating some populations as sufficiently "productive" to be integrated into capitalist labor regimes while relegating other populations as "surplus." Racialization is central to processes of differentiation.[4] Racial capitalist production and reproduction include multiple relations of accumulation, both free and unfree forms of exploitation, and modes of dispossession and elimination in the sourcing of new capital, markets, and political technologies to pacify dominated populations and classes.[5]

In the context of Palestine, Andy Clarno argues, racial capitalism is inseparable from, and intertwined with, settler colonialism. According to Clarno, "at the core of the concept of racial capitalism is the recognition that racialization and capital accumulation are mutually constitutive processes that combine in dynamic, context-specific formations."[6] Accordingly, Israeli settler colonialism and apartheid ought to be theorized in the context of specific formations of racial capitalism in Palestine, wherein Palestinians are racialized as inferior, exploitable, and dispensable. Settler colonialism is a system of domination that is premised on the exploitation of Indigenous peoples while maintaining elimination as the primary goal.[7] Elimination and exploitation are both central to the Israeli settler-colonial economy, whereby Palestinians are seen as dispensable but, at the same time, are instrumental to Israel's ability to globally market its weapons as "combat tested" to client states and militaries.[8]

This chapter examines Zionist settler colonialism in Palestine through the analytical framework of racial capitalism.[9] It focuses on Elbit Systems and on the experience of Palestine Action to explore how racial capitalism reproduces and maintains the Israeli settler colonization of Palestine by advancing both the elimination of Palestinians and the use of Palestinians and their bodies as sites of militarized accumulation. In doing so, it builds on theorizations of settler colonialism as a necropolitical structure that is intertwined with the politics of race and racial capitalism to illuminate the shifting patterns of racialization, accumulation, and domination in Israeli settler colonialism, and the ways in which global geographies of racial capitalism are reproduced through settler colonialism in Palestine.[10] Through the focus on Elbit, the chapter sheds light on the ways in which relations of racial capitalism take both local and global forms in the racialization of Palestinians as inherent to militarized accumulation. The chapter also draws on the author's guerrilla activist research and involvement with Palestine Action[11] to explicate how transnational solidarity activist resistance in Britain constitutes political intimacies[12] that can generate decolonial praxis and global solidarities that disrupt both settler colonization in Palestine and the systemic relations of racial capitalism that sustain it.

## ELBIT SYSTEMS: NECROPOWER AND SETTLER COLONIALISM IN PALESTINE

Based in Haifa, Elbit Systems is Israel's largest arms manufacturer and security company.[13] In 2023, it ranked as the twenty-first largest arms company in the world.[14] The company mostly operates in the military sector of aerospace, land and naval systems, security, intelligence, and surveillance services.[15] Elbit's second-largest customer, after the US government, is the Israeli Ministry of Defense. The company supplies up to 85 percent of the land-based equipment and unmanned aerial vehicle (UAV) drones used by the Israeli military.[16] In 2021, around 22 percent of Elbit's profits came from Israel.[17]

Elbit is one of Israel's largest and fastest growing private military companies. In 2018, it took over the former state-run Israeli arms company Israeli Military Industries (IMI), previously the sole producer of small-caliber ammunition to the Israeli military—a role that Elbit now fills.[18] Elbit markets its small-caliber ammunition models as "combat proven" by the Israeli and US militaries.[19] Its purchase of IMI is part of both the increasing privatization of the Israeli settler-colonial military regime[20] and the growing popularity of Elbit's "combat proven" brand with states and militaries globally. The sale of IMI to Elbit was conditioned on the relocation of IMI's facilities from the center of Israel to the Ramat Beka military zone in the Naqab. The relocation is part of a wider Israeli plan to Judaize the Naqab by moving military bases to the area, thus contributing to the dispossession and ethnic cleansing of the Palestinian Bedouin.[21]

Elbit has played a key role in both defining and maintaining Israel's place on the global stage. Israel has gained a position in the international system as a lucrative entrepôt for the securing of weapons and security systems for the purposes of managing warehoused—often migrant and refugee—surplus populations, and of reinforcing systems of domestic policing and surveillance. These practices have emerged as the primary modes that define racial capitalism's accumulation patterns under neoliberal regimes.[22] From its outset, Israel was designed as a colonial capitalist economy premised upon a racialized division of labor.[23] After the Nakba, the ethnic cleansing of 800,000 Palestinians from Palestine in 1948,[24] the newly formed State of Israel depended upon Palestinian labor as a cheap and racialized workforce.[25] This racialized system of settler-colonial capitalism frequently requires successive rounds of primitive accumulation, crucial in capturing new lands, labor, and resources for capitalist development.[26] The primary logic of racial capitalism in the service of settler colonialism operates "to shore up continued access to Indigenous peoples' territories for the purposes of state formation, settlement, and capitalist development."[27]

Analyses of Zionist colonization in Palestine must be theoretically attentive to the global and local shifts in the diverse strategies of settler-colonial domination and racial capitalist patterns of accumulation. The neoliberal restructuring of the Israeli economy involved an accelerated process of privatization[28] and growing specialization in the production of high-tech weapons systems and surveillance technologies.[29] Israel's reliance upon the exploitation of racialized Palestinian labor has depended on the needs of Israeli capitalism. In line with a segregationist mindset that followed the Oslo Accords (manifested in the slogan "We [Israelis] here and they [Palestinians] there"), the entrenching of Palestinian dependency on the Israeli economy and the underdevelopment of the Palestinian economy[30] was followed by restrictions on employment permits provided to Palestinians from Gaza and the West Bank allowing them to work in Israel. These restrictions "tightened from 1993 to 1996, abated from 1997 to 1999, intensified again after 2000, and bifurcated after 2006 when Israel began increasing the number of permits for the West Bank and eliminated permits altogether for the Gaza Strip."[31]

The gradual process of confining Palestinians to reservations as a racialized surplus population that is no longer needed as cheap labor corresponded with the rise of Israel's high-tech economy, as embedded in the necropolitical nature of Israeli settler colonialism. Achille Mbembe argues that the Foucauldian concept of biopower, the assertion of state power over the biological reproduction and regulation of the lives and bodies of its subject populations, does not capture contemporary forms of state power that submit life to the power of death.[32] Mbembe employs the concept "necropower" to particularly account for "the various ways in which, in our contemporary world, weapons are deployed in the interest of maximally destroying persons and creating death-worlds."[33] Israel's settler colonization of Palestine, especially Gaza, represents, according to Mbembe, the most accomplished form of such necropower. As a system of "late-modern" colonial occupation, Israel's necropolitical settler-colonial regime "differs in many ways from early-modern occupation, particularly in its combining of the disciplinary, the biopolitical, and the necropolitical."[34]

By reducing the demand for a racialized Palestinian workforce, neoliberal restructuring in Israel has depended upon the expansion of necropolitical death-worlds for the purpose of more effectively eliminating the increasingly unneeded Palestinians. However, concomitant colonial and necropolitical processes for disposing of redundant populations do not mean that Palestinians are not exploited under Israeli settler-colonial capitalism.

While the Israeli economy, since the Oslo Accords, no longer depends on cheap Palestinian labor, current racial capitalist configuration renders Palestinians an (in)dispensable source for settler-colonial capital and militarized accumulation. This is done through the testing of new weapons and technologies on Palestinians, which is central to Israel's strategy of marketing weapons as "combat proven" and for the benefit of Israel's neoliberal securocratic war economy.[35] As Clarno makes clear: "Racial formation shapes the production of surplus populations by differentially valuing human life and marking some people as disposable. Yet it is important to recognize that even populations experiencing extreme levels of unemployment are not beyond the dynamics of racial capitalism."[36]

Elbit Systems plays a primary role in manufacturing this necropolitical structure. For example, Elbit's drones are regularly deployed in routine bombings and invasions of Gaza and in extrajudicial assassinations of Palestinian civilians and members of the Hamas government.[37] The assassination of Hamas commander Ahmed Jabari at the beginning of Israel's 2012 invasion of Gaza, carried out by an Elbit Hermes 450 drone, is one example.[38] During Israel's 2014 invasion of Gaza, the Israeli Air Force attempted to "operationalize as many capabilities as possible" of Hermes 450 and Hermes 900 drones. As reported by the Israeli Air Force, "UAV squadrons flew nonstop during the operation and every aircraft was crucial to the success of the mission."[39] Like its other technological and weapons systems, Elbit's drones are marketed as "field tested" and "combat proven."[40] Elbit continues to play a key role in Israel's necropolitical domination over Gaza and, according to the Israeli Air Force, "there is not a moment in the day or night that a UAV is not in the sky."[41] Elbit drones are also deployed in surveillance, intelligence gathering, and house arrests in the West Bank. Elbit's UAV Skylark drone was deployed during the so-called "Brothers Come Home" Israeli attacks in June and July 2014, when scores of Palestinians were arbitrarily arrested.[42]

Elbit's technology is integral to the management of death and the creation of death-worlds in Gaza. Its pioneering of new forms of militarized violence is integral to what is described by Eyal Weizman[43] as the "politics of verticality," whereby late-modern colonial occupation functions through a layered system of constant surveillance and control, from the dispersed geographies that segregate Palestinian towns and villages from one another into a system of "splintering occupation," to the occupation of the sky itself.[44] The inability to discern if the drone is there for surveillance or to carry out a military strike conditions the lives of Palestinians in Gaza to what Ruth Wilson Gilmore[45] describes as the necropolitical "vulnerability to premature death." In the West Bank, settler-colonial structuring constructs a complex interlocking system of splintering occupation through

> checkpoints, enclosures, watchtowers, trenches, all manner of demarca-
> tions that in many cases have no other function than to intensify the en-
> claving of entire communities, without ever fully succeeding in keeping
> away those considered a threat. This is the case with all those Palestin-
> ian towns that are literally surrounded by areas under Israeli control.[46]

Reminiscent of the Bantustan system under South African apartheid, settler territorialization works to orchestrate the ongoing expansion of Israeli set- tlements in such a way as to simultaneously dispossess Palestinians while disciplining and containing them, as dispensable "native surplus" popula- tions, to ever-dwindling ghettos, while using their bodies as sites for capital accumulation.[47]

Elbit is one of the main suppliers of the "smart walls" technology for the apartheid wall and checkpoint system in the West Bank and for the auto- mated surveillance wall around the Gaza Strip.[48] It supplies electronic de- tection fence systems,[49] including fifteen miles of electronic security walls around East Jerusalem, fitted with day and night cameras combined with laser range finders and sensor detection systems.[50] Furthermore, according to Who Profits—an independent research center focusing on exposing the involvement of Israeli and international corporations in the Israeli coloniza- tion of Palestine—in December 2019, Elbit was contracted by the Israeli Min- istry of Interior to develop, maintain, and operate its Rotem-Reut database system deployed at Israel's international borders and at Israeli checkpoints across the West Bank, East Jerusalem, and Gaza.[51]

Crucially, this system of necropolitical confinement and segregation requires the production and maintenance of Indigenous Palestinians as racially inferior, thus reproducing Jewish racial and settler superiority.[52] According to Somdeep Sen, race operates as a structuring relation under- pinning the colonization of Palestine. He argues that "Fanon's racialized characterization of the relationship between the colonized and the colonizer can also be treated as a metaphor for the 'racial regime' that orders the lives of Palestinians living under Israel's settler colonial rule."[53] Drawing from Patrick Wolfe,[54] Ronit Lentin articulates Israeli settler colonialism as a "racial regime," a race-making project that rests on the dehumanization of Palestinians in order to rationalize its colonial domination.[55]

Elbit plays a significant role in the reproduction of the Zionist racial regime through supplying weapons and security technologies that maintain the segregation and containment of Palestinians within the necropolitical structure of Israeli settler colonialism. But its role in the racialization of Palestinians also extends to forms of ideological legitimation. As argued by Gargi Bhattacharyya,[56] in the context of contemporary iterations of US imperial discourse of the "war on terror," the figure of the "Palestinian terrorist" is used to legitimize the racialization of Palestinians as nonhumans and as security threats. It is situated at the heart of global racializing discourses of counterterrorism, which primarily target Arabs, North Africans, and Muslims. For example, the Israeli philosopher Asa Kasher, author of the Israeli military's ethics code, uses such discourses to justify the targeting of civilians: "We must understand that a new kind of war demands new principles of action. The old principle that distinguished between combatants and civilians is no longer relevant, now that we are fighting Palestinian terrorists who operate from within Palestinian populated areas."[57] The blurring of the line between combatants and civilians in the contemporary proliferation of drone warfare and assassination campaigns extends beyond Israel. Gregoire Chamayou shows how Israeli legal and military doctrine, developed specifically with regard to Gaza, has informed US legal and ethical discourses on the use of drone warfare, rationalizing extrajudicial assassinations and the killing of civilians as "collateral damage."[58]

Elbit's role in racializing Palestinians as security threats that must be targeted and eliminated does not merely sustain Israel's ability to maintain its necropolitical settler-colonial regime. Elbit, which markets its weaponry and military technologies through discourses of security and counterterrorism, also describes itself as a pioneer in global securitization. According to its company profile: "The global war on terror, along with the threats posed by urban warfare, demand smooth interoperability among forces on all fronts. . . . As an acknowledged leader in the field, we build on over three decades of experience in training and simulation programs."[59] In establishing itself as a leader in the field, Elbit—a hybrid of a private company and an arm of Israel's security industrial complex—uses the Palestinians to market its weapons and technology as "combat proven" to states increasingly defined by homeland security, border militarization, and counterterrorism. As put by Uzi Landau, the former Israeli minister of interior, Israel is a "laboratory for fighting terror."[60]

Elbit's deep involvement in the settler colonization of Palestine should therefore be understood as part of the global relationships of racial capitalism. The continuing accumulation of capital on a global scale, through the production of racial difference, leads to a process that resigns Palestinians to necropolitical realities of exploitability and disposability. Elbit provides the means for subjugating and dispossessing Palestinians, as well as the technology that allows Israel to play a leading role in the global arms and security markets with client states all over the world. This dual role was exemplified most explicitly during the 2014 assault on Gaza, where the operability of Elbit's Hermes 900 drone was accelerated so as to take advantage both of its military capabilities and of the marketing opportunities that the "combat proven" label would accrue.[61] Since 2014, the Hermes 900 has increasingly become one of Elbit's most successful products, as evidenced by the number of contracts the company has secured for its procurement. This includes a US$300 million contract to supply Hermes 900 tactical drones to "an unspecified country in Asia," suspected to be India,[62] and a contract to supply the Brazilian Air Force with additional Hermes drones.[63]

Racialized as disposable surplus populations, Palestinians are continuously embroiled in necropolitical geographies wherein "vast populations are subjected to living conditions that confer upon them the status of the living dead."[64] Thus, Palestinians are faced not only with resisting death or colonial dispossession but also with a system that attempts to construct them as sites of accumulation through their very bodies and lives, as testing sites for Israel's war economy.[65] Not satisfied with the mere elimination of the Indigenous Palestinians, Israel seeks to commodify, market, and export this violence globally, merchandising its securocratic war with the Palestinians to increasingly militarized states aiming to control domestic unrest as a result of inequality and precarity, as well as global refugee flows and what are seen as security threats. By using colonized Palestine as a laboratory for testing its weapons and security technologies, Elbit both commodifies its role in Israeli settler colonialism through its "combat proven" brand and acts as a global provider of technologies of repression and pacification, exemplifying not only Israel's regime of neoliberal colonial capitalism but also global processes of racial capitalist accumulation through militarization, as further detailed in the next section.

## PALESTINE AS LABORATORY FOR MILITARIZED ACCUMULATION

Settler-colonial sites have long been used as laboratories for developing new techniques of social control, population management, counterinsurgency, and political violence.[66] As has been noted widely—as opposed to the Eurocentric historical teleology, according to which developments within Europe diffuse outward into the colonial periphery—in practice, organized modes of repression have largely developed within colonial sites and circulated back to the metropole, or across the dividing line between settler society and the "frontier."[67] According to David Lloyd and Patrick Wolfe,

> To the extent that Israel's regime in Palestine recapitulates and extends earlier models of settler colonial dispossession and domination, recalling the earlier cases of North America and Australasia, its function as a program for contemporary state forms not only supplies new technologies and practices of regulation and segregation but also highlights the continuities between the logics of settler colonialism and those of the neoliberal state globally.[68]

Such processes also hold true for the ongoing reproduction of racial capitalism at a global level. As Lisa Lowe argues, racial capitalism not only emerged out of settler-colonial processes of primitive accumulation, Indigenous dispossession, and racialized systems of labor, but also continues to underpin contemporary patterns of accumulation under neoliberalism and the shift toward local and global systems defined by containing and disciplining warehoused, racialized, surplus populations.[69] John Collins argues that we need to think of "Global Palestine," a framework that situates Palestine at the intersection of a series of global processes that prefigure transformations taking place in the contemporary structures of capitalism and state violence.[70] Through this lens, Palestine functions as a unique space of contestation for understanding not only the settler-colonial logics of the past, but also the global processes that sustain settler colonialism in Palestine in the present. By theorizing Global Palestine through the framework of racial capitalism, we can begin to see how Israel's model of containing Palestinians to be exploitable by the weapons of arms companies such as Elbit Systems informs future techniques of governance and modes of racialized capital accumulation. As Bhattacharyya argues, racial capitalism requires ever-shifting modes of exploitation for its accumulation patterns toward the ever-increasing racialized disposability of dispossessed and unneeded populations.[71]

Israel relies upon keeping Palestinians within a liminal necropolitical constellation of overlapping systems of exploitation, racialization, and settler-colonial domination. This system of necropolitical capitalist exploitation subsequently constitutes a process that William Robinson terms "militarized accumulation" or "accumulation by repression."[72] Following Robinson, I therefore propose that "Global Palestine" is reproduced by a global system of racial capitalism defined by ruling international classes and imperial states requiring unprecedented levels of capital accumulation and global inequality, while being increasingly dependent upon the proliferation of militarism and repression.[73] It is through this emerging system of militarized accumulation that Palestinians, in becoming increasingly dispensable to the Israeli economy as a source of cheap racialized labor, have become instrumental to Israel's economy and its "niche" role in the transnational military industrial complex. Asking "Where would [Israel] be without the occupation and the regional conflict it generates?," Jeff Halper argues that Israel's political and economic niche under neoliberal capitalism requires the colonization and subjugation of the Palestinians in order to market itself as a model that can be replicated all over the world. This serves purposes of both domestic and global forms of pacification and securitization, whereby Israel functions as the "enforcement arm of transnational capitalism, ensuring the smooth flow of capital and resources while addressing challenges to its hegemony."[74]

Within this interlocking local and global matrix of racial capitalism, Elbit plays a key role as a global supplier of the military and security technologies required for the purposes of maintaining a smooth flow of capital, resources, and social pacification, as well as in solidifying Israel's political power in the international sphere. Some examples: Elbit's Hermes 450 drones have been procured by the US Customs and Border Protection agency for surveillance along the Mexico border.[75] The use of Elbit's drones not only in military strikes and assassinations, but also in developing forms of "vertical sovereignty" modelled on their deployment in Palestine, is becoming increasingly popular globally. Elbit drones are also purchased by both the European Union and the UK Maritime and Coastguard Agency. The EU border agency Frontex has awarded Elbit contracts worth up to €100 million for military-grade Hermes 900 drones for the purpose of monitoring the Mediterranean for "every sea craft involved in any form of irregular or illegal activities at sea."[76] Elbit was awarded a £990,000 contract for a "Drone Demonstration and Development Project" by the UK Maritime and Coastguard Agency, taking part in flight demonstrations for the purpose of exhibiting "Search and Rescue (SaR) capabilities and the use of long-range unmanned capabilities in civilian airspace."[77] The UK National Police Air Service has also carried out trials with Elbit drones, researching their potential uses for domestic British policing.[78]

Elbit's role in border surveillance technologies is not limited to supplying UAV drones; it also extends to the sale of surveillance towers and electronic security technologies. Companies such as Elbit play a central role in the global proliferation of such militarized borders.[79] A key example is the US-Mexico border wall.[80] In 2019, Customs and Border Protection issued contracts worth up to US$187 million to Elbit's US division to provide hundreds of electronic surveillance towers equipped with radar and sensor systems modelled on those used by the apartheid annexation wall in the West Bank and the automated electronic border fence around the Gaza Strip.[81] Viewing Global Palestine through the role that Elbit plays in the global proliferation of military and security technologies is further evidenced by the role Elbit has played since 2014 in turning the Tohono O'odham Native reservation in southern Arizona into a militarized occupation of mass surveillance.[82] Elbit participated in the construction of ten integrated surveillance towers in a US$26 million contract on Tohono O'odham land, creating a system of "persistent surveillance" whereby border agents have "administered beatings, used pepper spray, pulled people out of vehicles, shot two Tohono O'odham men under suspicious circumstances, and entered people's homes without warrants."[83] As pointed out by one of the reservation's Indigenous residents: "Now we won't be able to go anywhere near here without the big U.S.-Israeli eyes monitoring us, watching our every move. . . . It is apartheid here."[84]

According to Bobby Brown, senior director of Customs and Border Protection at Elbit's US division, the company's ultimate goal is to build a "layer" of electronic surveillance equipment across the entire perimeter of the United States, where, "over time, we'll expand not only to the northern border, but to the ports and harbors across the country."[85] Israel—and, by extension, Elbit—is thus regarded by the United States and a number of its arms companies and border agencies as a key strategic partner; weapons and security technologies produced by Israeli and US companies can be tested in the field in Palestine and used at the Mexico border against migrants, racialized communities, and colonized Indigenous peoples for the benefit of both settler colonies.[86]

The use of Elbit's drones and technology around the world is not confined to borderization, extending to areas including military strikes and assassinations. Elbit's UAV drones are known for their use by Israel as instruments of targeted assassinations of Palestinian leaders. Targeted assassinations—effectively extrajudicial executions—have been adopted as a key strategy employed by the US military under former president Barack Obama in Afghanistan, Iraq, and elsewhere.[87] As former US secretary of defense Donald Rumsfeld stated in 2001, "the techniques used by the Israelis against the Palestinians could quite simply be deployed on a larger scale."[88] Likewise, Elbit's drones have been deployed by the British Army in both Afghanistan and Iraq since 2007, while its SkyStriker Suicide Drone was deployed in 2020 by the Azerbaijani military in Nagorno-Karabakh, where illegal cluster munitions, identified as Israeli made, were used against civilian targets.[89] Elbit has also been developing a close relationship with India, supplying it with weapons and technologies for use in its military occupation of Jammu and Kashmir.[90] Between 2014 and 2020, India was the largest importer of Israeli weapons.[91] In 2018, the Adani Defence branch of the Indian multinational company Adani Global joined Elbit in the development of a UAV drone manufacturing facility in Hyderabad.[92]

Elbit's global flow of arms and technologies exposes how Global Palestine is imbued in contemporary patterns of racial capitalism's systems of exploitation and accumulation across geographies. Osuri and Zia[93] para-phrase Palestinian scholar Nadera Shalhoub-Kevorkian,[94] who argues that Israel serves as a laboratory for global configurations of militarized accu-mulation wherein "the bodies, lands, and even deaths of those occupied and colonized become another resource, another commodity, in late modern capitalism's necropolitical arms trade."[95] Global Palestine exposes the logic of racial capitalism through the ways in which it renders exploitable differ-ent geographies, populations, and bodies by "seizing upon colonial divisions, identifying particular regions for production and others for neglect, certain populations for exploitation and still others for disposal."[96]

To summarize, settler colonialism and the necropolitical and racial con-struction of Palestinians as exploitable subjects of militarized accumulation should be understood through the ongoing shifts in racial capitalism's ac-cumulation patterns and Palestine's role as prefiguring the current global order. As Collins argues,[97] "Palestine is located at the intersection of two sets of global processes that symbolize not only the profundity of the structural injustices that are being confronted today, but also the resilience and cre-ativity with which many people are confronting those injustices."[98] Palestin-ian resilience is complemented by acts of global solidarity and resistance, as discussed in the concluding section.

## PALESTINE ACTION AND DECOLONIAL SOLIDARITY PRAXIS

Since the summer of 2020, Palestine Action has been engaged in a sustained direct action campaign against Elbit Systems sites across Britain. This cam-paign is aimed at highlighting Elbit's role in the settler colonization of Pales-tine and its position in exporting Israel's model of militarized accumulation globally.[99]

Emerging out of a political context in Britain that continues to attempt the repression of Palestine solidarity activism, compounded by Britain's on-going complicity with Israeli apartheid and colonialism, Palestine Action activists have come together to campaign against this complicity. Activists employ a repertoire of direct action strategies, hold weekly protests, and mo-bilize members of local communities living near the sites of Elbit's factories in Oldham, Shenstone, Tamworth, and Sandwich. Palestine Action activists, along with members of the local communities, have consistently targeted

Elbit's factory sites with the aim of halting production for days and some-times weeks, costing Elbit millions of pounds in damages and production losses. The frequency and sustained nature of the direct action campaign is focused specifically on exposing, disrupting, and destroying the flow of weapons and components used for the production of drones, tanks, and mil-itary gear that serve the Israeli military, as well as border administrations and militaries across the world.

Palestine Action's activism ranges from short hit-and-run tactics to lon-ger-lasting actions, such as covering buildings in red paint to symbolize the blood that the company's technologies and profits are complicit in spilling; causing low-level property damage and adding graffiti; seeking to occupy factory roofs, gates, and sites (with some occupations lasting several days); and smashing factory windows, air-conditioning systems, and security cam-eras. All these actions aim to disrupt, for as long as possible, the ability of the factories to work. Rooftop occupations have occurred simultaneously with mass community protests outside the factories. The most famous direct action was a six-day occupation of Elbit's subsidiary UAV Tactical Systems in Leicester during the May 2021 bombing of Gaza. On the sixth day of the Pal-estine Action rooftop occupation of the factory, hundreds of people from the community protested outside the gates and barricaded the police officers inside, refusing to let them leave with the detained activists for a number of hours.

Palestine Action also targeted LaSalle Investment Management, the property management company that hosts Elbit's offices, as well as compa-nies such as Arconic in Birmingham, which also supplied the cladding that allowed for the Grenfell Tower fire that killed more than seventy people in London in 2017. Another company targeted was the chemicals company Solvay in Wales. Both Arconic and Solvay supply materials for manufac-turing Elbit's drones and weaponry. The victory in shutting down the Elbit subsidiary Ferranti Technologies in Oldham, mentioned at the start of this chapter, was achieved through a sustained campaign that combined strate-gies of direct action and local community mobilization.

Moving beyond the BDS campaign's focus on boycotting Israeli goods, Palestine Action aims to confront Israeli settler colonialism through tar-geting the international relations of racial capitalism that sustain it. Such a model of activism radicalizes the possibilities of international solidarity by exposing, targeting, and disrupting the transnational flow of technologies of violence exchanged across geographies, between Britain, the United States, and Israel. Palestine Action provides a concrete example of employing an internationalist strategy while engaging in direct action at the local level. As stated by the network's cofounder Huda Ammori, "the idea of boycott divestment and sanctions, essentially that's what we're doing, sanctions, through direct action."[100]

## CONCLUSION

As Palestinian novelist and revolutionary Ghassan Kanafani reminds us: "Imperialism has laid its body over the world. . . . Wherever you strike it, you damage it, and you serve the world revolution."[101] This chapter used the lens of racial capitalism to theorize the racialization of the Palestinians by Zionist colonialism, positioning the Israeli private arms company Elbit Systems at the center of Israel's necropolitical technologies for manufacturing and marketing Israel's "battle tested" weapons and security systems to global buyers. Elbit systems and its role in sustaining militarized accumulation therefore play a key role in enabling Israel to continue the racialization and colonization of the Palestinians.

Palestine Action offers a model of internationalist activism by employing a model that is situated "within an assemblage of transnational and translocal solidarity networks."[102] Such a resistance model considers the liberation of Palestine as a prerequisite for global liberation against racial capitalism and exemplifies what Noura Erakat terms the "seeds for a decolonial future,"[103] generating new forms of radical, global, and decolonial internationalism.[104] As the Palestinian people continue their resistance against settler colonialism, Palestine Action is generating new radical practices that advance the BDS movement further by centering racial capitalism as the target in its decolonial solidarity praxis.

*Nine*

# ZIONIST RACIALIZED SEXUAL POLITICS AND PALESTINIAN REFUSAL

RONIT LENTIN

IN 2018, THE STATE OF ISRAEL, AN AFFILIATE NON-EUROPEAN member of the European Broadcasting Union, was represented at the Eurovision Song Contest by the unconventional pop star Netta Barzilai. Her song, "I Am Not Your Toy, You Stupid Boy," which was performed by Barzilai wearing a glittery corset and a kimono and interspersing the verses with arm flaps, beatboxing, and chicken noises, and which, she said, was inspired by the #MeToo movement, won the contest. Barzilai, described as a "plus-size performer who completely owns her space and rocks her originality—goofy faces, chicken noises, and all—with stunning confidence,"[1] is an unusual Eurovision star. She was much admired by people in Israel, from small children to the gay community,[2] for her in-your-face performance and for breaking with accepted body and gender norms. Barzilai's hypersexualized self-representation and her song were interpreted by the media as refusing patriarchal domination.[3] I propose, however, that the performance and the song were about more than popular music or the challenge to gender and body stereotypes. They should, rather, be linked to three central aspects of sexual

184

and gender politics in Israel and Palestine that must be understood within the broader context of imperialism, colonialism, and settler colonialism as deeply racialized.

The first aspect of this broader context is Israel's boast of gender and LGBTQ+ equality, including making military service mandatory for men, women, and queers. The Israeli myth of gender and queer equality, however, ignores Israel being a patriarchal Jewish theocracy[4] and obscures the profound inequalities between Palestinian, Ashkenazi Jewish, and Arab/Mizrahi Jewish women[5] and between Israeli Jewish and Palestinian queers.[6] Zionist settler colonialism is premised on a racialized contrast between Israel as a progressive Western state and Palestinian society as backward, patriarchal, homophobic, lacking gender equality, and needing rescue. The second aspect is Israel's perennial refusal to be anyone's "toy" in its defiance of international law and UN conventions—a refusal that, coupled with its assertion of white Jewish supremacy, explains its determination to commit the genocide in Gaza in plain view. The third is the contradiction between Barzilai's refusal to service patriarchy and the highly sexualized nature of Israeli society, where everyday practices of gender-based violence, rape culture, and pinkwashing are pervasive and normalized.

Four years before her Eurovision victory, Barzilai, then an Israeli Defense Forces (IDF) conscript, sang with the IDF Navy entertainment troupe at Israel's 2014 Independence Day celebrations.[7] That was just two months before the "Protective Edge" assault on the besieged Gaza enclave in July that resulted in the Israeli military murdering 2,251 Palestinians, including 551 children; injuring 11,231 Palestinians, including 3,436 children; and destroying 18,000 housing units.[8] These numbers are much lower than the many thousands of Palestinian people, most of them civilians, who would be killed by the IDF during the Gaza genocide: according to an article published in the British medical journal *The Lancet,* by July 2024 the number of both direct and indirect deaths resulting from Israel's genocide was estimated at 186,000 people.[9]

About a year after Barzilai's Eurovision win, twelve Israeli teenage boys were accused by a nineteen-year-old British tourist of gang-raping her in the Cypriot resort town of Ayia Napa. The most significant aspect of the case was the widespread Israeli support for the accused teenagers, who were given a hero's welcome when they returned home.[10]

I interpret these seemingly unrelated occurrences—Israel's assaults on the Gaza Strip and the Gaza genocide, Barzilai's "Not Your Toy" winning the 2018 Eurovision Song Contest, and the 2019 rape case in Cyprus—as links in Israel's colonization chain, characterized, inter alia, by its defiant refusal to abide by international law. At one end of the refusal spectrum stands Barzilai, whose performance signaled a gendered, perhaps even feminist, refusal to serve as patriarchy's handmaiden, upholding the fabricated image of "Brand Israel" as a haven of gender and LGBTQ+ rights.[11] At the other end of the spectrum stand the repeated genocidal attacks on Gaza, part of Israel's ongoing permanent war against the Palestinians,[12] and its refusal to be anyone's "toy." Israel's exceptionalist refusal was explicitly stated by its first prime minister, David Ben-Gurion, who said already in 1955, "Our future depends not on what the gentiles will say, but on what the Jews will do."[13] This refusal has been repeated many times since as successive Israeli politicians have insisted that Israel is entitled to commit any aggressions against the Palestinians in "self-defense," evoking Jewish victimhood, particularly with regard to the Holocaust, despite the absurdity of claiming self-defense against an occupied population. The latest iteration of the refusal followed the International Court of Justice issuing a series of provisional measures against Israel in January 2024. The extreme right-wing minister for national security, Itamar Ben-Gvir, called the international body "antisemitic," declaring: "The decision of the antisemitic court in The Hague proves what was already known: This court does not seek justice, but rather the persecution of Jewish people. They were silent during the Holocaust and today they continue the hypocrisy and take it another step further."[14]

Between the two is the rape case in Cyprus, but also the controversy regarding the accusations against Hamas for allegedly raping Israeli women during its attack on October 7, 2023. The debates surrounding the accusations illustrate Israel's rape culture, which, according to journalist Natasha Roth-Rowland, is a direct consequence of the colonization of Palestine: "Israelis have lived with the example that one's desire for something is worth more than what—or whom—may be harmed in the quest to pursue it. The idea that something is there for the taking simply because one covets it is toxic, contagious."[15]

Finalizing this chapter while the Gaza genocide is ongoing makes the writing angrier, for which I make no apologies, and renders some of the analysis murkier, particularly in light of the heated debates regarding the unsubstantiated accusations that Hamas engaged in mass rapes of Israeli women, as confirmed by, inter alia, the UN Independent International Commission of Inquiry on the Occupied Palestinian Territory[16]—debates that I argue emanate from the racist Israeli obsession with Palestinian men as inherently violent rapists. The chapter begins by arguing that Zionists have employed sexual politics as a racializing strategy since the nineteenth-century invention of the "new (muscular) Jew," the masculinized European Ashkenazi Zionist antithesis of both feminized diaspora Jews[17] and racialized Palestinian (as well as non-European Arab-Jewish) masculinities and femininities. The racialization of sexual politics continues in present-day Israel, where Palestinian women, men, and queers are racialized in gender-specific ways. I then suggest that Israel strategically deploys the myth of gender and LGBTQ+ equality in order to juxtapose Israeli modernity with Palestinian patriarchal backwardness and thus justify the ongoing colonization of Palestine. The use of sexual politics as a racializing strategy resonates with what Honaida Ghanim calls "thanatopolitics"—the management of death and destruction.[18] The chapter foregrounds heteronormativity, as evidenced by homonationalism, rape culture, and pinkwashing, and concludes by outlining some examples of the gendered refusal of, and resistance to, colonial Israel's racial rule.

## FROM ZIONISM'S MASCULINE "NEW JEW" TO ISRAEL'S RAPE CULTURE

The racial state of Israel[19] controls women's gender roles while at the same time feminizing racialized and colonized men. Israel's racialized sexual politics is exemplified by its reproductive regime, which incentivizes childbearing in Jewish families while actively working to reduce Palestinian procreation.[20] Israel also controls nonwhite Jewish procreation, as evidenced by the administration of the controversial contraceptive Depo Provera to Ethiopian Jewish women while in transit camps on their way to Israel.[21]

According to Alana Lentin,[22] race is a "technology for the management of human difference, the main goal of which is the production, reproduction, and maintenance of white supremacy," and should be thought of in terms of what it does, not what it is. Gender is likewise a performative rather than an identity category, as argued by Judith Butler.[23] While conceptualizing gender as performative is useful, we should bear in mind that in the case of Palestinians, gender and race are co-performed—made visible and permissible—by the fact of being colonized and racialized. Moreover, Israel's claim to be a haven of gender and LGBTQ+ equality rests on the premise of heteronormativity that is rooted in white/European/Jewish supremacy, which uses the state regulation of sexuality to designate which individuals are "fit" for the full privileges of citizenship.[24] This resonates with the Israeli regulation of reproduction and childbearing, which differentiates between (fully human) European Jews, (not-quite-human) non-European Arab and Black Jews and Palestinian citizens, and (nonhuman) occupied and colonized Palestinian subjects. This division is, of course, more complex, as argued by Alexander Weheliye[25] in a more general context in his analysis of racial assemblages.

Israel's sexual exceptionalism also involves what Jasbir Puar terms "homonationalism"—a form of national homosexuality that racializes Palestine and Palestinian queers, who are excluded by the colonizing state from the remit of LGBTQ+ equality.[26] Strategies of pinkwashing are employed by Israel's use of its arguably stellar LGBTQ+ rights to deflect attention from, and to justify its colonization of, Palestine.[27] Pinkwashing in the Palestinian context, Puar further argues, functions dually, "as a form of discursive preemptive securitization that marshals neo-orientalist fears of Palestinians as backward, sexually repressed terrorists, and as an intense mode of subjugation of Palestinians under settler colonial rule."[28] The view of Palestinian men as sexually repressed violent terrorists resurfaced in the Israeli claims regarding the alleged rapes by Hamas on October 7 and functions to deflect attention from, and forms part of the discursive justification of, the racialization of the Palestinians.

Theorizing women as key to reproducing nations is apt in the case of the racial construction of Jewish Israel, where the 1950 Law of Return initially granted people born to Jewish mothers the right to "return" to the State of Israel with automatic citizenship rights. This assumes that Jewish people are "returning" to their historical homeland rather than colonizing Palestine, fixating Israel's foundation on racial discrimination. Challenged as racially discriminatory against Palestinians born on the land and not allowed the right of return, the Law of Return was amended in 1970 to include the children and grandchildren of Jews. Both the original law and the amendment have racial implications: by including the children and grandchildren of Jews, the amendment was reminiscent of the Nazi Nuremberg Laws.[29] In 1991, the Law of Return was further relaxed to admit non-Jewish relatives of immigrant Russian Jews.[30] However, Netanyahu's far-right government voiced demands to eliminate the "grandparent clause," which, its ultraorthodox members argued, "is causing a significant drop in the percentage of Jews living in Israel, endangering Israel's continuity as the Jewish state."[31] Racial sexual politics is played out in Israel, where the ruling European Ashkenazi Zionist masculinity controls Palestinian but also Jewish women and Arab Jews. As Nahla Abdo argues, white Ashkenazi-European Jewish feminist members of the Zionist settler-colonial elite control the epistemological sphere through representing the "other"—Palestinian, as well as Mizrahi-Arab, women and men.[32]

Like antisemitism, Zionism constructs Jewish people as a biological race-nation that, according to Zionism's European ideologues, required its own homeland, which was to be a replica of Europe away from Europe.[33] In this homeland, European Jews would overcome their racialization and become white, consolidating their racial supremacy over Palestinians but also over non-European Jews. Zionist leaders, Raphael Falk argues, committed Zionism to a concept of race as colonial nationalism and invented the "new Jew," Max Nordau's "Jewry of Muscle," the active, warlike antithesis of the feminized, "degenerate" European diaspora Jew.[34] Escaping from Europe, Ashkenazi "new Jews" became akin to European gentiles, whose antisemitic contempt for diaspora Jews is replicated in Euro-Ashkenazi Israelis' contempt for Palestinians, but also for Arab, Mizrahi, and Black Ethiopian Jewish Israelis.

Crucially, the Zionist "new Jew" was not merely a racial construction deriving from colonialism, social Darwinism, and eugenics. It was also a masculine construction drawing on historical images of biblical and post-biblical male Judean heroism and on internalized antisemitic stereotypes of diaspora degeneracy.[35] According to Todd Samuel Presner, European Zionist body ideals of masculinity and militancy, which shared the cultural and intellectual roots of fascist body ideals, posited women as reproducing the species and men as reproducing the state—a gendered dichotomy deeply embedded in Israeli culture, despite claims to gender equality.[36] Ironically, while Palestine and the Palestinians were feminized in Zionist discourse, in contrast with the hypermasculinized heterosexual ideal of the Israeli Jew, Laura Khoury, Seif Dana, and Ghazi-Walid Falah posit the feminization of Palestine through the metaphor "Palestine as a woman and women as Palestine," as found in popular Palestinian literature.[37]

Although it is hard to imagine a time when Israeli Jews were not muscular and masculine and when homoerotic bonding was not central to Israeli militarism, the militarization of Israeli society is the key—alongside the racialization of Palestinians and non-European Jews—to controlling vanquished, occupied, and besieged Palestinian populations. Indeed, militarization and the Israeli military are the central building blocks of Israeli state and society, as argued by Haim Bresheeth-Zabner.[38] Yet, despite the increasing participation of women in combat duties—seen by Israeli feminists as a desirable accomplishment[39]—sexual harassment is rampant in the Israeli military.[40] And militarism facilitates Israel's rape culture, which targets Palestinian and Jewish women alike. At the same time, it is also weaponized against Palestinian men, who are often accused of sexually assaulting and harassing Jewish women for "nationalist motives."[41] The widespread belief in Palestinian men as sexual predators and rapists was evident in the Israeli media debates about the allegations that Hamas combatants engaged in a systematic campaign of rapes of Israeli women during the October 7 attack, discussed later.

My discussion of Israel's rape culture must begin with the consistent denial—for racist reasons—of the prevalence of rapes of Palestinian women by Israeli soldiers ever since the 1948 Nakba. Telling in this respect is the statement by the Israeli left-wing journalist and political activist Uri Avnery, a veteran of the 1948 war, regarding rapes during the Nakba: "I knew we committed nearly every human atrocity . . . everything apart from rape and sexual abuse . . . for racist reasons. Having sex with an Arab woman was considered demeaning."[42] Israeli feminist scholar Tal Nitsan reiterates Avnery's denial by alleging that her interviews with male IDF soldiers stationed in occupied Palestine's population centers "prove" that rapes of Palestinian women were rare and that, rather than sexually abusing Palestinian women, the soldiers "de-womanized" them as sexually unattractive, inhuman, polluting, and impure.[43]

While the Israeli colonization of Palestine did not entail campaigns of mass rapes intended to alter the ethnic composition of the Palestinian population—as in the former Yugoslavia, where the Serbs engaged in mass rapes of Bosnian Muslim women as part of their ethnic cleansing project[44]—the rape of Palestinian women by Israeli soldiers during the Nakba was widespread. These rapes did not go unnoticed at the time, but their denial continues. In fact, they have been documented by journalists and scholars. Aviv Lavie wrote about the brutal 1949 gang rape of a young Bedouin girl by a group of Israeli soldiers who later executed her.[45] Israeli historian Ilan Pappé lists three sources for reports on rapes during the Nakba: international organizations such as the United Nations and the Red Cross, the Israeli archives (which indicate that Ben-Gurion "seems to have been informed about each case and entered them in his diary"), and oral history testimonies by Palestinian victims and Israeli perpetrators.[46]

Despite the ongoing denials, and although Palestinians have also denied the rapes for cultural and psychological reasons,[47] rape was used broadly and tactically by Israeli soldiers during the Nakba. Though no statistics exist, Palestinian feminist scholar Nadera Shalhoub-Kevorkian told *Al Arabiya News* that Palestinian families she interviewed told her that they fled their homes in 1948 because of the rapes.[48] Palestinian writer Salman Natour told me in a 2006 interview that, just as the notorious 1948 Deir Yassin massacre was meant as a "warning to all the Palestinians that a similar fate awaited them if they refused to abandon their homes and take flight," Palestinian women were afraid of being raped and were "concerned about their honour."[49] Likewise, Palestinian scholar Isis Nusair writes that the women she interviewed who were first- and second-generation Nakba survivors told her of their fears of rape and the violation of honor. Although most of them chose to speak only indirectly about the rapes, "the gendered impact of these events was present at nearly everything the women said."[50]

Having interviewed Palestinian women in Israeli jails, Abdo argues that many Palestinian women prisoners experience sexual abuse, molestation, the threat of rape, and rape.[51] According to the Palestinian Authority Prisoners' Affairs Commission, Palestinian women prisoners continue to be subjected to abuse and torture in the special section of Hasharon prison called Al-Maabar, an isolation unit where they are often held for weeks.[52]

Shalhoub-Kevorkian argues that rape and the threat of rape remain relevant to understanding the position of Palestinian women under Israeli rule.[53] In 2016, an Israeli army officer was indicted by a military court for raping a Palestinian woman and for accepting bribes for granting entry and work permits to Palestinian women.[54] And, in 2024, the prevalence of rape and sexual abuse of Palestinian women prisoners was confirmed by a panel of UN experts who have seen "credible allegations" that Palestinian women and girls were subjected to sexual assaults, including rape, while in Israeli detention, and were calling for a full investigation.[55] Evidence also emerged of rapes of Palestinian male prisoners with metal sticks in the Israeli Sde Teiman detention center—which was established specifically to hold captives from Gaza after October 7—and a leaked report by the UN Relief and Works Agency for Palestinian Refugees in the Near East confirmed the death of at least one prisoner as a result of rape.[56]

Furthermore, despite the Jewish religious prohibition of extramarital sex, raping Palestinian women has been repeatedly sanctioned by Jewish religious leaders. The IDF's Rabbi Colonel Eyal Karim, though declaring that "drafting girls is totally forbidden," stated in 2016 that in times of war it is permissible for soldiers to "have sex with comely gentile [Palestinian] women against their will."[57] Rapes of Palestinian women and men by Israeli soldiers illustrate the racialization of the Palestinian gendered body by the Israeli colonial culture of violence.

Accusing Palestinian men of sexually assaulting Jewish women is an essential part not only of the Israeli rape culture but also of the Zionist desire to maintain the purity of the Jewish race. In July 2023, the Israeli parliament passed an amendment to the Hate Crimes Law, doubling the punishment for sexual harassment offences with "nationalistic motivation." According to Israeli legal scholar Orit Kamir, this is a racist amendment, serving the Zionist view of women as sex objects symbolizing the national honor, and warning "other" men against sullying it.[58] Framing Palestinian men as sexually aggressive has been employed by extreme right-wing Jewish anti-"miscegenation" groups such as Lehava, whose supporters often carry placards with the slogan "Miscegenation Is a Holocaust," warning Palestinians, in Arabic, "Don't even think about a Jewish girl" and warning Jewish women, in Hebrew, 'Beware the goys—they will defile you.'"[59]

The racialization of Palestinian men as sexual predators was further evident following the October 7 Hamas attack. In November 2023, Israel launched an international campaign accusing Hamas of engaging in systematic rapes of Israeli women and using rape as a weapon of war. These accusations were widely reported by major international media outlets, and by human rights organizations, all without testimonies or independent verification of sources. Most of the accusations were later debunked.[60] At the time of writing, two UN reports addressed the Israeli allegations. The first, by the UN Special Representative on Sexual Violence in Conflict, Pramila Patten, published in March 2024, found "reasonable grounds to believe that conflict-related sexual violence occurred in multiple locations, including rape and gang rape in at least three locations in southern Israel," but Patten was unable to verify other reports of rape or speak to any survivors/victims. Her report recommended an international investigation, which Israel is refusing to allow.[61] The second report, by the Independent International Commission of Inquiry on the Occupied Palestinian Territory, published in June 2024, found that sexual and gender-based violence did occur but that the commission was unable to independently verify allegations of rape. The commission "did not find credible evidence, however, that [Palestinian] militants received orders to commit sexual violence."[62] However, it did find that "the frequency, prevalence and severity of sexual and gender-based crimes perpetrated against Palestinians since 7 October across the OPT [Occupied Palestinian Territories] indicate that specific forms of SGBV [sexual and gender-based violence] are part of ISF [Israeli Security Forces] operating procedures."[63] By July 2024, there was no evidence to suggest that Hamas engaged strategically, systematically, and in a widespread manner in mass rape as a weapon of war.[64] Furthermore, the Palestinian American journalist Ali Abunimah argues that the Israeli campaign is based on "emotional manipulation, outlandish claims, distortion, and an appeal to racist notions that Palestinians are inherently violent and cruel." Abunimah's detailed analysis shows that these allegations continue the long history of colonizers portraying Black, colonized, and enslaved men as savage brutes predisposed to sexual violence against white and settler women, and that the rape of white women by Black men was considered by colonizers as the "most terrible crime."[65]

Some commentators argue that the rape accusations served as one of the engines of the Gaza genocide. I maintain that they emanate from Israel's rape culture and the racialization of Palestinian men as sexual predators. Furthermore, regarding racialized Palestinian but also Mizrahi/Arab Jewish men as sexual aggressors consolidates white European Ashkenazi Jewish supremacy. One example is *Chanshi*, a 2022 television series featuring an American Ashkenazi Orthodox woman migrating to Israel to seek sex with Mizrahi Israeli soldiers. The series epitomizes the racialization of Mizrahi/Arab Jewish men as primitive and sexually aggressive, justifying the control of oriental bodies while shirking responsibility for their racialization.[66] Linking another gang rape of an Israeli teenager by a group of Mizrahi men in the Israeli resort of Eilat in 2020 with the racialization of Mizrahi men, Eness Elias argues that

> the invasion of the Mizrahi man into the Ashkenazi territory is an Ashkenazi nightmare that has for years blocked the entry of Mizrahi masculinity into the [Israeli] mainstream. . . . The Eilat rape was criticized by everyone, but it was also used to frame Mizrahi men as the perpetrators of Israel's rape culture.[67]

## THANATOPOLITICS: KILLING THE PALESTINIAN (FEMALE) BODY

The debates regarding gender-based violence and Israel's rape culture focus on, inter alia, the frequent murders of Palestinian women in Israel by their partners. Juxtaposing the 2020 gang rape in Eilat and the murder of a Palestinian woman, Nora Ka'abiya, by her husband, Palestinian journalist Sheren Falah Sa'ab wrote: "We women are unprotected, both inside and outside the home; and the situation is particularly tough for Palestinian women."[68] Focusing on the scant media attention to Ka'abiya's murder, Falah Sa'ab wonders whether the murder of a Palestinian woman is not "sexy" enough to warrant media coverage, and whether gender-based violence in Palestinian society is considered "part of their culture" and the problem of the women themselves, and of Palestinian society.

Focusing on the frequent murders of Palestinian women for so-called family honor, Palestinian sociologist Manar Hasan criticizes Israeli feminists for attributing these murders to Palestinian patriarchal structures. She argues that the murders are bound up with the interests of the colonizing Israeli state. Quite apart from the inadequate policing of gender-based violence in Palestinian society, Hasan argues that the state colludes with the heads of Palestinian *hamulas* (extended families), as demonstrated by the handing over—back to their families—of Palestinian women who had escaped their families in fear of being murdered by their male relatives. Such collusion, Hasan insists, "is a product of conscious social and political control whose price tag is minimal: no more than a few female corpses per year."[69] And, I would add, this colonial collusion indicates the racialization by Jewish Israel of Palestinian society as backward, patriarchal, and inherently violent.

In *Killing the Black Body*, African American scholar Dorothy Roberts chronicles the war against Black reproduction by regulating and killing the Black female body, from the slavery era to the present.[70] Palestinian sociologist Honaida Ghanim documents Israel's gender-based violence as expressed by the detention of pregnant Palestinian women on their way to give birth at the Israeli military checkpoints in the West Bank. Analyzing population management under Israel's colonial rule, Ghanim moves beyond Foucauldian theories of biopolitics, proposing instead thanatopolitics—the management of death and destruction—as a more appropriate analytical framework.[71] Ghanim's analysis is upheld by several reports, including by the Office of the UN High Commissioner for Human Rights, documenting the deaths of pregnant women and their newborn babies at IDF checkpoints.[72] It is also upheld by reports of the terror experienced by women waiting to give birth during Israel's assaults on Gaza in 2009, 2012, and 2014,[73] and by the near total destruction of the Gaza healthcare system, endangering, among others, the 50,000 pregnant women living in Gaza and the 180 babies being born each day during the Gaza genocide.[74]

Extending the concept of thanatopolitics, Shalhoub-Kevorkian uses the term "femicide" to describe the murders of Palestinian women and the placing of women who live with the permanent threat of being killed on what she terms "death row" in the context of Israeli racial settler colonialism. The violence of both poverty and the occupation, she argues, means that "the more Palestinian men have suffered at the hands of the Israeli occupiers (e.g., beatings, incarceration, humiliation), the more they have been prone to vent their anger and feelings of helplessness."[75] The term "femicide," she insists, enables us to explore the process leading to the deaths of Palestinian women, who often pay the highest price for the racialization of Palestinians and the colonization of Palestine.

Writing about the harm caused by the frequent publication of images of violence against Black people in the United States, African American scholar Marc Lamont Hill argues that the ordinariness of these images forces Black people to engage with their most traumatic experiences of racialization. At the same time, the images may undermine collective outrage. Black vulnerability, he adds, does not provoke the same sympathy, outrage, or political response as does the vulnerability of white Americans targeted by violence. As a result, "the more we see it, the easier it is to be *un*bothered by it."[76] Similarly, frequent media and social media reports and images of Israel's violence against Palestinians, including the murders of Palestinian women by Palestinian men, augment Palestinian vulnerability yet leave most Israelis *un*bothered. This has become more obvious since the October 7 Hamas attack and the onset of the Gaza genocide, moving many Israelis to call for the intensification of the destruction of Gaza "until victory."

However, Palestinians must be seen not as mere victims of the Israeli racial colony but rather as agents of active resistance, and representations of Israel's relentless violence may in fact mobilize Palestinian women, men, and queers to rise against its colonial violence. More specifically, Lamont Hill argues that the mediatized murders of Black women in the United States do not inspire the same response as the equally mediatized murders of cis-hetero Black men.[77] I am not sure whether this is also the case with the response to the mediatized murders of Palestinian women, as opposed to the murders of Palestinian men. However, one thing is certain: Palestinian women have always been involved in resisting the Israeli colonization of Palestine through acts of gendered resistance and refusal.

## CONCLUSION

This chapter juxtaposed the heteronormative construction of the cis-hetero masculine "new Jew" and the feminization of Palestine, the prevalence of gender-based violence and rape culture in Israel, and the specific violence against Palestinian women, on the one hand, and the contradiction between Israel branding itself as a haven of gender and LGBTQ+ equality, and its use of sexual politics in the ongoing colonization of Palestine and the racializa-tion of the Palestinians, on the other. To conclude, I focus on resistance and refusal as the other side of the sexual politics coin.

The Hamas act of resistance on October 7 has been condemned as a "crime against humanity" by Israel but also by many Western intellectu-als. Writing in the *London Review of Books*, and calling the Hamas attack a "vengeful pathology," Adam Shatz displays, according to Abdaljawad Omar, a "moral aversion to Palestinian resistance" and a "reductionist view of re-sistance itself, equating it to 'primordial instincts' and unchecked passions while dismissing other possibilities." Instead, Omar argues that resistance "is and always was a hopeful pathology, even when it fails to snatch a victory." In line with dismissing Palestinian men as savages and sexual predators, Omar argues that the profane Palestinian fighter remains an orientalist trope, con-fined "within legal constructs and liberal narratives of victimhood, which offers only a superficial treatment of agency, civil resistance and nonvio-lence, ignoring the harsh realities Palestinians face and the conditions that breed Palestinian liberation organizations."[78]

Resistance is central to the anticolonial struggle, in Palestine as else-where. However, Black studies scholar Alexander Weheliye's philosophical insistence that concepts such as resistance, body, and gender binaries are not sufficient when race is positioned front and center in analyzing subjec-tion and dehumanization motivates me to focus on refusal rather than resis-tance. Building on the writ of habeas corpus, Weheliye coins the term *habeas viscus* ("you shall have the flesh") to signify political violence as using the flesh to sustain its brutality.[79] The flesh, as the configuration of the human, he argues, is the fuel that animates racialized assemblages of subjection that are unable to annihilate practices of freedom and liberation, which cannot be understood merely in terms of resistance and agency because this lexicon blinds us to real possibilities of freedom.

Unlike Weheliye, however, Palestinians, including Palestinian feminists, insist on retaining the lexicon of resistance, agency, and the body, as I now show before moving to addressing resistance as refusal. Palestinian women have always been partners in resisting and fighting the Zionist colonization, whether as villagers, workers, teachers, trade unionists, activists, or armed freedom fighters.[80] Khoury, Dana and Falah posit Palestinian women's *embodied* resistance, which "has redefined gender roles," and write that Palestinian women's bodies become "trans-border bodies that cross territorial boundaries." I juxtapose their use of the term "body" with aspects of Weheliye's use of the more concrete term "flesh." While the occupation dispersed actual Palestinian bodies, their common refugee status and the representation of women in popular literature, Khoury, Dana and Falah argue, "formed a collective gender identity."[81] Using the metaphor of "Palestine as a woman" in popular Palestinian literature, they deconstruct gender binaries in "doing [invaluable] resistance" and argue that while the hidden transcripts of resistance require women to remain at home, in occupied Palestine the home itself becomes a site of resistance.[82]

Shalhoub-Kevorkian argues that, in Palestine, resistance becomes an everyday act. She theorizes the enfleshed bodies of Palestinian women becoming the occupation's battlefield by describing, inter alia, how, when facing the threat of house demolitions, Palestinian women often sleep in their day clothes to avoid being caught in their nightclothes by Israeli soldiers. Militarization, she writes, constructs Palestinian women as boundary markers, and they often become "punching bags" for men both inside and outside the home.[83] Through Palestinian women's narratives, the occupation itself assumes a gender, and Shalhoub-Kevorkian describes the embodied, gendered, social blockages facing women in occupied East Jerusalem as the "politics of militarized dismemberment."[84] Though such blockages often "amputate" their ability to access justice, Shalhoub-Kevorkian shows that, for most of the women, refusing the occupation is not necessarily about resistance but rather about survival and *sumud* (perseverance).

As I am watching, with increasing pain and horror, the genocide committed by Israel against Gaza's women, children, and men, thinking about resistance cannot be limited to the Hamas fighting. I therefore opt for using the term "refusal." Just as Israeli sexual politics must be understood in the context of settler colonialism, part of which is Israel's refusal to observe international law, relentlessly turning all criticism—including the hearing by the International Court of Justice of South Africa's genocide case against it[85]—into accusations of antisemitism, so too is refusal a key component of the sexual politics of the colonized. On the one hand, Israeli sexual politics as refusal is exemplified by Netta Barzilai's "Not Your Toy" refusing patriarchal domination, or by female IDF soldiers refusing to accept a military backseat, preferring to participate enthusiastically alongside male soldiers in the colonization of Palestine, the racial subjugation of the Palestinians, and the Gaza genocide.[86] On the other hand, Palestinian sexual politics is epitomized by everyday acts of refusal by Palestinian women and queers opposing colonization and refusing to remain silent in the face of genocide.

A poignant example of sexual politics as refusal is Palestinian queers opposing Israel's homonational colonial regime and pinkwashing strategies. Lana Tatour focuses on the struggle of the Palestinian queer (PQueer) movement that began organizing in '48 Palestine in the early 2000s.[87] Tatour examines how the racialized and sexualized dimensions of Israel's settler-colonial violence and domination shape PQueer subjectivities and engender forms of sexual politics as refusal. She conceptualizes PQueer refusal as emancipatory in that it responds to both the liberal violence of the settler state and the liberal politics of the global LGBTQ+ movement, and shows how PQueer refusal strategies have developed in relation to—and against—the Israeli LGBTQ+ community, homonationalism, the homocolonial practice of pinkwashing, and what Joseph Massad calls the Gay International.[88] Tatour's study of the PQueer movement illuminates the study of the gendered Palestinian refusal of Zionist colonialism, which often overlooks the gendered and sexualized dimensions of colonial domination and colonized refusal. It is a useful illustration of the role played by sexual politics both in the racialization of the Palestinians and in the Palestinians' refusal to partake in colonial Israel's heteronormative performance of gender.

*Ten*
# ANTISEMITISM AND THE PROXIFICATION OF ANTIRACISM

ALANA LENTIN

FOR MANY YEARS, I DIDN'T WANT TO WRITE ABOUT ANTISEMITISM. WHEN I brought out my short primer, *Racism*, in 2008, my editor asked me to include a chapter on antisemitism, so I did, but I linked it to Islamophobia. In 2019, when I was writing my book *Why Race Still Matters*, the original structure did not include anything on antisemitism. But, during the writing process, I decided to focus the fourth and final chapter on antisemitism and its political usages—which had been brought to the fore by various events, including the "antisemitism crisis" engulfing the British Labour Party at the time.[1] I ended up finding the discussion of antisemitism useful for thinking through race as relational, and racisms in their various guises as codependent:

> Zoning in on antisemitism draws together the various components of this book: the resurgent fusion of race and genetics, the redrawing of the definitional boundaries of racism, and the dismissal of the "merely cultural" as "factionalizing, identitarian and particularistic" (Butler 1998: 33). It opens questions that are imbricated in the racial; questions of nation, belonging and loyalty, of the inextricability of race from the

colonial, of what constitutes whiteness and white supremacy, and of solidarity and its absence.[2]

Earlier, I had also written about antisemitism for a chapter on its role in the interpretation of the meaning of race after the murderous attacks on the French satirical newspaper *Charlie Hebdo*.[3] Until *Why Race Still Matters*, the little I had written on antisemitism expressed my ambivalence about doing so. In 2017, I wrote:

> The route to talking about antisemitism is necessarily paved with caveats: both the impossibility of decoupling from actions carried out in the name of all Jews and the relative inconsequentiality of antisemitism when confronted with the unbearable magnitude of racism faced by Black people, Muslims, migrants and refugees in the societies I have lived in and studied.[4]

However, I also wrote that I felt that the rise in antisemitism, exponential in the wake of Trumpism, had given me license to reflect on my own position vis-à-vis race as a white European Jewish woman with a past and present as a settler on occupied lands, first Palestine and now Gadigal.[5] How do I speak about antisemitism in a way that takes it seriously, both as an increasingly threatening form of political violence—both physical and discursive—and as the form of racism that, as I shall argue, often shapes and defines how and in what terms we can speak of other racisms? I want to write here, and to continue to write, about antisemitism, not only because I am threatened by it, but also because I want to show how according antisemitism the status of the master key of hate is detrimental to the fight to undo racisms.

My task is difficult because discussions of antisemitism lurch between this position and its opposite: that any talk of antisemitism today, particularly on the left, is manipulative and a weapon to disarm activism on behalf of Palestine. In this atmosphere, the opposition to antisemitism has become a proxy for real antiracist commitments: states actively engaged in repressing racialized people both at home and internationally can declare themselves antiracist via opposition to antisemitism. Groups on the far right of the political spectrum with fascist roots and connections also position themselves against antisemitism via their support for Israel and a shared Islamophobia.

Among leftists, too, concerns about antisemitism are dismissed when the left promotes itself as inherently antiracist, allowing for at times careless, at times dangerous amalgamations to be made between Jews and the global capitalist elite, and of all Jews as agents of the Zionist state.

In what follows, I begin by arguing that we must go beyond pointing out the hypocritical double standards that accompany discussions of racism in general and antisemitism in particular. I then widen the perspective on these urgent problems, first by looking at the role that the exceptionalization of antisemitism via the "event" of the Shoah (the Holocaust) has played for the constitution of antiracism. I examine the dead end of philosemitism as an effective challenge to antisemitism, before explaining how dominant anti-antisemitism acts as a proxy for antiracism in ways that are deeply damaging to anticolonialist and antiracist thought and practice. I conclude by arguing that we need to resist the moralist tone of most declarative challenges to antisemitism and place the struggle instead within an anticolonial framework that relates antisemitism to other forms of racism, centers the material over the affective, and is adamant about the possibility of defying both antisemitism and Zionism. This is urgent because, as Valentina Pisanty writes, today it has become normalized for right-wing actors to declare support for Israel and for this to stand in for a form of opposition to antisemitism, while at the same time "rehabilit[ating] the ancient calumny of the Jewish plot to take over the world."[6] On the other hand, the generalized failure of what we can broadly term the antiracist left to pay close attention to how antisemitism relates to other forms of racism and how it may be possible to build alliances with Jews in ways that take our concerns about antisemitism seriously, while staying firmly opposed to Zionism, means that we are poorly equipped to challenge this increasingly dominant right-wing line. Today, it has become urgent to theorize antisemitism as mutually constitutive of other forms of racism, and as a key feature of the architecture of the racial-colonial—not only for Jews, who come increasingly under attack, but in the general aim of attacking racism beyond empty speech.

## BEYOND HYPOCRISY

On February 5, 2021, the International Criminal Court (ICC) announced that it had jurisdiction to start a criminal investigation against Israel for war crimes. Israeli prime minister Benjamin Netanyahu responded with a staged video message. Staring down the camera and gesturing emphatically with his hands, he declared: "When the ICC investigates Israel for fake war crimes, this is pure anti-Semitism." He went on to assert that "the court established to prevent atrocities like the Nazi Holocaust against the Jewish people is now targeting the one state of the Jewish people."[7]

By this logic—one which Netanyahu, who has declared himself leader of world Jewry, constantly reiterates—an attack on Israel is an attack on all Jews. From the opposing perspective, of course, all Jews, wherever they may be in the world and whatever their connection to Israel, if any, are responsible for its war crimes. Speaking soon after the ICC's announcement, the French decolonial intellectual Houria Bouteldja remarked that this is how antisemitism is created, by giving the false impression that Jews and Israel are one and the same.[8] A similar point was made by the Jewish philanthropist George Soros when he remarked, in 2003, that "the policies of the Bush administration and the Sharon administration" had contributed to the resurgence of antisemitism in Europe. For this, and for his support of organizations "permeated by antisemitism," such as Black Lives Matter, Soros has today become the target of increasingly shrill right-wing—including Zionist—opprobrium.[9]

Herein lies the hypocrisy. Netanyahu openly mocks the victims of the Shoah by cynically using their deaths to protect Israel against investigation for its own practices of state murder, land theft, and exploitation of Indigenous Palestinians. But he and other prominent Zionists also join forces with antisemites such as the Hungarian prime minister, Victor Orbán, whose campaign of state-sanctioned antisemitism fixates on Soros as the prototypical figure of the all-powerful, maleficent Jewish banker. For Netanyahu, Orbán is an ally in the fight against antisemitism and against the "threat of radical Islam," which "could endanger the world."[10] As antisemitism is written out of the history of Europe and transposed onto that of Arabs and Muslims, Netanyahu can say that it was the grand mufti of Jerusalem—not Hitler—who was responsible for the extermination of the Jews of Europe.[11] The comfort Israel and its allies have had with the Euro-American extreme right in Poland and Hungary, and with Donald Trump during his time in office, cheapens their performatively reverent speech evoking the Shoah. For these hard-liners, and also for many of their liberal critics,[12] the purported antisemitism of both the Arab states and Muslim people around the world excuses that of their far-right bedfellows—political leaders, fringe parties, and right-wing pundits alike. The fact that Jews were torn from their homes in North Africa and West Asia, first by European colonists and then by Israel with the aim of demographic Jewish hegemony, is rarely introduced to complicate the official origin story of Arab and Muslim antisemitism.[13]

Protests in the dying days of Trump's first presidency, against what he and his supporters claimed was a rigged election result, often included participants waving Israeli flags. Despite the antisemitic conspiracy theories to which many Trump supporters subscribe, white nationalist visions align firmly with those of Israel as a state that "embodies the strong arm of xenophobic nationalism and militarized masculinity, unapologetically pushing back invading ethno-religious Others, expanding its territory, and protecting its heritage in bold defiance of a chorus of liberal outcry."[14] As the right-wing Jewish pundit Ben Shapiro tweeted with regard to Ann Coulter, her antisemitic remarks are "awful, nonsensical . . . [but she] is also super pro-Israel, and has always been so, so I won't lose sleep."[15]

In addition to the obvious hypocrisy of the selective anti-antisemitism of the Israeli state and its supporters, public conversations about the place accorded antisemitism—in comparison, for example, to anti-Blackness or Islamophobia—also emphasize a pick-and-choose attitude toward anti-racism. For example, following the publication in October 2020 of the Equalities and Human Rights Commission report on antisemitism in the British Labour Party, it was remarked that a higher prevalence of Islamophobia and anti-Black racism within both major political parties in the United Kingdom had not received proportionate attention.[16] The Board of Deputies of British Jews, among others, responded to allegations of antisemitism in the Labour Party by repeating that "this wouldn't happen to any other minority." However, a report by the Labour Muslim Network found that a quarter of the 422 Muslim Labour Party members surveyed had experienced Islamophobia firsthand.[17]

Obviously, hypocrisy and selective antiracism were at play, and those criticizing the double standards of both Israel's racism and the disproportionate attention given to antisemitism in the public discourse are entirely correct. However, homing in on hypocrisy is a distraction from a closer examination of what this means about how we interpret and challenge both antisemitism itself and racism and ongoing coloniality more broadly, as well as the links between them. In general, racism is imbued with double standards, but it increasingly seems that there is no other language in which to talk about it. Of course, it is true that placing different expectations on differently racialized groups and individuals is a key way in which racism functions to discriminate and degrade. But I am increasingly dissatisfied with the assumption that drives the exposure of hypocrisy: that the mere laying bare of the patent unfairness of the application of different rules and norms to people on the basis of race will bring about a change. As Gavan Titley has said in relation to racism and freedom of speech, "Of course [the right's] politics is absolutely riven with hypocrisy, but it doesn't work because of hypocrisy."[18] Rather, the hypocrisy is beside the point because of the valence of particular understandings of what constitutes democratic exchange in Titley's account, and definitions of racism in my discussion here. Only once we have relented to dwell on the hypocrisy and have understood the particular political function of a fixation—far from new, but particularly heightened—with Jews and antisemitism can we start to undo the harm done by this philosemitism to the Palestinian cause, and to the antiracist struggle more broadly.

## THE EXCEPTIONALIZATION OF ANTISEMITISM AND THE (RE)DEFINITION OF RACISM

Shoah remembrance as a public ritual and civic duty has eclipsed knowledge of the history of antisemitism, which itself has been reduced to a unique and aberrant event.[19] The detachment of the Shoah from the longer durée of antisemitism and the function "The Jew" had for the racial formation of Europe[20] strongly inform the idea of the Shoah, and, by extension, antisemitism, as anomalous to the story of European, and thus world, progress. The severing of the Shoah from the racializing logics that came to define Europe in opposition both to its internal "others" and to the global majority in the colonial era makes it available to dominant narratives of racism as exception. As I have previously written, Europe's silence about race and its treatment as a taboo subject has contributed to the lack of a public language for talking about its significance for European self-understandings.[21] The construction of the Shoah as exceptional played a significant role in creating this taboo.

The gravity of the genocide, often construed as a mass experiment in eugenics decoupled from the structurally colonial conditions that birthed and
nurtured racial "science," made it untouchable. Michael Rothberg reminds
us that the treatment of the Shoah as exceptional grew in part out of the
relative silence that surrounded it in the early years that followed, the Shoah
taking several decades to become enshrined in public memory in Europe
and beyond. However, the insistence on the Shoah's uniqueness did serve to
"separat[e] it off from other histories of collective violence." The struggle to
connect these, not only to oppose "a hierarchy of suffering"[22] but also to place
the Shoah within the history of coloniality, continues to define public and
scholarly treatment of its legacies.

The Shoah's growth in significance in Europe's telling of history to itself
necessitated the narrative of exception and uniqueness. To see it otherwise,
and to place it in the context of a past and continuous present of race as intrinsic to the formation of colonial modernity and white European supremacy, would entail a reckoning with its meaning with which neither Europe
nor its offshoots in the settler colonies were willing to contend. Instead,
the Shoah—firmly secured in the past—along with other "exceptional" examples, most frequently slavery and apartheid, become the prototype for
racism as states gradually folded the maxim of "never again" into their public
pronouncements without considering what this really implies.

The exceptionalization of the Shoah, and consequently antisemitism,
sits within this landscape: racism is "frozen" in "past events" to which all
other instances can be compared.[23] This pastness of "real racism" sits un-
comfortably with the undeniable presence of systemic racialized exploitation and discrimination across the Global North, as well as the proliferation
of increasingly extremist ideological stances both on the fringes and in the
mainstream of discourse and politics. This racism is open to what Titley calls
debatability, its legitimacy to be named as such constantly subject to question.[24] One of the main ways in which racism is made debatable is through
its comparison to the events of the "real racism" of the past, allowing the
experiences of racialized people today to be scrutinized in perpetual comparison. As I have argued, on this basis the public discourse is shaped by a
narrative of "not racism," a form of discursive racist violence in which not
only is the existence of structurally racist conditions and effects constantly

questioned, but racism is redefined from a hegemonically white perspective that construes it as exceptional and irrational.[25] The tactic of separating so-called real racism from what are portrayed as the exaggerated complaints of those who face racism in a time that many have decided is "postrace" is a familiar one. For example, the Black Lives Matter protests of 2020 were met with dismissals of antiracism and even of critical race theory as extremist ideologies.[26] This rhetoric often refers, as the British writer David Goodhart did in 2017, to the "normal definition" of racism, from which current versions are said to have drifted. For Goodhart, this "normal definition" refers to "irrational hatred, fear or contempt for another group," severing these attitudes from anti-immigrant sentiment, which he sees as justifiable, from institutional racism, and most certainly from colonialism, which is deemed long past.[27] Likewise, the theme of irrationality often accompanies the public discourse on antisemitism and the Shoah, which are treated as incomprehensible hatreds, expunged of politics.

The narrowing of racism to select prototypes, therefore, and its characterization as an irrational attitude held by individuals frees it from what Miri Song has called its "historical basis, severity and power."[28] Rather than seeing race and racism as central to the history of Europe,[29] as imbricated in the development and spread of capitalism,[30] and as a central technology of colonial rule that continues to shape the relationship, both conceptual and material, of Europeanness and non-Europeanness,[31] racism is seen as the bad attitude of irrational, morally repugnant people. Hence, racism has been dislodged from these roots and attached to those it has historically subjugated; the new racists are Black and Brown, and, particularly, Muslim.[32] Their racism, we are told, is apparent in their ungratefulness as migrants, their failure to integrate into the societies of their "hosts," and their temerity to protest in the "wrong way" against the discrimination and exploitation they face. Specifically, their racism is manifested through antisemitism, which, being the main prototype for "real racism," is seen as dragging it back to the present from a dormant past for which Europeans have atoned and from which they have moved on.

Hence, in variants of what the French political theorist Pierre-André Taguieff called the "new Judeophobia," an alliance of Muslims and anti-Zionists is said to have displaced European elites to become the real antisemites of today.[33] My argument is not that antisemitism is never to be found among these groups. Indeed, while it is important to delineate clearly the differences between antisemitism and criticism of Israel, in order to oppose the manipulation of their amalgamation in instruments such as the International Holocaust Remembrance Alliance definition of antisemitism, this does not negate the fact that many opponents of Israel interchange anti-Zionism and antisemitism. However, these antisemitic statements are not made exclusively by members of racialized minority groups and are often just as likely to be found among the "white left" as they are in majority-white organizations in general. However, while we must not deresponsibilize those who express antisemitism, we should acknowledge the role played by Zionism in making Jews and Israel interchangeable. We should also pay close attention to the hierarchies of racism, at the pinnacle of which antisemitism has been placed, and how this serves a hegemonic account that displaces the origins of racism and transposes responsibility for it onto the shoulders of its current victims. Not only does the detachment of antisemitism from its European roots serve the agenda of the European states in the face of Black and Brown resistance to ongoing racism,[34] it also has the effect of tethering Jewishness to whiteness and obscuring the existence of Jews of color and the harms done against them under colonialism and ongoing racist structures, as I now turn to demonstrating in the case of France.[35]

## THE POLITICAL UTILITY OF PHILOSEMITISM IN THE ADVANCE OF STATE RACISM: THE CASE OF FRANCE

Antisemitism, I have suggested, represents the pinnacle of the hierarchy of racisms because it is both exceptional and of the past. The dominant strategy of Euro-America in response to antisemitism after the Shoah was to reduce its long history to the Nazi genocide as a singular event, to detach it from past and continuing racial-colonial rule, and, with the dominance of pro-Zionism and Islamophobia, to locate it as primarily the preserve of Arabs, Muslims, anti-Zionists, and often—via the looming caricatures of Elijah Muhammad or, more recently, the case of the Black British grime artist Wiley—Black people.[36] As I have remarked, this characterization of antisemitism is accompanied by a general recalibration of racism as not, or no longer, a European or a white problem, but one that increasingly holds white people—including, in this vision of things, Jews—in its sights, thus obscuring the different experiences of Black and Arab Jews with regard to everyday and systemic racism.[37] For example, in an article on the "Decolonialism Observatory," a French website set up to track the activities of decolonial and race critical intellectuals, Yana Grinshpun argues that to be antiwhite is to be antisemitic, anti-Western, and anti-Zionist, thus erasing white Christian antisemitism as well as racism against Jews of color.[38] By the same token, the International League Against Racism and Anti-Semitism, or LICRA, one of the oldest French antiracist organizations, which was originally established to campaign against anti-Jewish pogroms, sees "antiwhite racism" as a problem on a par with racism against those racialized as, for example, Black, Brown, Muslim, and Roma. This deracination and universalization of racism serves to delegitimize the struggle of racialized people against state violence, as well as systemic exploitation and discrimination.

In the French case in particular, the elevation of antisemitism above other forms of racism and the cementing together of "antiwhiteness" and attacks on Jews is part of a general campaign against antiracist thought and action that has become acute under President Emmanuel Macron—one that manipulates antisemitism in its service. It is important to note that it was not always concern for antisemitism that motivated the folding of Jews into the nation and into whiteness. It was the expansion of the nation-state, liberal ideology, and colonial rule that undergirded the postrevolutionary French state's need to domesticate the Jews through an emancipation that was experienced by the Orthodox Ashkenazi as an imposition from above.[39] This need was further evident in the 1870 Crémieux Decree, which granted French citizenship to colonized Algerian Jews but not to Muslims—the first step in the de-Arabization of non-European Jews, later completed by Zionism.[40] Neither the emancipation of the Jews nor their becoming French erased the political antisemitism of the late nineteenth century, which mapped onto older forms of Christian Judeophobia.[41] Bkouche notes that it was the Holocaust that made white people out of Jews, reminding us of Catholic monarchist Georges Bernanos's "terrible words" that "after the massacre it was no longer possible to be antisemitic," as though if it were not for the Holocaust, antisemitism could have continued as usual.[42]

What Bouteldja calls "state philosemitism" emerged when Europe realized that it had applied colonialist procedures on its own soil and, as Aimé

Césaire put it, no longer "merely" against "the Arabs of Algeria, the 'coolies' of India, and the [Blacks] of Africa."[43] It does not denote actual love of Jews or concern with antisemitism against all Jews. If that were the case, the antisemitism waged against anti-Zionist Jews, Black Jews, Jews of color, and all those who do not fit into a template of what the modern Jewish subject of the post-Holocaust looks like would be equally protected. The philosemitic defense of Jews and Israel relies on the tacit acceptance of the idea of Jews as perennial foreigners so that even while Jews are being defended, French citizens and Jews are always talked about as separate in official discourse. This reveals how "'Jews' as a category are still not a fully legitimate part of the nation and its identity."[44] For example, in 2004, President Jacques Chirac noted the rise in racist attacks against "our Jewish or Muslim compatriots, *or sometimes quite simply against the French.*"[45] The defense of Jews, then, takes on the most antisemitic of characteristics, the assumption that Jewish loyalty always lies beyond the nation. Arguably, official protection of Israel at all costs is not detached from the antisemitic will for Jews to leave the diaspora, this certainly being a major driver in the rise of Christian Zionism.[46]

State philosemitism thus takes independent agency away from Jews and "unilaterally squeezes us between the forces of power and the popular masses."[47] This positioning is what permits Jews in France to become what Bouteldja has referred to as the "*dhimmis* of the Republic," the *dhimmis* being those Jews and Christians who were accorded protected status under Arab rule in the past.[48] Positioned as such, Jews become aligned with the needs of the state and whiteness and are, to evoke Frantz Fanon, stripped of the capacity for "ontological resistance."[49] It is not that Jews (particularly white, Western Jews), like colonized Africans, are denied permission to define ourselves independently. Rather, just as the white man needs the Black man to define himself, so too the Jew becomes someone for others.

This could be seen in the context of the French National Assembly's passage in February 2021 of the so-called Samuel Paty article of the anti-separatism law, which drew on the association of antisemitism with the purported separatism from French society and its values of mainly Muslim minorities. Paty, a schoolteacher, was murdered in a heinous act by a young man of Chechen origin in October 2020. The law allows for anyone who disrespects the "values of the French republic"—it names "radical Islamism" in particular—to be imprisoned for three years or face a fine of €45,000. The almost unanimous vote in favor of the law came after a campaign targeting what are portrayed as "indigenist teachings" imported into France from North America and infiltrating French schools and universities. The education minister, Jean-Michel Blanquer, accused academics who have, as President Macron put it, "encouraged the ethnicization of social issues" of "intellectual complicity with terrorism."[50] This view is supported by the over one hundred signatories of a manifesto that claimed, in October 2020, that "indigenist, racialist, and 'decolonial' ideologies," imported from North America, were responsible for "conditioning" the violent extremist who murdered Paty. For the representatives of the dominant culture in France, the law against separatism is necessary, to cite Macron, due to the insufficiencies of integration and of "our fight against discrimination, and racism, such as antisemitism," which have bred "our enemy." Here, Macron singles out antisemitism among racisms, claiming that it was the failure to act against it that created the conditions for the murder of Paty (not himself Jewish). Within the conservative Jewish milieu, the murder was interpreted as a natural culmination of the "war on Jews," which has now spread to all spheres of French life.[51] The antiseparatism law—which is, as the Frantz Fanon Foundation has said, a "new demonstration of the coloniality of power" targeting racialized communities already disproportionately policed and punished—participates in driving a further wedge between Jews and other racialized people with whom we should be in solidarity against the incursions of both state and popular racism.[52]

## CREATING ANTIRACIST PROXIES

As the French case makes clear, the state and a whole host of civil society actors, including some of the oldest antiracist organizations, use concern with antisemitism—seen as equivalent to anti-Zionism and as a problem not of European elites but of Muslim minorities and decolonial activists and thinkers—to justify repressive state action against racialized communities. The fight against antisemitism acts as a proxy for a real opposition to racism, with even right-wing actors able to portray themselves as the "real antiracists" because of their performative opposition to antisemitism. In this vision of things, opposition to Muslims and Islamism—the two often being interchanged—and support for repressive laws and policies against them are presented as antiracist because they are said to protect Jews. Whether Jews participate in such calls for repressive measures (and many do) is immaterial to the fact that official opposition to antisemitism acts to whitewash state racism. Clearly, then, this hegemonic anti-antisemitism can also target Jews as either Black or Brown and thus coming within the sights of the repressive and discriminatory forces of the state, or for engaging in thought that goes counter to the dominant ideological frame. In a different setting, such has been the case for Jews, including Israelis, in Germany in recent years. In one example, a closed discussion group organized by Israeli Jewish women in Berlin, the School for Unlearning Zionism, came under public attack as promoting the Boycott, Divestment, Sanctions movement, which was categorized as antisemitic by the Bundestag in 2019.[53]

The tightening of restrictions on critics of Israel should be seen as consistent with the broader repression of antiracist expression that theorizes race in terms of ongoing coloniality and white supremacy, rather than as individual moral wrongdoing. This has wider implications for progressive movements writ large. For example, in 2019, France's National Assembly adopted the International Holocaust Remembrance Alliance definition of antisemitism, which includes "denying the Jewish people their right to self-determination," among other criticisms of Israel, as examples of antisemitism.[54] The catalyst for adopting the definition came after "new philosopher" Alain Finkielkraut was verbally abused by protestors aligned with the *gilets jaunes* grassroots movement for economic justice, who were identified as pro-Palestine supporters—an incident that was hegemonically interpreted as an antisemitic attack.[55]

Pointing out the role played by antisemitism in delegitimizing antiracism and other liberationist politics, however, must be approached with care. From the antisemitic viewpoint, Jews, as Gavin Langmuir writes, are chimerical—"monsters which, although dressed syntactically in the clothes of real humans, have never been seen and are projections of mental processes unconnected with the real people of the outgroup."[56] But antisemitism too has a chimeric quality in the way it is discussed today, readily lending itself to the needs of those who mobilize it as either ubiquitous or a straw man. On the one hand, antisemitism has become a tool with which to disarm political opposition from the left. On the other hand, antisemitism is a *mere* weapon whose mention automatically triggers distrust. This was the simplistic binary cleaved in the case of the "antisemitism crisis" that engulfed the British Labour Party under Jeremy Corbyn. As David Renton rightly argues, because supporters of Corbyn, who was alternately accused of abetting or excusing antisemitism, were disproportionately concerned with the affairs of the party over the principles of antiracism, any existence of antisemitism was automatically dismissed as rightist weaponization.[57] From the other side, those who manipulated the existence of antisemitism in order to attack Corbyn, be it from within or outside the Labour Party, often did not have the concerns of actual Jews at heart. Jews, both for antisemites and for those who manipulate antisemitism for other than antiracist ends, are what David Smith calls "ghostly, walking tropes. They are representations of people, not people per se."[58]

The swing then between the outright dismissal of antisemitism and its manipulation in the interests of states or political actors is of no service in the struggle against it. Antisemitic conspiracy fantasies have grown in the digital media age,[59] exploding exponentially in the midst of the global coronavirus pandemic.[60] Yet, as I have shown, the allegiances between outright conspiratorial antisemites and pro-Zionists, including many conservative Jews, thwarts our ability to mount an antiracist challenge to this newly energized antisemitism. Opponents of antisemitism, Jewish or otherwise, are faced with poorly articulated definitions of antisemitism that see it as fixed in time. As Renton argues, the leftist vision of antisemitism as unchanged since the 1920s and restricted to the furthest corners of the right wing[61] does not recognize that this was never the case, nor that antisemitism, like racism, changes "shape, size, contours, purpose, function—with changes in the economy, the social structure, the system and, above all, the challenges, the resistances of that system."[62] So, defenders of Corbyn, rather than using the opportunity to examine how racisms of all kinds manifest within the Labour Party as a structurally white institution, repeatedly stated that it was the most "anti-racist party," and that accusations of antisemitism were nothing but right-wing smears.[63]

The official opposition to antisemitism, which, as we have seen, ties it to anti-Zionism and to race critical and decolonial thought, and the right of racialized people, particularly Muslims, to oppose state racism, becomes a proxy for real engagement with an antiracist politics. As a consequence, there is a failure at both ends of the political spectrum to engage antisemitism as a real political force. Rather, whether antisemitism is real or an imaginary weapon becomes the conflict that organizes the debate, to the detriment both of Jews ourselves and of the potential to build solidarities with other racialized subjects. This debate is not about antisemitism or racism at all. Rather, these topics are proxies through which those within institutions struggle over power. The question should not be whether antisemitism exists, or whether it is more or less threatening than other forms of racism. Antisemitism exists because the extent to which it is a core ideology at the heart of Euromodernity has not been confronted, just as there is a refusal to confront race in general as a political force. The very posing of such questions, from either side of the political divide, serves as a means to avoid confronting the effects of race, coloniality, and racism on both the local and global scales.

## CONCLUSION

Appealing to the morality of abhorring antisemitism is appealing to those faced with what can at times be career-ending accusations from Zionists and philosemites against those who criticize Israel. Such was the response of the Cameroonian philosopher Achille Mbembe, around whom controversy erupted in 2020 when a right-wing German politician accused him of relativizing the Holocaust after he was announced as an opening speaker for a regional cultural festival. The criticisms of Mbembe focused on his essay "The Society of Enmity," in which he draws comparisons between apartheid South Africa and both the Israeli occupation and the Shoah—though he heavily qualifies the latter comparison, saying that it took place "in an extreme fashion and within a quite different setting."[64] Yet merely placing apartheid and the Shoah side-by-side—never does he equate them—was enough in Germany for Mbembe to be accused of antisemitism.

In a subsequent interview, Mbembe said in response that "the idea that I might harbor hatred and prejudice against any other human being, or any constituted state as such, is totally repugnant."[65] The impulse to appeal to morals—even to people who cynically and selectively deploy antiracism—is understandable; of course, where we stand on racial injustice is bound up with our personal morality. However, to question the effectiveness of this approach in a landscape that has reduced the discussion of racism and antisemitism to one of personal morality rather than politics, it is useful to contrast it with the case of Houria Bouteldja. Bouteldja has continuously faced accusations of antisemitism in her role as the former spokesperson for the Party of the Indigenous of the Republic, from which she has now resigned, and after the publication of her book *Whites, Jews and Us: Towards a Politics of Revolutionary Love.*[66]

In a recent case, an article that Bouteldja published on the leftwing French website *Mediapart* was removed after a public outcry accused her of antisemitism. Bouteldja wrote about the antisemitism directed toward April Benayoum, a French beauty queen crowned Miss Provence, whose father is from Israel. She denounced the antisemitic attacks on Benayoum in no uncertain terms. However, she also used the case to distinguish between antisemitism and criticism of Israel, which had been amalgamated in most accounts of the attacks. Inviting Miss Provence to take a position against the state, rather than her Israeli origins necessitating that she defend it, Bouteldja wrote:

> One can be the daughter of an Israeli and position oneself against the colonial reality of Israel. One cannot be Israeli innocently. [Bouteldja here paraphrases the great anticolonial writer and leader Aimé Césaire, who wrote: "No one colonizes innocently, and no one can colonize without impunity."[67]] However, by making the choice to stand with the anticolonial struggle, [Benayoum] can be sure that the decolonial movement would welcome her with open arms.[68]

Here, Bouteldja rejects a Zionist discourse that sees only one possible fate for Jews: to be inexorably tied to a racist, colonial state that occupies another people in our name, even as we deny or even attempt to dismantle it. To be an anticolonial Jew is anathema, not only to the communal gatekeepers who stand steadfast with the racial colony of Israel, but also to those gentiles who use our tragedy to exculpate their own continuing complicity with racism and colonialism at home and abroad. This binding of Jewishness to Israel works antisemitically to deny Jews the capacity to defy this destiny.

But in insisting on the noninnocence of Miss Provence, Bouteldja also ac-
cuses herself, arguing that the fight against racism must be multidirectional
and introspective. In an article written after her cancellation by *Mediapart*,[69]
she reminded us that she too has declared culpability:

> No French person is innocent, starting with me. . . . Not only am I not
> innocent—because I am French—but I am also a criminal. Therefore,
> I allowed myself to judge Miss Provence not innocent because I had
> already conducted my own trial and had already been served my sen-
> tence. . . . My crime rests on one tangible fact: the share of imperialist rev-
> enues between the Western ruling classes and the white, and to a lesser
> extent non-white, working classes.[70]

Yet this materialist conception of race, which emphasizes its structural
nature and its exploitative effects, does not register with those who hear
racism only in one key: the moral one. This moralistic antiracism focuses
on the attitudes of individuals detached from the structures that produce
them. This dominant understanding of racism couches it in terms of personal wrongdoing, of unsavory and outdated attitudes, refusing to see race
as bound up with colonialism, such as that of the Zionist state. Only in this
moral conception is it possible to conflate anti-Zionism, a form of opposition to colonial domination, with antisemitism, a form of racism that, like
all racisms, is inextricable from colonialism. Responding to accusations of
antisemitism using the language of morality therefore runs the risk of being
unable to disentangle antisemitism and anti-Zionism; more broadly, it can
recompound the antimaterialist view of racism, rather than unsettling it.

What the contrast between the cases of Bouteldja and Mbembe shows is
that appeals to morals have little effect on those who view antisemitism and
its epitome, the Shoah, as purely moral matters, decoupled from the coloni-
ity of race. Decontextualized and depoliticized, antisemitism and the Shoah
have been recast as a trauma at the heart of whiteness. From this perspective, there are two types of antisemitism: good and bad, just as there are good
and bad Jews. Bad antisemitism is presented as "real"; it exists among the
far right, the far left, and Muslims. In contrast, "good antisemitism," which
treats Jews as a racialized subaltern group in service to the state, is left intact.
Bad Jews are those who refuse to allow antisemitism to be instrumentalized

in the service of racial rule. We are anti-Zionist and struggle against racism in all its forms.[71] The bad Jew who refuses to sit in her accorded place is the thorn in the side of the racial state. Therefore, although, as Cohen rightly remarks, white Jews are not external to Euro-American states and elites,[72] it is possible for anticolonialist Jews acting collectively to undermine the role we are assigned under globalized racial rule. For Jews to participate in the top-down project to quell anticolonial resistance and race-critical and decolonial thought, in what is suggested to be Jewish interest, is a ruse. Instead, we must oppose the alignment of opposition to antisemitism with structural white interests, including those of the State of Israel, by reconnecting with what Santiago Slabodsky calls our "barbarian history," the history that ties us to the other subjects of racial rule.[73]

*Eleven*

# MARTIN LUTHER KING AND THE STRUGGLE FOR PALESTINIAN RIGHTS

DAVID PALUMBO-LIU

WHY EMBARK UPON THE IMPOSSIBLE TASK OF DISCOVERING WHAT THE Reverend Martin Luther King Jr. would have thought, had he lived to see how the Israeli occupation of Palestinian territories developed and how that occupation has now turned into what the International Court of Justice has determined to be a plausible case of genocide?[1] The answer is simple: without a thoughtful reflection, rooted in the values in which King actually believed, the Zionist claim that King is one of theirs persists as a tool to delegitimize the case for Palestinian rights. I take my cue in pursuing this task from Hajar Yazdiha, whose book *The Struggle for the People's King: How Politics Transforms the Memory of the Civil Rights Movement* mounts an impressive critique of how white supremacists and others have appropriated and distorted King's words. Yazdiha analyzes "rival social movements' strategic uses and misuses of the memory of the civil rights movement," showing that "in these battles to shape the direction of the societal future, the long trajectories of these reckonings and counterreckonings become apparent."[2] In this chapter, I trace the nature and trajectory of King's ideas as they might help us see how the moral basis of his vision for civil rights can be applied to the Palestinian case and Israel's 2023 genocidal war on Gaza.

Despite being reviled as a rabble-rouser and troublemaker by much of white America, and regarded as an inciter of violence and named "the most dangerous man in America" by the Federal Bureau of Investigation,[3] King was awarded the Nobel Peace Prize in 1964. In 1983, a federal holiday was created to commemorate his life. An ordained minister, a proponent of non-violent civil disobedience, and an orator of brilliance and eloquence, King has become the iconic figure of civil rights in the United States, and those on all sides of the political spectrum have been anxious to secure his posthumous endorsement of their views. Defenders of the State of Israel are no exception. In particular, many of them have used King's words both to endorse Israel's settler colonial project and to support their contention, made in order to discredit the cause of Palestine, that advocates for Palestinian rights are antisemites.

Before addressing these assertions, it is important to consider two things that complicate our understanding of how King's beliefs might be applied to the present situation in Palestine. The first is something that Michael R. Fischbach treats in detail in his book *Black Power and Palestine: Transnational Countries of Color*. In the fourth chapter, entitled "Balanced and Guarded: Martin Luther King Jr. on the Arab-Israeli Tightrope," Fischbach explains the political dilemma King faced with regard to speaking out on Palestine: he was caught between militant members of the Black Power movement with whom he had to work, and long-standing Jewish American allies who had been pillars of the civil rights movement. Therefore, one can take both King's silence on the matter of Palestine and his comments echoing Zionist talking points (for example, that Palestine was a land without people for a people without land) in at least two ways: as sincere expressions of belief (positive and negative), or as cautiously applied silence or speech. Or even both. However, one episode illustrates that King was stuck in more than simply a political quandary. Fischbach writes:

> In the spring of 1965 the American Jewish Committee proposed a trip to Israel, where King would be a guest of the Israeli government. He accepted this invitation in May of 1965 but never acted on it.... King did not accept these invitations, but about that same time, he began developing

plans to travel to the Middle East on his own. He started planning a huge pilgrimage of American Christians who would travel both to Israel and the West Bank in late 1967. King must have been affected deeply enough by his own pilgrimage to the Holy Land that he wanted to return in the company of others, although on his own terms, not as an honored guest of Israeli and Jewish groups.[4]

King told his aides what would happen "if he went ahead with the pilgrimage after Israel's lightning victory and occupation of the Christian holy sites in Jerusalem and the West Bank in the first week of June 1967":

> "I'd run into the situation where I'm damned if I say this and I'm damned if I say that no matter what I'd say, and I've already faced enough criticism including pro-Arab. . . . I just think that if I go, the Arab world, and of course Africa and Asia for that matter, would interpret this as endorsing everything that Israel has done, and I do have questions of doubt. . . . I don't think I could come out unscathed." Too much was at stake: his vision of how to continue the fight for civil rights, how to respond to the challenges to that vision posed by rival Black Power militants, his need to speak out against war and uphold the principle of nonviolence, and his need to maintain good ties with Jewish supporters.[5]

The fact that the apostle of nonviolence had come out strongly against the American war in Vietnam in his famous speech "A Time to Break Silence," delivered at the Riverside Church in New York in April 1967, was another reason why it was becoming increasingly difficult for King to be associated with Israel's preemptive strike and subsequent military occupation of Arab territory—territory that included the holiest shrines in Christianity. King was also worried about Israel becoming "smug and unyielding" after its massive victory.[6]

Before I delve into this passage, something needs mentioning with regard to "Jewish supporters." Then, as today, the tendency has been to act as if all Jewish Americans are uniformly Zionists, and therefore King had to be especially cautious when speaking about Palestine. In fact, during his lifetime, King might well have found non-Zionists and anti-Zionists among his Jewish allies. In his recent book *Our Palestine Question: Israel and American Jewish*

*Dissent 1948–1978*, Geoffrey Levin tells of rabbis such as Morris Lazaron and Elmer Berger, who were vocal advocates for Palestinian rights. He explains that in the 1960s and 1970s, there were numerous Jewish American organizations—such as the American Jewish Alternative to Zionism and the Committee on New Alternatives in the Middle East—that were deeply involved in non-Zionist or anti-Zionist work.[7] These organizations were building on the work of similar Jewish American groups that came into existence at the same time as the State of Israel—some even argued for the Palestinian right of return and were openly hostile to the equation of Judaism with Zionism. Indeed, as Levin points out, some felt that such an equation was dangerous to the State of Israel, as well as to Jews in the diaspora. All the more reason to believe that had he lived longer, and perhaps visited Palestine on his own, King would have felt more compelled to speak out for Palestinian rights.

Returning to Fischbach's account, what we see here is not just the "tightrope" that King had to walk, but also his ardent interest in witnessing history with his own eyes, unblinkered by State "guidance." King had to understand directly what was going on—this would help him find the right words to say, or not to say. His commitment was for justice for all, and this required both historical accuracy and political vision. I choose the words "witnessing" and "vision" purposefully, for this allows me to make my point about the second issue that complicates our understanding of King and Palestine. What is lost in many of these debates is the fact that King worked within the prophetic tradition.

As Kenyatta R. Gilbert notes, "King used a prophetic voice in his preaching—the hopeful voice that begins in prayer and attends to human tragedy. Indeed, the best of African-American preaching is three-dimensional—it is priestly, it is sage, it is prophetic."[8] Cornel West asserts that "King's radical love was Christocentric in content and black in character. Like the Christocentric language of the Black Church that produced the radical King—Jesus as the Bright and Morning Star against the backdrop of the pitch darkness of the night."[9] One can see this facet of King's oratory most famously in his 1963 "I Have a Dream" speech,[10] but his use of the phrasing regarding "the arc of the moral universe"[11] perhaps illustrates his commitment to the prophetic tradition even more, for it shows that his words are often borrowed from others in that tradition.

As Mychal Denzel Smith points out:

> "The arc of the moral universe is long, but it bends toward justice" is King's clever paraphrasing of a portion of a sermon delivered in 1853 by the abolitionist minister Theodore Parker. . . . In that sermon, Parker said: "I do not pretend to understand the moral universe. The arc is a long one. My eye reaches but little ways. I cannot calculate the curve and complete the figure by experience of sight. I can divine it by conscience. And from what I see I am sure it bends toward justice."[12]

Smith points out that by evoking the words of an abolitionist, King was mobilizing the prophetic tradition to activist purposes. There was no chance that King believed that the arc would result in justice without human beings subscribing to and acting on a program of liberation. Therefore, I argue, extracting (and often decontextualizing, or only partially citing) King's words (or silences) can result in an image of King as a Zionist. But to do this would be to erase violently the very living and prophetic tradition that King saw as his calling. I assert that that prophetic tradition is exactly the liberatory ethos that clearly and decisively separates King from both secular Zionists and Christian Zionism.

If we understand this, we can make a case not for "where Martin Luther King really stood" (the title of one Zionist piece), but for where his words would lead us today. Simply put, those who would make King into a Zionist seek to lock him into a narrow, archived message that supports their case. This chapter suggests that we instead let King's words flow into the present, guided by the virtues and values he embraced and for which he died, and into the future of Palestinian liberation.

### KING'S ACTIVISM

It has been argued that there were two major phases of King's activism, the first being his work on Black rights, which is closely identified with Selma and the civil rights movement, and a second phase wherein he expanded his scope to include a set of broader rights. During this period, King took on the issue of equality for all, the antiwar movement, conflicts in the Middle East, and housing and economic rights. He became increasingly concerned with legal forms of segregation, whereby inequality and the denial of all sorts of rights to different groups of people were hardwired into the legal architecture of the state. While there may have been a temporal division between these two phases, there was no moral or ethical discontinuity. King's struggles for equality, freedom, and rights for all would logically extend to Palestine. Nevertheless, advocates for Israel freeze King in time and into the image they have created for him.

There are two main elements in the case for King as a Zionist. First, the supporters of Israel take King's genuine criticisms of antisemitism and bend them to incriminate pro-Palestinian activism. Second, they use an oft-cited remark that King made to support Israel's need for security, but omit his remark in that same interview about the need for Arab security. By citing one and not the other, they erase the very reason that King put them side by side: for him, the two were interdependent. Furthermore, they take words that King uttered at a point in history when the occupation of Palestinian territories was only at its start and when the full contours of what was to follow— the destruction of more and more Palestinian villages and the construction of more and more illegal settlements—were still blurred. As the case for "security" increasingly took the shape of violent acts of ethnic cleansing and the destruction of property and infrastructure, any chance of "security" for Palestinians was erased as well. King's support for Israel is best understood as support for the idea of a secure homeland for the Jewish people, where Jews could find safe harbor from the horrors of the Holocaust during World War II, and from any chance that they would suffer another genocide. In no case should it be seen as an endorsement of Israel perpetrating its own genocide against the Palestinians. Similarly, his criticism of antisemitism should not be used to protect Zionism from criticism, which is how it has been used by Zionists.

Those making these claims cite a letter that King supposedly wrote to an "anti-Zionist friend":

> You declare, my friend; that you do not hate the Jews, you are merely "anti-Zionist." . . . And I say, let the truth ring forth from the high mountain tops, let it echo through the valleys of God's green earth: When people criticize Zionism, they mean Jews. . . . Anti-Semitism, the hatred of the Jewish people, has been and remains a blot on the soul of mankind. In this we are in full agreement. So know also this: anti-Zionist is inherently anti-Semitic, and ever will be so.[13]

Taken at face value, this does appear to be unequivocal. However, serious doubt has been raised as to the authenticity of the text. This passage supposedly originated from a piece entitled "Letter to an Anti-Zionist Friend" in an August 1967 issue of the *Saturday Review*.[14] But researchers have found no letter from King in any of the four August 1967 issues of that magazine. Some have claimed that the letter was also published in a book by King entitled *This I Believe: Selections from the Writings of Dr. Martin Luther King Jr.* But, according to the *Electronic Intifada*, "no such book was listed in the bibliography provided by the King Center in Atlanta, nor in the catalogs of several large public and university libraries."[15] A search of all electronic databases (including that of Stanford University's Martin Luther King, Jr. Research and Education Institute) confirms this.

There is no doubt whatsoever that, in the historical persecution of the Jewish people, King saw a terrible case of injustice. But he also used it as an analogy for other cases worldwide of bigotry, racism, and genocide. That is, antisemitism did not have a privileged status above all other forms of bigotry. Speaking before the Convention of the American Jewish Congress in 1958, King stated:

> Every Negro leader is keenly aware, from direct and personal experience, that the segregationists make no fine distinctions between the Negro and the Jew. The irrational hatred motivating his actions is as readily turned against Catholic, Jew, Quaker, Liberal and One-Worlder, as it is against the Negro. . . . [Their] aim is to maintain through cruel segregation groups whose uses as scapegoats can facilitate their political and social rule over all people. Our common fight is against these deadly enemies of democracy, and our glory is that we are chosen to prove that courage is a characteristic of oppressed people, however cynically and brutally they are denied full equality and freedom.[16]

Here, King not only draws the connection between the racism that plagued the Black community and that which affected the Jewish community, but also extends the analogy to all peoples suffering from persecution and anti-democratic forces. It is precisely King's ability to sympathize with the plight of all oppressed people—regardless of race, religion, or ethnicity—that leads one to believe that sympathy for Palestinians would not be beyond his scope of interest, nor would vibrant criticism of the sources of their oppression.

In particular, Israel's denial of democratic rights and equality to Palestinians and others (such as African asylum seekers and non-Jewish migrants) would have been in contradiction to the State of Israel that King imagined.

The second—and the most substantial and most often deployed—element that Zionists rely on in arguing that King would support Israel is a statement they use to show that he prioritized Israel's security. The most highly cited text is a 1968 interview he did with his close friend, Rabbi Abraham Joshua Heschel, which reads in part:

> On the Middle East crisis, we have had various responses. The response of some of the so-called young militants again does not represent the position of the vast majority of Negroes. There are some who are color-consumed and they see a kind of mystique in being colored, and anything non-colored is condemned. We do not follow that course in the Southern Christian Leadership Conference, and certainly most of the organizations in the civil rights movement do not follow that course.
>
> I think it is necessary to say that what is basic and what is needed in the Middle East is peace. Peace for Israel is one thing. Peace for the Arab side of that world is another thing. Peace for Israel means security, and we must stand with all of our might to protect its right to exist, its territorial integrity. I see Israel, and never mind saying it, as one of the great outposts of democracy in the world, and a marvelous example of what can be done, how desert land almost can be transformed into an oasis of brotherhood and democracy. Peace for Israel means security and that security must be a reality.
>
> On the other hand, we must see what peace for the Arabs means in a real sense of security on another level. Peace for the Arabs means the kind of economic security that they so desperately need. These nations, as you know, are part of that third world of hunger, of disease, of illiteracy. I think that as long as these conditions exist there will be tensions, there will be the endless quest to find scapegoats. So there is a need for a Marshall Plan for the Middle East, where we lift those who are at the bottom of the economic ladder and bring them into the mainstream of economic security.[17]

What we find here is a series of interlocked comments that, taken together, form a more complex image of King's feelings about the Middle East. First, he sought to distance himself from young Black militants, for whom—in distinction from King's earlier statement on Black and Jewish suffering—an analog to their oppression was not the oppression of the Jews, but rather the Zionist oppression of the Palestinians. Nevertheless, as Fischbach points out, King found a way to articulate a position that was sympathetic to the Palestinians. He did so by aligning his efforts to improve the conditions of Black American life through economic means with a parallel attention to the economic security of Arabs. This demonstrates more than political finesse: it in fact aligns the Palestinian cause with the issues that were now much more on King's mind—the anticolonial war in Vietnam, and what would become the Poor People's March and all that it represented.

In this regard, it is useful to compare the 1968 interview with a 1967 statement found in "The Middle East Question," delivered by King at the Southern Christian Leadership Conference (SCLC) in Chicago in September. Again, supporters of Israel read this statement selectively, without acknowledging the fuller context and rationale behind it. They fail to note how King purposefully ties together diplomatic, political, and economic perspectives in ways that remain relevant today. Its basis lies not only in King's commitment to democracy but also in his understanding of material history:

> SCLC and Dr. King have repeatedly stated that the Middle East problem embodies the related questions of security and development. *Israel's right to exist as a state in security is incontestable. At the same time the great powers have the obligation to recognize that the Arab world is in a state of imposed poverty and backwardness that must threaten peace and harmony.* Until a concerted and democratic program of assistance is [effected], tensions cannot be relieved. Neither Israel nor its neighbors can live in peace without an underlying basis of economic and social development.
>
> At the heart of the problem are oil interests. As the American Jewish Congress has stated, "American policies in the Middle East have been motivated in no small measure by the desire to protect the $2,500,000,000 stake which U.S. oil companies have invested in the area." Some Arab feudal rulers are no less concerned for oil wealth and neglect the plight of their own peoples. The solution will have to be found in statesmanship by Israel and progressive Arab forces who in concert with the great powers recognize that fair and peaceful solutions are the concern of all humanity and must be found.[18]

King makes clear that security for Israel and development for Arabs go hand in hand. And, in this sense, it is wrong to think that King would extend an unconditional defense of Israeli actions for the sake of "security" then, or in the future, if it further worsened Arab poverty and oppression.

While Israel's advocates elide King's equal concern for Arab security, one of them actually does worse. Martin Kramer recognizes that aspect of King's statements, but only to claim that King would support Donald Trump's plan for Israel-Palestine:

> It is interesting to note that King's idea of "economic security" as a pre-condition of peace is still very much alive today. Indeed, rumors have floated that it forms the core of the much-anticipated "peace plan" devised by Jared Kushner on behalf of his father-in-law. If so, it would not be outrageous for the president to claim inspiration from King.[19]

This is perhaps the most egregious example of the kinds of distortions that Yazdiha critiques in her book.

Finally, Zionists wishing to claim King for their own are fond of citing his belief that Israel had a "right to exist," but it is crucial to acknowledge that this belief was inseparable from his belief that Israel was a democracy. Its right to exist was predicated on its being a democracy: "Peace for Israel means security, and we must stand with all of our might to protect its right to exist. . . . I see Israel, and never mind saying it, as one of the great outposts of democracy in the world."[20] What would King have said if he had witnessed Israel's abrogation of its responsibilities to actually be a democracy?[21] How would he have regarded the 2018 Nation-State Law passed by the Knesset as anything but antidemocratic? For that law declares, among other things, that "the right to exercise national self-determination in the State of Israel is unique to the Jewish people."[22]

Just as King probably would not have acquiesced to the notion that Israel's security could be based on its stealing of Palestinian land (Israel's justification of the occupation is, after all, that Israel is in a precarious position in the Middle East), so too he would have deplored the development of an apartheid state in Israel. It is this particular instantiation of Israeli statehood that would place it squarely within a constellation of similarly oppressive and undemocratic states and their similarly unjust practices.

## COLONIALISM, IMPERIALISM, AND SEGREGATION

Kramer offers an explanation of why King critiqued some cases of colonialism and imperialism but did not mention Israel-Palestine:

> King often broadly denounced imperialism and colonialism. But in choosing which foreign causes to champion, he consistently preferred those, from South Africa to Vietnam, in which peace would involve reconciliation across a clear racial divide. By King's criteria, the Palestine conflict lacked this marker: it was national or religious, but not racial.[23]

It is hard to reduce Vietnam to a "racial" war because, at its core, it was a civil war between two national groups, one communist and the other capitalist. It is also hard not to see the racial element in Israel-Palestine, where the war is predominantly between Western European Jews and Arab Palestinians. In any case, Kramer's essay again exemplifies the reductions performed by those Zionists who claim King as one of their own. In fact, King's growing understanding of international struggles led him to recognize the connection between colonialism and segregation.

King gives this account of his meeting with Ahmed Ben Bella, the leader of the Algerian War of Independence and the country's first elected president:

> For Ben Bella, it was unmistakably clear that there is a close relationship between colonialism and segregation. . . . Either we must solve our human relations dilemma occasioned by race and color prejudice— and solve it soon—or we shall lose our moral and political voice in the world community of nations. . . . We must face the inescapable fact that the shape of the world today does not afford us the luxury of an anemic democracy.[24]

Once again, we see the connection that King ceaselessly made between deprivation, poverty, and the denial of rights, and their threats to both peace and democracy.

In 1959, King delivered a speech mentioning one of his primary guiding stars, Mahatma Gandhi. He commented precisely on Gandhi's drawing of a parallel between colonialism and segregation, between India under British rule and South Africa under apartheid:

This was the exploitation that Mahatma Gandhi noticed years ago. And even more than that, these people were humiliated and embarrassed and segregated in their own land. There were places that the Indian people could not even go in their own land. The British had come in there and set up clubs and other places and even hotels where Indians couldn't even enter in their own land. Gandhi looked at all of this, and as a young lawyer, after he had just left England and gotten his law, received his law training, he went over to South Africa. And there he saw in South Africa, and Indians were even exploited there.

And one day he was taking a train to Pretoria, and he had first-class accommodations on that train. And when they came to took up the tickets, they noticed that he was an Indian, that he had a brown face, and they told him to get out and move on to the third-class accommodation, that he wasn't supposed to be there with any first-class accommodation. And Gandhi that day refused to move, and they threw him off the train. And there, in that cold station that night, he stayed all night, and he started meditating on his plight and the plight of his people. And he decided from that point on that he would never submit himself to injustice, or to exploitation.

It was there on the next day that he called a meeting of all of the Indians in South Africa, in that particular region of South Africa, and told them what had happened, and told them what was happening to them every day, and said that, "We must do something about it. We must organize ourselves to rid our community, the South African community, and also the Indian community back home, of the domination and the exploitation of foreign powers."[25]

Later, in a statement delivered at the 1962 American Negro Leadership Conference on Africa, King went so far as to assert: "Colonialism and segregation are nearly synonymous . . . because their common end is economic exploitation, political domination, and the debasing of human personality."[26] In one particular instance, the manner in which King expressed this belief bears importantly on today's discussions regarding Palestine. According to the King Institute, "King believed South Africa was home to 'the world's worst racism' and drew parallels between struggles against apartheid in South

Africa and struggles against 'local and state governments committed to "white supremacy'" in the southern United States."[27]

In his sermon "The American Dream," delivered at the Ebenezer Baptist Church in 1965, King tells a remarkable story. During a trip to India, he is presented as an example of an "American untouchable":

> The principal introduced me and then as he came to the conclusion of his introduction, he says, "Young people, I would like to present to you a fellow untouchable from the United States of America." And for the moment I was a bit shocked and peeved that I would be referred to as an untouchable.
>
> Pretty soon my mind dashed back across the mighty Atlantic. And I started thinking about the fact that at that time no matter how much I needed to rest my tired body after a long night of travel, I couldn't stop in the average motel of the highways and the hotels of the cities of the South. I started thinking about the fact that no matter how long an old Negro woman had been shopping downtown and got a little tired and needed to get a hamburger or a cup of coffee at a lunch counter, she couldn't get it there. I started thinking about the fact that still in too many instances, Negroes have to go to the back of the bus and have to stand up over empty seats. I started thinking about the fact that my children and the other children that would be born would have to go to segregated schools. I started thinking about the fact: twenty million of my brothers and sisters were still smothering in an airtight cage of poverty in an affluent society. I started thinking about the fact: these twenty million brothers and sisters were still by and large housed in rat-infested, unendurable slums in the big cities of our nation, still attended inadequate schools faced with improper recreational facilities. And I said to myself, "Yes, I am an untouchable, and every Negro in the United States of America is an untouchable." And this is the evilness of segregation: it stigmatizes the segregated as an untouchable in a caste system. We hold these truths to be self-evident, if we are to be a great nation, that all men are created equal. God's black children are as significant as his white children. "We hold these truths to be self-evident." One day we will learn this.[28]

Among many other things, what is remarkable about this speech is King's moment of resentment at being called an "untouchable." He reveals then just how infectious bigotry can be. The fact that he pauses and reflects upon that act of bigotry on his part indicates that he was open to setting aside learned prejudices and examining that point of identification objectively. Indeed, if King could extend that empathy and understanding to Dalits in India and to Blacks in America, he could extend it too to Palestinians and objectively evaluate their case.

King certainly did so with regard to the Japanese Americans who had been interned during World War II. In fact, King saw state-backed segregation precisely as fascist:

> I don't have any faith in the whites in power responding in the right way.... They'll treat us like they did our Japanese brothers and sisters in World War II. They'll throw us into concentration camps. The Wallaces and the Birchites will take over. The sick people and the fascists will be strengthened. They'll cordon off the ghetto and issue passes for us to get in and out.[29]

Here, King displays his willingness to draw a historical analogy between the oppressions faced by different racial minorities. We would uphold King's principles by supposing that he would extend his analogy to the Palestinians, as well as to interned Japanese Americans. After all, Palestinians are relegated into ghettos and required to have "passes" for passage in or out; there are separate roadways for Jews and Palestinians; Palestinians are dispossessed of their homes and lands; and Palestinians are deprived of equal rights. It is impossible to believe that this would square in any way with the freedom and equality that King fought for all his life.

A critique of Israel as an international criminal in its illegal seizure of Palestinian territories, a recognition of its colonial, segregationist, and apartheid project, and a radical rethinking of his support for Israel as a non-democratic—indeed, antidemocratic and even fascist—state, would be consistent with King's overall project, which was for freedom for all:

> The determination of Negro Americans to win freedom from every form of oppression springs from the same profound longing for freedom that motivates oppressed peoples all over the world. The rhythmic beat of deep discontent in Africa and Asia is at bottom a quest for freedom and human dignity on the part of people who have long been victims of colonialism.[30]

King was far from dematerializing colonial and imperial ideologies. But those ideologies, and their material effects, inform his precise understanding of a global, and raced, interdependent economy. Consider this excerpt from a 1967 sermon:

> Don't forget in doing something for others that you have what you have because of others. Don't forget that. We are tied together in life and in the world. And you may think you got all you got by yourself. But you know, before you got out here to church this morning, you were dependent on more than half of the world. You get up in the morning and go to the bathroom, and you reach over for a bar of soap, and that's handed to you by a Frenchman. You reach over for a sponge, and that's given to you by a Turk. You reach over for a towel, and that comes to your hand from the hands of a Pacific Islander. And then you go on to the kitchen to get your breakfast. You reach on over to get a little coffee, and that's poured in your cup by a South American. Or maybe you decide that you want a little tea this morning, only to discover that that's poured in your cup by a Chinese. Or maybe you want a little cocoa, that's poured in your cup by a West African. Then you want a little bread and you reach over to get it, and that's given to you by the hands of an English-speaking farmer, not to mention the baker. Before you get through eating breakfast in the morning, you're dependent on more than half the world. That's the way God structured it; that's the way God structured this world. So let us be concerned about others because we are dependent on others.[31]

It should go without saying that in all these exchanges, King would stress the importance of economic freedom and independence, the centrality of the human dimension. The illegal blockade that the Israeli government has placed on Gaza, and the conditions under which Palestinians labor, would surely not escape his disapprobation.

Ultimately, and most importantly, not only did King diagnose a global condition of struggles against colonialism and imperialism and for democracy, he also called on the global community to form lines of solidarity with these struggles:

> We are challenged to rise above the narrow confines of our individualistic concerns to the broader concerns of all humanity. The new world is a world of geographical togetherness. . . .

If we are to speed up the coming of the new age we must have the moral courage to stand up and protest against injustice wherever we find it.[32]

Note here that King is certainly not anti-British, anti-French, or anti-Dutch, but he is decidedly against the systematic practices undertaken by those governments to colonize their subjects and deny them rights. So, it is not at all unreasonable that King might criticize any government while cherishing its people, and it is entirely reasonable to believe that he would answer his own call for solidarity with all oppressed peoples. In statement after statement cited here, there is no doubt that King would regard the Palestinians as an oppressed people.

The fact that King explicitly linked colonialism, imperialism, fascism, and segregation, as well as economic injustice and antidemocratic suppression, and saw them all as global phenomena, suggests that he would indeed make connections broadly in ways that would similarly transcend any allegiance to one nation. In this respect, we should now turn to the largest organized solidarity campaign for Palestinian rights—the Boycott, Divestment, Sanctions (BDS) movement.

Consider the fact that when King insisted that struggles for freedom demand work at the international level, he chose the South African apartheid state as an exemplary case:

An international emergency which involves the poor, the dispossessed, and the exploited of the whole world. . . .

Even entrenched problems like the South African government and its racial policy could be tackled on this level. . . . Indeed, although it is obvious that nonviolent movements for social change must internationalize, because of the interlocking nature of the problems they all face, and because otherwise those problems will breed war, we have hardly begun to build the skills and the strategy, or even the commitment, to planetize our movement for social justice.[33]

In that regard, he might well have been a supporter of BDS, which has, since its beginnings, noted its indebtedness to the antiapartheid movement. Several things lead me to make this claim, including the following three factors.

First, given King's interest in the specific role of the church as a moral beacon, he would have seen how numerous religious groups—such as the Mennonite Church USA, the Presbyterian Church (USA), the United Church of Christ, the pension fund of the United Methodist Church, and several Quaker branches (including the American Friends Service Committee)—have partially or completely divested from Israeli businesses in the Occupied Palestinian Territories.[34] Second, the 2016 statement from the Movement for Black Lives supporting the Palestinians and all people living under oppression resoundingly echoes King's spirit:

> The Movement for Black Lives stands with the Palestinian people and especially those in Gaza, that have been engaging in resistance at the Gaza border. As we watched the brutal attacks on these brave activists which continued during and after the opening of the U.S. embassy in Jerusalem, we were painfully reminded of what happens when Black people, here in the U.S., decide to resist. We know that the United States government sends the same weapons to Tel Aviv as it sends to Ferguson, and hundreds of other cities across the country. We know that police officers in the United States learn the tactics of war from Israeli police forces, who come annually to train U.S. officers in methods of oppression, surveillance and murder. We understand that we are connected to the Palestinian people by our shared demand for recognition and justice and our long histories of displacement, discrimination and violence. . . .
>
> We stand on the side of those fighting for the freedom of Black people, Palestinians and oppressed people all around the world.[35]

Finally, the current global protests against Israeli genocide and apartheid bear witness to the reach and strength of King's expansive vision.

## CONCLUSION

> We must use time creatively, in the knowledge that the time is always ripe to do right.
>
> —Martin Luther King Jr.[36]

At the start of this chapter, I argued that King's words should be seen within the prophetic tradition. I suggested that freezing those words in time and voiding their application to today's world betrays that tradition. To be sure, we embark on an uncertain path if we too quickly set aside history. Appropriating King's eloquence to serve our purposes without thorough grounding in the full context of their utterance is dangerous and deceptive. Still, there is no doubt that the debates on King's legacy will continue so long as there is interest, and, even in this case, we can see the usefulness of King's legacy in provoking debate and dissent.

But, ultimately, King would want us to look to the future, along the trajectory of a moral universe carried along by international civil society. What we find today is concrete proof that the mission has found worldwide volunteers. As I write this, in the spring of 2024, the world witnesses the explosion of the "Student Intifada," in protest of Israel's genocide in Gaza and in support of Palestinian liberation, starting in the United States but now spreading globally. The central feature of this movement is the demand that universities "disclose and divest"—that is, disclose and divest their holdings in companies that aid, abet, and profit off Israel's genocidal attacks on Gaza and its ethnic cleansing of the West Bank. At the time of writing, the attacks have left more than 40,000 Palestinians dead—70 percent of whom are women and children—and destroyed schools, hospitals, universities, libraries, mosques, and churches. The movement's demands emanate from student encampments, which are nonviolent autonomous zones carved out of university spaces. Make no mistake, they are directly inherited from King.

In 1968, the year of his assassination, King was planning the Poor People's Campaign. A central feature was to be "Resurrection City,"

> an ambitious direct action campaign with the purpose of expanding the national conversation about Civil Rights in America. His idea was to gather people from around the country and from different races and ethnic backgrounds who shared a common struggle—the problems of poverty. Dr. King's original plan involved an unpermitted (and illegal) occupation of the National Mall by the poor, making the realities of economic inequality visible to the nation's leaders right on their doorsteps. King envisioned mass arrests of the protestors which he hoped would stir sympathy among the American public.[37]

After King's death, the project was realized by Reverend Ralph Abernathy and others—including Jesse Jackson, who stated that "Resurrection City cannot be seen as a mudhole in Washington, but *it is rather an idea unleashed in history.*"[38] In this chapter, I have looked not at the archive of King's statements on Palestine and the Palestinians, which are admittedly sparse for some of the reasons I have suggested, but, rather, at the legacy of words and actions that King did set out for us to witness, and from which to draw our conclusions. It is up to each of us to keep the faith he placed in us.

# Acknowledgments

We want to begin by acknowledging the Traditional Owners and Custodians of the stolen Gadigal and Bedegal land on which a significant part of our work on this book was done. We pay our respects to Elders past and present and acknowledge that sovereignty has never been ceded. As we witness the genocide in Gaza from so-called Australia, we are reminded that settler colonialism has always been premised on genocide, and that liberation is interconnected.

This book is a collective effort. We started working on it in 2019, and so our deepest gratitude is to the contributors for their patience. It has been a pleasure and an honor to work with such a brilliant group of scholars who have been so generous with their time and engagement and from whom we have learned a great deal. As we conclude this project, the genocide in Gaza continues. We especially want to acknowledge the toll that this horrifying period has taken on the Palestinians involved in this book: Yasmeen Abu-Laban, Seraj Assi, Noura Erakat, and Sherene Seikaly. We thank them for their commitment and their labor.

At Stanford University Press, we thank Kate Wahl, our editor, who believed in the project from the beginning and whose vision and meticulous attention to detail helped shape the final product. We also thank Laleh Khalili and Sherene Seikaly, the coeditors of the Stanford Studies in Middle Eastern and Islamic Societies and Cultures series in which this book is published, for their care and support for the book. Seikaly also offered thoughtful engagement and incisive feedback, reminding us that Palestine was never an island and must be located within regional and global histories, and that Palestine has much to contribute to, and not just benefit from, the study of race. To the anonymous reviewers who read the book with great generosity and offered valuable feedback, thank you.

Our immense gratitude to the Palestinian artist Tayseer Barakat for allowing us to use his incredibly powerful art on the cover of this book. We thank Gil Hochberg for pointing us to Barakat's work and the piece selected for the cover, as well as Naif Shaqqur and Majd Kayyal for their help and advice.

We also thank the Faculty of Arts, Design and Architecture and the School of Social Sciences at the University of New South Wales, where Lana is based, for their generous support. This support has been indispensable to our ability to finish the book. We thank Michelle Nichols, who helped prepare the manuscript for submission. We would be lost without her.

We would also like to offer our individual thanks.

From Lana: I thank Ronit Lentin, who planted the initial seed for this book. I am grateful to Dirk Moses, Sherene Seikaly, Jumana Bayeh, and the anonymous reviewers for reading and commenting on the introduction with care and intellectual rigor, and to Noura Erakat for our conversations on race, Zionism, and settler colonialism. My gratitude also to the participants in the workshop "Race, Religion, and the Question of Palestine," run and hosted by the Center for Palestine Studies and generously funded by the Institute for Religion, Culture and Public Life, both at Columbia University. This was such an invigorating space, and the conversations we had stayed with me as I was working on the book. I am grateful to Lila Abu-Lughod for suggesting that we create this space at CPS to discuss race and Palestine, and it was an honor to co-convene the workshop together with Nadia Abu El-Haj. Maya Wind and Brenna Bhandar kindly invited me to present my work on race, racism, and the question of Palestine at the University of British Columbia. I thank Maya and Brenna and the participants for a wonderful and stimulating conversation.

To Randa Abdel-Fattah, Paula Abboud, Jumana Bayeh, Na'ama Carlin, Sara Dehm, and Sara Saleh for their friendship and care, which have sustained me, especially since October 2023. To my sisters, Duna and Adan, and my parents, Misbah and Amal, who always hold me and have space for me. And to Noam Peleg and our gorgeous kids, Neal and Minah, for being a source of infinite love and strength. I cannot help but hold onto you even tighter as we witness the unbearable pain of the hundreds of thousands of Palestinians in Gaza losing their loved ones. I hope we get to live in a more humane and less cruel world.

And from Ronit: My work on this book has above all been inspired by the Palestinian people's steadfastness and their ongoing resistance to the Zionist colonization of Palestine; I owe them a debt of admiration and my deepest gratitude. I was also inspired by the international Palestine solidarity movement, in particular the Ireland Palestine Solidarity Campaign, Jews for Palestine Ireland, and the Tzedek Collective in so-called Australia. Special thanks to activists Fatin Al Tamimi, Kevin Squires, Zoe Lawlor, John Reynolds, and David Landy in Ireland; to Haim Bresheeth Zabner and Yosefa Loshitzky in London; to my dearest friends, the late Eli Aminov and Nitza Aminov, in Jerusalem; and to Rand Khatib and Ryan Al Natour in Sydney.

My writing and pro-Palestine activism owe to many Palestinian scholar activists, in particular Nahla Abdo, Nadera Shalhoub-Kevorkian, Steven Salaita, Ali Abunimah, Toufic Haddad, Honaida Ghanim, Abdaljawad Omar, Haidar Eid, and Muhannad Ayyash—my thanks to them and to so many other inspiring Palestinian theorists. Finally, my most sincere thanks to race scholars Alana Lentin and Kieron Turner for keeping me focused and helping me to expand my knowledge and understanding.

*Notes*

**Preface**

1. *Application of the Convention on the Prevention and Punishment of the Crime of Genocide in the Gaza Strip (South Africa v. Israel)*, International Court of Justice, Order of January 26, 2024, https://www.icj-cij.org/sites/default/files/case-related/192/192-20240126-ord-01-00-en.pdf.

2. *South Africa vs. Israel*, Application Instituting Proceedings, December 29, 2023, 68, https://www.icj-cij.org/sites/default/files/case-related/192/192-20231228-app-01-00-en.pdf.

3. *South Africa vs. Israel*, Application Instituting Proceedings, 60.

4. *South Africa vs. Israel*, Application Instituting Proceedings, 60.

5. *South Africa vs. Israel*, Application Instituting Proceedings, 61.

6. Ghassan Abu Sitta (@GhassanAbuSitt1), "Like a criminal suspecting that his accomplaces want to throw him under-the-bus, Netanyahu is in Congress to remind the US political ellite that this is as much their genocide as it is his," X, July 25, 2024, 4:05 a.m., https://x.com/GhassanAbuSitt1/status/1816172874081632656.

7. Seraj Assi, "Israeli Soldiers Flaunt War Crimes on Social Media. Why Aren't They Held Accountable?" *Truthout*, July 21, 2024, https://truthout.org/articles/israeli-soldiers-flaunt-war-crimes-online-why-arent-they-held-accountable/.

8. "Israel-Gaza War in Maps and Charts: Live Tracker," *Al Jazeera*, last accessed July 25, 2024, https://www.aljazeera.com/news/longform/2023/10/9/israel-hamas-war-in-maps-and-charts-live-tracker.

9. Rasha Khatib, Martin McKee, and Salim Yusuf, "Counting the Dead in Gaza: Difficult but Essential," *Lancet*, July 5, 2024, https://www.thelancet.com/journals/lancet/article/PIIS0140-6736(24)01169-3/fulltext.

10. "Report Projects Excess Deaths Due to Gaza Crisis," London School of Hygiene & Tropical Medicine, February 23, 2024, https://www.lshtm.ac.uk/newsevents/news/2024/report-projects-excess-deaths-due-gaza-crisis.

11. Save the Children, "The Missing Children of Gaza," last accessed July 25, 2024, https://www.savethechildren.net/gaza-missing-children?utm_campaign=gaza&utm_medium=social&utm_source=twitter.

12. Arwa Mahdawi, "An Israeli Bomb Destroyed 4,000 Embryos at a Gaza IVF Centre. Where Is the Outrage?" April 20, 2024, https://www.theguardian.com/commentisfree/2024/apr/20/israel-destroyed-embryos-bombing-ivf-center-gaza.

13. "Doctors in Gaza Report a Rise in Miscarriages as Pregnant Women Face Severe Stress and a Lack of Food," ActionAid USA, June 6, 2024, https://www.actionaidusa.org/news/doctors-in-gaza-report-a-rise-in-miscarriages-as-pregnant-women-face-severe-stress-and-a-lack-of-food/.

14. Francesca Albanese, *Anatomy of a Genocide: Report of the Special Rapporteur on the Situation of Human Rights in the Palestinian Territories Occupied since 1967* (advance unedited version), UN Doc. A/HRC/55/73 (March 25, 2024), 1, https://www.ohchr.org/sites/default/files/documents/hrbodies/hrcouncil/sessions-regular/session55/advance-versions/a-hrc-55-73-auv.pdf.

15. Integrated Food Security Phase Classification, "The Gaza Strip: IPC Acute Food Insecurity Analysis May–September 2024," *IPC Global Initiative—Special Brief*, July 10, 2024, https://www.ipcinfo.org/ipcinfo-website/countries-in-focus-archive/issue-105/en/; "Israel-Gaza War in Maps and Charts."

16. "Israel: Starvation Used as Weapon of War in Gaza," Human Rights Watch, December 18, 2023, https://www.hrw.org/news/2023/12/18/israel-starvation-used-weapon-war-gaza.

17. Malu Cursino, "Israeli Protesters Block Aid Trucks Destined for Gaza," BBC, May 14, 2024, https://www.bbc.com/news/articles/cg3o0jek94zo.

18. UN Office of the High Commissioner for Human Rights, "UN Experts Condemn 'Flour Massacre,' Urge Israel to End Campaign of Starvation in Gaza," press release, March 5, 2024, https://www.ohchr.org/en/press-releases/2024/03/un-experts-condemn-flour-massacre-urge-israel-end-campaign-starvation-gaza.

19. Ruth McHugh-Dillon, "Malnourished Children in Gaza 'Don't Have the Energy to Cry': UNICEF," SBS News, March 18, 2024, https://www.sbs.com.au/news/podcast-episode/malnourished-children-in-gaza-dont-have-the-energy-to-cry-unicef/q11ypc4ke; "Israel's Forced Starvation in Gaza Has Killed Dozens of Children," *Al Jazeera*,

June 3, 2024, https://www.aljazeera.com/program/newsfeed/2024/6/3/israels-forced-starvation-in-gaza-has-killed-dozens-of-children.

20. Hossam Shabat (@HossamShabat), "We are slowly dying, . . ." X, July 23, 2024, https://x.com/hossamshabat/status/1815462846676799534?s=12.

21. "Hamas Leader Killed—Latest: War Enters 'Worrying New Phase' as Hamas Leader Killed and Iran Vows Revenge," Sky News, July 31, 2024, https://news.sky .com/story/israel-gaza-latest-hamas-war-updates-sky-news-blog-12978800?postid =6906216#liveblog-body.

22. United Nations, "Press Conference by Secretary-General António Guterres at United Nations Headquarters," November 6, 2023, https://press.un.org/en/2023/ sgsm22021.doc.htm.

23. Peter Beaumont and Julian Borger, "Gaza a 'Living Hell' after Heavy Winter Rains Drench Makeshift Tents," December 14, 2023, https://www.theguardian.com/world/ 2023/dec/13/gaza-a-living-hell-after-heavy-winter-rains-drench-makeshift-tents.

24. "UN Aid Mission Witnesses 'Apocalyptic' Scenes in Gaza City, with Most Basic Supplies Non-Existent," UN News, July 12, 2024, https://news.un.org/en/audio/ 2024/07/1152041#.

25. "Gaza Has Become a Graveyard for Thousands of Children," UNICEF, October 31, 2023, https://www.unicef.org/press-releases/gaza-has-become-graveyard-thousands -children.

26. "UNICEF Geneva Palais Briefing Note—Gaza: The World's Most Dangerous Place to Be a Child," UNICEF, December 19, 2023, https://www.unicef.org/press-releases/ unicef-geneva-palais-briefing-note-gaza-worlds-most-dangerous-place-be-child.

27. Lana Tatour, "How Human Rights Organizations Are Aiding the Israeli Assault on Gaza," *Mondoweiss*, December 12, 2023, https://mondoweiss.net/2023/12/ how-human-rights-organizations-are-aiding-the-israeli-assault-on-gaza/.

28. Sherene Seikaly, "From the Editor," *Journal of Palestine Studies* 53, no. 1 (2024): 1–6, https://doi.org/10.1080/0377919X.2024.2359289.

29. Gaza Academics and Administrators, "Open Letter by Gaza Academics and University Administrators to the World," *Al Jazeera*, May 29, 2024, https://www .aljazeera.com/opinions/2024/5/29/open-letter-by-gaza-academics-and-university -administrators-to-the-world.

30. Malaka Shwaikh, "Against 'Resilience,'" *London Review of Books*, January 23, 2024, https://www.lrb.co.uk/blog/2024/january/against-resilience.

31. International Convention on the Elimination of All Forms of Racial Discrimination, December 21, 1965, 660 UNTS 195.

32. *Legal Consequences Arising from the Policies and Practices of Israel in the Occupied Palestinian Territory, Including East Jerusalem*, International Court of

Justice, Advisory Opinion of July 19, 2024, https://www.icj-cij.org/sites/default/files/case-related/186/186-20240719-adv-01-00-en.pdf.

## Introduction

I am grateful to Dirk Moses, Sherene Seikaly, Jumana Bayeh, and the anonymous readers for their careful, generous, and incisive feedback on the introduction. I also thank Ronit Lentin for reading multiple versions, and I specifically acknowledge her contribution to the section on racial capitalism. All errors are mine.

1. "Israel's Occupation of Palestinian Territory Is 'Apartheid': UN Rights Expert," *UN News*, March 25, 2022, https://news.un.org/en/story/2022/03/1114702.

2. B'Tselem's analysis and its favoring of ethnicity over race is in line with other analyses by Israeli scholars. For critiques of Israeli scholarship and their focus on ethnicity, see Nahla Abdo, *Women in Israel: Race, Gender and Citizenship* (London: Zed Books, 2011); Ronit Lentin, *Traces of Racial Exception: Racializing Israeli Settler Colonialism* (London: Bloomsbury Academic, 2018); Lana Tatour, "Domination and Resistance in Liberal Settler Colonialism: Palestinians in Israel between the Homeland and the Transnational" (PhD diss., University of Warwick, 2016).

3. B'Tselem, *A Regime of Jewish Supremacy from the Jordan River to the Mediterranean Sea: This Is Apartheid* (2021), 8.

4. Amnesty International, *Israel's Apartheid against Palestinians: A Cruel System of Domination and a Crime against Humanity* (2022), 54.

5. Human Rights Watch, *A Threshold Crossed: Israeli Authorities and the Crimes of Apartheid and Persecution* (2021), 36.

6. Human Rights Watch, *A Threshold Crossed*, 36.

7. Human Rights Watch, *A Threshold Crossed*, 35.

8. Human Rights Watch, *A Threshold Crossed*, 37–38.

9. UN Human Rights Council, *Report of the Special Rapporteur on the Situation of Human Rights in the Palestinian Territories Occupied since 1967*, UN Doc. A/HRC/49/87 (August 12, 2022), 9.

10. Amnesty International, *Israel's Apartheid against Palestinians*, 74.

11. John Reynolds, this volume.

12. Saree Makdisi, "Apartheid / ~~Apartheid~~ / []," *Critical Inquiry* 44, no. 2 (2018): 310–11.

13. Saree Makdisi, "Author Talk with Saree Makdisi," Better Read than Dead, March 5, 2023, https://www.betterreadevents.com/events/author-talk-with-saree-makdisi.

14. Alana Lentin, *Why Race Still Matters* (Cambridge: Polity, 2020).

15. Loubna Qutami, "Moving beyond the Apartheid Analogy in Palestine and South Africa," *Middle East Report Online*, February 3, 2020, https://merip.org/2020/02/moving-beyond-the-apartheid-analogy-in-palestine-and-south-africa-trump/.

16. The book uses "race critical theory," rather than "critical race theory." In the literature on race, "critical race theory" is described as arising from the discipline of law, critical legal traditions, and civil rights struggles, while "race critical theory" is associated with the wider history of racial theorizations in the critical tradition: see Philomena Essed and David Theo Goldberg, eds., *Race Critical Theories* (Malden, MA: Blackwell, 2002). "Race critical theory" takes on board theorists such as W. E. B. Du Bois, Oliver Cromwell Cox, Cedric Robinson, Frantz Fanon, and Stuart Hall, among others, and is indebted to feminist thinkers such as Audre Lorde, Gloria Anzaldúa, Angela Davis, Gloria Joseph, bell hooks, and Hazel Carby, among others, to think about race and racism, their social and intellectual conditions, their causes and effects, and their interplay with other socially significant expressions, such as class and gender.

17. Qutami, "Moving beyond the Apartheid Analogy"; Lana Tatour, "Why Calling Israel an Apartheid State Is Not Enough," *Middle East Eye*, January 18, 2021, https://www.middleeasteye.net/opinion/why-calling-israel-apartheid-state-not-enough.

18. Tatour, "Why Calling Israel an Apartheid State Is Not Enough."

19. Edward W. Said, *The Question of Palestine* (New York: Vintage, 1979); Fayez Sayegh, "Zionist Colonialism in Palestine (1965)," *Settler Colonial Studies* 2, no. 1 (2012): 206–25; Elia Zureik, *The Palestinians in Israel: A Study in Internal Colonialism* (London: Routledge, 1979).

20. Omar Jabary Salamanca, Mezna Qato, Kareem Rabie, and Sobhi Samour, "Past Is Present: Settler Colonialism in Palestine," *Settler Colonial Studies* 2, no. 1 (2012): 1–8.

21. On Israel as an ethnic state and an ethnocracy, see As'ad Ghanem, "State and Minority in Israel: The Case of Ethnic State and the Predicament of Its Minority," *Ethnic and Racial Studies* 21, no. 3 (1998): 428–48; Amal Jamal, "Strategies of Minority Struggle for Equality in Ethnic States: Arab Politics in Israel," *Citizenship Studies* 11, no. 3 (2007): 263–82; Nadim Rouhana, *Palestinian Citizens in an Ethnic Jewish State: Identities in Conflict* (New Haven, CT: Yale University Press, 1997); Oren Yiftachel, *Ethnocracy: Land and Identity Politics in Israel/Palestine* (Philadelphia: University of Pennsylvania Press, 2006).

22. On Israel as a racial settler-colonial state, see Nadia Abu El-Haj, "Racial Palestinianization and the Janus-Faced Nature of the Israeli State," *Patterns of Prejudice* 44, no. 1 (2010): 27–41; Lentin, *Traces of Racial Exception*; Makdisi, "Apartheid / ~~Apartheid~~ / []"; Tatour, "Domination and Resistance."

23. For analysis that employs settler colonialism but sustains a focus on ethnicity, see Mazen Masri, *The Dynamics of Exclusionary Constitutionalism: Israel*

*as a Jewish and Democratic State* (Oxford: Hart, 2017); Nadim Rouhana, ed., *Israel and Its Palestinian Citizens: Ethnic Privileges in the Jewish State* (Cambridge: Cambridge University Press, 2017).

24. For work on race, security, and surveillance, see Nadera Shalhoub-Kevorkian, *Security Theology, Surveillance and the Politics of Fear* (Cambridge: Cambridge University Press, 2015); Elia Zureik, *Israel's Colonial Project in Palestine: Brutal Pursuit* (London: Routledge, 2015). For work on racial capitalism, see Muhannad Ayyash, "Colonial Racial Capitalism and Violence: Theorising the Relationship between Empire and Israeli Settler Colonialism," *Journal of Holy Land and Palestine Studies* 23, no. 2 (2024): 205–20; Andy Clarno, *Neoliberal Apartheid: Palestine/Israel and South Africa after 1994* (Chicago: University of Chicago Press, 2017). For work on law, race, and property, see Brenna Bhandar, *Colonial Lives of Property: Law, Land, and Racial Regimes of Ownership* (Durham, NC: Duke University Press, 2018); and Noura Erakat, "Whiteness as Property in Israel: Revival, Rehabilitation, and Removal," *Harvard Journal on Racial & Ethnic Justice* 31 (2015): 69–103. For work on the racialization of Israeli settler colonialism, see Yasmeen Abu-Laban and Abigail B. Bakan, *Israel, Palestine and the Politics of Race: Exploring Identity and Power in a Global Context* (London: I. B. Tauris, 2019); Lentin, *Traces of Racial Exception*; and Patrick Wolfe, *Traces of History: Elementary Structures of Race* (London: Verso, 2016). For work on citizenship and race, see Yael Berda, *Colonial Bureaucracy and Contemporary Citizenship: Legacies of Race and Emergency in the Former British Empire* (Cambridge: Cambridge University Press, 2023); Lana Tatour, "Citizenship as Domination: Settler Colonialism and the Making of Palestinian Citizenship in Israel," *Arab Studies Journal* 27, no. 2 (2019): 8–39. For work on Black-Palestinian solidarity, see Noura Erakat and Marc Lamont Hill, "Black-Palestinian Transnational Solidarity," *Journal of Palestine Studies* 48, no. 4 (2019): 7–16; Keith Feldman, *A Shadow over Palestine: The Imperial Life of Race in America* (Minneapolis: University of Minnesota Press, 2015); Michael R. Fischbach, *Black Power and Palestine: Transnational Countries of Color* (Stanford, CA: Stanford University Press, 2018); and Maha Nassar, "Palestinian Engagement with the Black Freedom Movement prior to 1967," *Journal of Palestine Studies* 48, no. 4 (2019): 17–32. For work on the imperial politics of race, see Seraj Assi, *The History and Politics of the Bedouin: Reimagining Nomadism in Modern Palestine* (New York: Routledge, 2018); and Sherene Seikaly, "The Matter of Time," *American Historical Review* 124, no. 5 (2019): 1681–88. For work on race and labor, see Nimrod Ben Zeev, "Palestine along the Colour Line: Race, Colonialism, and Construction Labour, 1918–1948," *Ethnic and Racial Studies* 44, no. 12 (2021): 2190–212. For work on anti-Palestinian racism, see Yasmeen Abu-Laban and Abigail B. Bakan, "Anti-Palestinian Racism and Racial Gaslighting," *Political Quarterly* 93, no. 3 (2022): 508–16; M.

Muhannad Ayyash, "The Toxic Other: The Palestinian Critique and Debates about Race and Racism," *Critical Sociology* 49, no. 6 (2022): 953–66, https://doi.org/10.1177/08969205221130415; Liz Fekete, "Anti-Palestinian Racism and the Criminalisation of International Solidarity in Europe," *Race & Class* 66, no. 1 (2024): 99–120, https://doi.org/10.1177/03063968241253708; and Maha Nassar, "*Exodus*, Nakba Denialism, and the Mobilization of Anti-Arab Racism," *Critical Sociology* 49, no. 6 (2022): 1037–51, https://doi.org/10.1177/08969205221132878. For work on gender and race, see Frances S. Hasso, *Buried in the Red Dirt: Race, Reproduction, and Death in Modern Palestine* (Cambridge: Cambridge University Press, 2021); and Sarah Ihmoud, "Policing the Intimate: Israel's Anti-Miscegenation Movement," *Jerusalem Quarterly*, no. 75 (2018): 91–103. For work on refugees and race, see Shaira Vadasaria, "1948 to 1951: The Racial Politics of Humanitarianism and Return in Palestine," *Oñati Socio-Legal Series* 10, no. 6 (2020): 1242–69. For work on health and race, see Danya M. Qato, "Introduction: Public Health and the Promise of Palestine," *Journal of Palestine Studies* 49, no. 4 (2020): 8–26; Yara M. Asi, Mienah Z. Sharif, Bram Wispelwey, Nadia N. Abuelezam, A. Kayum Ahmed, and Goleen Samari, "Racism as a Threat to Palestinian Health Equity," *Health Equity* 8, no. 1 (2024): 371–75; Osama Tanous, Bram Wispelwey, and Rania Muhareb, "Beyond Statelessness: 'Unchilding' and the Health of Palestinian Children in Jerusalem," *Statelessness & Citizenship Review* 4, no. 1 (2022): 88–112; and Osama Tanous, Yara Asi, Weeam Hammoudeh, David Mills, and Bram Wispelwey, "Structural Racism and the Health of Palestinian Citizens of Israel," *Global Public Health* 18, no. 1 (2023): 1–22.

25. Rana Barakat, "Writing/Righting Palestine Studies: Settler Colonialism, Indigenous Sovereignty and Resisting the Ghost(s) of History," *Settler Colonial Studies* 8, no. 3 (2018): 350 (emphasis in original).

26. Said, *The Question of Palestine*, 122.

27. Stuart Hall, *The Fateful Triangle: Race, Ethnicity, Nation* (Cambridge, MA: Harvard University Press, 2017).

28. It is important to note that the UN report is different from the reports of B'tselem, Human Rights Watch, and Amnesty International in that it addresses settler colonialism in its analysis of Israel's apartheid regime. For critiques on how the apartheid reports overlook settler colonialism, see Soheir Assad and Rania Muhareb, "Dismantle What? Amnesty's Conflicted Messaging on Israeli Apartheid," *Institute for Palestine Studies* (blog), February 15, 2022, https://www.palestine-studies.org/en/node/1652565; Noura Erakat, "Beyond Discrimination: Apartheid Is a Colonial Project and Zionism Is a Form of Racism," *EJIL: Talk!* (blog), July 5, 2021, https://www.ejiltalk.org/beyond-discrimination-apartheid-is-a-colonial-project-and-zionism-is-a-form-of-racism/; Noura Erakat and John Reynolds, "We

Charge Apartheid? Palestine and the International Criminal Court," *Third World Approaches to International Law Review*, April 20, 2021, https://twailr.com/we-charge -apartheid-palestine-and-the-international-criminal-court/; Noura Erakat and John Reynolds, "Understanding Apartheid," *Jewish Currents*, November 1, 2022, https:// jewishcurrents.org/understanding-apartheid; Reynolds, this volume; Tatour, "Why Calling Israel an Apartheid State Is Not Enough"; Lana Tatour, "Amnesty Report: The Limits of the Apartheid Framework," *Middle East Eye*, February 8, 2022, https://www .middleeasteye.net/opinion/israel-amnesty-apartheid-report-limits-framework.

29. Lentin, *Traces of Racial Exception*.

30. Abdo, *Women in Israel*, 17.

31. Lentin, *Why Race Still Matters*, 9.

32. Wolfe, *Traces of History*, 22.

33. Barnor Hesse, "Preface: Counter-Racial Formation Theory," in *Conceptual Aphasia in Black: Displacing Racial Formation*, ed. P. Khalil Saucier and Tryon P. Woods (Lanham, MD: Rowman & Littlefield, 2016), viii.

34. Hall, *The Fateful Triangle*, 53–55.

35. Ann Laura Stoler, *Race and the Education of Desire: Foucault's History of Sexuality and the Colonial Order of Things* (Durham, NC: Duke University Press, 1995), 27.

36. Alexander G. Weheliye, *Habeas Viscus: Racializing Assemblages, Biopolitics, and Black Feminist Theories of the Human* (Durham, NC: Duke University Press, 2014), 4.

37. Weheliye, *Habeas Viscus*, 8.

38. Samera Esmeir, *Juridical Humanity: A Colonial History* (Stanford, CA: Stanford University Press, 2012), 9.

39. Hortense Spillers, "Mama's Baby, Papa's Maybe: An American Grammar Book," *Diacritics* 17, no. 2 (1987): 67.

40. Katherine McKittrick, ed., *Sylvia Wynter: On Being Human as Praxis* (Durham, NC: Duke University Press, 2015).

41. Frantz Fanon, *Black Skin, White Masks* (London: Pluto, 1967), 4. See Sylvia Wynter, "Towards the Sociogenic Principle: Fanon, Identity, the Puzzle of Conscious Experience, and What It Is Like to Be 'Black,'" in *National Identities and Socio-Political Changes in Latin America*, ed. Mercedes F. Durán-Cogan and Antonio Gómez-Moriana (New York: Routledge, 2001), 53.

42. On Fanon's approach to the question of the human, see Esmeir, *Juridical Humanity*, 6–8.

43. Sylvia Wynter and Katherine McKittrick, "Unparalleled Catastrophe for Our Species? Or, to Give Humanness a Different Future: Conversations," in *Sylvia Wynter:*

*On Being Human as Praxis*, ed. Katherine McKittrick (Durham, NC: Duke University Press, 2015), 23.

44. Azfar Shafi and Ilyas Nagdee, *Race to the Bottom: Reclaiming Antiracism* (London: Pluto, 2022), 9–12.

45. Wolfe, *Traces of History*, 53.

46. Hall, *The Fateful Triangle*.

47. Lentin, *Why Race Still Matters*, 5.

48. On the occlusion of race in Israeli scholarship, see Lentin, *Traces of Racial Exception*.

49. Lentin, *Why Race Still Matters*, 10–11.

50. Shafi and Nagdee, *Race to the Bottom*, 10.

51. Lentin, *Traces of Racial Exception*.

52. Zureik, *Israel's Colonial Project*, 5.

53. Joseph Massad, "The End of Zionism: Racism and the Palestinian Struggle," *Interventions* 5, no. 3 (2003): 440.

54. Ibrahim Abu-Lughod and Baha Abu-Laban, eds., *Settler Regimes in Africa and the Arab World: The Illusion of Endurance* (Wilmette, IL: Medina University Press, 1974), xx.

55. Yasser Arafat, Speech to the UN General Assembly in New York, November 13, 1974, United Nations: The Question of Palestine, https://www.un.org/unispal/document/auto-insert-187769/.

56. UN General Assembly, Resolution 3379, Elimination of All Forms of Racial Discrimination, UN Doc. A/RES/3379(XXX) (November 10, 1975).

57. Noura Erakat, this volume.

58. Steven Salaita, *Inter/Nationalism: Decolonizing Native America and Palestine* (Minneapolis: University of Minnesota Press, 2016); Linda Tabar, "From Third World Internationalism to 'the Internationals': The Transformation of Solidarity with Palestine," *Third World Quarterly* 38, no. 2 (2017): 414–35.

59. On the theorization of race as a technology of power, see Lentin, *Why Race Still Matters*.

60. Sayegh, "Zionist Colonialism in Palestine," 214–15 (emphasis in original).

61. Sayegh, "Zionist Colonialism in Palestine," 215 (emphasis in original).

62. Sayegh, "Zionist Colonialism in Palestine," 217 (emphasis in original).

63. For settler colonialism and the logic of elimination, see Patrick Wolfe, "Settler Colonialism and the Elimination of the Native," *Journal of Genocide Research* 8, no. 4 (2006): 387–409.

64. Ghassan Kanafani, *On Zionist Literature*, trans. Mahmoud Najib (Oxford: Ebb Books, 2022), 54.

65. Kanafani, *On Zionist Literature*, 35.

66. Edward W. Said, "Zionism from the Standpoint of Its Victims," *Social Text* 1, no. 1 (1979): 11 (emphasis in original).

67. Said, "Zionism from the Standpoint," 28.

68. Theodor Herzl, *The Jewish State* (1896; New York: Dover, 1988), 23. See also Rashid Khalidi, *The Hundred Years' War on Palestine: A History of Settler Colonialism and Resistance, 1917–2017* (New York: Metropolitan Books, 2020).

69. David T. Goldberg, "Racial Palestinianization," in *Thinking Palestine*, ed. Ronit Lentin (London: Zed Books, 2008), 43.

70. Shira Robinson, *Citizen Strangers: Palestinians and the Birth of Israel's Liberal Settler State* (Stanford, CA: Stanford University Press, 2013), 13.

71. Raphael Falk, *Zionism and the Biology of the Jews* (Tel Aviv: Resling, 2006).

72. Said, "Zionism from the Standpoint," 26.

73. Sherene Seikaly, *Men of Capital: Scarcity and Economy in Mandate Palestine* (Stanford, CA: Stanford University Press, 2015), 4.

74. Julia Elyachar, "Relational Finance: Ottoman Debt, Financialization, and the Problem of the Semi-Civilized," *Journal of Cultural Economy* 16, no. 3 (2023): 323–36, https://doi.org/10.1080/17530350.2023.2189146.

75. Seikaly, *Men of Capital*, 5.

76. Khalidi, *The Hundred Years' War*, 11.

77. Seikaly, *Men of Capital*, 5.

78. Seikaly, "The Matter of Time," 1683.

79. Quoted in Goldberg, "Racial Palestinianization," 42–43 (emphasis added by Goldberg).

80. Khalidi, *The Hundred Years' War*, 43.

81. Khalidi, *The Hundred Years' War*, 55.

82. Shlomo Sand, "The Invention of the Jewish People," in *Pretending Democracy: Israel, an Ethnocratic State*, ed. Na'eem Jeenah (Johannesburg: Afro-Middle East Centre, 2012), 27–52.

83. Nadia Abu El-Haj, *The Genealogical Science: The Search for Jewish Origins and the Politics of Epistemology* (Chicago: University of Chicago Press, 2012).

84. Aaron Rabinowitz, "Israeli High Court Allows DNA Testing to Prove Judaism," *Haaretz*, January 24, 2020, https://www.haaretz.com/israel-news/2020-01-24/ty-article/.premium/israeli-high-court-allows-dna-testing-to-prove-judaism/0000017f-e13b-d804-ad7f-f1fb85f90000.

85. Abu El-Haj, *The Genealogical Science*, 16.

86. Abu El-Haj, *The Genealogical Science*, 17.

87. Abu El-Haj, *The Genealogical Science*, 18 (emphasis in original).

88. Sand, "The Invention of the Jewish People," 36–37.

89. Ihmoud, "Policing the Intimate," 92–93. On racialized sexual politics, see also Ronit Lentin, this volume.

90. Nadeem Karkabi, "The Impossible Quest of Nasreen Qadri to Claim Colonial Privilege in Israel," *Ethnic and Racial Studies* 44, no. 6 (2021): 966–86.

91. JTA, "Palestinian Requests to Convert to Judaism Rejected Automatically," *Jerusalem Post*, April 1, 2016, https://www.jpost.com/arab-israeli-conflict/palestinian -requests-to-convert-to-judaism-rejected-automatically-449987.

92. Shira Robinson, *Citizen Strangers*, 9.

93. Ella Shohat, "Sephardim in Israel: Zionism from the Standpoint of Its Jewish Victims," *Social Text* 19/20 (1988): 1–35.

94. Joseph Massad, "Zionism's Internal Others: Israel and the Oriental Jews," *Journal of Palestine Studies* 25, no. 4 (1996): 53–68.

95. On the distinction between white supremacy and Jewish supremacy in the context of the Mizrahim, see Lihi Yona, "The Color of Racism: What Many Get Wrong about Race Relations in Israel," +972 *Magazine*, June 24, 2018, https://www.972mag .com/the-color-of-racism-what-many-get-wrong-about-race-relations-in-israel/.

96. As'ad Ghanem, "Mizrahi (Oriental) Jews and the Ashkenazi System: Incorporation versus Separation Politics," in *Ethnic Politics in Israel: The Margins and the Ashkenazi Centre* (London: Routledge, 2010), 60–78; Sami Shalom Chetrit, *Intra-Jewish Conflict in Israel: White Jews, Black Jews* (London: Routledge, 2010); Tatour, "Domination and Resistance."

97. Charles W. Mills, *The Racial Contract* (Ithaca, NY: Cornell University Press, 1997), 127 (emphasis in original).

98. Goldberg, "Racial Palestinianization," 33.

99. Quoted by Michael R. Fischbach in this volume.

100. On racial capitalism, see Clarno, *Neoliberal Apartheid*; Darryl Li, "On Law and Racial Capitalism in Palestine," *Law and Political Economy Project* (blog), June 15, 2021, https://lpeproject.org/blog/on-law-and-racial-capitalism-in-palestine/; Danya M. Qato, "Introduction." On race and labor regimes, see Nimrod Ben Zeev, "'We Built This Country': Palestinian Citizens in Israel's Construction Industry, 1948–73," *Jerusalem Quarterly* 84 (2020): 10–46; Ben Zeev, "Palestine along the Colour Line"; Nimrod Ben Zeev, "Toward a History of Dangerous Work and Racialized Inequalities in Twentieth-Century Palestine/Israel," *Journal of Palestine Studies* 51, no. 4 (2022): 89–96. On race and land, see Bhandar, *Colonial Lives of Property*. On the security industrial complex, see Nivi Manchanda and Sharri Plonski, "Between Mobile Corridors and Immobilizing Borders: Race, Fixity and Friction in Palestine/Israel," *International Affairs* 98, no. 1 (2022): 183–207; Kieron Turner, this volume. On race

and economic development, see Alaa Tartir, Tariq Dana, and Timothy Seidel, eds., *Political Economy of Palestine: Critical, Interdisciplinary, and Decolonial Perspectives* (Cham, Switzerland: Palgrave Macmillan, 2021).

101. Susan Koshy, Lisa Marie Cacho, Jodi A. Byrd, and Brian Jordan, eds., *Colonial Racial Capitalism* (Durham, NC: Duke University Press, 2022), 5.

102. Brenna Bhandar and Rafeef Ziadah, "Acts and Omissions: Framing Settler Colonialism in Palestine Studies," *Jadaliyya*, January 14, 2016, https://www.jadaliyya.com/Details/32857/Acts-and-Omissions-Framing-Settler-Colonialism-in-Palestine-Studies; Koshy et al., *Colonial Racial Capitalism*.

103. Robin D. G. Kelley, "What Did Cedric Robinson Mean by Racial Capitalism?" *Boston Review,* January 12, 2017, https://www.bostonreview.net/articles/robin-d-g-kelley-introduction-race-capitalism-justice/; Cedric J. Robinson, *Black Marxism: The Making of the Black Radical Tradition* (1983; Chapel Hill: University of North Carolina Press, 2000).

104. Haider Eid and Andy Clarno, "Rethinking Our Definition of Apartheid: Not Just a Political Regime" Al Shabaka Policy Paper, August 27, 2017, https://al-shabaka.org/briefs/rethinking-definition-apartheid-not-just-political-regime/.

105. Koshy et al., *Colonial Racial Capitalism*, 1.

106. Azanian Manifesto (1984), South African History Online, https://www.sahistory.org.za/sites/default/files/archive-files/AvSep84.1684.8098.001.001.Sep1984.15.pdf.

107. Koshy et al., *Colonial Racial Capitalism*, 5–7 (emphasis in original). On capitalism as a colonial relation, see also Glen Sean Coulthard, *Red Skin, White Masks: Rejecting the Colonial Politics of Recognition* (Minneapolis: University of Minnesota Press, 2014).

108. Clarno, *Neoliberal Apartheid*, 9.

109. Gilmore, quoted in Koshy et al., *Colonial Racial Capitalism*, 2 (emphasis in original).

110. With the growing identification of the Bedouin as Indigenous, there is a tendency to view them as inherently anticapitalist. But, as Nora Barakat shows in her book *Bedouin Bureaucrats*, under Ottoman rule, the Bedouin were also part of the capitalist transformation, they accumulated land, and they were part of the slave trade in the region: Nora Elizabeth Barakat, *Bedouin Bureaucrats: Mobility and Property in the Ottoman Empire* (Stanford, CA: Stanford University Press, 2023).

111. Seikaly, *Men of Capital*, 8.

112. Beshara Doumani, *Rediscovering Palestine: Merchants and Peasants in Jabal Nablus, 1700–1900* (Berkeley: University of California Press, 1995), 8. See also Barakat, *Bedouin Bureaucrats*.

113. See Khalidi, *The Hundred Years' War*, 17; Seikaly, *Men of Capital*, 8; Doumani, *Rediscovering Palestine*.

114. Doumani, *Rediscovering Palestine*.

115. While the focus in this section is on land and labor as central features of racial capitalism and settler colonialism, the relevance of racial capitalism extends to other areas—for example, Israel's prison industry and its profiting from the incarceration of Palestinians; the function of gentrification in cities such as Jaffa, Akka, and Haifa as a colonial modality of displacement and dispossession; Israel's tourism industry in '48 and '67 Palestine; and the recent neoliberal agenda of incorporating '48 Palestinians into Israel's high-tech industry.

116. Koshy et al., *Colonial Racial Capitalism*, 5.

117. Said, "Zionism from the Standpoint," 38.

118. Joseph Massad, "Jewish National Fund: A Century of Land Theft, Belligerence and Erasure," *Middle East Eye*, February 1, 2023, https://www.middleeasteye.net/opinion/colonial-chutzpah-jewish-national-fund.

119. Munir Fakher Eldin, "The Middle Class and the Land Struggle in Palestine: Revisiting the Colonial Encounter in the Beisan Valley, 1908–1948," *Comparative Studies of South Asia, Africa, and the Middle East* 43, no. 3 (2023): 251, https://doi.org/10.1215/1089201X-10896552.

120. Eldin, "The Middle Class and the Land Struggle," 249.

121. Eldin, "The Middle Class and the Land Struggle," 257.

122. Said, "Zionism from the Standpoint," 38.

123. Erakat, "Whiteness as Property in Israel," 84. For a database of discriminatory laws, see Adalah: The Legal Center for Arab Minority Rights in Israel, "The Discriminatory Laws Database," September 25, 2017, http://www.adalah.org/en/content/view/7771.

124. On the use of citizenship as a means for the expulsion of Palestinians from their land, see Robinson, *Citizen Strangers*; Tatour, "Citizenship as Domination." On citizenship as an instrument of (Jewish) capital accumulation, see Areej Sabbagh-Khoury, "Citizenship as Accumulation by Dispossession: The Paradox of Settler Colonial Citizenship," *Sociological Theory* 40, no. 2 (2022): 151, https://doi.org/10.1177/07352751221095474.

125. Erakat, "Whiteness as Property in Israel," 71.

126. Basic Law: Israel—The Nation-State of the Jewish People, https://main.knesset.gov.il/EN/activity/documents/BasicLawsPDF/BasicLawNationState.pdf.

127. Cheryl I. Harris, "Whiteness as Property," *Harvard Law Review* 106, no. 8 (1993): 1709.

128. On Jewishness as property, see Rabea Eghbariah, "Jewishness as Property under Israeli Law," *Law and Political Economy Project* (blog), July 9, 2021,

https://lpeproject.org/blog/jewishness-as-property-under-israeli-law/. It is also important to note that the production of Jewishness as property has been joined by the production of (Ashkenazi) whiteness as property, with Ashkenazi Jews benefiting the most from stolen Palestinian land and property.

129. On the relationship between whiteness and property in Israel, see Erakat, "Whiteness as Property in Israel."

130. Bhandar, *Colonial Lives of Property*.

131. Adalah, "The Discriminatory Laws Database."

132. Sabri Jiryis, *The Arabs in Israel, 1948–1966*, trans. Marie Dobson (Beirut: Institute for Palestine Studies, 1969); Sabri Jiryis, "Domination by the Law," *Journal of Palestine Studies* 11, no. 1 (1981): 67–92.

133. Said, "Zionism from the Standpoint," 43.

134. "Israel Is Set to Approve 4,000 Settler Units in Occupied West Bank," *Al Jazeera*, May 6, 2022, https://www.aljazeera.com/news/2022/5/6/israel-set-to -approve-4000-settler-units-in-occupied-west-bank.

135. See, for example, Nir Hasson, "Only 7% of Jerusalem Building Permits Go to Palestinian Neighborhoods," *Haaretz*, December 7, 2015, 2–15, https:// www.haaretz.com/israel-news/2015-12-07/ty-article/.premium/only-7-of-jlem -building-permits-go-to-palestinian-neighborhoods/0000017f-f5fe-d460-afff -fffeb87f0000; UN Relief and Works Agency for Palestine Refugees in the Near East, "Demolition Watch," accessed July 24, 2024, https://www.unrwa.org/ demolition-watch.

136. Bhandar, *Colonial Lives of Property*, 2.

137. Alexandre Kedar, Ahmad Amara, and Oren Yiftachel, *Emptied Lands: A Legal Geography of Bedouin Rights in the Negev* (Stanford, CA: Stanford University Press, 2018).

138. Gershon Shafir, *Land, Labour and the Origins of the Israeli-Palestinian Conflict, 1882–1914* (Cambridge: Cambridge University Press, 1989).

139. On the creation of the "new Jew," see Sahar Huneidi, *Race in Early Zionist Thought: Max Nordau, Arthur Ruppin and Ephraim Lilien and the Creation of the "New Jew"* (London: Bloomsbury Academic, forthcoming); Ronit Lentin, *Israel and the Daughters of the Shoah: Reoccupying the Territories of Silence* (Oxford: Berghahn Books, 2000); Shafir, *Land, Labour and the Origins*.

140. Quoted in Ghassan Kanafani, *The 1936–39 Revolt in Palestine* (New York: Committee for a Democratic Palestine, 1972), 16.

141. Kanafani, *The 1936–39 Revolt*; Zvi Ben-Dor Benite, this volume.

142. Kanafani, *The 1936–39 Revolt*, 13.

143. Kanafani, *The 1936–39 Revolt*, 13. See also Elia Zureik, "Toward a Sociology of the Palestinians," *Journal of Palestine Studies* 6, no. 4 (1977): 3–16.

144. Charles W. Anderson, "State Formation from Below and the Great Revolt in Palestine," *Journal of Palestine Studies* 47, no. 1 (185) (2017): 39–40. On the role of the Palestinian capitalist elite, see also Seikaly, *Men of Capital.*

145. Ben Zeev, "We Built This Country"; Zureik, *The Palestinians in Israel.*

146. Yael Berda, *Living Emergency: Israel's Permit Regime in the Occupied West Bank* (Stanford, CA: Stanford University Press, 2017).

147. Adriana Kemp and Rebecca Raijman, *Workers and Foreigners: The Political Economy of Labour Migration in Israel* (Jerusalem: Van Leer Institute, 2008).

148. Abu El-Haj, "Racial Palestinianization."

149. Jeff Halper, *Israel, the Palestinians and Global Pacification* (London: Pluto, 2015); Turner, this volume.

150. Eid and Clarno, "Rethinking Our Definition of Apartheid"; see also Manchanda and Plonski, "Between Mobile Corridors and Immobilizing Borders."

151. Eid and Clarno, "Rethinking Our Definition of Apartheid," 3.

152. Kareem Rabie, *Palestine Is Throwing a Party and the Whole World Is Invited: Capital and State Building in the West Bank* (Durham, NC: Duke University Press, 2021), 5.

153. Tartir, Dana, and Seidel, *Political Economy of Palestine*, 5. See also Clarno, *Neoliberal Apartheid.*

154. Clarno, *Neoliberal Apartheid.* By "post-apartheid South Africa," I mean the country after the formal end of the apartheid regime. Clearly, as many scholars have pointed out, the apartheid legacy still shapes South Africa today.

155. Qutami, "Moving beyond the Apartheid Analogy."

156. Ayyash, "The Toxic Other"; Abu-Laban and Bakan, "Anti-Palestinian Racism"; Fekete, "Anti-Palestinian Racism"; Palestine Legal, "Palestine Legal Files Title VI Complaint against George Washington University for Years-Long, Hostile Anti-Palestinian Environment," news release, February 15, 2023, https://palestinelegal.org/news/tag/Anti-Palestinian+racism; Dania Majid, *Anti-Palestinian Racism: Naming, Framing and Manifestations* (Arab Canadian Lawyers Association, 2022).

157. On Western denial, see Saree Makdisi, *Tolerance Is a Wasteland: Palestine and the Culture of Denial* (Oakland: University of California Press, 2022).

158. Mezna Qato, "Anti-Palestinianism (Noun)," Twitter, November 24, 2020, https://twitter.com/meznaqato/status/1331123975909494784?lang=es.

159. Abu-Laban and Bakan, "Anti-Palestinian Racism," 509.

160. Ayyash, "The Toxic Other," 1.

161. Concerns have been raised about the dangers of anti-Palestinian racism becoming an exceptionalist concept. This concern, however, is insufficient reason to give up on the concept altogether. As Palestinian tradition and present activism show,

we can recognize anti-Palestinian racism without necessarily exceptionalizing it. Palestinians have been doing so for decades and continue today to see their struggle as intersectional and to follow intersectional understandings of anti-Palestinian racism. This is evident in forming alliances and expressing solidarity with movements such as Black Lives Matter and with Indigenous peoples in North America and Australia.

162. JPS, quoted in Mahmoud Darwish, "Anti-Arab Prejudice in Europe," *Journal of Palestine Studies* 3, no. 4 (1974): 166.

163. Darwish, "Anti-Arab Prejudice in Europe," 166. See also Makdisi, *Tolerance Is a Wasteland*; Said, *The Question of Palestine*.

164. See Abu El-Haj, "Racial Palestinianization," 30.

165. See Neve Gordon, "Antisemitism and Zionism: The Internal Operations of the IHRA Definition," *Middle East Critique* (2024): 3–7, https://doi.org/10.1080/19436149.2024.2330821.

166. Nadia Abu El-Haj, "Palestine Is the Exception to Free Speech and Academic Freedom at Barnard," *Mondoweiss*, October 30, 2023, https://mondoweiss.net/2023/10/palestine-is-the-exception-to-free-speech-and-academic-freedom-at-barnard/ (emphasis in original).

167. Susan Beckerleg, "African Bedouin in Palestine," *African and Asian Studies* 6, no. 3 (2007): 289–303; Darryl Li, "Translator's Preface: A Note on Settler Colonialism," *Journal of Palestine Studies* 45, no. 1 (2015): 69–76.

168. On Black-Palestinian solidarity, see Kristian Davis Bailey, "Black-Palestinian Solidarity in the Ferguson-Gaza Era," *American Quarterly* 67, no. 4 (2015): 1017–26; Erakat and Lamont Hill, "Black-Palestinian Transnational Solidarity"; Fischbach, *Black Power and Palestine*.

169. See, for example, Anti-Blackness Roundtable, "Roundtable on Anti-Blackness and Black-Palestinian Solidarity," *Jadaliyya*, June 3, 2015, https://www.jadaliyya.com/Details/32145.

170. Middle East Studies Association, "MESA Board Statement in Solidarity with the Uprisings against Systemic Racism and Anti-Blackness," June 29, 2020, https://mesana.org/advocacy/letters-from-the-board/2020/06/29/mesa-board-statement-in-solidarity-with-the-uprisings-against-systemic-racism-and-anti-blackness.

171. Seikaly, "The Matter of Time"; Sherene Seikaly, *From Baltimore to Beirut: On the Question of Palestine* (forthcoming).

172. Jaclynn Ashly, "Afro-Palestinians Talk Heritage and Resistance," *Al Jazeera*, August 5, 2017, https://www.aljazeera.com/features/2017/8/5/afro-palestinians-talk-heritage-and-resistance; Sara Hassan, "The Hidden Resistance of African-Palestinians," *TRT World*, May 15, 2019, https://www.trtworld.com/magazine/the-hidden-resistance-of-african-palestinians-26671; Marc Lamont Hill, "From

Ferguson to Palestine," *Biography* 41, no. 4 (2018): 942–57; Fayida Jailler, "The History of Afro-Palestinians, Past and Present," *Travel Noire*, May 27, 2021, https://travelnoire.com/history-afro-palestinians-past-and-present.

173. Beckerleg, "African Bedouin in Palestine," 290–91; Lamont Hill, "From Ferguson to Palestine," 946; Jailler, "The History of Afro-Palestinians."

174. Ashly, "Afro-Palestinians Talk"; Jailler, "The History of Afro-Palestinians."

175. Lamont Hill, "From Ferguson to Palestine."

176. Quoted in Lamont Hill, "From Ferguson to Palestine," 947 (emphasis in original).

177. Lamont Hill, "From Ferguson to Palestine," 947.

178. On slavery in Palestine, see Seikaly, *From Baltimore to Beirut*. On slavery in the Middle East, see Chouki El Hamel, *Black Morocco: A History of Slavery, Race, and Islam*, African Studies Series (New York: Cambridge University Press, 2013); Eve Troutt Powell, *Tell This in My Memory: Stories of Enslavement from Egypt, Sudan, and the Ottoman Empire* (Stanford, CA: Stanford University Press, 2012); Ehud R. Toledano, *As If Silent and Absent* (New Haven, CT: Yale University Press, 2008); Terence Walz and Kenneth M. Cuno, eds., *Race and Slavery in the Middle East: Histories of Trans-Saharan Africans in Nineteenth-Century Egypt, Sudan, and the Ottoman Mediterranean* (Cairo: American University in Cairo Press, 2010); John Hunwick and Eve Troutt Powell, *The African Diaspora in the Mediterranean Lands of Islam* (Princeton, NJ: Markus Weiner, 2002); Ahmad Alawad Sikainga, *Slaves into Workers: Emancipation and Labor in Colonial Sudan* (Austin: University of Texas Press, 1996); Gokh Amin Alshaif, "Black and Yemeni: Myths, Genealogies, and Race," in *Racial Formations in Africa and the Middle East: A Transregional Approach* (POMEPS Studies 44, Project on Middle East Political Science, September 2021), 129–34; Beeta Baghoolizadeh, *The Color Black: Enslavement and Erasure in Iran* (Durham, NC: Duke University Press, 2024); Zachary Mondesire, "Race after Revolution: Imagining Blackness and Africanity in the 'New Sudan,'" *Racial Formations in Africa and the Middle East: A Transregional Approach* (POMEPS Studies 44, Project on Middle East Political Science, September 2021); Taylor Moore, "Betraying Behita: Superstition and the Paralysis of Blackness in Out el Kouloub's Zanouba," *International Journal of Middle East Studies* 54, no. 1 (2022): 149–58.

179. Safa Abu-Rabia, "Is Slavery Over? Black and White Bedouin Women in the Naqab (Negev)," in *Struggle and Survival in Palestine/Israel*, ed. Mark LeVine and Gershon Shafir (Berkeley: University of California Press, 2012), 277–88. According to the World Population Review, the number of Bedouin residents in Rahat in 2024 is 84,015: "Rahat Population 2024," *World Population Review*, accessed July 1, 2024, https://worldpopulationreview.com/world-cities/rahat-population.

180. On the Dom (Romani), see Arpan Roy, "A Space of Appearance: Romani Publics and Privates in the Middle East," *Anthropological Theory* 24, no. 2 (2024): 175–200, https://doi.org/10.1177/14634996231194214; Arpan Roy, "The Returns of Life: 'Making' Kinship in Life and Death," *Anthropological Theory* 20, no. 4 (2020): 484–507, https://doi.org/10.1177/1463499619894427.

## Chapter 1

This chapter expands claims we made in Yinon Cohen and Neve Gordon, "Israel's Bio-Spatial Politics: Territory, Demography and Effective Control," *Public Culture* 30, no. 2 (2018): 199–220. We acknowledge equal contribution.

1. Shlomo Gazit, *The Carrot and the Stick: Israel's Policy in Judaea and Samaria, 1967–68* (New York: B'nai B'rith Books, 1995).

2. Michel Foucault, *"Society Must Be Defended": Lectures at the Collège de France, 1975–1976*, ed. Mauro Bertani and Alexandro Fontana, trans. David Macey (New York: Macmillan, 2003).

3. Edward Said, *The Question of Palestine* (New York: Vintage Books, 1980), 36; see also Nadia Abu El-Haj, *Facts on the Ground: Archaeological Practice and Territorial Self-Fashioning in Israeli Society* (Chicago: University of Chicago Press, 2008); Nadia Abu El-Haj, *The Genealogical Science: The Search for Jewish Origins and the Politics of Epistemology* (Chicago: University of Chicago Press, 2012); Saree Makdisi, "The Architecture of Erasure," *Critical Inquiry* 36, no. 3 (2010): 519–59.

4. Ghazi-Walid Falah, "Dynamics and Patterns of the Shrinking of Arab Lands in Palestine," *Political Geography* 22, no. 2 (2003): 179–209.

5. Yinon Cohen, "Spatial Politics and Socioeconomic Gaps between Jews and Palestinians in Israel," *Israeli Sociology* 17, no. 1 (2015): 7–31 (in Hebrew).

6. Patrick Wolfe, "Settler Colonialism and the Elimination of the Native," *Journal of Genocide Research* 8, no. 4 (2006): 387–409.

7. Fayez A. Sayegh, *Zionist Colonialism in Palestine* (Beirut: Palestine Liberation Organization Research Center, 1965).

8. Ilan Pappe, *The Ethnic Cleansing of Palestine* (New York: Simon and Schuster, 2006).

9. Alana Lentin, "Europe and the Silence about Race," *European Journal of Social Theory* 11, no. 4 (2008): 487–503.

10. Areej Sabbagh-Khoury, "The Internally Displaced Palestinians in Israel," in *The Palestinians in Israel: Readings in History, Politics and Society*, ed. Nadim N. Rouhana and Areej Sabbagh-Khoury (Haifa: Mada al Carmel, 2011), 26–46.

11. Yinon Cohen, "From Haven to Heaven: Changing Patterns of Immigration to Israel," in *Challenging Ethnic Citizenship: German and Israeli Perspectives on Immigration*, ed. Daniel Levy and Yfaat Weiss (New York: Berghahn Books, 2002), 36–56.

12. Elia Zureik, *The Palestinians in Israel: A Study in Internal Colonialism* (New York: Routledge, 1979).

13. Ahmad Sa'di, *Thorough Surveillance: The Genesis of Israeli Policies of Population Management, Surveillance and Political Control towards the Palestinian Minority* (Manchester, UK: Manchester University Press, 2013).

14. Rassem Khamaisi, "Mechanism of Land Control and Territorial Judaization of Israel," in *In the Name of Security*, ed. Majid Al-Haj and Uri Ben-Eliezer (Haifa: Haifa University Press, 2003), 421–49.

15. Geremy Forman and Alexandre Kedar, "From Arab Land to 'Israel Lands': The Legal Dispossession of the Palestinians Displaced by Israel in the Wake of 1948," *Environment and Planning D: Society and Space* 22, no. 6 (2004): 809–30.

16. Alexander Kedar and Oren Yiftachel, "Land Regime and Social Relations in Israel," in *Realizing Property Rights*, ed. Hernando de Soto and Francis Cheneval, vol. 1 of Swiss Human Rights Book (Zurich: Rüffer and Rub, 2006), 129–46.

17. Yehouda Shenhav, *The Arab Jews: A Postcolonial Reading of Nationalism, Religion, and Ethnicity* (Stanford, CA: Stanford University Press, 2006).

18. Ella Shohat, "Sephardim in Israel: Zionism from the Standpoint of Its Jewish Victims," *Social Text*, nos. 19–20 (1988): 1–35.

19. Kedar and Yiftachel, "Land Regime and Social Relations."

20. Nicola Perugini and Neve Gordon, *The Human Right to Dominate* (Oxford: Oxford University Press, 2015); Rashid Khalidi, *The Hundred Years' War on Palestine: A History of Settler Colonialism and Resistance, 1917–2017* (New York: Metropolitan Books, 2020).

21. Noura Erakat, *Justice for Some: Law and the Question of Palestine* (Stanford, CA: Stanford University Press, 2020).

22. Cohen, "From Haven to Heaven."

23. Kenneth Prewitt, *What Is "Your" Race? The Census and Our Flawed Efforts to Classify Americans* (Princeton, NJ: Princeton University Press, 2013).

24. Shohat, "Sephardim in Israel."

25. Cohen, "From Haven to Heaven."

26. Lana Tatour, "Citizenship as Domination: Settler Colonialism and the Making of Palestinian Citizenship in Israel," *Arab Studies Journal* 27, no. 2 (2019): 8–39.

27. *Ornan v. Ministry of Interior*, District Court of Jerusalem, OM 6092/07, July 5, 2008, paras. 58, 14.

28. Ian Lustick, "Israel as a Non-Arab State: The Political Implications for Mass Immigration of Non-Jews," *Middle East Journal* 53, no. 3 (1999): 417–33.

29. David Sibley, "Purification of Space," *Environment and Planning D: Society and Space* 6, no. 4 (1988): 409–21.

30. Israel Central Bureau of Statistics, Statistical Abstract of Israel, No. 74, Table 2.13, September 12, 2023.

31. Naama Blatman-Thomas, "Commuting for Rights: Circular Mobilities and Regional Identities of Palestinians in a Jewish-Israeli Town," *Geoforum* 78 (2017): 22–32.

32. Chanina Porat, *The Bedouin-Arab in the Negev between Migration and Urbanization, 1948–1973* (Beersheba: Negev Center for Regional Development, Ben-Gurion University, 2009) (in Hebrew).

33. Ismael Abu-Saad, "Spatial Transformation and Indigenous Resistance: The Urbanization of the Palestinian Bedouin in Southern Israel," *American Behavioral Scientist* 51, no. 12 (2008): 1713–54; Mansour Nasasra, *The Naqab Bedouins: A Century of Politics and Resistance* (New York: Columbia University Press, 2017).

34. Ahmad Amara, Ismael Abu-Saad, and Oren Yiftachel, eds., *Indigenous (In)Justice: Human Rights Law and Bedouin Arabs in the Naqab/Negev* (Cambridge, MA: Harvard University Press, 2012); Michal Rotem and Neve Gordon, "Bedouin Sumud and the Struggle for Education," *Journal of Palestine Studies* 46, no. 4 (2017): 7–27.

35. Ahmad Amara, "The Negev Land Question: Between Denial and Recognition," *Journal of Palestine Studies* 42, no. 4 (2013): 27–47.

36. Neve Gordon, *Israel's Occupation* (Berkeley: University of California Press, 2008).

37. Abu El-Haj, *Facts on the Ground*, 19.

38. Jerusalem Institute for Policy Research, *Statistical Yearbook of Jerusalem: 2024*, ed. Yair Assaf-Shapira (2024), https://jerusaleminstitute.org.il/yearbook/#/4273.

39. Tamara Tawfiq Tamimi, "Revocation of Residency of Palestinians in Jerusalem: Prospects for Accountability," *Jerusalem Quarterly*, no. 72 (2017): 37–47.

40. Jerusalem Institute for Policy Research, *Statistical Yearbook*.

41. B'Tselem, *The Quiet Deportation Continues: Revocation of Residency and Denial of Social Rights of East Jerusalem Palestinians* (September 1998), https://www.btselem.org/publications/summaries/199809_quiet_deportation_continues.

42. Human Rights Watch, *A Threshold Crossed: Israeli Authorities and the Crimes of Apartheid and Persecution* (2021), 188.

43. Neve Gordon and Moriel Ram, "Ethnic Cleansing and the Formation of Settler Colonial Geographies," *Political Geography* 53 (2016): 20–29.

44. Tom Segev, *1967: Israel, the War, and the Year That Transformed the Middle East*, trans. Jessica Cohen (New York: Metropolitan Books, 2007), 410.

45. Avi Raz, *The Bride and the Dowry: Israel, Jordan, and the Palestinians in the Aftermath of the June 1967 War* (New Haven, CT: Yale University Press, 2012).

46. Gazit, *The Carrot and the Stick*.

47. Sami Tayeb, "The Palestinian McCity in the Neoliberal Era," *Middle East Report*, no. 290 (2019): 24–28.

48. Gordon, *Israel's Occupation*, 23.

49. "Moshe Dayan's Eulogy for Roi Rutenberg—April 19, 1956," Jewish Virtual Library, https://www.jewishvirtuallibrary.org/moshe-dayan-s-eulogy-for-roi-rutenberg-april -19-1956#:~:text=Let%20us%20not%20cast%20the,fathers%20dwelt%2C%20into %20our%20estate

50. Sara Roy, *The Gaza Strip: The Political Economy of De-Development* (Washington, DC: Institute for Palestinian Studies, 1995).

51. Gordon, *Israel's Occupation*.

52. Meron Benvenisti and Shlomo Khayat, *The West Bank and Gaza Atlas* (Jerusalem: West Bank Data Base Project, 1988), 112–13; Roy, *The Gaza Strip*, 175–81.

53. Yehezkel Lein, "Behind the Barrier: Human Rights Violations as a Result of Israel's Separation Barrier" (B'Tselem Position Paper, March 2003).

54. Eyal Weizman, *Hollow Land: Israel's Architecture of Occupation* (London: Verso, 2012), 132.

55. Peace Now, "Data," accessed July 20, 2024, https://peacenow.org.il/en/ settlements-watch/settlements-data/population.

56. Marco Allegra, Ariel Handel, and Erez Maggor, eds., *Normalizing Occupation: The Politics of Everyday Life in the West Bank Settlements* (Bloomington: Indiana University Press, 2017).

57. Tatour, "Citizenship as Domination."

58. Gordon, *Israel's Occupation*.

59. Neve Gordon and Muna Haddad, "The Road to Famine in Gaza," *New York Review of Books*, March 30, 2024, 1.

60. Nasasra, *The Naqab Bedouins*.

61. Cohen, "Spatial Politics and Socioeconomic Gaps," 14–15.

62. Rotem and Gordon, "Bedouin Sumud."

63. Negev Coexistence Forum for Civil Equality, *Home Demolitions in Bedouin Communities Negev-Naqab, Israel 2021–2022* (2023), https://www.dukium.org/wp -content/uploads/2023/10/Home-Demolition-Report-2021-2022_ENG_02.pdf.

64. Brenna Bhandar, *Colonial Lives of Property: Law, Land, and Racial Regimes of Ownership* (Durham, NC: Duke University Press, 2018), 115–48.

65. Thabet Abu-Ras, "Land Disputes in Israel: The Case of the Bedouin in the Negev," *Adalah Newsletter* 24 (2006): 1–10 (in Hebrew).

66. *Abu-Madigam v. Israel Land Administration*, HCJ 2887/04, decided April 14, 2007.

67. Rotem and Gordon, "Bedouin Sumud."

68. Emily McKee, "Performing Rootedness in the Negev/Naqab: Possibilities and Perils of Competitive Planting," *Antipode* 46, no. 5 (2014): 1172–89.

69. Jewish National Fund USA, "Community Building—Our Blueprint Negev Strategy," accessed July 20, 2024, https://www.jnf.org/our-work/community -building/our-blueprint-negev-strategy.

70. Michael Hauser Tov, "Israel Approves Four Jewish Desert Communities in Tense Cabinet Meeting," *Haaretz,* March 27, 2022.

71. Adalah: The Legal Center for Arab Minority Rights in Israel, "Israel's Destruction of Umm al-Hiran Reminiscent of Darkest of Regimes Such as Apartheid-Era South Africa," April 11, 2018, https://www.adalah.org/en/content/ view/9467.

72. Foucault, *"Society Must Be Defended."*

73. Michael Zanger-Tishler, "Ethnoracial Classification and the Israeli Central Bureau of Statistics: Constructing Palestinian Criminality in Israel (1990–2019)," *Ethnic and Racial Studies* 45, no. 15 (2022): 2867–91, https://doi.org/10.1080/01419870 .2022.2042351.

74. Hadeel Assali, "Diary: Palestinians in Paraguay," *London Review of Books* 45, no. 10 (May 18, 2023), https://www.lrb.co.uk/the-paper/v45/n10/hadeel-assali/diary; Segev, *1967.*

75. Segev, *1967,* 534.

76. "Will Rabin's Dream of Gaza Being Swallowed by the Sea Come True?" *Middle East Monitor,* September 21, 2015, https://www.middleeastmonitor.com/20150921 -will-rabins-dream-of-gaza-being-swallowed-by-the-sea-come-true/.

77. B'Tselem, "Fatalities," accessed July 20, 2024, https://statistics.btselem.org/ en/all-fatalities/by-date-of-incident?section=women&tab=overview.

78. Human Rights Watch, *"I Can't Erase All the Blood from My Mind": Palestinian Armed Groups' October 7 Assault on Israel* (July 17, 2024), https://www.hrw.org/ report/2024/07/17/i-cant-erase-all-blood-my-mind/palestinian-armed-groups -october-7-assault-israel.

79. Mark Landler, "'Erase Gaza': War Unleashes Incendiary Rhetoric in Israel," *New York Times,* November 15, 2023.

80. United Nations, "10,000 People Feared Buried under the Rubble in Gaza," *UN News,* May 2, 2024, https://news.un.org/en/story/2024/05/1149256.

81. Nicola Perugini and Neve Gordon, "'Medicide' in Gaza and International Law: Time for Banning the Bombing of Hospitals" (Policy Paper Series, Institute of Palestine Studies, 2024).

82. World Health Organization, *oPt Emergency Situation Update,* no. 33 (October 7, 2023–June 6, 2024), https://www.emro.who.int/images/stories/Sitrep_-_issue_33 .pdf?ua=1&ua=1.

83. ReliefWeb, "Education under Attack in Gaza, with Nearly 90% of School Buildings Damaged or Destroyed, and No University Left Standing," April 16, 2024, https://reliefweb.int/report/occupied-palestinian-territory/education-under-attack-gaza-nearly-90-school-buildings-damaged-or-destroyed-and-no-university-left-standing.

84. Forensic Architecture, "'No Traces of Life': Israel's Ecocide in Gaza 2023–2024," 2024, https://forensic-architecture.org/investigation/ecocide-in-gaza.

85. Gordon and Haddad, "The Road to Famine."

86. Hagar Shezaf, "Since the War Began, Entire Areas of the West Bank Have Been Emptied of Their Palestinian Communities," *Haaretz*, May 5, 2024.

87. *Application of the Convention on the Prevention and Punishment of the Crime of Genocide in the Gaza Strip* (*South Africa v. Israel*), International Court of Justice, Order, May 24, 2024, para. 32, https://www.icj-cij.org/case/192; Convention on the Prevention and Punishment of the Crime of Genocide, December 9, 1948, 78 UNTS 276.

88. Suhad Bishara, "Land and Law in Palestine/Israel: Settler Colonial Perspectives on Jewish Territorial Domination" (PhD diss., King's College London, 2022).

89. Blatman-Thomas, "Commuting for Rights."

90. Raef Zreik, "The Day the 'Jewish State Bill' Would Take Effect, . . ." *Tarabut*, March 1, 2018, http://www.tarabut.info/en/articles/article/israel-nationality-law-2018/.

91. Adalah: The Legal Center for Arab Minority Rights in Israel, "The Discriminatory Laws Database," September 25, 2017, http://www.adalah.org/en/content/view/7771.

92. Basic Law: Israel—The Nation-State of the Jewish People (emphasis added), https://main.knesset.gov.il/EN/activity/documents/BasicLawsPDF/BasicLawNationState.pdf.

## Chapter 2

1. Hagai El-Ad, interview on *Occupied Thoughts* (podcast), Foundation for Middle East Peace, January 12, 2021; B'Tselem, *A Regime of Jewish Supremacy from the Jordan River to the Mediterranean Sea: This Is Apartheid* (2021).

2. Yesh Din, *The Israeli Occupation of the West Bank and the Crime of Apartheid* (June 2020).

3. Human Rights Watch, *A Threshold Crossed: Israeli Authorities and the Crimes of Apartheid and Persecution* (2021).

4. Noura Erakat, "Beyond Discrimination: Apartheid Is a Colonial Project and Zionism Is a Form of Racism," *EJIL: Talk!* (blog), July 5, 2021; Noura Erakat and John Reynolds, "We Charge Apartheid? Palestine and the International Criminal Court,"

*Third World Approaches to International Law Review—TWAILR: Reflections* 33 (April 2021); Lana Tatour, "Why Calling Israel an Apartheid State Is Not Enough," *Middle East Eye*, January 18, 2021.

5. Yesh Din, *The Israeli Occupation*, 5.

6. John Reynolds, "Third World Approaches to International Law and the Ghosts of Apartheid," in *The Challenge of Human Rights: Past, Present and Future*, ed. David Keane and Yvonne McDermott (Cheltenham, UK: Edward Elgar, 2012), 194–218.

7. Red Nation, "Land Back, with Nickita Longman, Emily Riddle, & Lindsay Nixon," *The Red Nation Podcast*, October 5, 2020.

8. Ronnie Kasrils, "Birds of a Feather: Israel and Apartheid South Africa—Colonialism of a Special Type," in *Israel and South Africa: The Many Faces of Apartheid*, ed. Ilan Pappé (London: Zed Books, 2015), 23–42.

9. Christopher Gevers, "'Unwhitening the World': Rethinking Race and International Law," *UCLA Law Review* 67, no. 6 (2021): 1658.

10. Lana Tatour, "The Culturalisation of Indigeneity: The Palestinian-Bedouin of the Naqab and Indigenous Rights," *International Journal of Human Rights* 23, no. 10 (2019): 1569–93.

11. United Nations, International Convention on the Elimination of All Forms of Racial Discrimination, December 21, 1965, 660 UNTS 195, art. 1 (emphasis added).

12. John Dugard and John Reynolds, "Apartheid, International Law and the Occupied Palestinian Territory," *European Journal of International Law* 24 (2013): 867–913; John Quigley, "Apartheid Outside Africa: The Case of Israel," *Indiana International & Comparative Law Review* 2 (1991): 221–51.

13. Tatour, "Why Calling Israel an Apartheid State Is Not Enough."

14. United Nations, International Convention on the Suppression and Punishment of the Crime of Apartheid, November 30, 1973, 1015 UNTS 243.

15. Yesh Din, *The Israeli Occupation*, 5.

16. B'Tselem, *A Regime of Jewish Supremacy*, 8.

17. Tshepo Madlingozi, "Social Justice in a Time of Neo-Apartheid Constitutionalism: Critiquing the Anti-Black Economy of Recognition, Incorporation and Distribution," *Stellenbosch Law Review* 28 (2017): 123–47.

18. Andy Clarno, *Neoliberal Apartheid: Palestine/Israel and South Africa after 1994* (Chicago: University of Chicago Press, 2017).

19. Keith Feldman, *A Shadow over Palestine: The Imperial Life of Race in America* (Minneapolis: University of Minnesota Press, 2015), 229.

20. Fayez A. Sayegh, *Zionist Colonialism in Palestine* (Beirut: Research Center, Palestine Liberation Organization, 1965), 27.

21. Sayegh, *Zionist Colonialism*, 27.

22. Sayegh, *Zionist Colonialism*, 27–28.

23. Sayegh, *Zionist Colonialism*, 21.

24. See Noura Erakat, this volume.

25. Hasan Sa'b, *Zionism & Racism* (Beirut: Research Center, Palestine Liberation Organization, 1965), 31.

26. Sabri Jiryis, *The Arabs in Israel*, trans. Inea Bushnaq (New York: Monthly Review, 1976), 239.

27. Elia Zureik, *The Palestinians in Israel: A Study in Internal Colonialism* (London: Routledge, 1979), 16–17.

28. Al-Hadaf, "The Parallel Racist Entities: Israel and South Africa," *Al-Hadaf* 2 (1971): 90, cited in Andy Clarno, *Neoliberal Apartheid: Palestine/Israel and South Africa after 1994* (Chicago: University of Chicago Press, 2017), 207.

29. Al-Hadaf, "Israel and South Africa," *Al-Hadaf* 3 (1972): 135.

30. Nabil Shaath, "Filastin al-Ghad" [The Palestine of tomorrow], *Shu'un Filastiniya* 1, no. 2 (1971): 5–23.

31. Popular Front for the Liberation of Palestine, "South Africa: Profiting from Apartheid," *PFLP Bulletin* 45 (December 1980): 35.

32. "Human Rights in Israel," *Journal of Palestine Studies* 4, no. 3 (1975): 164, 168.

33. Regina Sharif, "Right versus Power," *Journal of Palestine Studies* 4, no. 4 (1975): 114.

34. Alfred T. Moleah, "Violations of Palestinian Human Rights: South African Parallels," *Journal of Palestine Studies* 10, no. 2 (1981): 14–16.

35. Rashid Khalidi, "The Palestinian Dilemma: PLO Policy after Lebanon," *Journal of Palestine Studies* 15, no. 1 (1985): 88–103.

36. Haydar 'Abd Al-Shafi, "The Oslo Agreement: An Interview with Haydar 'Abd Al-Shafi," *Journal of Palestine Studies* 23, no. 1 (1993): 15.

37. United States Department of Justice, *Report of the Attorney General to the Congress of the United States on the Administration of the Foreign Agents Registration Act of 1938, as Amended for the Calendar Year 1972* (Washington, DC: Government Printing Office, 1973), 101.

38. Palestine Research Center, *Israeli Racism* (Beirut: Research Center, Palestine Liberation Organization, 1975), 8.

39. Hanna Dib Nakkara, "Israeli Land Seizure under Various Defense and Emergency Regulations," *Journal of Palestine Studies* 14, no. 2 (1985): 13–34.

40. John Reynolds, *Empire, Emergency and International Law* (Cambridge: Cambridge University Press, 2017).

41. Palestine Research Center, *Israeli Racism*, 12.

42. Palestine Research Center, *Israeli Racism*, 14–16.

43. Erakat, this volume.

44. Walter Lehn, ed., *Zionism and Racism: Proceedings of an International Symposium* (Tripoli: International Organization for the Elimination of All Forms of Racial Discrimination, 1977), vii.

45. Edward W. Said, "Intellectual Origins of Imperialism and Zionism," in *Zionism and Racism: Proceedings of an International Symposium*, ed. Walter Lehn (Tripoli: International Organization for the Elimination of All Forms of Racial Discrimination, 1977), 125.

46. Said, "Intellectual Origins," 129.

47. Edward W. Said, *The Question of Palestine* (New York: Vintage, 1979), 37.

48. Edward W. Said, *The Politics of Dispossession: The Struggle for Palestinian Self-Determination, 1969–1994* (New York: Vintage, 1996), 340.

49. Edward W. Said, *The End of the Peace Process: Oslo and After* (New York: Vintage, 2000), 285–86.

50. Ali Abunimah, "Apartheid and Israel: Similarities," *Chicago Maroon*, March 2, 2001.

51. Azmi Bishara, "A Short History of Apartheid." MIFTAH—The Palestinian Initiative for the Promotion of Global Dialogue and Democracy, January 13, 2004.

52. Bishara, "A Short History."

53. Leila Farsakh, "Israel: An Apartheid State?" *Le Monde Diplomatique*, November 2003.

54. Leila Farsakh, "Independence, Cantons, or Bantustans: Whither the Palestinian State?" *Middle East Journal* 59, no. 2 (2005): 230–45; Leila Farsakh, *Palestinian Labour Migration to Israel: Labour, Land and Occupation* (New York: Routledge, 2005), 2, 135, 134–72.

55. Leila Farsakh, "Apartheid, Israel and Palestinian Statehood," in *Israel and South Africa: The Many Faces of Apartheid*, ed. Ilan Pappé (London: Zed Books, 2015), 162.

56. Amneh Badran, *Zionist Israel and Apartheid South Africa: Civil Society and Peace Building in Ethnic-National States* (London: Routledge, 2009).

57. See, among many others, Samer Abdelnour, "Beyond South Africa: Understanding Israeli Apartheid," *Al-Shabaka*, April 4, 2013; Nadia Abu El-Haj, "Racial Palestinianization and the Janus-Faced Nature of the Israeli State," *Patterns of Prejudice* 44, no. 1 (2010): 27–41; Yasmeen Abu-Laban and Abigail B. Bakan, "Israel/Palestine, South Africa and the 'One-State Solution': The Case for an Apartheid Analysis," *Politikon* 37, no. 2 (2010): 331–51; Ghada Ageel, ed., *Apartheid in Palestine: Hard Laws and Harder Experiences* (Edmonton: University of Alberta Press, 2016);

Salem Barahmeh, "Palestinians Are Fighting to Dismantle Apartheid, Not Just Annexation," *+972 Magazine*, June 29, 2020; Omar Barghouti, *Boycott, Divestment, Sanctions: The Global Struggle for Palestinian Rights* (Chicago: Haymarket Books, 2011); Raef Zreik and Azar Dakwar, "What's in the Apartheid Analogy? Palestine/Israel Refracted," *Theory & Event* 23, no. 3 (2020): 664–705; Randa Farah, "Refugee Camps in the Palestinian and Sahrawi National Liberation Movements: A Comparative Perspective," *Journal of Palestine Studies* 38, no. 2 (2009): 76–93; Honeida Ghanim, ed., *Israel and the Apartheid: A View from Within* (Ramallah: Madar, 2018); Yara Hawari, "Apartheid from Within? The Palestinian Citizens of Israel," *Al-Shabaka*, November 2017; Nadia Hijab and Ingrid Jaradat Gassner, "Talking Palestine: What Frame of Analysis? Which Goals and Messages?" *Al-Shabaka*, April 12, 2017; Amjad Iraqi, "Unlike South Africa, the World Is Giving Israel a Pass on Apartheid," *+972 Magazine*, July 26, 2019; Saree Makdisi, "Apartheid / Apartheid / [ ]," *Critical Inquiry* 44, no. 2 (2018): 304–30; Yousef Munayyer, "This Duck Is an Apartheid Duck," *Daily Beast*, April 24, 2012; Walid Salem, "Apartheid, Settler Colonialism and the Palestinian State 50 Years On," *Palestine-Israel Journal of Politics, Economics, and Culture* 22, no. 2/3 (2017): 112–18; Raef Zreik, "Palestine, Apartheid and the Rights Discourse," *Journal of Palestine Studies* 34, no. 1 (2004): 68–80; Elia Zureik, *Israel's Colonial Project in Palestine: Brutal Pursuit* (London: Routledge, 2016).

58. Yesh Din, *The Israeli Occupation*, 5.

59. Yesh Din, *The Israeli Occupation*, 5.

60. For example, Rinad Abdulla, "Colonialism and Apartheid against Fragmented Palestinians: Putting the Pieces Back Together," *State Crime Journal* 5, no. 1 (2016): 51–80; Amjad Alqasis, "Israeli Apartheid: A Means to an End, Not an Endgoal," *Al-Majdal* 48 (2012): 14–17; Jamil Dakwar, "It's Simple Apartheid," *Al-Ahram Weekly*, December 21–27, 2006; Noura Erakat, "The Structural Roots of Israeli Apartheid," *Al-Jazeera*, October 28, 2013; Erakat, "Beyond Discrimination"; Sahar Francis, "Denial of the Right to Life and Liberty of Person as an Act of Apartheid," *Al-Majdal* 47 (Autumn 2011); Hassan Jabareen, "The Israeli Regime of *Hafradah*," *Fasl al-Maqal*, April 11, 2008 (English translation published in *Adalah Newsletter* 47); Hazem Jamjoum, "Not an Analogy: Israel and the Crime of Apartheid," *The Electronic Intifada*, April 3, 2009; Victor Kattan, "The Russell Tribunal on Palestine and the Question of Apartheid," *Al-Shabaka*, November 2011; Mazen Masri, "Entrenching Apartheid: The Netanyahu-Trump Annexation Plan," *EUI Global Citizenship Observatory*, May 14, 2020; Rania Muhareb, "Apartheid, the Green Line, and the Need to Overcome Palestinian Fragmentation," *EJIL: Talk!* (blog), July 7, 2021; Nimer Sultany, "Don't Call It Discrimination," *Guardian*, April 30, 2007.

61. For example, Al-Haq, *Discrimination Is Real: Discriminatory Israeli Policies in Israel, the Occupied Territories and Occupied East Jerusalem* (paper presented to the World Conference Against Racism, Durban, South Africa, August 28–September 7, 2001); Al-Haq and Adalah, "Al Haq and Adalah Hold Symposium on New Legal Research Study: Occupation, Colonialism, Apartheid? A Re-Assessment of Israel's Practices in the Occupied Palestinian Territories under International Law," *Adalah Newsletter* 63 (August 2009); Al-Haq–Law in the Service of Man, BADIL Resource Center for Palestinian Residency and Refugee Rights, the Palestinian Center for Human Rights, Al Mezan Centre for Human Rights, Addameer Prisoner Support and Human Rights Association, the Civic Coalition for Palestinian Rights in Jerusalem, the Cairo Institute for Human Rights Studies, and Habitat International Coalition–Housing and Land Rights Network, *Joint Parallel Report to the United Nations Committee on the Elimination of Racial Discrimination on Israel's Seventeenth to Nineteenth Periodic Reports* (November 10, 2019); BADIL, "Overcoming the Ongoing Nakba: BDS & the Global Anti-Apartheid Movement," *Al-Majdal* 38 (Summer 2008); BADIL, "Israel and the Crime of Apartheid: Towards a Comprehensive Analysis," *Al-Majdal* 47 (Autumn 2011); LAW, *Apartheid, Bantustans, Cantonization: The ABC of Oslo* (Jerusalem: LAW—The Palestinian Society for the Protection of Human Rights & the Environment, 1998); Stop the Wall, "The Wall" (Ramallah: Stop the Wall, 2002); Palestinian Boycott, Divestment and Sanctions National Committee, "United Against Apartheid, Colonialism and Occupation," Palestinian Civil Society's Strategic Position Paper for the Durban Review Conference, Geneva, April 20–24, 2009, October 2008.

62. Zreik, "Palestine, Apartheid and the Rights Discourse," 68.

63. Organization of African Unity, Resolution 77 (XII), Resolution on the Question of Palestine, AHG/Res. 77 (XII) (August 1, 1975).

64. Thomas Sankara, "What Is the Nonaligned Movement Doing?" (speech at the Nonaligned Summit, Harare, September 3, 1986), in *Thomas Sankara Speaks: The Burkina Faso Revolution 1983–1987* (Atlanta: Pathfinder, 2007), 306.

65. Noura Erakat, "Whiteness as Property in Israel: Revival, Rehabilitation, and Removal," *Harvard Journal on Racial & Ethnic Justice* 31 (2015): 69–103, 71.

66. Mark Marshall, "Rethinking the Palestine Question: The Apartheid Paradigm," *Journal of Palestine Studies* 25, no. 1 (1995): 16.

67. Erakat, "Whiteness as Property."

68. Rabea Eghbaria, "Jewishness as Property under Israeli Law," *Law & Political Economy Project*, July 9, 2021.

69. Stuart Hall, "Race, the Floating Signifier" (lecture at Goldsmiths College, University of London, 1997), published as "Race—The Sliding Signifier," in *The Fateful Triangle: Race, Ethnicity, Nation* (Cambridge, MA: Harvard University Press, 2017), 31–79.

70. Patrick Wolfe, *Traces of History: Elementary Structures of Race* (London: Verso, 2016).

71. Theodor Herzl, *The Jewish State* (Raleigh, NC: Hayes Barton, 1986), 18.

72. David Ben-Gurion, "'Israel—the Arab States,' consultation in the Prime Minister's office, 1 October 1952," 2446/7, Israel State Archives, quoted in Avi Shlaim, "Israel, the Great Powers, and the Middle East Crisis of 1958," *Journal of Imperial and Commonwealth History* 12, no. 2 (1999): 178.

73. Said, *The Question of Palestine*, 18–19.

74. Said, *The Question of Palestine*, 122.

75. Aseel AlBajeh, "Decolonization from the Bottom Up," *This Week in Palestine*, May 2021, 36.

76. Jibran Majdalany, *On the Necessity for an Anti-Racialist Solution to the Palestine Conflict* (Beirut: Fifth of June Society, 1969), 6.

77. Majdalany, *On the Necessity*, 10

78. Majdalany, *On the Necessity*, 11.

79. Ahmed Abbes and Jonathan Rosenhead, "2021, the Year of Israeli Apartheid," *Mondoweiss*, July 27, 2021.

## Chapter 3

1. UN General Assembly, Resolution 3379, Elimination of All Forms of Racial Discrimination, UN Doc. A/RES/3379 (XXX) (November 10, 1975).

2. UN General Assembly, Resolution 46/86, Elimination of Racism and Racial Discrimination, UN Doc. A/RES/46/86 (December 16, 1991).

3. Noura Erakat, *Justice for Some: Law and the Question of Palestine* (Stanford, CA: Stanford University Press, 2019), 175–210.

4. Kristian Davis Bailey, "Black-Palestinian Solidarity in the Ferguson-Gaza Era," *American Quarterly* 67, no. 4 (2015): 1017–26; Noura Erakat, "Geographies of Intimacy: Contemporary Renewals of Black-Palestinian Solidarity," *American Quarterly* 72, no. 2 (2020): 471–96; Noura Erakat and Marc Lamont Hill, "Black-Palestinian Transnational Solidarity: Renewals, Returns, and Practice," *Journal of Palestine Studies* 48, no. 4 (2019): 7–16; Nadine Naber, "'The US and Israel Make the Connections for Us': Anti-Imperialism and Black-Palestinian Solidarity," *Critical Ethnic Studies* 3, no. 2 (2017): 15–30; Anti-Blackness Roundtable, "Roundtable on Anti-Blackness and Black-Palestinian Solidarity," *Jadaliyya*, June 3, 2015, https://www.jadaliyya.com/Details/32145.

5. UN Security Council, Resolution 242, UN Doc. S/RES/242 (November 22, 1967).

6. UN Doc. S/RES/242, para. 2(b).

7. Palestinian Liberation Organization, The Palestinian National Charter: Resolutions of the Palestine National Council, July 1–17, 1968, http://avalon.law.yale.edu/20th_century/plocov.asp.

8. Vijay Prashad, *The Darker Nation: A People's History of the Third World* (New York: New Press, 2007).

9. Prashad, *The Darker Nation.*

10. Antony Anghie, *Imperialism, Sovereignty, and the Making of International Law* (Cambridge: Cambridge University Press, 2004); Covenant of the League of Nations, June 28, 1919, art. 22.

11. Adom Getachew, *Worldmaking after Empire: The Rise and Fall of Self-Determination* (Princeton, NJ: Princeton University Press, 2019), 67.

12. Quoted in Getachew, *Worldmaking after Empire*, 80.

13. UN General Assembly, Resolution 1514, Declaration on the Granting of Independence to Colonial Countries and Peoples, UN Doc. A/RES/1514 (XV) (December 14, 1960).

14. Hamzah Baig, "'Spirit in Opposition': Malcolm X and the Question of Palestine," *Social Text* 37, no. 3 (2019): 47–71, https://doi.org/10.1215/01642472-7585050.

15. UN General Assembly, Resolution 3151, Policies of Apartheid of the Government of South Africa, UN Doc. A/RES/3151 (XXVIII) (December 14, 1973).

16. UN Security Council, Resolution 338, Ceasefire in the Middle East, UN Doc. S/RES/338(1973) (October 22, 1973).

17. James R. Stocker, *Spheres of Intervention: US Foreign Policy and the Collapse of Lebanon, 1967–1976* (Ithaca, NY: Cornell University Press, 2016), 122.

18. Erakat, *Justice for Some*, 96–134.

19. UN General Assembly, Resolution 3237, Observer Status for the Palestine Liberation Organization, UN Doc. A/RES/3237 (XXIX) (November 22, 1974).

20. UN General Assembly, Resolution 3236, Question of Palestine, UN Doc. A/RES/3236 (November 22, 1974).

21. UN General Assembly, Resolution 1761, The Policies of Apartheid of the Government of the Republic of South Africa, UN Doc. A/RES/1761 (XVII) (November 6, 1962).

22. International Convention on the Suppression and Punishment of the Crime of Apartheid, November 30, 1973, 1015 UNTS 243 (Apartheid Convention).

23. UN Doc. A/RES/3151 (XXVIII).

24. Raymond Suttner, "Has South Africa Been Illegally Excluded from the United Nations General Assembly?" *Comparative and International Law Journal of Southern Africa* 17, no. 3 (1984): 279–301.

25. Spyros Blavoukos and Dimitris Bourantonis, *Chairing Multilateral Negotiations: The Case of the United Nations* (New York: Routledge, 2011), 51.

26. Declaration of Mexico on the Equality of Women and Their Contribution to Development and Peace, 1975, in United Nations, *Report of the World Conference of the International Women's Year, Mexico City, 19 June–2 July 1975*, UN Doc. E/CONF.66/34 (July 2, 1975), UN Sales No. E.76.IV.1 (1976), 2–7.

27. Declaration of Mexico on the Equality of Women, principles 24, 26.

28. United Nations, *Report of the World Conference of the International Women's Year*, para. 117.

29. United Nations, *Report of the World Conference of the International Women's Year*, para. 169.

30. Associated Press, "Africans Rebuff Arab Call for U.N. to Expel Israel," *New York Times*, August 2, 1975, https://www.nytimes.com/1975/08/02/archives/africans-rebuff-arab-call-for-un-to-expel-israel-africans-rebuff.html.

31. Naveed Ahmad, "The Palestine Liberation Organization," *The Middle East* 28, no. 4 (1975): 81–115, 104.

32. Organization of African Unity, Resolution 76 (XII), Resolution on the Middle East and Occupied Arab Territories, AHG/Res. 76 (XII) (August 1, 1975).

33. Organization of African Unity, Resolution 77 (XII), Resolution on the Question of Palestine, AHG/Res. 77 (XII) (August 1, 1975); UN General Assembly, Letter dated 13 October 1975 from the Permanent Representative of Tunisia to the United Nations addressed to the Secretary-General, UN Doc. A/10297 (October 16, 1975).

34. Organization of African Unity, AHG/Res. 77 (XII), arts. 1(c), 10.

35. Organization of African Unity, AHG/Res. 77 (XII), art. 11 (emphasis added).

36. UN Doc. A/RES/3379 (XXX).

37. Paul Hoffman, "Nonaligned Bloc Adds 4 Members," *New York Times*, August 27, 1975.

38. UN General Assembly, Resolution 3375, Invitation to the Palestine Liberation Organization to Participate in the Efforts for Peace in the Middle East, UN Doc. A/RES/3375 (XXX) (November 10, 1975).

39. UN General Assembly, Resolution 2919, Decade for Action to Combat Racism and Racial Discrimination, UN Doc. A/RES/2919 (XXVII) (November 15, 1972).

40. UN General Assembly, Resolution 3223, Decade for Action to Combat Racism and Racial Discrimination, UN Doc. A/RES/3223 (XXIX) (November 6, 1974).

41. UN GAOR, 30th Sess., Third Committee mtg., UN Doc. A/C.3/L.2157 (October 1, 1975).

42. UN GAOR, 30th Sess., Third Committee mtg., UN Doc. A/C.3/L.2159 (October 15, 1975).

43. Anis Al-Qasem, interview with the author via WhatsApp, December 31, 2018.

44. Anis Fawzi Kassim, interview with the author via Skype, July 16, 2016.

45. International Convention on the Elimination of All Forms of Racial Discrimination, December 21, 1965, 660 UNTS 195 (ICERD).

46. Fayez A. Sayegh, "Statements by the Late Dr. Fayez Sayegh," *Palestine Yearbook of International Law* 6 (1990): 144–79.

47. Nabil Shaath, interview with the author, Fatah Political Organization Building, Ramallah, West Bank, August 1, 2016.

48. Fayez A. Sayegh, *Zionist Colonialism in Palestine* (Beirut: Palestine Liberation Organization Research Center, 1965), 207.

49. Sayegh, *Zionist Colonialism*, 217.

50. Sayegh, *Zionist Colonialism*, 214.

51. Sayegh, *Zionist Colonialism*, 215.

52. Aziza Khazzoom, "The Great Chain of Orientalism: Jewish Identity, Stigma Management, and Ethnic Exclusion in Israel," *American Sociological Review* 68, no. 4 (2003): 490–94.

53. Humphrey L. Walz, "Zionism and Racism: Contrasting Perspectives and Perceptions," in *Zionism and Racism: Proceedings of an International Symposium*, ed. Walter Lehn (Tripoli: International Organization for the Elimination of All Forms of Racial Discrimination, 1977), 17–26.

54. Edward W. Said, "Intellectual Origins of Imperialism and Zionism," in *Zionism and Racism: Proceedings of an International Symposium*, ed. Walter Lehn (Tripoli: International Organization for the Elimination of All Forms of Racial Discrimination, 1977), 129.

55. Hasan Sa'b, *Zionism & Racism* (Beirut: Palestine Liberation Organization Research Center, 1965), 6.

56. Sa'b, *Zionism & Racism*, 5.

57. Sa'b, *Zionism & Racism*, 6.

58. Sa'b, *Zionism & Racism*, 23; see also Elmer Berger, *The Jewish Dilemma: The Case against Zionist Nationalism* (New York: Devin-Adair, 1945), 4–5.

59. UN GAOR, 30th Sess., 2400th plenary mtg., UN Doc. A/10330 (November 10, 1975), para. 328.

60. UN Doc. A/10330, paras. 324, 325.

61. UN Doc. A/10330, para. 326.

62. UN Doc. A/10330, para. 327.

63. ICERD, art. 1.

64. David Keane and Annapurna Waughray, "Introduction," in *Fifty Years of the International Convention on the Elimination of All Forms of Racial Discrimination* (Manchester, UK: Manchester University Press, 2017), 4.

65. Keane and Waughray, "Introduction," 4.

66. Natan Lerner, *The UN Convention on the Elimination of All Forms of Racial Discrimination*, rev. ed. (Leiden: Brill Nijhoff, 2014), 70–75.

67. Lerner, *The UN Convention*, 74.

68. Lerner, *The UN Convention*, 74.

69. Fayez A. Sayegh, "Statement Made at the 2134th Meeting of the Third (Social, Humanitarian and Cultural) Committee of the General Assembly on 17 October 1975," reprinted in *Palestinian Yearbook of International Law* 6 (1990): 144–66.

70. UN GAOR, 30th Sess., 2134th mtg., UN Doc. A/C.3/SR.2134 (October 17, 1975), para. 16.

71. UN Doc. A/C.3/SR.2134, para. 16.

72. Sayegh, "Statement Made," 157.

73. Sayegh, "Statement Made," 157; Ella Shohat, "Sephardim in Israel: Zionism from the Standpoint of Its Jewish Victims," in *On the Arab-Jew, Palestine, and Other Displacements* (London: Pluto, 2017).

74. Noura Erakat, "Whiteness as Property in Israel: Revival, Rehabilitation, and Removal," *Harvard Journal on Racial & Ethnic Justice* 31 (2015): 69–103.

75. UN Doc. A/C.3/SR.2134, para. 21; see also paras. 14, 16.

76. UN Doc. A/C.3/SR.2134, para. 59.

77. UN Doc. A/C.3/SR.2134, para. 25.

78. UN Doc. A/C.3/SR.2134, paras. 29, 38.

79. UN Doc. A/C.3/SR.2134, para. 42.

80. UN Doc. A/C.3/SR.2134, para. 53.

81. UN Doc. A/C.3/SR.2134, para. 54.

82. UN Doc. A/C.3/SR.2134, para. 68.

83. UN Doc. A/C.3/SR.2134, paras. 64, 65.

84. UN GAOR, 30th Sess., 2400th plenary mtg., UN Doc. A/10330 (November 10, 1975), para. 27.

85. UN Doc. A/10330, para. 39.

86. UN Doc. A/10330, para. 133.

87. UN Doc. A/10330, paras. 192, 163–65.

88. UN Doc. A/10330, paras. 115–25.

89. UN Doc. A/10330, para. 131.

90. UN Doc. A/10330, paras. 168, 171.

91. UN Doc. A/10330, para. 44.

92. UN Doc. A/10330, paras. 44–51.

93. UN Doc. A/10330, para. 339.

94. Al-Qasem, interview.

95. Patrick Wolfe, *Traces of History: Elementary Structures of Race* (London: Verso, 2016), 101.

96. Durban Review Conference, "The Durban Declaration and Programme of Action," 2009, https://www.un.org/en/durbanreview2009/ddpa.shtml.

97. Naomi Klein, "Minority Death Match," *Harper's Magazine*, August 25, 2009, https://harpers.org/archive/2009/09/minority-death-match/.

98. UN Committee on the Elimination of Racial Discrimination, Concluding Observations of the Committee on the Elimination of Racial Discrimination (Eightieth session, 2012), UN Doc. CERD/C/ISR/CO/14-16 (April 3, 2012).

99. UN Committee on the Elimination of Racial Discrimination, General Recommendation 19, The Prevention, Prohibition and Eradication of Racial Segregation and Apartheid (Forty-seventh session, 1995), UN Doc. A/50/18 at 140 (1995), reprinted in Compilation of General Comments and General Recommendations Adopted by Human Rights Treaty Bodies, UN Doc. HRI\GEN\1\Rev.6 (2003), 208, http://hrlibrary.umn.edu/gencomm/genrexix.htm.

100. UN Economic and Social Commission for Western Asia, "ESCWA Launches Report on Israeli Practices towards the Palestinian People and the Question of Apartheid," press release, March 15, 2017, https://www.unescwa.org/news/escwa-launches-report-israeli-practices-towards-palestinian-people-and-question-apartheid.

101. Reuters, "Senior U.N. Official Quits after 'Apartheid' Israel Report Pulled," March 18, 2017, https://www.reuters.com/article/us-un-israel-report-resignation/senior-u-n-official-quits-after-apartheid-israel-report-pulled-idUSKBN16O24X.

102. B'Tselem, *A Regime of Jewish Supremacy from the Jordan River to the Mediterranean Sea: This Is Apartheid* (2021), https://www.btselem.org/sites/default/files/publications/202101_this_is_apartheid_eng.pdf.

103. See John Reynolds, this volume.

104. See David Palumbo-Liu and Michael Fischbach, this volume.

105. Noura Erakat, "Extrajudicial Executions from the United States to Palestine," *Just Security*, August 7, 2020, https://www.justsecurity.org/71901/extrajudicial-executions-from-the-united-states-to-palestine/.

106. Jared Ball, Interview with Dr. Frank Wilderson, October 1, 2014, *i Mix What i Like!*, https://imixwhatilike.org/2014/10/01/frankwildersonandantiblackness-2/.

107. Erakat, "Extrajudicial Executions."

108. Cedric J. Robinson, *Black Marxism: The Making of the Black Radical Tradition* (Chapel Hill: University of North Carolina Press, 2000).

## Chapter 4

This chapter is based on Seraj Assi, "The Original Arabs: The Invention of the "Bedouin Race" in Ottoman Palestine," *International Journal of Middle East Studies* 50(2) (2018): 213–232. © Cambridge University Press, reproduced with permission.

1. John B. Glubb, *A Soldier with the Arabs* (New York: Harper, 1957), 29.

2. George W. Stocking, *Race, Culture, and Evolution: Essays in the History of Anthropology* (New York: Free Press, 1968), 39.

3. Patrick Wolfe, *Traces of History: Elementary Structures of Race* (London: Verso, 2016).

4. Clinton Bailey, *Bedouin Culture in the Bible* (New Haven, CT: Yale University Press, 2018).

5. Letter from Henry McMahon to Sharif Hussein, October 24, 1915, reprinted in Palestine Royal Commission, *Report* (Cmd. 5479, July 1937).

6. Anne Blunt and Wilfrid S. Blunt, *A Pilgrimage to Nejd, the Cradle of the Arab Race* (London: J. Murray, 1881), 261.

7. Christine Bolt, *Victorian Attitudes toward Race* (Toronto: University of Toronto Press, 1971); Catherine Hall, *Civilising Subjects* (Chicago: University of Chicago Press, 2002).

8. Wolfe, *Traces of History*.

9. Chandra Mallampalli, *Race, Religion, and Law in Colonial India: Trials of an Interracial Family* (Cambridge: Cambridge University Press, 2011).

10. Richard Burton, "Letters on the Survey II: From Captain R. F. Burton," *Palestine Exploration Fund Quarterly Statement* (January 1872).

11. Richard Burton and Charles Drake, *Unexplored Syria: Visits to the Libanus, the Tulúl El Safá, the Anti-Libanus, the Northern Libanus, and the 'Aláh*, 2 vols. (London: Tinsley Brothers, 1872).

12. Burton and Drake, *Unexplored Syria*, vol. 2, 227–378.

13. Burton and Drake, *Unexplored Syria*, vol. 2, 254.

14. Randolph Marcy, *The Prairie Traveler: A Hand-Book for Overland Expeditions* (London: Trübner and Co., 1863).

15. Thomas Wright, *The Life of Sir Richard Burton* (London: Everett & Co., 1906).

16. Johann Friedrich Blumenbach, *The Anthropological Treatise of Johann Friedrich Blumenbach* (London: Published for the Anthropological Society by Longman, Green, Longman, Roberts, & Green, 1865); Theodor Waitz, *Anthropology of Primitive Peoples* (London: Longman, Green, Longman, and Roberts, 1864).

17. Richard Burton, *Etruscan Bologna: A Study* (London: Smith, Elder, & Co., 1876), 188.

18. Isabel Burton, *The Life of Captain Sir Richard F. Burton* (London: Chapman & Hall, 1893), vol. 1, 251.

19. Richard Burton, *The Gold-Mines of Midian and the Ruined Midianite Cities* (London: C. Kegan Paul & Co., 1878), 157.

20. Burton, *The Gold-Mines of Midian*, 157.

21. Richard Burton, *Personal Narrative of a Pilgrimage to Al-Madinah and Meccah*, 2 vols. (1855; London: G. Bell and Sons, 1913), vol. 2, 86.

22. Burton, *Personal Narrative*, vol. 2, 76.

23. Burton, *Personal Narrative*, vol. 2, 77n2.

24. Burton, *Personal Narrative*, vol. 2, 80–81.

25. Burton, *Personal Narrative*, vol. 2, 81.

26. Burton, *Personal Narrative*, vol. 2, 79.

27. Burton, *Personal Narrative*, vol. 2, 84.

28. Richard, *The Gold-Mines of Midian*, 9–10.

29. Burton, *Personal Narrative*, vol. 2, 285.

30. Burton, *The Gold-Mines of Midian*, 154–55.

31. Richard Burton, *Scinde; or, The Unhappy Valley*, 2 vols. (London: Richard Bentley, 1851), vol. 2, 92.

32. Burton, *The Gold-Mines of Midian*, 155.

33. Gertrude Bell, *The Desert and the Sown* (New York: E. P. Dutton, 1907); Gertrude Bell, *The Arab War: Confidential Information for General Headquarters from Gertrude Bell* (London: Golden Cockerel, 1940); Blunt and Blunt, *A Pilgrimage to Nejd*.

34. William Roger Louis, *Ends of British Imperialism: The Scramble for Empire, Suez and Decolonization* (London: I. B. Tauris, 2006).

35. Rashid Khalidi, *British Policy towards Syria and Palestine, 1906–1914* (London: Published for the Middle East Centre, St. Antony's College, Oxford, by Ithaca Press, 1980).

36. Kathleen Howe, *Revealing the Holy Land: The Photographic Exploration of Palestine* (Santa Barbara, CA: Santa Barbara Museum of Art, 1977).

37. "Obituary: Colonel Claude Reignier Conder, R.E., LL.D.," *Geographical Journal* 35 (1910): 456–58.

38. Claude R. Conder and H. H. Kitchener, *The Survey of Western Palestine: Memoirs of the Topography, Orography, Hydrography, and Archæology* (London: Committee of the Palestine Exploration Fund, 1881).

39. Claude R. Conder, *Tent Work in Palestine: A Record of Discovery and Adventure*, 2 vols. (New York: D. Appleton, 1878).

40. Unsigned review of "Tent Work in Palestine," by Claude Regnier Conder, *University Magazine: A Literary and Philosophic Review* 2 (1878): 116, 118.

41. Claude R. Conder, *The Survey of Eastern Palestine* (London: Committee of the Palestine Exploration Fund, 1889).

42. Conder, *The Survey of Eastern Palestine.*

43. Dov Gavish, *A Survey of Palestine under the British Mandate 1920–1948* (London: RoutledgeCurzon, 2005), xvii.

44. Claude R. Conder, *Palestine* (London: G. Philip & Son, 1889), 21.

45. Conder, *Palestine*, 21.

46. Conder, *Palestine*, 230.

47. Conder, *Palestine*, 230.

48. Conder, *Palestine*, 110.

49. Conder, *Tent Work in Palestine*, vol. 2, 206.

50. Conder, *Tent Work in Palestine*, vol. 2, 206.

51. Conder, *Tent Work in Palestine*, vol. 2, 206 (emphasis added).

52. Conder, *Tent Work in Palestine*, vol. 2, 270–71 (emphasis added).

53. Conder, *Tent Work in Palestine*, vol. 2, 271.

54. Conder, *Tent Work in Palestine*, vol. 2, 272.

55. Conder, *Tent Work in Palestine*, vol. 2, 236–37.

56. Conder, *Tent Work in Palestine*, vol. 2, 237.

57. Conder, *Tent Work in Palestine*, vol. 2, 272.

58. Conder, *Tent Work in Palestine*, vol. 2, 235.

59. Conder, *Tent Work in Palestine*, vol. 2, 277.

60. Conder, *Tent Work in Palestine*, vol. 2, 269.

61. Unsigned review of "Tent Work in Palestine," 117.

62. Conder, *Tent Work in Palestine*, vol. 2, 208–9.

63. Claude R. Conder, *The Future of Palestine: A Lecture Delivered for the Palestine Exploration Fund* (London: Palestine Exploration Fund, 1892), reprinted as Claude R. Conder, "The Future of Palestine," in *Tent Work in Palestine: A Record of Discovery and Adventure*, 6th ed. (London: A. P. Watt & Son, 1895), 375–87.

64. Conder, "The Future of Palestine," 377.

65. Conder, "The Future of Palestine," 378–79.

66. Conder, *Tent Work in Palestine*, vol. 2, 332.

67. Conder, *Tent Work in Palestine*, vol. 2, 332.

68. Conder, *Tent Work in Palestine*, vol. 2, 332.

69. Conder, *Tent Work in Palestine*, vol. 2, 332.

70. Conder, "The Future of Palestine," 376.

71. Conder, "The Future of Palestine," 384.

72. Conder, "The Future of Palestine," 383.

73. Conder, "The Future of Palestine," 382, 383.

74. For the Arab nationalist view, see Aref al-Aref and Harold Tilley, *Bedouin Love, Law and Legend* (Jerusalem: Cosmos, 1944).

75. Philip Hitti begins his 1943 account *The Arabs* with a chapter on "The Original Arabs: The Bedouin," while George Antonius's seminal 1938 *Arab Awakening* is replete with references to the Bedouin as the "original Arab race." See Philip K. Hitti, *The Arabs: A Short History* (Princeton, NJ: Princeton University Press, 1943); George Antonius, *The Arab Awakening: The Story of the Arab National Movement* (London: Hamilton, 1938).

76. Seraj Assi, *The History and Politics of the Bedouin: Reimagining Nomadism in Modern Palestine* (New York: Routledge, 2018).

77. Seraj Assi, "Are the Bedouin of Palestine a Lost Tribe of Israel?" *Haaretz*, September 12, 2018, https://www.haaretz.com/middle-east-news/2018-09-12/ty-article-opinion/.premium/are-the-bedouin-of-palestine-a-lost-tribe-of-israel/0000017f-f006-dc28-a17f-fc372d8d0000.

## Chapter 5

1. Haim Golan, ed., *The Poale-Zion Commission in Palestine 1920*, 2 vols. (Ramat Ef'al: Yan Tabenkin, 1989) (in Hebrew).

2. Shlomo Tivoni, *Rishonim ve-nahshonim: sipuro shel shevet ha-Tsayarim be-Zikhron Ya'akov* (Netanyah: ha-Agudah ve-hevrah ve-tarbut, 1993), 141 (in Hebrew).

3. Robert Alter, *Modern Hebrew Literature* (New York: Behrman House, 1975), 141.

4. Shmuel Yavnieli, "Le-Takanat Matsav He-Temanim," *Ha-Adama* 1 (1919): 80–95.

5. In this chapter, I am using all three terms interchangeably, according to context.

6. Theodor Herzl, *The Jewish State* (1896; New York: Dover, 1988), 86.

7. Etan Bloom, *Arthur Ruppin and the Production of Pre-Israeli Culture* (Leiden: Brill, 2011), 93–95, 225–29; Raphael Falk, *Zionism and the Biology of the Jews* (New York: Springer, 2017), 97–100.

8. See Yinon Cohen and Yitchak Haberfeld, *Rising Wage Inequality and the Wage-Gap between Mizrahim and Ashkenazim* (Tel-Aviv: Pinhas Sapir Center for Development, 2002).

9. For example, Moshe Behar and Zvi Ben-Dor Benite, eds., *Modern Middle Eastern Jewish Thought: Writings on Identity, Politics, and Culture 1893–1958* (Waltham, MA: Brandeis University Press, 2013); Moshe Behar and Zvi Ben-Dor Benite, "The Possibility of Modern Middle Eastern Jewish Thought," *British Journal of Middle Eastern Studies* 41, no. 1 (2014): 43–61; Sami Shalom Chetrit, *Intra-Jewish Conflict in Israel: White Jews, Black Jews* (London: Routledge, 2010); Yehouda Shenhav, *The Arab*

*Jews: A Postcolonial Reading of Nationalism, Religion, and Ethnicity* (Stanford, CA: Stanford University Press, 2006); Ella Shohat, *On the Arab-Jew, Palestine, and Other Displacements: Selected Writings* (London: Pluto, 2017).

10. Smadar Lavie, "Writing against Identity Politics: An Essay on Gender, Race, and Bureaucratic Pain," *American Ethnologist* 39 (2012): 780–804.

11. Ronit Lentin, *Traces of Racial Exception: Racializing Israeli Settler Colonialism* (London: Bloomsbury, 2018), 83–84.

12. Lentin, *Traces of Racial Exception*, 87–88; see also Alexander G. Weheliye, *Habeas Viscus: Racializing Assemblages, Biopolitics, and Black Feminist Theories of the Human* (Durham, NC: Duke University Press, 2014).

13. Nadia Abu El-Haj, *The Genealogical Science: The Search for Jewish Origins and the Politics of Epistemology* (Chicago: University of Chicago Press, 2012).

14. Patrick Wolfe, *Traces of History: Elementary Structures of Race* (London: Verso, 2016), 239–72.

15. Wolfe, *Traces of History*, 259.

16. Following Gershon Shafir, *Land, Labor, and the Origins of the Israeli-Palestinian Conflict, 1882–1914* (Berkeley: University of California Press, 1996).

17. Shafir, *Land, Labor, and the Origins*.

18. Golan, *The Poale-Zion Commission*, vol. 1, 19.

19. Golan, *The Poale-Zion Commission*, vol. 2, 37; Tivoni, *Rishonim ve-nahshonim*, 141.

20. Shmuel Yavnieli, "Avodat Ha-Tehiyya ve-Yehudei Ha-Mizrah," *Ha-Po'el Ha-Tsa'ir*, June 7, 1910.

21. Shmuel Yavnieli, *Masa Le-Teman* (Tel Aviv: Mappai Press, 1951).

22. Bat-Zion Eraqi Klorman, "Yemeni Jews and the Labor Movement: Cultural-Ideological Distinction or Ethnic and Economic Discrimination—Comments on Yosef Gorny's Article: 'The Strength and Weaknesses of Constructive Paternalism: The Second Aliyah Leaders' Image of the Yemenite Jews,'" *Katharsis* 2 (2004): 53–68 (in Hebrew); Yosef Gorny, "The Strengths and Weaknesses of 'Constructive Paternalism': The Second Aliyah Leaders' Image of the Yemenite Jews," *Cathedra: For the History of Eretz Israel and Its Yishuv* 108 (2003): 131–62; Nitza Druyan, "A Zionist Mission to Yemen, in a Distorted Mirror," *Peamim* 18 (1984): 137–40; Yehuda Nini, *Socialist Zionism* (Tel-Aviv: Friends of the Histadrut, 1972); Yehuda Nini, *Early Aliya from Yemen: Immigration without Organization* (Tel-Aviv: Friends of the Histadrut, 1976).

23. Yavnieli, *Masa Le-Teman*, 149–60 and passim.

24. Yavnieli, *Masa Le-Teman*, 14–17.

25. Yavnieli, *Masa Le-Teman*, 125–49 and passim.

26. R. B. Serjeant and Ronald Lewcock, *Sana'ā': An Arabian Islamic City* (London: World of Islam Festival Trust, 1983).

27. Yavnieli, *Masa Le-Teman*, 16.

28. Sven Beckert, *Empire of Cotton: A Global History* (New York: Alfred A. Knopf, 2015).

29. Yavnieli, *Masa Le-Teman*, 17.

30. Nitza Druyan, *Be-'en "marvad ḳesamim": 'ole-Teman be-Erets Yiśra'el, 1881–1914* (Jerusalem: Makhon Ben-Tsvi, 1981) (in Hebrew); Druyan, "A Zionist Mission to Yemen."

31. Zeev Smilanski, "Hebrew or Arab Workers," pt. 1, *Ha-Shiloah*, July 2, 1908, 71–79 (pt. 2, *Ha-Shiloah*, November 1, 1908, 461–69), 71.

32. Smilanski, "Hebrew or Arab Workers," 71.

33. Smilanski, "Hebrew or Arab Workers," 71–76.

34. Smilanski, "Hebrew or Arab Workers," 74.

35. Smilanski, "Hebrew or Arab Workers," 75.

36. Smilanski, "Hebrew or Arab Workers," 76.

37 Smilanski, "Hebrew or Arab Workers," 74–75.

38. Smilanski, "Hebrew or Arab Workers," 77.

39. Smilanski, "Hebrew or Arab Workers," 77–78.

40. Smilanski, "Hebrew or Arab Workers," 76.

41. Smilanski, "Hebrew or Arab Workers," 75.

42. Hapoel Hatzair, Historical Jewish Press Digital Archive, 1907–25, accessed June 25, 2024, https://www.nli.org.il/he/discover/newspapers/jpress.

43. Shafir, *Land, Labor, and the Origins*, 95.

44. Smilanski, "Hebrew or Arab Workers," 78.

45. Smilanski, "Hebrew or Arab Workers," 78–79.

46. Smilanski, "Hebrew or Arab Workers," 75.

47. Raziel Mamet, "Yemeni Jewry's Settlements in Israel," in *Se'i yonah: Yehude Teman be-Yiśra'el*, ed. Shalom Seri (Tel-Aviv: AmOved/Agudat "E'eleh be-tamar," 1984), 181 (in Hebrew).

48. Tivoni, *Rishonim ve-nahshonim*, 142.

49. Tivoni, *Rishonim ve-nahshonim*, 142.

50. Tivoni, *Rishonim ve-nahshonim*, 143.

51. Judges 19–21.

52. Tivoni, *Rishonim ve-nahshonim*, 143–44.

53. Rosa Luxemburg, "Introduction to Political Economy," in *The Complete Works of Rosa Luxemburg*, vol. 1, *Economic Writings 1*, ed. Peter Hudis, trans. David Fernbach, Joseph Fracchia, and George Shriver (London: Verso, 2013), 275–76.

54. Rosa Luxemburg, "Introduction to Political Economy," 236–73.

55. Rosa Luxemburg, "Introduction to Political Economy," 211.

56. Tivoni, *Rishonim ve-nahshonim*, 144.

57. Yehuda Nini, *Temene Kinneret: He-hayit o halamti halom 1912–1931* (Tel Aviv: 'Am 'Oved, 1996) (in Hebrew).

58. Nini, *Temene Kinneret*, 14.

59. Shoshana Madmoni-Gerber, *Israeli Media and the Framing of Internal Conflict: The Yemenite Babies Affair* (New York: Palgrave Macmillan, 2014), 30–34.

60. Golan, *The Poale-Zion Commission*, vol. 2, 61.

61. Moshe Behar and Zvi Ben-Dor Benite, eds., *Modern Middle Eastern Jewish Thought: Writings on Identity, Politics, and Culture 1893–1958* (Waltham, MA: Brandeis University Press, 2013), 224.

62. Ofra Yeshua-Lyth, *Politically Incorrect: Why a Jewish State Is a Bad Idea*, rev. English ed. (Bloxham, UK: Skyscraper, 2016), 255.

63. Abraham Abbas, "From Ingathering to Integration: The Communal Problem in Israel," in *Modern Middle Eastern Jewish Thought: Writings on Identity, Politics, and Culture 1893–1958*, ed. Moshe Behar and Zvi Ben-Dor Benite (Waltham, MA: Brandeis University Press, 2013), 247.

## Chapter 6

This chapter is equally and jointly written by the coauthors. We acknowledge the support of the Social Sciences and Humanities Research Council of Canada. For their constructive comments on an earlier draft, we thank the editors and anonymous reviewers.

1. United Nations Relief and Works Agency for Palestine Refugees in the Near East (UNRWA), "UNRWA Situation Report #107 on the Situation in the Gaza Strip and the West Bank, Including East Jerusalem," May 14, 2024, https://www.unrwa.org/resources/reports/unrwa-situation-report-107-situation-gaza-strip-and-west-bank-including-east-Jerusalem.

2. Rasha Khatib, Martin McKee, and Salim Yusuf, "Counting the Dead in Gaza: Difficult but Essential," *Lancet*, July 5, 2024, https://www.thelancet.com/journals/lancet/article/PIIS0140-6736(24)01169-3/fulltext.

3. International Court of Justice, "Application of the Convention on the Prevention and Punishment of the Crime of Genocide in the Gaza Strip (South Africa v. Israel)," Press Release No. 2024/3, January 12, 2024, https://www.icj-cij.org/sites/default/files/case-related/192/192-20240112-pre-01-00-en.pdf.

4. Francesca Albanese, *Anatomy of a Genocide: Report of the Special Rapporteur on the Situation of Human Rights in the Palestinian Territories Occupied Since 1967*

(advance unedited version), UN Doc. A/HRC/55/73 (March 25, 2024), 1, https://www
.ohchr.org/sites/default/files/documents/hrbodies/hrcouncil/sessions-regular/
session55/advance-versions/a-hrc-55-73-auv.pdf.

5. Rashid Khalidi, *The Hundred Years' War on Palestine: A History of Settler Colonialism and Resistance, 1917–2017* (New York: Picador, 2020), 58.

6. Khalidi, *The Hundred Years' War*, 75–76.

7. Nihad Boqa'i, "Palestinian Internally Displaced Persons Inside Israel: Challenging the Solid Structures," *Palestine-Israel Journal of Politics, Economics and Culture* 15–16, no. 3 (2008): 1–16.

8. UN General Assembly, Resolution 194, Palestine—Progress Report of the United Nations Mediator, UN Doc. A/RES/194(III) (December 11, 1948).

9. Abigail B. Bakan and Yasmeen Abu-Laban, "The Israel/Palestine Racial Contract and the Challenge of Anti-Racism: A Case Study of the United Nations World Conference against Racism," *Ethnic and Racial Studies* 44, no. 12 (2021): 2167–89.

10. See Leila Abu-Lughod and Ahmad H. Sa'di, *Nakba: Palestine, 1948, and the Claims of Memory* (New York: Columbia University Press, 2007).

11. Convention Relating to the Status of Refugees, July 28, 1951, 189 UNTS 137.

12. UN General Assembly, Resolution 428(V), Statute of the Office of the United Nations High Commissioner for Refugees, UN Doc. A/RES/428(V) (December 14, 1950).

13. Rashid Khalidi, "Truth, Justice and Reconciliation: Elements of a Solution to the Palestinian Refugee Issue," in *The Palestinian Exodus, 1948–1998*, ed. Ghada Karmi and Eugene Coltran (London: Ithaca, 1999), 239.

14. Protocol Relating to the Status of Refugees, January 31, 1967, 606 UNTS 267. See also Stephen Castles, "The International Politics of Forced Migration," in *Fighting Identities: Race, Religion and Ethno-Nationalism*, ed. Leo Panitch and Colin Leys (London: Merlin Press, 2002), 178.

15. Yasmeen Abu-Laban, "What UNRWA Tells Us about Refugees and the United Nations," in *Does the UN Model Still Work? Challenges and Prospects for the Future of Multilateralism*, ed. Kim Fontaine-Skronski, Valériane Thool, and Norbert Eschborn (Leiden: Brill, 2023), 250–65.

16. Julian Borger, "Israel Still Has No Proof of UNRWA Terrorist Claims—But Damage to Aid Agency Is Done," *Guardian*, April 22, 2024, https://www.theguardian
.com/world/2024/apr/22/israeli-allegations-of-unrwa-staff-links-to-terrorism-cost
-aid-agency-dearly.

17. UNRWA, "UNRWA: Claims versus Facts," May 2024, 7, https://www.unrwa
.org/unrwa-claims-versus-facts-february-2024.

18. Yasmeen Abu-Laban, "Redefining the International Refugee Regime: UNHCR, UNRWA and the Challenge of Multigenerational Protracted Refugee Situations," in *Research Handbook on the Law and Politics of Migration*, ed. Catherine Dauvergne (Cheltenham, UK: Edward Elgar, 2021), 310–22.

19. Abigail B. Bakan and Yasmeen Abu-Laban, "Anti-Palestinian Racism, Antisemitism, and Solidarity: Considerations towards an Analytic of Praxis," *Studies in Political Economy* 105, no. 1 (2024): 107–22; Yasmeen Abu-Laban and Abigail B. Bakan, "Anti-Palestinian Racism and Racial Gaslighting," *Political Quarterly* 93, no. 3 (2022): 508–16; Arab Canadian Lawyers Association, *Anti-Palestinian Racism: Naming, Framing and Manifestations*, prepared by Dania Majid (April 25, 2022), https://www.canarablaw.org/our-work; Sherene H. Razack, *Casting Out: The Eviction of Muslims from Western Law and Politics* (Toronto: University of Toronto Press, 2008).

20. Sharry Aiken and Stephanie J. Silverman, "Decarceral Futures: Bridging Immigration and Prison Justice towards an Abolitionist Future," *Citizenship Studies* 25, no. 2 (2021): 141–61.

21. Nadia Abu El-Haj, *Facts on the Ground: Archaeological Practice and Territorial Self-Fashioning in Israeli Society* (Chicago: University of Chicago Press, 2001); Noura Erakat, *Justice for Some: Law and the Question of Palestine* (Stanford, CA: Stanford University Press, 2019); Edward W. Said, *The Question of Palestine* (New York: Vintage, 1992); Patrick Wolfe, *Traces of History: Elementary Structures of Race* (New York: Verso, 2016).

22. Ghada Ageel, ed., *Apartheid in Palestine: Hard Laws and Harder Experiences* (Edmonton: University of Alberta Press, 2016); Richard Falk and Virginia Q. Tilley, "Israeli Practices towards the Palestinian People and the Question of Apartheid," *Palestine and the Israeli Occupation* 1, no. 1 (2017): 1–65; Human Rights Watch, *A Threshold Crossed: Israeli Authorities and the Crimes of Apartheid and Persecution* (2021).

23. Bakan and Abu-Laban, "Anti-Palestinian Racism, Antisemitism, and Solidarity."

24. Ilan Pappé, *The Ethnic Cleansing of Palestine* (Oxford: Oneworld, 2006); UNRWA, *Annual Operational Report 2019* (2020), https://www.unrwa.org/sites/default/files/content/resources/aor_2019_eng.pdf; Shaira Vadasaria, "1948–1951: The Racial Politics of Humanitarianism and Return in Palestine," *Onati Socio-Legal Series* 10, no. 6 (2020): 1242–69.

25. Albanese, *Anatomy of a Genocide*.

26. Khalidi, *The Hundred Years' War*, 9.

27. Yasmeen Abu-Laban and Abigail B. Bakan, *Israel, Palestine and the Politics of Race: Exploring Identity and Power in a Global Context* (London: I. B. Tauris, 2020);

Mazen Masri, *The Dynamics of Exclusionary Constitutionalism: Israel as a Jewish and Democratic State* (Oxford: Hart Publishing, 2017).

28. Charles W. Mills, *The Racial Contract* (Ithaca, NY: Cornell University Press, 1997); Carole Pateman and Charles Mills, *Contract and Domination* (Malden, MA: Polity, 2007).

29. Abu-Laban and Bakan, *Israel, Palestine and the Politics of Race*; Erakat, *Justice for Some*; Khalidi, *The Hundred Years' War*; Muna S. Tareh, "On the Violence of Self-Determination: The Palestinian Refugee as the Ontological Other," *Arab Studies Quarterly* 42, no. 3 (2020): 181–225; Vadasaria, "1948–1951"; Albanese, *Anatomy of a Genocide*.

30. Abigail B. Bakan, "Race, Class and Colonialism: Reconsidering the 'Jewish Question,'" in *Theorizing Anti-Racism: Linkages in Marxism and Critical Race Theories*, ed. Abigail B. Bakan and Enakshi Dua (Toronto: University of Toronto Press, 2014), 252.

31. Wolfe, *Traces of History*, 247.

32. Bakan, "Race, Class and Colonialism."

33. UN General Assembly, Resolution 217A(III), Universal Declaration of Human Rights, UN Doc. A/810 (December 10, 1948).

34. Abu El-Haj, *Facts on the Ground*.

35. Nur Masalha, *The Bible and Zionism: Invented Traditions, Archaeology and Post-Colonialism in Israel-Palestine* (London: Zed Books, 2007).

36. Pappé, *The Ethnic Cleansing of Palestine*.

37. See Noura Erakat and Mouin Rabbani, eds., *Aborted State? The UN Initiative and New Palestinian Junctures* (Washington, DC: Tadween, 2013); Loureen Sayej, "Palestinian Refugees and the Right of Return in International Law," *Oxford Human Rights Hub*, May 14, 2018, https://ohrh.law.ox.ac.uk/palestinian-refugees-and-the-right-of-return-in-international-law/; United Nations Information System on the Question of Palestine, "The Question of Palestine," accessed July 1, 2021, https://www.un.org/unispal/data-collection/.

38. UNRWA, "What We Do," accessed September 29, 2021, https://www.unrwa.org/what-we-do.

39. Ricardo Bocco, "UNRWA and the Palestinian Refugees: A History within a History," *Refugee Survey Quarterly* 28, nos. 2–3 (2010): 231, https://www.unrwa.org/userfiles/201006109359.pdf.

40. Bakan and Abu-Laban, "The Israel/Palestine Racial Contract," 2172.

41. Boqa'i, "Palestinian Internally Displaced Persons."

42. James G. Lindsay, "Fixing UNRWA: Repairing the UN's Troubled System of Aid to Palestinian Refugees" (Policy Focus 91, Washington Institute for Near East Policy, January 2009).

43. Khalidi, *The Hundred Years' War*.

44. Cathryn Costello, "On Refugeehood and Citizenship," in *The Oxford Handbook of Citizenship*, ed. Ayelet Shachar, Rainer Bauböck, Irene Bloemraad, and Maarten Vink (Oxford: Oxford University Press, 2017), 719.

45. BADIL Resource Center for Palestinian Residency and Refugee Rights, *Survey of Palestinian Refugees and Internally Displaced Persons 2016–2018* (2020), xiv.

46. Abu-Laban, "Redefining the International Refugee Regime"; "Biden Administration to Restore Aid to Palestinians," BBC, January 27, 2021, https://www.bbc.com/news/world-middle-east-55824227.

47. Borger, "Israel Still Has No Proof."

48. UNRWA, "UNRWA: Claims versus Facts."

49. Julian Borger and Ruth Michaelson, "Israel Lodges Proposal with UN for Dismantling of Palestinian Relief Agency," *Guardian*, March 31, 2024, https://www.theguardian.com/world/2024/mar/31/israel-plan-un-dismantle-palestinian-relief-agency-unwra.

50. Nur Masalha, *The Politics of Denial: Israel and the Palestinian Refugee Problem* (London: Pluto, 2003).

51. Masalha, *The Politics of Denial*, 1–2.

52. White House, "Peace to Prosperity: A Vision to Improve the Lives of the Palestinian and Israeli People" (January 2020), https://www.un.org/unispal/document/peace-to-prosperity-a-vision-to-improve-the-lives-of-the-palestinian-and-israeli-people-us-government-peace-plan/.

53. Yossi Yonah, "Israel's Immigration Policies: The Twofold Fact of the 'Demographic Threat,'" *Journal of the Study of Race, Nation and Culture* 10, no. 2 (2004): 195–218.

54. Muhannad Ayyash, *A Hermeneutics of Violence: A Four-Dimensional Conception* (Toronto: University of Toronto Press, 2019), 213.

55. Joseph A. Massad, *The Persistence of the Palestinian Question: Essays on Zionism and the Palestinians* (London: Routledge, 2006), 82.

56. Yosefa Loshitzky, *Identity Politics on the Israeli Screen* (Austin: University of Texas Press, 2001), 50.

57. Haim Bresheeth-Zabner, *An Army Like No Other: How the Israel Defense Forces Made a Nation* (London: Verso, 2020), 4.

58. Bakan, "Race, Class and Colonialism."

59. See Alana Lentin, this volume.

60. Karen Brodkin, *How Jews Became White Folks and What That Says about Race in America* (New Brunswick, NJ: Rutgers University Press, 1998).

61. Daniel Boyarin, "Outing Freud's Zionism: Or, the Bitextuality of the Diaspora Jew," in *Queer Diasporas*, ed. Cindy Patton and Beningno Sanchez-Eppler (Durham, NC: Duke University Press, 2000), 71–79, 92.

62. Wolfe, *Traces of History*, 249.

63. Massad, *The Persistence of the Palestinian Question*, 83.

64. Abu-Laban and Bakan, *Israel, Palestine and the Politics of Race*; Orna Sasson-Levy, "A Different Kind of Whiteness: Marking and Unmarking of Social Boundaries in the Construction of Hegemonic Ethnicity," *Sociological Forum* 28, no. 1 (2013): 27–50.

65. Bakan, "Race, Class and Colonialism," 258.

66. Diva K. Stasiulis and Abigail B. Bakan, *Negotiating Citizenship: Migrant Women in Canada and the Global System* (Toronto: University of Toronto Press, 2005); Lana Tatour, "Citizenship as Domination: Settler Colonialism and the Making of Palestinian Citizenship in Israel," *Arab Studies Journal* 27, no. 2 (2019): 8–39.

67. Tatour, "Citizenship as Domination."

68. Sasson-Levy, "A Different Kind of Whiteness," 32; Ronit Lentin, "Palestinian Lives Matter: Racialising Israeli Settler-Colonialism," *Journal of Holy Land Palestine Studies* 19, no. 2 (2020): 133–49.

69. Wolfe, *Traces of History*, 250.

70. Nicole Chavez, Emanuella Grinberg, and Eliott C. McLaughlin, "Pittsburgh Synagogue Gunman Said He Wanted All Jews to Die, Criminal Complaint Says," CNN, October 31, 2018, https://www.cnn.com/2018/10/28/us/pittsburgh-synagogue-shooting/index.html.

71. Abu-Laban and Bakan, *Israel, Palestine and the Politics of Race*; Bakan, "Race, Class and Colonialism"; Judith Butler, *Parting Ways: Jewishness and the Critique of Zionism* (New York: Columbia University Press, 2012); Said, *The Question of Palestine*; see also Alana Lentin, this volume.

72. Mills, *The Racial Contract*.

73. Bakan, "Race, Class and Colonialism"; Brodkin, *How Jews Became White Folks*; Matthew F. Jacobson, *Whiteness of a Different Color: European Immigrants and the Alchemy of Race* (Cambridge, MA: Harvard University Press, 1998); Cynthia Levine-Rasky, "White Privilege: Jewish Women Writing and the Instability of Categories," *Journal of Modern Jewish Studies* 7, no. 1 (2008): 51–66; David Roediger, *The Wages of Whiteness: Race and the Making of the American Working Class* (London: Verso, 2007).

74. Noah Lewin-Epstein and Yinon Cohen, "Ethnic Origin and Identity in the Jewish Population of Israel," *Journal of Ethnic and Migration Studies* 45, no. 11 (2019): 2132.

75. Joseph A. Massad, "Zionism's Internal Others: Israel and the Oriental Jews," *Journal of Palestine Studies* 25, no. 4 (1996): 53–68; Nissim Mizrachi and Hanna

Herzog, "Participatory Destigmatization Strategies among Palestinian Citizens, Ethiopian Jews and Mizrahi Jews in Israel," *Ethnic and Racial Studies* 35, no. 3 (2012): 418–35; Ella Shohat, "The Invention of the Mizrahim," *Journal of Palestine Studies* 29, no. 1 (1999): 5–20.

76. Wolfe, *Traces of History*, 252.

77. Ilan Pappé, *Israel* (London: Routledge, 2018), 51.

78. Youssef Courbage, "Reshuffling the Demographic Cards in Israel/Palestine," *Journal of Palestine Studies* 28, no. 4 (1999): 21–39, 28.

79. Wolfe, *Traces of History*, 253.

80. Gadi Ben Ezer, *The Ethiopian Jewish Exodus: Narratives of the Migration Journey to Israel 1977–1985* (London: Routledge, 2002); Alon Burstein and Liora Norwich, "From a Whisper to a Scream: The Politicization of the Ethiopian Community in Israel," *Israel Studies* 23, no. 2 (2018): 25–50; Yonathan Paz, "Ordered Disorder: African Asylum Seekers in Israel and Discursive Challenges to an Emerging Refugee Regime" (Research Paper No. 205, UNHCR, 2011), 8, https://www .unhcr.org/research/working/4d7a26ba9/ordered-disorder-african-asylum-seekers -israel-discursive-challenges-emerging.html; Hadas Yaron, Nurit Hashimshony-Yaffe, and John Campbell, "'Infiltrators' or Refugees? An Analysis of Israel's Policy towards African Asylum-Seekers," *International Migration* 51, no. 4 (2013): 144–57.

81. Maayan Ravid, "Making Their Lives Miserable: Structural Violence and State Racism towards Asylum Seekers from Sudan and Eritrea in Israel," *State Crime* 11, no. 1 (2022): 128–48.

82. Albanese, *Anatomy of a Genocide*.

83. Masalha, *The Bible and Zionism*.

84. Ageel, *Apartheid in Palestine*; Brenna Bhandar, *Colonial Lives of Property: Law, Land and Racial Regimes of Ownership* (Durham, NC: Duke University Press, 2018); Uri Davis, *Apartheid Israel: Possibilities for the Struggle Within* (New York: Zed Books, 2003); Wolfe, *Traces of History*.

85. Abu-Laban, "Redefining the International Refugee Regime."

86. "Report: Israel to Shut UNRWA Schools in East Jerusalem," *Times of Israel*, January 20, 2019, https://www.timesofisrael.com/report-israel-to-shut-unrwa -schools-in-east-jerusalem/.

Chapter 7

1. Rudyard Kipling, "The White Man's Burden," in *Rudyard Kipling's Verse: Inclusive Edition, 1885–1918* (Toronto: Copp Clark, 1919), 373–74.

2. W. E. B. Du Bois, "Forethought," in *The Souls of Black Folk: Essays and Sketches* (Chicago: A. C. McClurg, 1903), http://www.gutenberg.org/files/408/408-h/408-h.htm.

3. W. E. B. Du Bois, "Suez," 1956, W. E. B. Du Bois Papers, Special Collections and University Archives, University of Massachusetts Amherst Libraries, https://credo.library.umass.edu/view/pageturn/mums312-b237-i029/#page/1/mode/1up.

4. Michael R. Fischbach, *Black Power and Palestine: Transnational Countries of Color* (Stanford, CA: Stanford University Press, 2018).

5. George Breitman, ed., *Malcolm X Speaks* (New York: Grove, 1965), 48, 50.

6. Breitman, *Malcolm X Speaks*, 36.

7. Breitman, *Malcolm X Speaks*, 50.

8. Eric C. Lincoln, *The Black Muslims in America*, rev. ed. (Boston: Beacon, 1973), 249.

9. Lincoln, *The Black Muslims*, 177.

10. Malcolm X, "Zionist Logic," *Egyptian Gazette*, September 17, 1964.

11. Frantz Fanon, *The Wretched of the Earth*, trans. Constance Farrington (New York: Grove, 1968), 213.

12. Stokely Carmichael (Kwame Ture) with Ekwueme Michael Thelwell, *Ready for Revolution: The Life and Struggle of Stokely Carmichael (Kwame Ture)* (New York: Scribner, 2003), 558–59.

13. James Forman, *The Making of Black Revolutionaries: A Personal Account* (New York: Macmillan, 1972), 496.

14. "The Palestine Problem: Test Your Knowledge," *SNCC Newsletter*, June–July 1967, 4.

15. "SNCC and the Arab-Israeli Conflict," *The Movement*, September 1967, 2.

16. Author's interview with Randa Khalidi al-Fattal, Beirut, June 24, 2012.

17. Stokely Carmichael (Kwame Ture), *Stokely Speaks: From Black Power to Pan-Africanism* (Chicago: Lawrence Hill, 2007), 161.

18. Carmichael, *Stokely Speaks*, 138, 142.

19. "Drawing Lessons: H. Rap Brown and Stokely Carmichael Addresses at Newton Rally," audio recording, February 17, 1968, Pacifica Radio/UC Berkeley Social Activism Sound Recording Project.

20. "Politics, Minority Report, Omar Ahmed," 1968, Black Power Conference Reports, *Black Nationalism and the Revolutionary Action Movement: The Papers of Muhammad Ahmad (Max Stanford)*, Archives Unbound Series, Gale Cengage (subscription required), file: Black Power Conference 1968, 1969.

21. "An Appeal by Black Americans against United States Support of the Zionist Government of Israel," advertisement, *New York Times*, November 1, 1970.

22. Eldridge Cleaver, *Soul on Ice* (New York: Dell, 1968), iii.

23. Federal Bureau of Investigation, "The Fedayeen Impact—Middle East and United States," June 1970, 39, https://archive.org/details/FedayeenImpactMiddleEastAndUnitedStatesJune1970/page/n4/mode/2up.

24. John Suiter, "Will the Machine-Gunners Please Step Forward," *Berkeley Barb*, August 15–21, 1969, 10–11.

25. Jeff Gerth, "Interview with David Hilliard," *Black Panther*, February 17, 1970, 4.

26. "Black Panther Party Statement on Palestine," September 18, 1970, University of California, Berkeley, Bancroft Library, Eldridge Cleaver Papers, carton 5, folder 9.

27. "Fat'h Speaks to Africa," *Black Panther*, October 11, 1969, 4.

28. "Yassir Arafat—Commander of Al Fat'h, Palestine: Voices of Rebellion," *Black Panther*, December 20, 1969, 15.

29. Hebrew for "Sons of the Covenant," the oldest and largest Jewish service organization in the world: *Britannica*, last updated May 21, 2024, https://www .britannica.com/topic/Bnai-Brith.

30. Jay Kaufman, "Thou Shalt Surely Rebuke Thy Neighbor," in *Black Anti-Semitism and Jewish Racism*, intro. Nat Hentoff (New York: Schocken, 1970), 51.

31. Author's interview with Courtland Cox via telephone, October 15, 2015.

32. "SNCC and the Arab-Israeli Conflict," 2.

33. Junebug Jabo Jones, "The Mid-East and the Liberal Reaction," *SNCC Newsletter*, September–October 1967, 5–6.

34. John Suiter, "Will the Machine-Gunners," 11.

35. "Our Enemy's Friends Are Also Our Enemies," *Black Panther*, August 9, 1969, 12–13.

36. Connie Matthews, "Will Racism or International Proletarian Solidarity Conquer?" *Black Panther*, April 25, 1970, 16.

37. William Jelani Cobb, ed., *The Essential Harold Cruse: A Reader* (New York: Palgrave, 2002), 76–77.

38. Harold Cruse, *Rebellion or Revolution?* (New York: William Morrow, 1968), 75.

39. Askia Muhammad Touré, "A Song in Blood and Tears," *Negro Digest/Black World*, November 1971, 20.

40. Haki R. Madhubuti, "A Poem for a Poet," in *Groundwork: New and Selected Poems, Don L. Lee/Haki R. Madhubuti from 1966–1996* (Chicago: Third World, 1996), 88.

41. Shirley Graham Du Bois, "Confrontation in the Middle East," *Black Scholar* 5, no. 3 (1973): 37.

42. Graham Du Bois, "Confrontation," 37.

43. "Why I Left America: Conversation: Ida Lewis and James Baldwin," in *New Black Voices: An Anthology of Contemporary Afro-American Literature,* ed. Abraham Chapman (New York: Penguin. 1972), 412.

44. See Zvi Ben-Dor Benite, this volume.

45. Ella Shohat, "Sephardim in Israel: Zionism from the Standpoint of Its Jewish Victims," *Social Text* 19/20 (Autumn 1988): 6.

46. Tom Segev, *1949: The First Israelis* (New York: Free Press, 1986), 157.

47. Henriette Dahan Kalev, "Colorism in Israel: The Construct of a Paradox," *American Behavioral Scientist* 62, no. 14 (2018): 2101, 2104.

48. Orna Sasson-Levy, "A Different Kind of Whiteness: Marking and Unmarking of Social Boundaries in the Construction of Hegemonic Ethnicity," *Sociological Forum* 28, no. 1 (2013): 29.

49. Noura Erakat, "Whiteness as Property in Israel: Revival, Rehabilitation, and Removal," *Harvard Journal on Racial & Ethnic Justice* 31 (2015): 72.

50. Yosef Waksman, "The Panthers Dream to Fight Together with the Arabs against the Establishment," *Maariv*, April 11, 1972 (in Hebrew), reprinted in *Documents from Israel, 1967–1973: Readings for a Critique of Zionism*, ed. Uri Davis and Norton Mezvinsky (London: Ithaca, 1975), 122.

51. Sami Shalom Chetrit, *Intra-Jewish Conflict in Israel: White Jews, Black Jews* (Abingdon, UK: Routledge, 2010), 119.

52. Chetrit, *Intra-Jewish Conflict*, 120.

53. Waksman, "The Panthers Dream," 120.

54. Kokhavi Shemesh, "This Is My Opinion," *Matzpen*, January 1973 (in Hebrew), reprinted in *Documents from Israel, 1967–1973: Readings for a Critique of Zionism*, ed. Uri Davis and Norton Mezvinsky (London: Ithaca, 1973), 115–16.

55. Black for Palestine, accessed June 20, 2020, http://www.blackforpalestine .com/.

56. Institute by Reut and Anti-Defamation League, *The Assault on Israel's Legitimacy—The Frustrating 20X Question: Why Is It Still Growing? Condition, Direction and Response*, Version A (January 2017), https://www.jewishpublicaffairs .org/wp-content/uploads/sites/10/2015/09/The-20X-Question-Strategic-Framework -vs-DLG-and-BDS-By-Reut-Group-and-ADL.pdf.

57. Michael R. Fischbach, "What Color Are Israeli Jews? Intersectionality, Israel Advocacy, and the Changing Discourse of Color and Indigeneity," in *Selected Racial Boundaries: The Social Life of Blackness in Israel*, ed. Uri Dorchin and Gabriella Djerrahian (Abingdon, UK: Routledge, 2021), 236–55.

58. David Schraub, "White Jews: An Intersectional Approach," *AJS Review* 43, no. 2 (2019): 406.

59. Hen Mazzig, "Op-Ed: No, Israel Isn't a Country of Privileged and Powerful White Europeans," *Los Angeles Times*, May 20, 2019, https://www.latimes.com/ opinion/op-ed/la-oe-mazzig-mizrahi-jews-israel-20190520-story.html.

60. Mazzig, "Op-Ed."

61. Ruth Frankenberg, *White Women, Race Matters: The Social Construction of Whiteness* (Minneapolis: University of Minnesota Press, 1993), 236.

62. Dana Weiler-Polak, "Israel Enacts Law Allowing Authorities to Detain Illegal Migrants for up to 3 Years," *Haaretz*, June 3, 2012, https://www.haaretz.com/israel-s -new-infiltrators-law-comes-into-effect-1.5167886.

63. Jason Williams, quoted in Deborah Barfield Berry and Joey Garrison, "Biden, Facing Backlash over War in Gaza, Is Losing Support from Some Young Black Voters," *USA Today*, December 17, 2023, https://www.usatoday.com/story/news/ politics/elections/2023/12/17/young-black-voters-want-biden-to-speak-up-more-for -palestinians/71936147007/.

64. Cori Bush, "Remarks Introducing Ceasefire Now Resolution," October 16, 2024, https://bush.house.gov/imo/media/doc/remarks_introducing_ceasefire_now _resolution.pdf; Clyde McGrady, "From Ferguson to Gaza: How African Americans Bonded with Palestinian Activists," *New York Times*, February 6, 2024, https://www .nytimes.com/2024/02/06/us/african-americans-palestinian.html.

65. Movement for Black Lives, "The Movement for Black Lives Calls for an Immediate End to the U.S.-Backed Occupation of Palestine," October 2023, https://m4bl.org/statements/movement-for-black-lives-statement-on-us-backed -occupation-of-palestine/.

66. Willie Dwayne Francois III, "For Many Black Church Leaders, It's about Seeing God in Gaza," Faith & Leadership, Duke Divinity School, Duke University, May 14, 2024, https://faithandleadership.com/many-black-church-leaders-its-about -seeing-god-gaza.

67. Bob Dylan "The Times They Are A-Changin'" (1963), https://www.bobdylan .com/songs/times-they-are-changin/.

**Chapter 8**

1. Shir Hever, "Elbit Systems: The Israeli Arms Company under Fire from Activists," *Middle East Eye*, January 14, 2022, https://www.middleeasteye.net/news/ israel-uk-elbit-systems-arms-company-under-fire-activists.

2. Cedric J. Robinson, *Black Marxism: The Making of the Black Radical Tradition* (1983; Chapel Hill: University of North Carolina Press, 2000), 26.

3. Robinson, *Black Marxism*, 26.

4. Gargi Bhattacharyya, *Rethinking Racial Capitalism: Questions of Reproduction and Survival* (London: Rowman & Littlefield, 2018), 11–16.

5. Robinson, *Black Marxism*, xxviii; see also Lisa Lowe, *The Intimacies of Four Continents* (Durham, NC: Duke University Press, 2015), 150; Patrick Wolfe, *Traces of History: Elementary Structures of Race* (London: Verso, 2016), 20–23.

6. Andy Clarno, *Neoliberal Apartheid: Palestine/Israel and South Africa after 1994* (Chicago: University of Chicago Press, 2017), 9.

7. Sai Englert, "Settlers, Workers, and the Logic of Accumulation by Dispossession," *Antipode* 52, no. 6 (2020): 1654. On the relationship between Indigenous people and capitalist proletarianization, see Glen Coulthard, *Red Skin, White Mask: Rejecting the Colonial Politics of Recognition* (Minneapolis: University of Minnesota Press, 2014). On the shifting structure of settler-colonial labor regimes, see Robin D. G. Kelley, "The Rest of Us: Rethinking Settler and Native," *American Quarterly* 69, no. 2 (2017): 267–76.

8. Jeff Halper, *War against the People: Israel, the Palestinians and Global Pacification* (London: Pluto, 2015).

9. Robinson, *Black Marxism*.

10. See Ronit Lentin, *Traces of Racial Exception: Racializing Israeli Settler Colonialism* (London: Bloomsbury, 2018); Fayez Sayegh, "Zionist Colonialism in Palestine (1965)," *Settler Colonial Studies* 2, no. 1 (2012): 206–25. On race and settler colonialism, see Wolfe, *Traces of History*. On necropolitics, see Achille Mbembe, *Necropolitics* (Durham, NC: Duke University Press, 2019). On racial capitalism, see Bhattacharyya, *Rethinking Racial Capitalism*; Robinson, *Black Marxism*.

11. Kieron Turner, "Disrupting Coloniality through Palestine Solidarity: Decolonising or Decolonial Praxis?" *Interfere* 3 (2022): 6–34, https://interferejournal .org/wp-content/uploads/2022/12/2-disrupting-coloniality-through-palestine -solidarity-decolonising-or-decolonial-praxis-kieron-turner.pdf.

12. Chandni Desai and Linda Tabar, "Decolonization Is a Global Project: From Palestine to the Americas," *Decolonization: Indigeneity, Education & Society* 6 (2017): i–xix; Goldie Osuri and Ather Zia, "Kashmir and Palestine: Archives of Coloniality and Solidarity," *Identities* 27, no. 3 (2020): 249–66.

13. Therezia Anderson and Tom Cooper, *Gaza: Life beneath the Drones* (London: Freedom, 2015), 20–21; Who Profits, "Elbit Systems," last modified October 12, 2021, https://www.whoprofits.org/company/elbit-systems/#:~:text=In%202020%2C %20the%20Israeli%20Ministry,sales%20directly%20to%20the%20IMOD.

14. "Top 100 for 2023," *Defense News*, 2021, accessed May 24, 2024, https://people .defensenews.com/top-100/.

15. Who Profits, "Elbit Systems' Complicity in the Assault on Gaza 2014," November 2014, https://www.whoprofits.org/publications/report/105?elbit-systems-complicity -in-the-assault-on-gaza-2014.

16. Corporate Watch, "Elbit Systems: Company Profile," February 6, 2019, https://corporatewatch.org/elbit-systems-company-profile-2/; Who Profits, "Elbit Systems."

17. Elbit Systems, *Company Profile* (2021), https://elbitsystems.com/company -profile/#p=1.

18. Corporate Watch, "Elbit Systems"; Elbit Systems, "Elbit Systems Awarded a $144 Million Contract from the Israeli MOD to Supply Small Caliber Ammunition,"

press release, January 1, 2020, https://elbitsystems.com/pr-new/elbit-systems-awarded-a-144-million-contract-from-the-israeli-mod-to-supply-small-caliber-ammunition/.

19. Elbit Systems, *Elbit Systems Land Small Caliber Ammunition Portfolio: Advanced Ammunition Solutions* (2019), 2, https://elbitsystems.com/media/Catalog-Small-Caliber-Ammunition_13_Web.pdf.

20. Shir Hever, *The Privatization of Israeli Security* (London: Pluto, 2018), 168.

21. Who Profits, "Elbit Systems."

22. David Lloyd and Patrick Wolfe, "Settler Colonial Logics and the Neoliberal Regime," *Settler Colonial Studies* 6, no. 2 (2016): 111; Harsha Walia, *Border and Rule: Global Migration, Capitalism and the Rise of Racist Nationalism* (Chicago: Haymarket Books, 2021).

23. Nahla Abdo and Nira Yuval-Davis, "Palestine, Israel, and the Zionist Settler Project," in *Unsettling Settler Societies: Articulations of Gender, Race, Ethnicity and Class*, ed. Daiva Stasialus and Nira Yuval-Davis (London: Sage, 1995).

24. Rashid Khalidi, *The Hundred Years' War on Palestine: A History of Settler Colonialism and Resistance, 1917–2017* (New York: Metropolitan Books, 2020).

25. See Zvi Ben-Dor Benite, this volume; Nimrod Ben Zeev, "Palestine along the Colour Line: Race, Colonialism, and Construction Labour, 1918–1948," *Ethnic and Racial Studies* 44, no. 12 (2021): 2190–212.

26. Englert, "Settlers, Workers, and the Logic"; Siddhant Issar, "Theorising 'Racial/Colonial Primitive Accumulation': Settler Colonialism, Slavery and Racial Capitalism," *Race & Class* 63, no. 1 (2021): 23–50.

27. Coulthard, *Red Skin, White Mask*, 125.

28. Hever, *The Privatization of Israeli Security*.

29. Halper, *War against the People*, 68.

30. Somdeep Sen, *Decolonising Palestine: Hamas between the Anticolonial and the Postcolonial* (Ithaca, NY: Cornell University Press, 2020), 45.

31. Clarno, *Neoliberal Apartheid*, 40; for more on the permit regime, see Yael Berda, *Living Emergency: Israel's Permit Regime in the Occupied West Bank* (Stanford, CA: Stanford University Press, 2017).

32. Mbembe, *Necropolitics*, 67.

33. Mbembe, *Necropolitics*, 92.

34. Achille Mbembe and Libby Meintjes, "Necropolitics," *Public Culture* 15, no. 1 (2003): 27, https://muse.jhu.edu/article/39984.

35. Bhattacharyya, *Rethinking Racial Capitalism*, 19; Halper, *War against the People*, 39–40.

36. Clarno, *Neoliberal Apartheid*, 15.

37. Corporate Watch, "Elbit Systems"; Robert Mackey, "Secret Israeli Report Reveals Armed Drone Killed Four Boys Playing on Gaza Beach in 2014," *The Intercept*, August 11, 2018, https://theintercept.com/2018/08/11/israel-palestine-drone-strike -operation-protective-edge/.

38. Anderson and Cooper, *Gaza*.

39. Israeli Air Force, "The IAF's New UAV: The 'Hermes 900' Is Operational Once Again," November 10, 2015, https://www.iaf.org.il/4427-45608-en/IAF.aspx.

40. Corporate Watch, "Elbit Systems"; Elbit Systems, *Elbit Systems Land Small Caliber Ammunition Portfolio*, 24–25; Elbit Systems, "Elbit Systems Awarded a Follow-On Contract to Supply Hermes™ 900 Unmanned Aircraft Systems to the Brazilian Air Force," press release, January 5, 2022, https://elbitsystems.com/pr-new/ elbit-systems-awarded-a-follow-on-contract-to-supply-hermes-900-unmanned -aircraft-systems-to-the-brazilian-air-force/.

41. Israeli Air Force, "The IAF's New UAV."

42. Who Profits, "Elbit Systems."

43. Eyal Weizman, *Hollow Land: Israel's Architecture of Occupation* (London: Verso, 2007), 19.

44. Mbembe, *Necropolitics*, 81–82; Weizman, *Hollow Land*, 12–14.

45. Ruth Wilson Gilmore, "Abolition Geography and the Problem of Innocence," in *Futures of Black Radicalism*, ed. Gaye T. Johnson and Alex Lubin (London: Verso, 2017), 225.

46. Mbembe, *Necropolitics*, 43.

47. Lloyd and Wolfe, "Settler Colonial Logics."

48. Todd Miller, *More Than a Wall: Corporate Profiteering and the Militarization of US Borders* (September 2019), https://www.tni.org/files/publication-downloads/ more-than-a-wall-report.pdf.

49. Who Profits, "Elbit Systems."

50. Miller, *More Than a Wall*, 50.

51. Who Profits, "Elbit Systems."

52. Sen, *Decolonising Palestine*, 64–66.

53. Sen, *Decolonising Palestine*, 66; Frantz Fanon, *The Wretched of the Earth* (London: Penguin, 1963).

54. Wolfe, *Traces of History*, 27.

55. Lentin, *Traces of Racial Exception*, 88.

56. Gargi Bhattacharyya, "Globalizing Racism and the Myths of the Other in the 'War on Terror,'" in *Thinking Palestine*, ed. Ronit Lentin (London: Zed Books, 2008), 46–49.

57. Quoted in Honaida Ghanim, "Thanatopolitics: The Case of the Colonial Occupation in Palestine," in *Thinking Palestine*, ed. Ronit Lentin (London: Zed Books, 2008), 74–75.

58. Gregoire Chamayou, *A Theory of the Drone* (London: New Press, 2015), 132.

59. Elbit Systems, *Company Profile*, 18.

60. Quoted in Noura Erakat, *Justice for Some: Law and the Question of Palestine* (Stanford, CA: Stanford University Press, 2019), 197.

61. Halper, *War against the People*, 104–05.

62. EurAsian Times Desk, "Watch: Has India Signed a Deal with Israel to Procure Hermes 900 Drones from Elbit Systems?" *EurAsian Times*, March 4, 2021, https://eurasiantimes.com/which-asian-country-signed-a-300mn-drone-deal-with-israeli-firm-elbit/.

63. Elbit Systems, "Elbit Systems Awarded a Follow-On Contract."

64. Mbembe, *Necropolitics*, 92.

65. Bhattacharyya, *Rethinking Racial Capitalism*, 17–20; Halper, *War against the People*.

66. Lloyd and Wolfe, "Settler Colonial Logics," 111–15.

67. John Collins, *Global Palestine* (London: Hurst and Company, 2011), 2–4; James Trafford, *The Empire at Home: Internal Colonies and the End of Britain* (London: Pluto, 2020), 12; Wolfe, *Traces of History*; Elia Zureik, "Settler Colonialism, Neoliberalism and Cyber Surveillance: The Case of Israel," *Middle East Critique* 29, no. 2 (2020): 221.

68. Lloyd and Wolfe, "Settler Colonial Logics," 116.

69. Lowe, *The Intimacies of Four Continents*.

70. Collins, *Global Palestine*, 2–6.

71. Bhattacharyya, *Rethinking Racial Capitalism*, 177–80.

72. William I. Robinson, *The Global Police State* (London: Pluto, 2020).

73. Robinson, *The Global Police State*, 3.

74. Halper, *War against the People*, 4–5.

75. Miller, *More Than a Wall*, 22.

76. Kaamil Ahmed, "EU Accused of Abandoning Migrants to the Sea with Shift to Drone Surveillance," *Guardian*, October 28, 2020, https://www.theguardian.com/global-development/2020/oct/28/eu-accused-of-abandoning-migrants-to-the-sea-with-shift-to-drone-surveillance.

77. UK Government, "Drone Demonstration and Development Project," Contracts Finder, July 2, 2020, https://www.contractsfinder.service.gov.uk/Notice/713d488e-6c55-4293-9a10-9759a2191dad?origin=SearchResults&p=1.

78. Sam Lewis, "National Police Air Service Tests Potential of Drone Technology," *Commercial Drone Professional*, September 14, 2020, https://www.commercialdroneprofessional.com/national-police-air-service-tests-potential-of-drone-technology/.

79. Jimmy Johnson, "A Palestine-Mexico Border," June 29, 2012, NACLA, https://nacla.org/blog/2012/6/29/palestine-mexico-border.

80. Walia, *Border and Rule*, 80.

81. Will Parrish, "The U.S. Border Patrol and an Israeli Military Contractor Are Putting a Native American Reservation under 'Persistent Surveillance,'" Stop the Wall, August 26, 2019, https://book.stopthewall.org/the-u-s-border-patrol-and-an-israeli-military-contractor-are-putting-a-native-american-reservation-under-persistent-surveillance/.

82. Parrish, "The U.S. Border Patrol."

83. Parrish, "The U.S. Border Patrol."

84. Quoted in Parrish, "The U.S. Border Patrol."

85. Quoted in Parrish, "The U.S. Border Patrol."

86. Hever, *The Privatization of Israeli Security*, 142.

87. Erakat, *Justice for Some*, 192.

88. Quoted in Chamayou, *A Theory of the Drone*, 32.

89. See Anderson and Cooper, *Gaza*, 22; Amnesty International, "Armenia/Azerbaijan: Civilians Must Be Protected from Use of Banned Cluster Bombs," October 5, 2020, https://www.amnesty.org/en/latest/news/2020/10/armenia-azerbaijan-civilians-must-be-protected-from-use-of-banned-cluster-bombs/; Seth J. Frantzman, "Israel Revolutionized Azerbaijan's Drone Arsenal. Are the Weapons Working?" *Jerusalem Post*, July 21, 2020, https://www.jpost.com/jpost-tech/israel-revolutionized-azerbaijans-drone-arsenal-are-the-weapons-working-635829.

90. BDS India, *Israel-India Military Relations: Ideological Paradigms of Security* (January 2020), https://peoplesdispatch.org/wp-content/uploads/2020/01/India-Israel-Military-Relations-2020_compressed.pdf.

91. Visualizing Palestine 101, "Global Complicity in Israel's Arms Industry," V1.1, November 2019, https://101.visualizingpalestine.org/visuals/global-complicity-israels-arms-industry; Stockholm International Peace Research Institute, "SIPRI Arms Transfers Database," last modified March 15, 2021, https://www.sipri.org/databases/armstransfers.

92. Osuri and Zia, "Kashmir and Palestine," 257.

93. Osuri and Zia, "Kashmir and Palestine."

94. Nadera Shalhoub-Kevorkian, "Human Suffering in Colonial Contexts: Reflections from Palestine," *Settler Colonial Studies* 4, no. 3 (2014): 277–90; Nadera Shalhoub-Kevorkian, *Security Theology, Surveillance and the Politics of Fear* (Cambridge: Cambridge University Press, 2015).

95. Quoted in Osuri and Zia, "Kashmir and Palestine," 257.

96. Lowe, *The Intimacies of Four Continents*, 156.

97. Collins, *Global Palestine*, 2.

98. Collins, *Global Palestine*, 2.

99. Palestine Action, "We Are Building a Nation-Wide Movement to End Complicity with Apartheid," September 1, 2020, https://www.palestineaction.org/we-are-building-a-nation-wide-movement-to-end-complicity-with-apartheid/.

100. Interview with the author, June 26, 2021.

101. Quoted in "Ghassan Kanafani: Voice of Palestine (1936–1972)," *Palestine Chronicle*, September 4, 2017, https://www.palestinechronicle.com/ghassan-kanafani-voice-of-palestine-1936-1972/.

102. Osuri and Zia, "Kashmir and Palestine," 260.

103. Noura Erakat, "Extrajudicial Executions from the United States to Palestine," *Just Security*, August 7, 2020, https://www.justsecurity.org/71901/extrajudicial-executions-from-the-united-states-to-palestine/.

104. Linda Tabar, "From Third World Internationalism to 'the Internationals': The Transformation of Solidarity with Palestine," *Third World Quarterly* 38, no. 2 (2017): 431.

**Chapter 9**

I thank Alana Lentin for sharpening my analysis of the obsession with the alleged rapes by Hamas.

1. Daniella Levy, "The Creative Resilience of Netta Barzilai," *The Rejection Survival Guide*, May 9, 2018, https://daniella-levy.com/rejectionsurvivalguide.com/2018/05/09/the-creative-resilience-of-netta-barzilai/.

2. Eran Swissa and Nir Wolf, "Netta's Shtick," *Israel Today*, April 19, 2018, https://www.israelhayom.co.il/article/550085.

3. Yvette Nahmia-Messinas, "'I Am Not Your Toy' and the End of Patriarchy," *Jerusalem Post*, June 11, 2018, https://www.jpost.com/opinion/i-am-not-your-toy-and-the-end-of-patriarchy-559719.

4. Barbara Swirski and Marilyn P. Safir, eds., *Calling the Equality Bluff: Women in Israel* (New York: Teachers College Press, 1993).

5. Nahla Abdo, *Women in Israel: Race, Gender and Citizenship* (London: Zed Books, 2011).

6. Sa'ed Atshan, *Queer Palestine and the Empire of Critique* (Stanford, CA: Stanford University Press, 2020).

7. Ran Boker, "Long before TOY: Watch Netta Barzilai Perform in an IDF Uniform," *Yediot Aharonot*, May 6, 2018, https://www.ynet.co.il/articles/0,7340,L-5253090,00.html.

8. UN Office for the Coordination of Humanitarian Affairs, "Key Figures on the 2014 Hostilities," June 23, 2015, https://www.ochaopt.org/content/key-figures-2014-hostilities.

9. Rasha Khatib, Martin McKee, and Salim Yusuf, "Counting the Dead in Gaza: Difficult but Essential," *Lancet* 404, no. 10449 (July 5, 2024): P237–68, https://www.thelancet.com/journals/lancet/article/PIIS0140-6736(24)01169-3/fulltext.

10. Nir Zadok, "When the Young Men Returned Home, the Arrival Hall Looked Like a Reception for Olympic Sportspeople," *Haaretz*, July 27, 2019, https://www.haaretz.co.il/news/law/.premium-1.7582598.

11. Ilan Pappé, *The Idea of Israel: A History of Power and Knowledge* (London: Verso, 2014), 214–305.

12. Ronit Lentin, *Traces of Racial Exception: Racializing Israeli Settler Colonialism* (London: Bloomsbury, 2018).

13. Jewish Virtual Library, "David Ben-Gurion: Selected Quotations," accessed October 2, 2020, https://www.jewishvirtuallibrary.org/select-quotations-of-david-ben-gurion.

14. "Ben Gvir Slams ICJ as Antisemitic, Says Israel Should Ignore Ruling on Provisional Measures," *Times of Israel*, January 26, 2024, https://www.timesofisrael.com/liveblog_entry/ben-gvir-slams-icj-as-antisemitic-says-israel-should-ignore-ruling-on-provisional-measures/.

15. Natasha Roth-Rowland, "Why Are So Many Israeli Women Subjected to Sexual Harassment?" *+972 Magazine*, March 3, 2016, https://www.972mag.com/why-are-so-many-women-subjected-to-sexual-harassment-in-israel/.

16. Report of the Independent International Commission of Inquiry on the Occupied Palestinian Territory, including East Jerusalem, and Israel, UN Doc. A/HRC/56/26 (June 10, 2024), https://www.ohchr.org/sites/default/files/documents/hrbodies/hrcouncil/sessions-regular/session56/a-hrc-56-crp-3.pdf.

17. Daniel Boyarin, *Unheroic Conduct: The Rise of Heterosexuality and the Invention of the Jewish Man* (Berkeley: University of California Press, 1997); Ronit Lentin, *Israel and the Daughters of the Shoah: Reoccupying the Territories of Silence* (New York: Berghahn Books, 2000).

18. Honaida Ghanim, "Thanatopolitics: The Case of the Colonial Occupation of Palestine," in *Thinking Palestine*, ed. Ronit Lentin (London: Zed Books, 2008), 65–81.

19. David Theo Goldberg, "Racial Palestinianization," in *Thinking Palestine*, ed. Ronit Lentin (London: Zed Books, 2008), 25–45; Lentin, *Traces of Racial Exception*.

20. Rhoda Ann Kanaaneh, *Birthing the Nation: Strategies of Palestinian Women in Israel* (Berkeley: University of California Press, 2002); Lana Tatour, "Domination and Resistance in Liberal Settler Colonialism: Palestinians in Israel between the Homeland and the Transnational" (PhD diss., University of Warwick, 2016); Lori Koffman, "Jewish Perspectives on Reproductive Realities," National Council of Jewish Women, 2018, https://www.ncjw.org/wp-content/uploads/2018/02/Jewish-Perspective-on-Reproductive-Realities-FORMATTED11.pdf.

21. Phoebe Greenwood, "Ethiopian Women in Israel 'Given Contraceptive without Consent,'" *Guardian*, March 1, 2013, https://www.theguardian.com/world/2013/feb/28/ethiopian-women-given-contraceptives-israel.

22. Alana Lentin, *Why Race Still Matters* (Cambridge: Polity, 2020), 5.

23. Judith Butler, "Performative Acts and Gender Constitution: An Essay in Phenomenology and Feminist Theory," *Theatre Journal* 40, no. 4 (1988): 519–31.

24. Eithne Luibhéid, *Pregnant on Arrival: Making the Illegal Immigrant* (Minneapolis: University of Minnesota Press, 2013), 3–6.

25. Alexander G. Weheliye, *Habeas Viscus: Racializing Assemblages, Biopolitics, and Black Feminist Theories of the Human* (Durham, NC: Duke University Press, 2014).

26. Jasbir K. Puar, "Homonationalism and Biopolitics," in *Out of Place: Interrogating Silences in Queerness/Raciality*, ed. Adi Kuntsman and Esperanza Miyake (York, UK: Raw Nerve Books, 2008), 14–15.

27. Jasbir K. Puar, *The Right to Maim: Debility, Capacity, Disability* (Durham, NC: Duke University Press, 2017), 96.

28. Puar, *The Right to Maim*, 96.

29. Rachael Gelfman Schultz, "The Law of Return," *My Jewish Learning*, accessed February 11, 2021, https://www.myjewishlearning.com/article/the-law-of-return/.

30. Patrick Wolfe, *Traces of History: Elementary Structures of Race* (London: Verso, 2016), 252.

31. Morton A. Klein, "Grandchild Clause Is Harming the Jewish State; Eliminate It—Opinion," *Jerusalem Post*, January 29, 2023, https://www.jpost.com/opinion/article-729920.

32. Abdo, *Women in Israel*, 4–5.

33. Raphael Falk, *Zionism and the Biology of Jews* (Tel Aviv: Resling, 2006), 18–19; Nadia Abu El-Haj, *The Genealogical Science: The Search for Jewish Origins and the Politics of Epistemology* (Chicago: University of Chicago Press, 2012).

34. Max Nordau, *Degeneration* (London: William Heinemann, 1895).

35. Boyarin, *Unheroic Conduct*.

36. Todd Samuel Presner, *Muscular Judaism: The Jewish Body and the Politics of Regeneration* (London: Routledge, 2007).

37. Laura Khoury, Seif Dana, and Ghazi-Walid Falah, "'Palestine as a Woman': Feminizing Resistance and Popular Literature," *Arab World Geographer* 16, no. 2 (2013): 147–76.

38. Haim Bresheeth-Zabner, *An Army Like No Other: How the Israel Defence Forces Made a Nation* (London: Verso, 2020).

39. Amira Hass, "The Brutal Mutation of Israeli Feminism," *Haaretz*, December 6, 2020, https://www.haaretz.co.il/blogs/shabahit/.premium-1.9351230.

40. Gili Cohen, "20% Increase in Reported Sexual Assaults in Israeli Army in 2016," *Haaretz*, January 30, 2017, https://www.haaretz.com/hblocked?returnTo= https%3A%2F%2Fwww.haaretz.com%2Fisrael-news%2F.premium-20-increase-in -reported-sexual-assaults-in-israeli-army-in-2016-1.5492356.

41. David Sheen, "Israel Weaponizes Rape Culture against Palestinians," *Electronic Intifada*, January 31, 2017, https://electronicintifada.net/content/israel -weaponizes-rape-culture-against-palestinians/19386.

42. Aviv Lavie, "It Was Decided and Executed: 'They Washed Her, Cut Her Hair, Raped Her and Killed Her': From Ben-Gurion's Diary, 22.6.49," *Haaretz*, October 28, 2005, https://www.haaretz.co.il/misc/1.920403.

43. Tal Nitsan, "The Boundaries of the Occupation: The Rarity of Rape in the Israeli-Palestinian Conflict" (MA thesis, 2006).

44. Euan Hague, "Rape, Power and Masculinity: The Construction of Gender and National Identities in the War in Bosnia-Herzegovina," in *Gender and Catastrophe*, ed. Ronit Lentin (London: Zed Books, 1997).

45. Lavie, "It Was Decided and Executed." See also Adania Shibli, *Minor Detail* (London: Fitzcarraldo Editions, 2020).

46. Ilan Pappé, *The Ethnic Cleansing of Palestine* (Oxford: Oneworld, 2006), 208–11.

47. Pappé, *The Ethnic Cleansing of Palestine*, 211.

48. "Re-exposed: A Horrific Story of Israeli Rape and Murder in 1949," *Al Arabiya News*, August 17, 2015, https://english.alarabiya.net/en/perspective/analysis/2015/ 08/17/RE-EXPOSED-A-horrific-story-of-Israeli-rape-and-murder-in-1949.

49. Ronit Lentin, *Co-Memory and Melancholia: Israelis Memorialising the Palestinian Nakba* (Manchester, UK: Manchester University Press, 2010), 139.

50. Isis Nusair, "Gendered Politics of Location of Three Generations of Palestinian Women in Israel," in *Displaced at Home: Ethnicity and Gender among Palestinians in Israel*, ed. Rhoda Ann Kanaaneh and Isis Nusair (Albany: State University of New York Press, 2010), 83–84.

51. Nahla Abdo, *Captive Revolution: Palestinian Women's Anti-Colonial Struggle within the Israeli Prison System* (London: Pluto, 2014), 161–62.

52. "Palestinian Female Prisoners Subjected to Torture and Abuse in Israeli Jails," *Days of Palestine*, December 24, 2021, https://daysofpalestine.ps/?p=8614.

53. "Re-exposed."

54. Judah Ari Gross, "IDF Removes Gag on 2016 Conviction of Officer for Raping Palestinian Woman," *Times of Israel*, October 20, 2021, https://www.timesofisrael .com/ending-censorship-idf-admits-officer-jailed-in-2017-raped-a-palestinian -woman/.

55. Julian Borger, "Claims of Israeli Sexual Assault of Palestinian Women Are Credible, UN Panel Says," *Guardian*, February 23, 2024, https://www.theguardian .com/world/2024/feb/22/claims-of-israeli-sexual-assault-of-palestinian-women-are -credible-un-panel-says.

56. Patrick Kingsley and Bilal Shbair, "Inside the Base Where Israel Has Detained Thousands of Gazans," *New York Times*, June 6, 2024, https://www.nytimes.com/ 2024/06/06/world/middleeast/israel-gaza-detention-base.html.

57. Jonathan Ofir, "Israeli Rabbi Who Advocated Rape of 'Comely Gentile Women' during War Becomes Chief Army Rabbi," July 12, 2016, https://mondoweiss .net/2016/07/israeli-advocated-becomes/.

58. Orit Kamir, "A Perfectly Racist Law That Sullies the Approach to Sexual Harassment with Patriarchal Nationalism," *Haaretz*, June 30, 2023, https://www .haaretz.co.il/opinions/2023-07-30/ty-article-opinion/.premium/00000189-a7ad -de97-af9f-efafa9d30000.

59. Jonathan Cook, "Israel's Lehava Stirs 'Anarchy' in Jerusalem," *Al Jazeera*, December 4, 2016, https://www.aljazeera.com/news/2016/12/04/israels-lehava-stirs -anarchy-in-jerusalem/?gb=true.

60. See The Short String, "CNN Report Claiming Sexual Violence on October 7 Relied on Non-Credible Witnesses, Some with Undisclosed Ties to Israeli Govt," *Mondoweiss*, December 1, 2023, https://mondoweiss.net/2023/12/cnn-report -claiming-sexual-violence-on-october-7-relied-on-non-credible-witnesses-some -with-undisclosed-ties-to-israeli-govt/; The Short String, "Family of Key Case in New York Times October 7 Sexual Violence Report Renounces Story, Says Reporters Manipulated Them," *Mondoweiss*, January 3, 2024, https://mondoweiss .net/2024/01/family-of-key-case-in-new-york-times-october-7-sexual-violence -report-renounces-story-says-reporters-manipulated-them/.

61. Office of the Special Representative of the Secretary-General on Sexual Violence in Conflict, *Mission Report: Official Visit of the Office of the SRSG-SVC to Israel and the Occupied West Bank, 29 January–14 February 2024,*

https://news.un.org/en/sites/news.un.org.en/files/atoms/files/Mission_report_of
_SRSG_SVC_to_Israel-oWB_29Jan_14_feb_2024.pdf.

62. Report of the Independent International Commission of Inquiry, para. 95.

63. Report of the Independent International Commission of Inquiry, para. 103.

64. Catherine Philp and Gabrielle Weiniger, "Israel Says Hamas Weaponised Rape. Does the Evidence Add Up?" *Times* (London), June 7, 2024, https://www.thetimes.com/magazines/the-times-magazine/article/israel-hamas-rape-investigation-evidence-october-7-6kzphszsj.

65. Ali Abunimah, "Watch: Debunking Israel's 'Mass Rapes' Propaganda," *Electronic Intifada*, December 4, 2023, https://electronicintifada.net/blogs/ali-abunimah/watch-debunking-israels-mass-rape-propaganda. See also Lana Tatour, "How Human Rights Organizations Are Aiding the Israeli Assault on Gaza," *Mondoweiss*, December 12, 2023, https://mondoweiss.net/2023/12/how-human-rights-organizations-are-aiding-the-israeli-assault-on-gaza/; Anwar Mhajne, "Understanding Sexual Violence Debates since 7 October: Weaponization and Denial," *Journal of Genocide Research* (30 May 2024), https://doi.org/10.1080/14623528.2024.2359851.

66. Hagar Shezaf, "Behind the 'Chanshi' Fantasies There Is a Sharp Statement about Sexual Harm," *Haaretz*, February 13, 2023, https://www.haaretz.co.il/gallery/mejunderet/2023-02-13/ty-article/.premium/00000186-4abd-d933-af9e-cbffe1350000.

67. Eness Elias, "The Ashkenazi Man's Nightmare between the Eilat Rape and the 'Asi Dispute," *Haaretz*, September 2, 2020, https://www.haaretz.co.il/gallery/galleryfriday/mizrachit/.premium-1.9121908.

68. Sheren Falah Sa'ab, "A Line Drawn between the Eilat Rape and 'Honour' Killing," *Haaretz*, August 31, 2020, https://www.haaretz.co.il/blogs/sherenf/BLOG-1.9117363.

69. Manar Hasan, "The Politics of Honor: Patriarchy, the State and the Murder of Women in the Name of Family Honor," *Journal of Israeli History* 21, nos. 1–2 (2002): 1–37.

70. Dorothy E. Roberts, *Killing the Black Body: Race, Reproduction and the Meaning of Liberty*, 20th anniversary ed. (1997; New York: Random House, 2017).

71. Ghanim, "Thanatopolitics," 65–66.

72. UN High Commissioner for Human Rights, *The Issue of Palestinian Pregnant Women Giving Birth at Israeli Checkpoints: Report of the High Commissioner for Human Rights*, UN Doc. A/HRC/7/44 (February 1, 2008).

73. Rasha Abou Jalal, "Gaza's Pregnant Women Suffer," *Al-Monitor*, November 30, 2014, https://www.al-monitor.com/pulse/originals/2014/11/gaza-pregnant-women-lack-medical-services.html.

74. "50,000 Women Pregnant in Gaza amid 'Decimation' of Its Health System," *Al Jazeera*, December 24, 2023, https://www.aljazeera.com/news/2023/12/24/50000 -women-pregnant-in-gaza-amid-decimation-of-its-health-system.

75. Nadera Shalhoub-Kevorkian, "Reexamining Femicide: Breaking the Silence and Crossing 'Scientific' Borders," in *Israeli Feminist Scholarship: Gender, Zionism, and Difference*, ed. Esther Fuchs (Austin: University of Texas Press, 2014), 292.

76. Marc Lamont-Hill, *We Still Here: Pandemic, Policing, Protest, and Possibility* (Chicago: Haymarket Books, 2020), 58–59.

77. Lamont Hill, *We Still Here*, 90.

78. Louis Allday, "An Interview with Abdaljawad Omar on October 7th and the Palestinian Resistance," in "For Palestine," *Ebb*, no. 1 (2024): 8–14.

79. Weheliye, *Habeas Viscus*, 2.

80. "Palestinian Women: The Backbone of Resistance," *Liberation School*, November 12, 2015, https://liberationschool.org/palestinian-women-the-backbone -of-resistance/.

81. Khoury, Dana and Falah, "Palestine as a Woman," 154–56.

82. Khoury, Dana and Falah, "Palestine as a Woman," 159–60.

83. Nadera Shalhoub-Kevorkian, *Militarization and Violence against Women in Conflict Zones in the Middle East: A Palestinian Case Study* (Cambridge: Cambridge University Press, 2009).

84. United Nations Women, *In the Absence of Justice: Embodiment and the Politics of Military Dismemberment in Occupied East Jerusalem* (December 2016), https:// unispal.un.org/pdfs/UNWOMENRPT_DEC16.pdf.

85. Bethan McKernan, "Israeli Officials Accuse International Court of Justice of Antisemitic Bias," *Guardian*, January 27, 2024, https://www.theguardian.com/ world/2024/jan/26/israeli-officials-accuse-international-court-of-justice-of -antisemitic-bias.

86. Ronnie Linder, "The Women Fighters Who Proved: The Army Received the Most Intensive 'Pilot' Imaginable," *Haaretz—The Marker*, March 1, 2024, https:// www.haaretz.co.il/weekend/2024-03-01/ty-article-magazine/.highlight/0000018d -f006-d7f4-a3dd-f60e415c0000.

87. Tatour, "Domination and Resistance."

88. Joseph Andoni Massad, "Re-Orienting Desire: The Gay International and the Arab World," *Public Culture* 14, no. 2 (2002): 361–85.

**Chapter 10**

1. David Renton, *Labour's Antisemitism Crisis: What the Left Got Wrong and How to Learn from It* (London: Routledge, 2021).

2. Alana Lentin, *Why Race Still Matters* (Cambridge: Polity, 2020), 136.

3. Alana Lentin, "Je suis Juif: Charlie Hebdo and the Remaking of Antisemitism," in *After Charlie Hebdo: Terror, Racism and Free Speech*, ed. Gavan Titley, Des Freedman, Gholam Khiabany, and Aurélien Mondon (London: Zed Books, 2017).

4. Lentin, *Why Race Still Matters*, 264.

5. The Gadigal are the people on whose land I reside. They are part of the Eora Nation, the area around what is now Sydney.

6. Valentina Pisanty, *The Guardians of Memory and the Return of the Xenophobic Right*, trans. Alastair McEwen (New York: CPL Editions, 2019), 21.

7. TOI Staff, "Netanyahu: An ICC Investigation of Israel Would Be 'Pure Anti-Semitism,'" *Times of Israel*, February 6, 2021, https://www.timesofisrael.com/netanyahu-an-icc-investigation-of-israel-would-be-pure-anti-semitism/.

8. La Perm, # 36, "Beur FM, antisémite?" February 7, 2021, https://fb.watch/3DmhUFWg27/.

9. Manfred Gerstenfeld, "George Soros's Negative Interactions with the Jewish World," *BESA Center*, October 26, 2020, https://besacenter.org/perspectives-papers/george-soros-jewish-world/.

10. Ilan Ben Zion, "Netanyahu Greets Hungary's Orban as 'True Friend of Israel,'" *AP News*, July 19, 2018, https://apnews.com/938bb193c0894691bf42a6457d1fae4c.

11. "Netanyahu: Hitler Didn't Want to Exterminate the Jews," *Haaretz*, October 21, 2015, https://www.haaretz.com/israel-news/netanyahu-absolves-hitler-of-guilt-1.5411578.

12. For example, critics of Israel's hardline politics, such as *Tikkun* magazine editor Rabbi Michael Lerner, are also able to cast Palestinians as actors in the Holocaust. Lerner wrote: "However much we may legitimately criticize Israeli policy toward the Palestinians, we must first acknowledge that the historic oppression of Jews helped create in them a pain so deep that many were unable to notice that, as they leapt from the burning building of Europe, they'd unintentionally landed on the back of another people. Surrounded by a world whose hostility has produced 2000 years of homelessness and oppression, and by a Palestinian people whose pain they are unable to acknowledge because of their own, Jews may find it hard to recognize that the existence of Israel renders them beneficiaries of great privilege or power. The terrible errors being made by Israel today are a consequence of sensitivity-dulling genocide—compounded by decades of implacable Arab hostility when it was the Jews who were stateless and living in displaced-persons camps and it was the Palestinians who were denying the Jews the right to enter Palestine." Michael Lerner, "The White Issue: 'Jews Are Not White,'" *Village Voice*, July 25, 2019 (originally published May 18, 1993), https://www.villagevoice.com/2019/07/25/the-white-issue-jews-are-not-white/.

13. Ariella A. Azoulay, "Algerian Jews Have Not Forgotten France's Colonial Crimes," *Boston Review*, February 10, 2021, http://bostonreview.net/global-justice/ariella-aisha-azoulay-benjamin-stora-letter.

14. Ben Lorber, "How the Israeli Flag Became a Symbol for White Nationalists," *+972 Magazine*, January 21, 2021, https://www.972mag.com/israeli-flag-white-nationalism-symbol/.

15. Ben Shapiro (@benshapiro), Twitter, September 17, 2015, 11:36 p.m., https://twitter.com/benshapiro/status/644505141299671041.

16. Michael Richmond, "Antiracism as Procedure," *Protocols*, no. 8 (2020), https://prtcls.com/article/richmond_labour-antisemitism/.

17. Ash Sarkar, "No Other Minority: Keir Starmer's Silence on the Islamophobia Report Speaks Volumes about Labour's Hierarchy of Racism," *Novara Media*, November 19, 2020, https://novaramedia.com/2020/11/19/no-other-minority-keir-starmers-silence-on-the-islamophobia-report-speaks-volumes-about-labours-hierarchy-of-racism/.

18. *Surviving Society*, episode 117, "Gavan Titley: Is Free Speech Racist?" SoundCloud, February 2, 2021, https://soundcloud.com/user-622675754/e117-gavan-titley-is-free-speech-racist.

19. Pisanty, *The Guardians of Memory*, 21.

20. Gil Anidjar, *The Jew, the Arab: A History of the Enemy* (Stanford, CA: Stanford University Press, 2003).

21. Alana Lentin, "Europe and the Silence about Race," *European Journal of Social Theory* 11, no. 4 (2008): 487–503.

22. Michael Rothberg, *Multidirectional Memory: Remembering the Holocaust in the Age of Decolonization* (Stanford, CA: Stanford University Press, 2009), 9.

23. Alana Lentin, "Racism in Public or Public Racism: Doing Anti-Racism in 'Post-Racial' Times," *Ethnic and Racial Studies* 39, no. 1 (2016): 33–48.

24. Gavan Titley, *Racism and Media* (London: Sage, 2019).

25. Lentin, *Why Race Still Matters*.

26. Cheryl Harris, "What Is Critical Race Theory and Why Is Trump Afraid of It?" *The Nation*, September 17, 2020, https://www.thenation.com/article/politics/trump-critical-race-theory/.

27. David Goodhart, "White Self-Interest Is Not the Same Thing as Racism," *Financial Times*, March 2, 2017, https://www.ft.com/content/220090e0-efc1-11e6-ba01-119a44939bb6; see also Eric Kaufmann, "'Racial Self-Interest' Is Not Racism: Ethno-Demographic Interests and the Immigration Debate" (working paper, Policy Exchange, March 2017).

28. Miri Song, "Challenging a Culture of Racial Equivalence," *British Journal of Sociology* 65, no. 1 (2014): 125.

29. David T. Goldberg, "Racial Europeanization," *Ethnic and Racial Studies* 29, no. 2 (2006): 331–64.

30. Cedric J. Robinson, *Black Marxism: The Making of the Black Radical Tradition* (London: Zed Books, 1983).

31. Barnor Hesse, "Racism's Alterity: The After-Life of Black Sociology," in *Racism and Sociology*, ed. Wulf D. Hund and Alana Lentin (Berlin: Lit Verlag, 2014).

32. Anna E. Younes, "Fighting Anti-Semitism in Contemporary Germany," *Islamophobia Studies Journal* 5, no. 2 (2020): 249–66.

33. Pierre-André Taguieff, *La Nouvelle judéophobie* (Paris: Fayard/Milles et une nuits, 2002).

34. Houria Bouteldja, *Les Blancs, les Juifs et nous: vers une politique de l'amour révolutionnaire* (Paris: La Fabrique éditions, 2016).

35. Azoulay, "Algerian Jews Have Not Forgotten."

36. Richmond, "Antiracism as Procedure."

37. Lewis R. Gordon, "Rarely Kosher: Studying Jews of Color in North America," *American Jewish History* 100, no. 1 (2016): 105–16.

38. Yana Grinshpun, "Décolonialisme et antisionisme à l'Université," *Observatorie du Décolonialisme*, January 24, 2021, http://decolonialisme.fr/?p=1609.

39. Ethan B. Katz, "An Imperial Entanglement: Anti-Semitism, Islamophobia, and Colonialism," *American Historical Review* 123, no. 4 (2018): 1190–209; Enzo Traverso, *Pour une critique de la barbarie moderne. Écrits sur l'histoire des Juifs et de l'antisémitisme* (Lausanne: Editions Page Deux, 1996).

40. Azoulay, "Algerian Jews Have Not Forgotten."

41. Jonathan Judaken, "Introduction," *American Historical Review* 123, no. 4 (2018): 1122–38.

42. Rudolf Bkouche, "Du philosémitisme d'Etat," UJFP, April 27, 2015, https://ujfp.org/du-philosemitisme-detat/.

43. Aimé Césaire, *Discourse on Colonialism*, trans. Joan Pinkham (New York: Monthly Review Press, 2000), 36.

44. Houria Bouteldja, "Racisme(s) et philosémitisme d'Etat ou comment politiser l'antiracisme en France?" *Parti des Indigenes de La République*, March 11, 2015, http://indigenes-republique.fr/racisme-s-et-philosemitisme-detat-ou-comment-politiser-lantiracisme-en-france-3/.

45. Bouteldja, "Racisme(s) et philosémitisme d'Etat" (emphasis added).

46. S. J. O'Donnell, "Antisemitism under Erasure: Christian Zionist Anti-Globalism and the Refusal of Cohabitation," *Ethnic and Racial Studies* 44, no. 1 (2021): 39–57.

47. Simon Assoun, "Simon, juif, antisioniste et gilet jaune," *Libération*," February 26, 2019, https://www.liberation.fr/debats/2019/02/26/simon-juif-antisioniste-et-gilet-jaune_1711777.

48. Bouteldja, *Les Blancs, les Juifs et nous*, 51.

49. Frantz Fanon, *Black Skin, White Masks* (London: Pluto, 1967).

50. Paola Pietrandrea, "Academic Freedom in the Context of France's New Approach to 'Separatism,'" *openDemocracy*, November 2, 2020, https://tinyurl.com/5q8dvjkq.

51. Israelvalley Desk, "Réactions en Israël après la mort de Samuel Paty. L'attentat islamiste commenté à Tel-Aviv," *Israelvalley*, October 17, 2020, https://israelvalley.com/2020/10/17/samuel-paty-decapite-lattentat-terroriste-a-conflans-largement-commente-en-israel/.

52. Frantz Fanon Foundation, "Separatism: A Step Further into Indignity," 2021, https://tinyurl.com/yzgb72ys.

53. Emily Dische-Becker, Sami Khatib, and Jumana Manna, "Palestine, Antisemitism, and Germany's 'Peaceful Crusade,'" *Protocols*, no. 8 (2020), https://prtcls.com/article/berlin-art-and-palestine-conversation/.

54. International Holocaust Remembrance Alliance, "IHRA Non-Legally Binding Working Definition of Antisemitism Adopted by the IHRA Plenary in Bucharest," May 26, 2016.

55. Houria Bouteldja and Alana Lentin, "We Are Not at Place de la République because, . . ." *openDemocracy*, February 28, 2019, https://www.opendemocracy.net/en/can-europe-make-it/we-are-not-at-place-de-la-r-publique-because/.

56. Gavin L. Langmuir, *History, Religion, and Antisemitism* (Berkeley: University of California Press, 1993), 109–10.

57. David Renton, *Labour's Antisemitism Crisis: What the Left Got Wrong and How to Learn from It* (London: Routledge, 2022).

58. David Norman Smith, "The Social Construction of Enemies: Jews and the Representation of Evil," *Sociological Theory* 14, no. 3 (1996): 221.

59. Daniel Allington, Beatriz L. Buarque, and Daniel Barker Flores, "Antisemitic Conspiracy Fantasy in the Age of Digital Media: Three 'Conspiracy Theorists' and Their YouTube Audiences," *Language and Literature* 30, no. 1 (2021): 78–102.

60. Matt Detzler, "An Old Libel—Coronavirus & Anti-Semitism," Trades Union Congress, August 24, 2020, https://www.tuc.org.uk/blogs/old-libel-coronavirus-anti-semitism.

61. Renton, *Labour's Antisemitism Crisis*.

62. Ambalavaner Sivanandan, *Communities of Resistance: Writings on Black Struggles for Socialism* (London: Verso, 1990), 64.

63. Maya Goodfellow, "To Fix Its Problems Now, Labour Must Face the Racism in Its Past," *Guardian*, March 8, 2019, https://www.theguardian.com/commentisfree/2019/mar/08/labour-party-racism-truth-past.

64. Achille Mbembe, "The Society of Enmity," *Radical Philosophy* 200 (November/December 2016): 25.

65. René Aguigah, "The Conviction and Conscience of Achille Mbembe," *New Frame*, April 23, 2020, https://www.newframe.com/the-conviction-and-conscience -of-achille-mbembe/.

66. Bouteldja, *Les Blancs, les Juifs et nous*; published in English as Houria Bouteldja, *Whites, Jews and Us: Towards a Politics of Revolutionary Love* (Cambridge, MA: MIT Press, 2017).

67. Aimé Césaire, *Discours sur le colonialisme* (Paris: Présence Africaine, 2017).

68. Houria Bouteldja, "L'anti-tatarisme des Palestiniens (et des banlieues) n'existe pas—A propos de Miss Provence et de l'antisémitisme (le vrai)," UJFP, December 26, 2020, https://ujfp.org/lanti-tatarisme-des-palestiniens-et-des-banlieues-nexiste -pas-a-propos-de-miss-provence-et-de-lantisemitisme-le-vrai/.

69. Houria Bouteldja, "Clavreul, Césaire et Moi. De l'innocence des uns et de la conscience des autres," UJFP, January 1, 2021, https://ujfp.org/clavreul-cesaire-et -moi-de-linnocence-des-uns-et-de-la-conscience-des-autres/.

70. Bouteldja, *Les Blancs, les Juifs et nous*.

71. Bouteldja and Lentin, "We Are Not at Place de la République."

72. Robert A. H. Cohen, "We Need to Decolonize Our Understanding of Antisemitism," *Patheos*, March 6, 2021, https://www.patheos.com/blogs/writingfromtheedge/2021/03/ we-need-to-decolonise-our-understanding-of-antisemitism/.

73. Santiago Slabodsky, *Decolonial Judaism: Triumphal Failures of Barbaric Thinking* (Basingstoke, UK: Palgrave Macmillan, 2015).

**Chpter 11**

1. *Application of the Convention on the Prevention and Punishment of the Crime of Genocide in the Gaza Strip* (*South Africa v. Israel*), International Court of Justice, https://www.icj-cij.org/case/192.

2. Hajar Yazdiha, *The Struggle for the People's King: How Politics Transforms the Memory of the Civil Rights Movement* (Princeton, NJ: Princeton University Press, 2023), 10.

3. Cornel West, "Introduction: The Radical King We Don't Know," in Martin Luther King Jr., *The Radical King*, ed. Cornel West (Boston: Beacon, 2014), x.

4. Michael R. Fischbach, *Black Power and Palestine: Transnational Countries of Color* (Stanford, CA: Stanford University Press, 2018), 77.

5. Fischbach, *Black Power and Palestine*, 71–72.

6. Fischbach, *Black Power and Palestine*, 81.

7. Geoffrey Levin, *Our Palestine Question: Israel and American Jewish Dissent 1948–1978* (New Haven, CT: Yale University Press, 2023).

8. Kenyatta R. Gilbert, "What Shaped King's Prophetic Vision?" *The Conversation*, January 15, 2017, https://theconversation.com/what-shaped-kings-prophetic-vision-71252.

9. West, "Introduction," xv.

10. Martin Luther King Jr., "I Have a Dream," speech delivered in Washington, DC, August 28, 1963, https://www.npr.org/2010/01/18/122701268/i-have-a-dream-speech-in-its-entirety.

11. For example, in his final Sunday sermon: Martin Luther King Jr., "Remaining Awake through a Great Revolution," sermon delivered at the National Cathedral, Washington, DC, March 31, 1968.

12. Mychal Denzel Smith, "The Truth about 'The Arc of the Moral Universe,'" *Huffington Post*, January 18, 2018, https://www.huffpost.com/entry/opinion-smith-obama-king_n_5a5903e0e4b04f3c55a252a4.

13. Quoted in Fadi Kiblawi and Will Youmans, "Israel's Apologists and the Martin Luther King Jr. Hoax," *Electronic Intifada*, January 18, 2004, https://electronicintifada.net/content/israels-apologists-and-martin-luther-king-jr-hoax/4955.

14. Kiblawi and Youmans, "Israel's Apologists."

15. David Palumbo-Liu, "What MLK Actually Thought about Israel and Palestine," *Jacobin*, February 10, 2019, https://jacobin.com/2019/02/martin-luther-king-israel-palestine-occupation.

16. Martin Luther King Jr., "Address Delivered at the National Biennial Convention of the American Jewish Congress," Miami Beach, May 14, 1958, Martin Luther King, Jr. Research and Education Institute, https://kinginstitute.stanford.edu/king-papers/documents/address-delivered-national-biennial-convention-american-jewish-congress.

17. Abraham Joshua Heschel, "Conversation with Martin Luther King," *Conservative Judaism* 22, no. 3 (1968): 12, https://www.rabbinicalassembly.org/sites/default/files/public/resources-ideas/cj/classics/1-4-12-civil-rights/conversation-with-martin-luther-king.pdf.

18. Martin Luther King Jr., "The Middle East Question," in *The Radical King*, ed. Cornel West (Boston: Beacon, 2014), 105–6.

19. Martin Kramer, "Where MLK Really Stood on Israel and the Palestinians," *Mosaic*, March 13, 2019, https://mosaicmagazine.com/observation/israel-zionism/2019/03/where-mlk-really-stood-on-israel-and-the-palestinians/.

20. Quoted in "Martin Luther King on Peace and Security for Israel," Jewish Virtual Library, accessed June 18, 2024, https://www.jewishvirtuallibrary.org/martin-luther-king-on-israel-s-security.

21. Noah Kulwin, "The Schism Is Finally Here," *Jacobin*, February 1, 2019, https://jacobinmag.com/2019/02/israel-democratic-party-aipac-palestine-occupation.

22. Raoul Wootliff, "Final Text of Jewish Nation-State Law, Approved by the Knesset Early on July 19," *Times of Israel,* July 18, 2018, https://www.timesofisrael.com/final-text-of-jewish-nation-state-bill-set-to-become-law/.

23. Kramer, "Where MLK Really Stood."

24. Martin Luther King Jr., "My Talk with Ben Bella," in *The Radical King*, ed. Cornel West (Boston: Beacon, 2014), 156.

25. Martin Luther King Jr., "Palm Sunday Sermon on Mohandas K. Gandhi," delivered at Dexter Avenue Baptist Church, Montgomery, Alabama, March 22, 1959, Martin Luther King, Jr. Research and Education Institute,_https://kinginstitute.stanford.edu/king-papers/documents/palm-sunday-sermon-mohandas-k-gandhi-delivered-dexter-avenue-baptist-church.

26. Quoted in "Apartheid," Martin Luther King, Jr. Research and Education Institute, accessed June 18, 2024, https://kinginstitute.stanford.edu/encyclopedia/apartheid.

27. "Apartheid."

28. Martin Luther King Jr., "The American Dream," sermon delivered at Ebenezer Baptist Church, Atlanta, July 4, 1965, in *A Knock at Midnight: Inspiration from the Great Sermons of Reverend Martin Luther King, Jr.*, ed. Clayborne Carson and Peter Holloran (New York: Warner Books, 1998), 90–91.

29. Alina Korn, "The Ghettoization of the Palestinians," in *Thinking Palestine*, ed. Ronit Lentin (London: Zed Books, 2008); Jenn M. Jackson, "Martin Luther King, Jr Was Radical: We Must Reclaim That Legacy," *Al Jazeera*, January 18, 2021, https://www.aljazeera.com/features/2021/1/18/martin-luther-king-jr-was-radical-we-must-reclaim-that-legacy.

30. Martin Luther King Jr., "Nonviolence and Racial Justice," February 6, 1957, Martin Luther King, Jr. Research and Education Institute, https://kinginstitute.stanford.edu/king-papers/documents/nonviolence-and-racial-justice.

31. Martin Luther King Jr., "The Three Dimensions of a Complete Life," sermon delivered at New Covenant Baptist Church, Chicago, April 9, 1967, in "Martin Luther King, Jr.: An Extraordinary Life," *Seattle Times*, https://projects.seattletimes.com/mlk/words-life.html.

32. Martin Luther King Jr., "Facing the Challenge of a New Age," address delivered at the First Annual Institute on Nonviolence and Social Change, Montgomery, Alabama, December 3, 1956, Martin Luther King, Jr. Research and Education Institute, https://kinginstitute.stanford.edu/king-papers/documents/facing-challenge-new-age-address-delivered-first-annual-institute-nonviolence.

33. Martin Luther King Jr., "Nonviolence and Social Change," November 1967, in *The Radical King*, ed. Cornel West (Boston: Beacon, 2014), 147–48.

34. Rick Gladstone, "United Church of Christ Approves Divestment to Aid Palestinians," *New York Times*, June 30, 2015, https://www.nytimes.com/2015/07/01/us/united-church-of-christ-to-divest-israel-to-aid-palestinians.html; Rick Gladstone, "US Church Puts 5 Banks from Israel on a Blacklist," *New York Times*, January 12, 2016, https://www.nytimes.com/2016/01/13/world/middleeast/us-church -puts-5-banks-from-israel-on-a-blacklist.html; "U.S. Mennonite Church Votes to Divest from Firms with Ties to Israeli Occupation," *Haaretz*, July 7, 2017, https://www .haaretz.com/us-news/u-s-mennonite-church-votes-to-divest-over-israeli-policy-1 .5492325; "US Presbyterian Church Votes Unanimously to Support BDS," *Palestine Chronicle*, June 27, 2018, http://www.palestinechronicle.com/us-presbyterian -church-votes-unanimously-to-support-bds/; American Friends Service Committee, "What You Should Know about AFSC's Support for the BDS Movement," January 7, 2019, https://www.afsc.org/blogs/news-and-commentary/what-you-should-know -about-afscs-support-bds-movement.

35. Movement for Black Lives, "The Movement for Black Lives Stands with the Palestinian People," *Al-Adab*, March 30, 2018, https://www.al-adab.com/ahmad/ar/ index.php/ar/test/other-articles/1743-the-movement-for-black-lives-stands-with -the-palestinian-people. See also Hamid Dabashi, "Black Lives Matter and Palestine: A Historical Alliance," *Al Jazeera*, September 6, 2016, https://www.aljazeera.com/ opinions/2016/9/6/black-lives-matter-and-palestine-a-historic-alliance/.

36. Martin Luther King Jr., *Why We Can't Wait* (New York: Harper & Row, 1964), 74.

37. National Park Service, "Resurrection City," last updated September 1, 2020, https://www.nps.gov/articles/resurrection-city.htm.

38. John Kelly, "Before Occupy D.C., There Was Resurrection City," *Washington Post*, December 2, 2011, https://www.washingtonpost.com/local/before-occupy-dc -there-was-resurrection-city/2011/12/01/gIQAoNqcPO_story.html (emphasis added).

# Index

| Stanford Studies in Middle Eastern and
| Islamic Societies and Cultures

*Lara Deeb and Sherene Seikaly, editors*

*For a complete listing of titles in this series, visit the
Stanford University Press website, www.sup.org.*

The authorized representative in the EU for product safety and compliance is:
Mare Nostrum Group
B.V Doelen 72
4831 GR Breda
The Netherlands

www.ingramcontent.com/pod-product-compliance
Lightning Source LLC
Chambersburg PA
CBHW020455270326
41926CB00008B/615

* 9 7 8 1 5 0 3 6 4 2 9 7 3 *